# Revenue Law
## Principles and Practice

James Kirkbride

LLB (Hons), MPhil, PGCE

and

## Abimbola A. Olowofoyeku

LLB (Hons), LLM, PhD

TUDOR

© James Kirkbride and Abimbola A. Olowofoyeku 1993, 1998

Published in Great Britain by Tudor Business Publishing Limited.

First published 1993
Second edition 1998

A CIP catalogue for this book is available from the British Library

ISBN 1 872807 08 9

The right of James Kirkbride and Abimbola A. Olowofoyeku to be
identified as the authors of this work has been asserted by them
in accordance with the Copyright, Designs and Patents Act 1988.

Typeset by Deltatype Ltd, Birkenhead, Merseyside.

Printed and bound in Great Britain by
Athenaeum Press Ltd, Newcastle upon Tyne.

# Contents

# Preface

Revenue Law textbooks have a reputation of being weighty, unwieldy tomes, filled with a mass of detail that is of no particular concern to students. Part of the problem is due to the fact that the subject area is itself very wide and the subject matter could be extremely complicated. But there is also a tendency for authors to attempt to cover every possible area of every possible topic, of every possible tax. This sometimes results in great width, but little depth – the reader knows a little about everything, but not enough about anything!

The development of this book emanates from concern to provide the reader with an in-depth analysis of the principles of Revenue Law in a focused manner. In so doing, our philosophy has been to sacrifice breadth for depth of coverage. We have not sought to cover every tax, or every area of the taxes that we have selected for coverage. This we have done in the hope that the reader will have access to a detailed analysis of selected areas of the law, while being insulated from a mass of unnecessary material.

We believe that students best understand the complexities of the subject if they are provided with an insight into the functions and reasons for the existence of the applicable rules. Hence we have in parts of this book sought to provide a discussion of the rules in their proper context, in order to facilitate a "principles"-based approach to the study of Revenue Law. This has often entailed detailed consideration of opinion and judicial comment.

We have, in the hope of encouraging an active approach to the reading and review of the text, provided a number of "self-check" questions at the end of each chapter. We have also included a chapter on examination preparation and techniques in order to assist students who, in spite of having a good understanding of the subject matter, fail to achieve matching examination results.

The book is intended primarily for undergraduate students in law, economics or accountancy, and students studying for professional qualifications in law and related disciplines. It should also appeal to the practitioner and academic searching for a quick insight into some of the complexities of Revenue Law.

# Preface to the Second Edition

This second edition follows the lead of the previous edition in seeking to present a "principles" approach to Revenue Law enabling the reader to consider an in-depth analysis of some of its complexities. Our opinion remains that students best understand the subject through a consideration of the functions and reasons for the existence of the applicable rules, in addition to a consideration of the rules themselves. Throughout the text we have sought to continue to provide an analysis of the law in addition to a consideration of the detail of the rules themselves. We hope this approach will appeal to both the practitioner and the student seeking to consider and comprehend the detail of Revenue Law.

In respect of the contents of this edition, we have decided to seek to bring the detail as up to date as possible. In addition, we decided to expand the chapters on corporation tax and on the history, functions and systems of taxation – the latter to include consideration of proposals for reform from the Institute of Fiscal Studies and from the Inland Revenue itself. The section on Capital Gains Tax has been substantially rewritten to reflect the many changes and developments in that area of the law.

Finally, a new chapter has been introduced on the income tax consequences of trusts and settlements. We hope this adds to the value of the book.

# Table of Cases

# Part One — General Principles

# 1

# Tax – history, functions and systems

Although the majority of this book is devoted to an examination of the principles and policy surrounding the direct taxes of income, capital gains, inheritance and corporation tax, it is important to develop an awareness of the history of taxation and the declared or presumed functions of tax. It is also of interest to be aware of the ad hoc nature of the UK tax system and opportunities and choices for reform. It is suggested that the sections on "functions" and on "systems" ought to be revisited once you have acquired and developed a working knowledge of the principles and operation of some of the direct taxes. Your ability to constructively analyse suggested reforms will be enhanced by your understanding of some of the substantive taxes.

The final part of this chapter considers some of the implications for revenue law of our membership of the European Communities.

## History and Functions

Income tax was introduced in this country by Pitt in 1799. [1] Its purpose was to finance the cost of the war against France. It was charged on the world-wide income of British residents and the British income of non-residents. This "temporary measure" was repealed in 1802 (a temporary peace in the war with France) but reintroduced by Addington in 1803. Addington made a number of adjustments and reforms to Pitt's system, in particular, Addington introduced a Schedular system of taxation and assessment—a system that remains today! [2] Peace in 1815 resulted in the expiration of the 1803 Act. A tax-free period was then enjoyed until 1842 when Peel re-imposed taxes broadly on the previous lines. Once again, it

---

[1] Although it should be noted that taxes and their influences might have been felt at an earlier time. For example, King John's demand for "scrutage" contributed to the crisis of 1215 and the subsequent submission and the issue of Magna Carta.

It should be appreciated that "tax" has proved difficult to define. The OECD's definition is, "the term taxes is confined to compulsory, unrequited payments to general government". This is perhaps the most useful working definition of tax.

[2] The details of today's Schedules are presented in later discussion.

was believed to be a "temporary" measure but was periodically re-imposed and remains today. The development of tax law and taxation has extended from pure income tax on individuals to encompass taxes on the income of companies (corporation tax) and taxes on the capital receipts and gains of individuals and companies through the introduction of capital gains tax, inheritance tax and corporation tax. As we shall see later, the various taxes and their methods of introduction and application have created many opportunities for tax planning and avoidance.

Apart from the above direct taxes introduced on the capital and income of individuals and companies, a number of indirect taxes have been introduced into the United Kingdom. Generally, indirect taxes do not apply directly to our income but are paid indirectly through our expenditure. For example, they are often found to be included in the final price we might pay for goods. Value added tax (VAT) is the more well-known and apparent indirect tax. It is also the tax that is causing concern at European level and is subject to reform.

Finally, it is interesting to note that although income tax in the United Kingdom reflected the development of many overseas systems of taxation—they also commenced life in response to the need to raise finances for periods of war and developed into a complex system imposing tax on most low income individuals—it has been suggested that the British tax system differs from its overseas equivalents in two ways. [1] First it raises taxes under a system of schedules [2]. Second, its system of collection at source is widespread and sophisticated. The PAYE system is a familiar example of the latter. A further example of collection at source and an indication of the system's expansion is apparent in the "net" interest payments received on ordinary building society and bank saving accounts. Collection at source necessarily results in a hidden cost. For example, one only needs to reflect on the administration costs to the employer of "agreeing" to act as tax collector through the imposition of the PAYE system.

## Functions and Principles of Taxation

It has been suggested that tax system has become the "maid of all work". [3]

---

[1] See S James and C Nobes, *The Economics of Taxation*, at Chapter 8.

[2] See later discussion of the Schedular system.

[3] In the Budget of March 1993, the Chancellor of the Exchequer announced that in looking for extra revenue he had to be guided by three principles:

" . . . that where possible money should be raised in a way that will not damage the working of the economy"

This description emphasises the range of functions that taxes and the tax system might perform or be asked to perform. These functions often include a combination of a management function, a redistributive function and a general need to raise revenue. We saw the need to raise revenue in the introduction of income tax to finance warfare. Today, that need might still be one of maintaining the armed forces along with a wider range of services such as law and order and education. But today the raising of revenue is not the sole function of tax—this was strikingly illustrated in the suggestion that a slight increase in income tax rates would compensate for any lost revenue that might ensue if we agreed the removal of capital gains tax and inheritance tax. Of course, the removal of capital gains tax and inheritance tax is unlikely. They exist for their own reasons and support other general objectives and functions of our tax system. In particular, they might make a contribution to the objective of affecting a redistribution of wealth.

The redistributive function will find differing degrees of support reflecting political persuasions and pressures. The progressive tax rates are often perceived as a reflection of the equitable imposition of higher rates of tax upon those who enjoy the greatest ability to pay those rates. Similarly, one could refer to the introduction of capital gains tax as an example of imposing tax on these who were fortunate enough to enjoy their "wealth" in a form other than as income. An interesting redistributive proposal was the suggestion that a number of tax deductions ought to be replaced by a system of tax credits. It was believed that "tax credits" would be much more useful to low income families [1]—particularly because the absence of taxable income removed the usefulness of a tax deduction.

Contribution to the management of the economy is a widely accepted function of taxation. Examples of this can be found in the way in which tax rules and allowances are used to control expenditure and inflation; and in the way in which we are encouraged to invest in the UK economy through tax exempt or advantageous savings schemes. For example, Personal Equity Plans (PEPs) have proliferated in the UK since their introduction in the late 1980s.

They provide an opportunity to invest in stocks and shares with the

" . . . this means reducing the value of allowances and broadening the tax base . . . and . . ."

" . . . that taxation should support social, health and environmental objectives".

[1] This was a recommendation of the Carter Report in respect of taxation in Canada. The Report of the Royal Commission on Taxation, RC Canada (1966).

The UK also considered a tax credit system in the 1972 Green Paper, "Proposals for a Tax Credit System".

advantages of tax-free profits. In introducing a "Saver's Budget" in 1986 the Chancellor of the Exchequer increased the annual limit on a PEP investment to £6,000 and limited the requirement that the monies must be invested in UK equities to 50% of the portfolio. The Chancellor declared his intention of encouraging long-term investment in share-ownership. In the same Budget, the Chancellor introduced the "Tax Exempt Special Savings Budget" (TESSA). These also have become very popular. The stated intention of the TESSA is to

> introduce a wholly new tax incentive which will reward saving and encourage people to build up a stock of capital.

The management of the economy and the use of tax often involves aspects of credit control, customs duties and to a lesser extent the control of, or influence on, behaviour. The latter is apparent in the investment and savings behaviour of PEPs and TESSAs, but might also include social behaviour such as taxation of alcohol, tobacco and car fuel.

## The Principles of Taxation

In developing a tax system to facilitate the above functions (or any other functions) it is normal to consider the "principles" upon which a tax system ought to be based. These principles are often the measure against which one would judge whether a tax system is good or bad. In considering and developing such principles, the accepted starting point is Adam Smith's proposed canons of taxation [1].

1. Equity—people should contribute taxes proportionate to their incomes and wealth.
2. Certainty—taxes should be certain and not arbitrary.
3. Convenience—the timing and manner of payment of taxes must be convenient.
4. Efficiency—the costs of collecting and imposing taxes must be kept to a minimum. The costs of collection should represent a small proportion of the revenue collected. The taxes should be efficient in that they do not distort behaviour—the principle of "neutrality".

Over the years, these canons of taxation have been reviewed and discussed and have occasionally been presented under similar or revised

[1] Adam Smith, *An Inquiry into the Nature and Causes of the Wealth of Nations* (1776).

headings. For example, in 1978 the Meade Committee considered the "Characteristics of a Good Tax Structure" as representing six heads [1]:

1. Incentives and economic efficiency
2. Distributional effects
3. International aspects
4. Simplicity and costs of administration and compliance
5. Flexibility and stability
6. Transitional problems.

The principles proposed by Adam Smith still dictate and influence thinking in this area. [2] We shall consider aspects of those principles together with aspects of the "characteristics" proposed by the Meade Committee, under four heads:

- efficiency
- incentives
- equity
- stability considerations.

Our choice of these "heads" reflects the economic influences on tax system and reform.

### (i) Efficiency

The efficiency of the tax system often involves consideration of its economic efficiency and contributions, and its efficiency measured in terms of administration and costs of compliance. The costs of compliance are the easier to appreciate and recognise. Adam Smith expressed concern over the proportional costs of collection. Similar concerns were expressed by the Meade Committee. The Committee emphasised the need to consider the potential costs of administrative complexity and the pure costs of administration. The latter should incorporate official administrative costs and also the (often neglected) tax compliance costs incurred by the private taxpayer. The Meade Committee believed that private compliance costs were often in excess of the official administrative costs—but were often ignored when judging and analysing the operation

---

[1] "The Structure and Reform of Direct Taxation": Report of a Committee chaired by Professor J E Meade, The Institute of Fiscal Studies (1978) at Chapter 2.

[2] For a useful introduction, see James and Nobes, *The Economics of Taxation*. See also, Kay and King, *The British Tax System*.

of the tax system. Examples of the private costs of compliance would include the costs of the employer in operating as a tax collector under the PAYE system; the costs imposed on a trader in complying with any VAT system; and the social costs to the community of the investment of manpower in developing a tax advisory and avoidance industry and the costs to the public sector in trying to hinder or prevent any process of tax avoidance. The process of tax change also brings with it the costs to the taxpayers and the authorities of adaption and response.

The actual costs of compliance ("the hidden costs of taxation") are more difficult to calculate than administrative costs, although attempted calculations and estimates do support the Meade Committee's conclusions that compliance costs are "substantial".[1] The Meade Committee's conclusions included the advice that we "tip the balance away from compliance costs on to official administrative costs" and develop a coherent tax system that is simple and easy to understand with the consequent advantages of acceptability.

Economic efficiency (or contributions) often invites recognition of what is known as the excess burden of taxation. Economists regard "efficiency" in terms of contributions to the "optimal allocation of scarce resources". Such an allocation demands the existence of perfect competition; and that market forces (supply and demand) dictate the price of goods and services and the allocation of scarce resources of factors of production. In the "real" world perfect competition does not exist and influences on supply or demand can distort allocations and price—with the accompanying inefficient effects on the economy. The imposition and use of tax can distort choices and subsequent allocations. It is that "distortion" that amounts to the "excess burden" of tax. The traditional example is the avoidance of Window Tax in 1747 when many taxpayers bricked-up their windows rather than pay tax. This "cost" resulted in a lack of amenity with no consequent benefit to the Government or the economy—it represented the excess burden of the Window Tax.

Similarly, the Meade Report refers to the "substitution effect" whereby taxes contribute to economic inefficiency by interfering with consumer choice. The Meade Report cites the examples of the

> wage earner reducing his hours of work in order to substitute untaxed leisure or do-it-yourself activity at home for taxed work;

[1] Sandford, *Hidden Costs of Taxation*, Institute of Fiscal Studies (1973), estimated compliance costs to represent 2.5–4.4 per cent of the revenue collected during 1970.

Similarly, it was reported in the *Financial Times* (28 November 1986) that compliance costs represented 3.3 per cent of the tax yield for 1983–84.

the housewife who may substitute untaxed domestic work for taxed earnings outside the home; and

the business executive who refuses promotion and thus substitutes his present occupation for the alternative more productive job, because the low post-tax increases in his earnings do not compensate for the social costs of moving.

These examples, and others, represent the loss or "costs" (the excess burden) of tax.

Two particular examples of "excess burden" that we will consider in detail in later chapters, are (i) the use of fringe benefits; and (ii) tax evasion and avoidance.

Fringe benefits represent those benefits in kind that employees receive instead of salary or income. The hope is that the benefits in kind will escape tax. If the "benefit" had been received as income or as part of the salary it would probably be taxable. We will examine in later chapters the detailed rules for the taxation and assessment of benefits in kind, but at this point it is important to appreciate the potential inefficiency of fringe benefits. If, for example, instead of receiving a company car (a fringe benefit) an employee was provided with the cash equivalent, he would then have the choice on how he might spend that money. That freedom of choice would accord with the economist's concept of "perfect competition" and his choice would better influence the factors of supply and demand and the allocation of scarce resources. For instance, he could choose to buy a cheaper form of transport (a used car) and invest the remainder or spend it on consumer goods of a different kind.

Tax evasion and avoidance is difficult to measure. The "loss" or "costs" represents the effort and the monies expanded in avoiding or even evading liability. It is estimated that evasion, and thus the "cost" and "loss", is widespread. For example, in 1979 the Chairman of the Board of Inland Revenue suggested that it was "not implausible" that tax evasion monies could amount to 7.5 per cent of the gross domestic product.

## (ii) Incentives

Many regard the concept and consideration of incentives as an aspect and measure of tax efficiency, and to that extent "incentives" belong to principle (i) above. "Incentives" examine the way in which the tax system should or does encourage people to work, save and invest, and accept risks of enterprise and innovation.

We previously mentioned the "substitution effect" of taxation and the taxpayer's surrender of work and effort in favour of other benefits such as leisure, hobby and do-it-yourself crafts. Similarly, the tax system might contribute to a substitution effect in relation to forms of business organisation. One might choose to operate as an unincorporated association rather than an incorporated business—depending upon the tax regimes and advantages. Alternatively, one might opt for a less profitable but relatively risk free business instead of the development of a risky venture, albeit that such a development would provide wider benefits to the economy and the community (if successful).

In relation to savings and investment, the "substitution effect" is often discussed in terms of the "double taxation of savings" : "savings" often come from earned income that has already been subject to taxation, and those savings and any interest returned will be subject to further tax. One can point to our discussion on PEPs and TESSAs as examples of government attempts to encourage savings and investment in a particular direction through the removal of a "double taxation" principle.

It is widely believed that an expenditure tax would provide a wider incentive to save essentially because it would, like PEPs and TESSAs, remove any "double taxation" fear.

In terms of incentive effects much discussion and emphasis is placed upon comparing the incentive effects of different forms of taxation. For example, it is widely believed that a progressive tax rate has potentially a higher disincentive effect on work effort than a proportional income tax system or a poll tax system. Similarly, it is believed that indirect taxes are more attractive to savers than progressive income tax rates which contribute to "double taxation".

The major difficulty in relation to incentives and tax is measurement. It is difficult to measure incentive responses to tax systems and change. For example, although there have been many studies whose conclusions and reports appear to support the widely believed views on incentives, tax rates and work effort, the methodology, precision and accuracy of the studies have caused concern.[1]

---

[1] See Atkinson and Stiglitz, *Lectures on Public Economies* (1980); Brown, *Taxation and the Incentive to Work* (1983).

*(iii) Equity*

Equity initially demands a consideration of whether a tax is "fair" and equitable. "Fairness" involves subjective judgments although some objective acceptance and perception of the "fairness" of a tax and a tax system is necessary in order to avoid adverse consequences. For example, evasion and taxpayer resistance to taxation can dramatically increase if the system or the tax is perceived to be unfair.

In considering "fairness" it is normal to recognise the importance of "horizontal" and "vertical" equity. "Horizontal" equity demands that tax systems treat equal people in equal circumstances in an equal way. "Vertical" equity permits discrimination between taxpayers in order to facilitate a redistribution between rich and poor. The Meade Committee reported that:

1. A good tax system should be horizontally equitable, ie should treat like with like.
2. A modern tax system must be so constructed as to be capable of use for vertical redistribution between rich and poor. [1]

An example of an equity argument supporting the introduction of a tax is apparent in the case of capital gains tax. During its introduction in 1964, the Chancellor of the Exchequer, stated that:

Capital gains confer much the same kind of benefit on the recipient as taxed earnings more hardly won. Yet earnings pay full tax while capital gains go free. This is unfair to the wage and salary earner. [2]

The development and promotion of "equity" of tax, incorporates problems of the definition of "income", "wealth" and "ability to pay". It also invites discussion of the need to consider tax capitalisation; distribution and the incidence of tax; inflation; and tax avoidance and evasion. Tax capitalisation involves tax benefits being incorporated in and reflected in the capital value of an asset. For example, mortgage interest relief has been reflected, over time, in the increased demand and price of housing. Once this has occurred, it becomes difficult and perhaps inequitable to remove the tax concession. In the instance of mortgage interest relief, those who had paid relief-inflated prices would suffer a capital loss.

[1] The Meade Committee Report (1978) at Chapter 2.
[2] Hansard, vol 710, col 245.

The distribution and incidence of tax is difficult to measure. It is assumed that a progressive tax rate coupled with the extension of tax beyond pure income tax has reflected a movement towards equality of liability. However, in determining equality of distribution it is important to appreciate the "incidence" of tax (who really pays for tax changes and increases). The "incidence" of tax might include the "economic" incidence in that the economy and the consumer might suffer if a progressive income tax induces more leisure and less work effort. The consumer might also suffer if the "incidence" is "shifted" from the producer to the consumer; for example, through the incorporation of tax rises into the market price of the product or service.

Inflation and its effects on "equity" is apparent in relation to both earned and unearned income. In relation to earned income it is important under a progressive tax rate system to make proportional adjustments to counter the effects of inflation. Thus, the Chancellor might seek to raise personal allowances and rate bands by the amount of inflation in order to seek to avoid any fall in "real incomes". In relation to unearned income, we find complex rules to allow an indexation system to apply to capital gains in order that taxpayers pay for "real" rather than inflationary gains.

Tax avoidance and tax evasion [1] often contribute to the "hidden costs" of taxation, but more importantly they have an adverse effect on redistribution because of the retention of wealth by those who successfully operate or contribute to avoidance schemes—an unintended distribution! In addition to the redistribution "inequity", widespread tax avoidance and tax evasion might contribute to the development of a perception of the "acceptability" of avoidance (or worse still, evasion!) which might find further wasteful avoidance and evasion. It is necessary for the legislature and the Courts to respond appropriately to artificial avoidance schemes in an attempt to curtail and prevent any perceptions of "acceptability"— unless, of course, we wish to follow some of our European partners in accepting evasion as a moral duty!

### (iv) Stability

We mentioned earlier that one of the functions of tax and tax systems is a contribution to the management of the economy. To economists and others, the use of the tax system in managing the economy ought to promote "stability". The Meade Report emphasised the need

---

[1] See later discussion on the concepts of evasion and avoidance.

for a certain stability in taxation in order that persons may be in a position to make reasonably far-sighted plans. Fundamental uncertainty breeds lack of confidence and is a serious impediment to production and prosperity. [1]

In promoting stability in the economy, taxation is a useful part of any government's armoury—yet, at a apparently contradictory level, taxation must allow flexibility and change. The flexibility and change is required in order to respond to different political views and changes and different trends and thinking in economic policy. The tax system must be able to respond and adjust to monetary policy or fiscal policy while providing and supporting economic stability. Economic stability and stabilisation demands recognition of the relative merits of the various taxes; the size of the tax base; the speed of adjustment and influence of tax changes (the "implementation" and "response lag"); and the development of built-in flexibility methods, such as progressive tax rates. Within these considerations it is clear that a good tax system must permit a change of emphasis in economic policy in order to reflect changes in government and thinking but appreciate that

[s]uch changes of emphasis will show themselves in the trade-off which is preferred among the various objectives of a good tax system. [2]

## Tax Reform

Tax reform requires a

tax system which looks like someone designed it on purpose. (W E Simon, former Secretary to US Treasury)

Such a system would, presumably, address the principles and functions of taxation and demonstrate and achieve appropriate distributions and contributions. In the United Kingdom we have, at times, seen aspects of reform and consolidation, but little in terms of a co-ordinated review and reform of our overall tax system and burdens [3]—perhaps, because the process of review and reform contains a number of fundamental

---

[1] The Meade Committee Report (1978).

[2] The Meade Committee Report (1978).

[3] We have experienced periods of consolidation, and periods of occasional and limited reforms, such as the reform of the unit of assessment to permit independent taxation of husband and wife (introduced on 6 April 1990).

difficulties. An interesting, unofficial review of the UK tax system was conducted by the Meade Committee, on behalf of the Institute of Fiscal Studies. [1] Although both the Committee and its Report have been subject to much criticism and comment, the Report is useful in identifying anomalies and areas of concern in the UK tax system, and in providing a comparison with an expenditure tax system. It is also believed that the Report will influence and make a contribution to future tax reform.

The Meade Committee was set up in mid-1975 and reported in 1978. Its brief was to "take a fundamental look at the UK tax structure". It must be noted that to make its task "manageable" the Committee quickly decided to exclude consideration of some taxes, in particular excise taxes, local rates, stamp duties, petroleum revenue taxes and aspects of value added tax. In reaching its conclusions, the Meade Committee considered that the present anomalies in the UK system ought not to remain and that it would be necessary to move to a pure income tax or to a pure expenditure tax. [2] The Committee, for reasons that we shall explore, preferred the option of an expenditure tax. An expenditure tax involves a calculation of an individual's consumption expenditure not an individual's expenditure *per se*. For example, one might start by calculating an individual's income for any period and add to that income any capital receipts and borrowing. This would enable us to calculate an individual's "spending power". Sensible and desirable spending in the form of savings and investment would then be deducted from that "spending power". The remaining balance would represent the individual's consumption expenditure and it is that "expenditure" (consumption) which would be subject to tax—progressive or otherwise. [3]

The concept of an expenditure tax is not new. It can be traced back to the writings of Thomas Hobbes and of John Stuart Mill. Nor is the concept of an expenditure tax confined to this country. In 1977 the US Treasury produced a "Blueprint for Basic Tax Reforms" based on expenditure tax principles; similarly in 1978 the Swedish Royal Commission on Taxation proposed reforms along the lines of an expenditure tax.

[1] The Meade Committee Report (1978). See also Kay & King, *The British Tax System.*

[2] The anomalies and concessions that concerned the Committee included, (i) the distortions in the capital markets through preferential treatment of some investments (eg pensions), (ii) the disincentive of progressive rate tax and the use of wasteful fringe benefits, (iii) the tax capitalisation problems of some concessions, such as mortgage interest relief.

Others have suggested that the UK tax system ought to be considered for reform because (i) the costs of administration are comparatively high, (ii) the system is not internationally compatible; and (iii) historically, the PAYE system is out-of-date and unnecessary.

[3] An "expenditure tax" ought to be regarded as (or even called) a "cash-flow income tax". See Kay, *Fiscal Studies*, Vol 7, No 4, page 9.

Despite these proposals the only known experience of expenditure tax systems were in India and Ceylon in the 1950s. In both instances, the systems were impractical and were abandoned—an event that was not considered by the Meade Committee.

The perceived advantages of an expenditure tax are that it would increase incentives to save and invest; it avoids the need to distinguish capital from income (although one would have to distinguish "saving" from "expenditure or consumption"); it would provide a base to tax an individual on what he takes out of (or "consumes") rather than on what he puts into the economy (although some economists believe "consumption" is economically beneficial and ought to be encouraged rather than penalised); and that it provides a basis for the development of a co-ordinated system of taxation based on proper principles rather than on ad hoc anomalies and concessions.

Even if one accepts the basis and principles of an expenditure tax, one wonders whether it is practically possible to consider its total introduction into the United Kingdom. For example, some tax concessions have been capitalised into assets. A sweeping removal of those concessions would remove the value of those assets and penalise those who had purchased or invested on the basis of existing concessions. Similarly, those individuals enjoying retirement might constantly be "taking out" of the economy monies to support their day-to-day activities. Those monies might derive from lifelong capital investments and pensions. To penalise such "consumption" might be perceived as inequitable. When he was Chancellor of the Exchequer, Mr N Lawson was caused to remark that a system of expenditure tax was "quite impracticable, even if it was desirable" (1984 Budget Speech).

Credit must be given to the Meade Committee in recognising possible transitional problems and responding by suggesting two alternative approaches to the introduction of an expenditure tax. The first approach involved the introduction of a universal expenditure tax based on the consumption principle and applicable to all taxpayers. The second approach involved the introduction of a two-tier expenditure tax. The lower tier would consist of a single rate of tax levied on expenditure or consumption through a form of value added tax (VAT or ITVAT as the Committee calls it). The upper tier would be a "universal expenditure tax" but limited in its "universal" application to higher rate taxpayers with higher levels of expenditure—a sort of surtax on the higher level consumers. It would be intended that over time the threshold for the application of the universal tax to those in the upper tier would eventually be lowered to a degree where the universal tax would be truly universal in its coverage and then the special VAT would be removed—proposal one, the favoured proposal, would then have been achieved.

As mentioned earlier, the Meade Committee and its Report were subject to criticism and comment. [1] Some critics referred to the unofficial nature and actual composition of the Committee; many critics commentated on the practical problems of the introduction of an expenditure tax—particularly transitional problems and the ultimately heavy reliance on a process of self-assessment; and some critics were concerned over the suggested benefits of an expenditure tax : some economists perceive that consumption is economically beneficial and ought not to be discouraged or penalised.

Similarly some particular (alleged) benefits of an expenditure-based tax have come under scrutiny. For example, it has been suggested that although an expenditure tax might increase the return to saving there was little evidence to suggest that it would substantially increase the level of saving. There is also some belief that expenditure tax would result in higher tax rates (needed to offset the loss of capital tax receipts) which in turn might present a disincentive to work, especially in instances of immediate consumption. Nor is it firmly believed that an expenditure tax would necessarily promote equity; a person's wealth might indicate a person's ability to pay but careful placing of that wealth (through exempt savings and investments) removes the obligation and liability to pay.

It is interesting to note that one of the driving forces behind the Meade Committee's appointment and proposals, the need to consider the removal of anomalies and concessions and the development of a co-ordinated and principled tax system, might itself be in danger should the Committee's proposals ever be formally adopted. It is clear that in any process of tax reform special interest groups are capable of obtaining ad hoc concessions and contribute to the development of anomalies through the process of "pressurising". There is little to suggest that such interest group concessions and anomalies would not be present in the process of change to an expenditure tax.

Finally, although there has not been a wholesale introduction of expenditure tax into the United Kingdom it is beginning to appear in the form of influencing recent tax developments. For example, the introduction of Personal Equity Plans (PEPs) in the 1986 Budget stirred the reaction that this represented

[1] See Prest 1978 BTR 176.

... the transfer of quoted shares from the category of "no fiscal privilege" to that of "Expenditure Tax" or better ... the principle that direct personal investment in equities is intended to be a privileged form of saving has now been clearly established ... [1]

## A Comprehensive Income Tax

The Meade Committee reported that the UK tax system fell somewhere between a pure (or comprehensive) income tax system and an expenditure tax system. Its principal reason for dismissing reform in favour of the former was that

... it would be extremely difficult, if not impossible, to introduce all the features of a comprehensive tax. In particular, we think that many of the measures which would theoretically be necessary to index the system for proper capital income adjustments against inflation would not be practicable. [2]

Despite any apparent practical difficulties, the development of a comprehensive income tax has been the subject of serious consideration—particular in Canada. [3] In essence a comprehensive income tax, often referred to as a tax on the "accretion of economic power", requires that tax is imposed on actual or imputed increases in wealth or economic power. The increase in wealth would include consideration of "wealth" at the beginning and at the end of the tax period together with a consideration of consumption during that period.

In 1966, the Carter Report [4] was presented to the Federal Government of Canada with the recommendation that a comprehensive income tax be introduced. The Report attracted the accolade that "[i]t must rank as the most comprehensive and detailed blueprint for tax reform ever created." [5]

The recommendations of the Carter Commission included the introduction of a new comprehensive base for income tax. This new base would

---

[1] J A Kay, *Fiscal Studies*, (1986) Vol 7, No 2, at page 35.

[2] The Meade Committee Report (1978) at p500.

[3] It must be recognised that the debate and discussions of the Carter Commission will influence the reform debate in other countries. This was apparent in the tax base rate reforms in the United States in 1986.

[4] The Report of the Royal Commission on Taxation, Canada, 1966. Chaired by Kenneth Le M Carter.

[5] Sandford, (1987) BTR 148.

enable tax to be imposed on all gains in purchasing power. Such gains, whether they occurred from actual or deemed capital disposals, would be classed as taxable "income". At the same time, the Commission proposed a general reduction of the tax rate: a reduction that could be achieved through the widening of the tax base.

Other recommendations of the Carter Commission included the integration of personal and corporate income tax and the removal of capital investment and allowance incentives. The latter were perceived as important in removing major sources of tax avoidance.

It is interesting to note that the Carter Commission considered the functions and principles of tax and was concerned at the need to reconcile any conflicts in terms of economic growth, stability, individual freedoms and government policy. The Commission's overriding objective in supporting the introduction of a comprehensive income tax was the promotion of "horizontal equity". It was the Commission's view that the development of "fair taxes should override all other objectives"—the comprehensive income tax was perceived as providing a good indicator and measure of the ability to pay.

Although the Carter Commission's Report was initially welcomed, it appears that little of it has been implemented or enacted.[1] Much of that "failure" must be accounted for by the particular political changes in Canada; however, it is probable that the Carter proposals, like the Meade Committee proposals, would face common problems and barriers in the process of tax reform. These include:

1. Pressures from special interest groups—we mentioned in relation to expenditure tax that anomalies and concessions could develop as a consequence of special interest groups. Examples of the "pressurising" that might be experienced are found in some of the responses to the Carter proposals. It is reported that the "business lobby" and the "farm lobby" made strong representation in respect of the proposed treatment of death and gift taxes. Similarly, one would expect that financial institutions in the UK would strongly respond to any attempts to remove mortgage interest relief—although the March Budget (1993) saw some weakening of the mortgage interest relief position.
2. Social and economic views—it has been suggested that one of the reasons why the Carter proposals may have failed to have been implemented is that the economic arguments and base of the proposals

---

[1] See Sandford, ibid.

are no longer "vogue". Social attitudes change in terms of priorities and "horizontal equity" might not now be appropriate. Regional policies, selective investment policies and redistribution might now be priorities. An extreme example of difference in social attitudes can be found in some jurisdictions where tax evasion is socially acceptable and often encouraged. By contrast, in the United Kingdom, tax evasion and avoidance is believed to attract social stigma.

3. Short-term political goods—it is clear that if any sweeping tax reforms are to succeed, they must enjoy political support. This need raises two problems. First, the proposals themselves ought to be as a consequence of political initiative and emanate from an official committee. The Meade Committee Report, initiated and appointed by the Institute of Fiscal Studies, failed to enjoy the necessary "official" status. Second, both the expenditure tax system and the comprehensive income tax system require a long-term commitment and ability to withstand public criticisms and concerns. Despite the long-term benefits of enjoying a tax system based on a coherent set of principles, it is highly probable that those who suffer during the transition would vehemently pursue their own short-term goals of defeating the changes and restoring their benefits. That "short termism" might also apply to the politicians. Apart from the amount of Parliamentary time that sweeping changes would absorb, it is unlikely that the Parliamentary term of a government would be sufficient to facilitate long term changes and withstand short-term unpopularity. Any attempt at introducing wholesale changes might realistically be viewed as political suicide.

British politicians used to be told that if they changed the tax system, the gainers would not thank them and the losers would not forgive them. If a Chancellor really wanted to make a reputation as tax reformer, he was advised to lie down until the feeling had passed. [1]

4. It has been suggested that tax reform in Britain will never substantially take place unless we reform the Inland Revenue first. [2] Criticism is directed at the dominant policymaking role performed by the Inland Revenue. Not only is this comparatively unique, but also inappropriate. The Inland Revenue does not possess the necessary awareness or

[1] J A Kay, *Fiscal Studies*, (1990), Vol 7, No 4, at p1.
[2] *Ibid* at p3.

expertise to contribute to and consider the socio-economic and political realities of reform—it is merely equipped to consider administrative criteria and perform administrative functions. It has been suggested that the Inland Revenue's role should be confined to the latter and that tax policy and reform should clearly be placed in the hands of the Treasury—perhaps assisted by a body of advisors. Recent developments, Mr Lamont's body of wise men, might constitute a tangible response to this area of criticisms and concerns. This body of independent tax advisors (the "wise men") has been continued by Mr Lamount's successors.

Finally, despite these procedural and process difficulties it is widely accepted that the "British tax system is complex, inefficient and unfair" and that reform is necessary.[1] The manner and method of reform is subject to opinion and debate but it is agreed that it must be coherent and based on principle; and probably incremental in approach and implementation.

## The Plain Language and Structure of Tax Legislation

One of the criticisms and perceived barriers to the reform of tax law is directed at the language and mass of detail of tax legislation: in fact it was reported that in November 1995 there were nearly 6,000 pages of Inland Revenue primary legislation, representing an increase of over 50 per cent since 1988.

A number of initiatives have been taken to address concerns over language, structure and volume. The Institute of Fiscal Studies set up a committee back in 1994 to examine these concerns. It subsequently recommended that a pilot project be adopted to see if an expensive rewrite could be justified: it estimated that a rewrite would take about five years and involve a team of up to 40 people. The Institute's Final Report on Tax Legislation was published in June 1996. In the meantime the Inland Revenue delivered to Parliament its report "The Path to Tax Simplification" in December 1995. Subsequently the Inland Revenue has published another consultative document (August 1996) setting out proposals for carrying out the review and rewrite recommended in the Institute of Fiscal Studies Final Report on Tax Legislation. The Revenue aims to make the rewritten laws as easy as possible to understand, through logical ordering of the provisions, directness of expression and clear and

[1] For a useful discussion on reform and principle see M Wilson, *Taxation*, Chapter 12.

simple layout. Difficult decisions exist in terms of layout: should it take an activity-based approach or one that reflects type of taxpayer, or type of tax or subject-base? Should it rewrite all the legislation at the same time and go for a "big-bang" introduction, or should it seek to reap the benefits of incremental reform through a staged introduction? Who should comprise the reform/rewrite team—public/private sector experts or a combination?

Whatever the answer to these and the many other questions raised by the reports, it is interesting to note the recognition of the problems and of the time-scale to achieve a revision of the problems of language, detail and volume. Perhaps the system and experiences of "self-assessment" might increase public awareness and experiences of the problem. One suspects that until public opinion is strong enough, successive governments will avoid the costs and disruption of a sweeping rewrite of tax legislation whatever the perceived long-term benefits.

## EC and International Influence

The operation, development and reform of our tax system must consider EC and international influences. International influences have always been present. For example, there is a need to consider comparative treatment of the taxation of individuals and corporations. High tax rates might result in emigration of individuals and corporations. Similarly, the tax treatment of capital will influence investment decisions and locations. It is clear that the tax-induced mobility of these factors of production will have a distorting effect on the locality and transfer of these factors—the tax system is not neutral but is influential in determining the allocation and location of scarce resources. One need only refer to the intentions of the government in the Republic of Ireland when it set a corporation tax of ten per cent in the hope of attracting manufacturing industry and corporations, to illustrate the distorting effect of taxation.

Other international effects of taxation include concerns over jurisdiction and enforcement. These involve the difficulty of negotiating double tax treaties and international co-operation. The fiscal and economic needs of some countries present difficult, and at times insurmountable, hurdles to co-operation on jurisdiction and enforcement matters. The OECD has a model code and agreement but this model is not binding and is often viewed as biased in favour of the economies of Western Europe. Other models have been suggested and developed, but they also suffer from perceived prejudice and favour.

Through its membership of the European Community, the United Kingdom has participated in the debate on aspects of tax reform in areas where barriers and distortions are apparent. It is important to appreciate that tax reform is necessary if the Community aims to facilitate the free movement of goods, services, people and capital and the freedom of establishment is to be fulfilled. This demands that the European Community considers and embarks on an ambitious harmonisation programme of both direct and indirect taxes. Thus far the Community has been progressing reform and harmonisation in areas of corporation tax and indirect tax in the form of VAT reforms. The Community's progress in the area of corporation tax reform will be considered at a later stage in the chapter on Corporation Tax—suffice to say at the moment that the Commission's progress has been slow and somewhat disappointing. The issue of indirect tax reforms has also been slow but is beginning to come to fruition. The operation and rates of VAT have had a distorting effect on the transfer of goods and services. [1] In a series of directives the European Community has accepted a framework for a common system of VAT and the Community countries are working toward the ultimate aim of a harmonised system of rate bands, although political difficulties remain. As part of the push for the creation of the "internal market", transitional measures came into force on 1 January 1993 and remain in force until 31 December 1996. These transitional measures involve a limited harmonisation and a response to the abolition of fiscal frontiers. The "measures" were included in the Finance Bill 1992 [2] and involve (broadly) amendments whereby exports from a member state to other European Community countries will no longer be subject to VAT, while imports from other European Community countries would be (an "acquisitions" principle). Tax charged in one Member State will be deductible in another Member State ("reverse charge" principle); whereas imports from non-EC countries will still be subject to taxation. The precise details of the operation of VAT are outside the scope of this work, but it is important for the reader to appreciate that VAT is one of those

---

[1] Since 1967, the Community has been working on the approximation of VAT and to this effect it adopted a long line of directives. For example, see the First and Second Directives (67/227/EEC and 67/228/EEC) which required Member States to adopt a system of VAT.

The comprehensive rules on VAT are to be found in the Sixth Directive (77/388/EEC) entitled "harmonisation of the laws of the Member States relating to turnover taxes—common system of value added tax and uniform basis of assessment". Numerous directives and decisions have been adopted to limit or amend Directive 77/388 (see Directive 83/181).

[2] The transitional system is an amendment of Directive 77/388 (Directive 91/680/EEC).

areas of taxation where we are beginning to experience EC-driven reforms.

*Self-Check Questions*

1. Identify and explain the characteristics of a good tax system.
2. What is an expenditure tax system? How does it differ from a comprehensive tax income system?
3. To what extent has the UK's membership of the European Communities influenced tax reform?

## Further Reading

Nelson-Jones J, *Tax Re-Distribution and Reality*, (1977) BTR 362–70.
Bensusan-Butt DM, *The Target for Tax Reform*, (1979) BTR 168–77.
Prest AR, *Proposals for a Tax-Credit System*, (1973) BTR 6–16.
Sandford C, *Carter Twenty Years On*, (1987) BTR 148.
Beighton LJH, *The Simplification of Tax Legislation*, (1996) BTR 50.

# 2

# The Territorial Scope

## Introduction

United Kingdom taxation is subject to a territorial limit, the cardinal principle being that the tax legislation does not extend beyond the jurisdiction. As far as income tax is concerned, this territorial aspect of income tax can be formalised into the propositions that either the source from which the taxable income is derived must be situated in the United Kingdom, or the person whose income is to be taxed must be resident in the United Kingdom.[1] The rules applicable in respect of other taxes are roughly similar, although they may differ in important respects. This chapter examines the concept of residence, and the other connecting factors which determine the liability of a person to United Kingdom taxation—i.e. ordinary residence, and domicile.

The terms "resident" and "ordinarily resident" are normally used in United Kingdom tax legislation, to describe a situation arising in a year of assessment, and not in relation to some longer or shorter period. The question that has to be decided is generally whether or not a person is resident or ordinarily resident in the United Kingdom in the year of assessment.[2] This is generally the same question that has to be decided in respect of the domicile of a person. The "United Kingdom" in this context refers to England, Scotland, Wales and Northern Ireland and does not include the Isle of Man and the Channel Islands.[3]

There are a number of general points to note with respect to the territorial scope of United Kingdom tax. Generally, a United Kingdom resident is taxable in respect of all income and capital gains wherever arising. Such a person will also be liable to inheritance tax, unless he is not domiciled in the United Kingdom and he has no United Kingdom property. A non-resident will be taxable on income arising from sources within the United Kingdom, and will be liable to capital gains tax, if he is

---

[1] Lord Herschell in *Colquhoun v Brooks* [1889] 14 App. Cas. 493 at 504.
[2] See Inland Revenue Statement of Practice, IR 20, para. 7.
[3] Inland Revenue Statement of Practice, IR 20, p3.

ordinarily resident, or if he is trading through a branch or agency in the United Kingdom and he disposes of assets used for the purposes of that branch or agency. There may be liability to inheritance tax unless the non-resident is also not domiciled here, and has no property here.

## Residence

Residence is the most important of the territorial connectors for liability to United Kingdom tax, but for all its importance, the term is not defined by statute. Since it has no special or technical meaning for tax purposes, it has to be given its plain and ordinary meaning. It was Viscount Cave LC who said in *Levene v IRC*[1]:

> ... the word "reside" is a familiar English word and is defined in the Oxford English Dictionary as meaning "to dwell permanently or for a considerable time, to have ones settled or usual abode, to live in a particular place". No doubt this definition must for present purposes be taken, subject to any modification which may result from the terms of the Income Tax Act and schedules, but, subject to that observation, it may be accepted as an accurate indication of the meaning of the word "reside".

The principal question with regard to residence is whether a person is resident in the United Kingdom or not, and not whether a person is resident in this country or in another country. That is to say, the question is: "is X resident in the United Kingdom?" and not for example, "is X resident in France or in the United Kingdom?", for X may well be resident in the United Kingdom for United Kingdom tax purposes while at the same time she may be resident in France under French law, and in Germany under German law. The Revenue and the courts in this country are not generally concerned with the last two situations, except perhaps in the context of double taxation agreements. As the Lord President said in *Cooper v Cadwalader*[2], it is not necessary in order for a person to be chargeable that he shall have his sole residence in the United Kingdom. Indeed, the Revenue have stated categorically:

> It is possible to be resident (or ordinarily resident) in both the UK and

---

[1] [1928] AC 217 at 222.
[2] [1904] 5 TC 101 at 106–107.

some other country (or countries) at the same time. If you are resident (or ordinarily resident) in another country, this does *not* mean that you cannot *also* be resident (or ordinarily resident) in the UK.[1]

Situations in which a person may be resident in the United Kingdom and in another country in the same year are normally covered by double taxation agreements. The United Kingdom has entered into such agreements with most of the other countries in the world, and new ones are being signed all the time.

Grammatically, the word "resident" indicates a quality of the person to be charged to tax—it is not descriptive of his property, real or personal.[2] The relation between a person and a place which is predicated by saying that a person "resides" there includes, *inter alia*, the element of time, duration, or permanence. However, that element, essential and importance as it is, is not the sole criterion[3], and thus whether a person is resident in the United Kingdom or not is essentially a question of fact and degree. The determination of whether or not the degree extends so far as to make a person resident or ordinarily resident here is for the Commissioners and it is not for the courts to say whether they would have reached the same conclusion.[4]

## The Residence of Individuals

*Introduction*

The determination of an individual's residence must be made for each relevant year of assessment (Viscount Cave in *Levene v IRC*). However, the courts may have regard to the taxpayer's conduct in years previous and subsequent to the relevant year of assessment in determining whether the taxpayer was resident in that year. The Revenue have produced a fairly detailed Statement of Practice on the residence and ordinary residence of individuals (IR 20), which contains a code of principles based largely on decisions in their favour. We shall refer to this code at various stages of our discussion.

The Revenue position is that, strictly speaking, each tax year must be

---

[1] IR 20, para. 1.4 (emphasis supplied).
[2] Per Viscount Sumner in *IRC v Lysaght* [1928] All ER 575 at 580.
[3] Lord President Clyde in *Reid v IRC* [1926] 10 TC 673 at 678.
[4] Per Lord Buckmaster in *IRC v Lysaght* [1928] All ER 575 at 582.

looked at as a whole, that a person is to be treated as either resident or not resident for the whole year, and that he cannot be regarded as resident for part of the year and not resident for the remainder.[1] The Revenue will however split the year, by concession[2], if the person is a new permanent resident; or if the person comes to the United Kingdom for at least two years (provided that he has not been ordinarily resident in the United Kingdom); or if the person has left the United Kingdom for permanent residence abroad (provided that in so doing he ceases to be ordinarily resident in the United Kingdom); or, subject to certain conditions,[3] if the person goes abroad under a contract of employment. In the first two cases the person is treated as resident only from the date of arrival in the United Kingdom, and in the last two, he is treated as not resident from the date of departure.

There are a number of factors (derived both from case law and the Inland Revenue code IR 20) which are applied in the determination of the residence status of an individual. Some of them are of conclusive effect in themselves, while some others, while not necessarily conclusive may, in combination with others, suffice to make an individual resident in the United Kingdom in a relevant year of assessment. Furthermore, some of the factors apply only to certain classes of individual while others apply generally. The discussion that follows examines these factors.

### Period of Physical Presence in the United Kingdom

Section 336(1) of the ICTA 1988 provides that an individual who is in the United Kingdom for some temporary purpose only and not with a view to establishing his residence there will not be charged to income tax as a person resident in the United Kingdom in any year of assessment, if he has not actually resided in the United Kingdom for a period equal in the whole to six months in that year.[4] The corollary to this is that if a person has actually resided in the United Kingdom for a period amounting to six months in any tax year, he will be taxed as a resident. This provision

---

[1] IR 20, para. 1.5.

[2] See ESC A11, 7 Feb. 1996.

[3] The conditions are that, the absence from the United Kingdom and the employment itself both extend beyond a complete tax year, and, any interim visits to the United Kingdom during the period do not amount to 183 days or more, in any tax year, or, an average of 91 days or more in a tax year. In this respect, the average will be taken over the period of absence up to a maximum of 4 years.

[4] See also s9(3) of the Taxation of Chargeable Gains Act 1992 for a similar provision in respect of Capital Gains Tax.

relates only to the taxation, under Schedule D, of profits or gains received in respect of foreign possessions or securities. However s336(2) extends the rule to tax charged under Cases I, II and III of Schedule E (income from offices, employments, etc.), and the revenue code IR 20 applies the rule generally. Under the IR 20, six months is equated with 183 days, whether or not the year is a leap year, and ignoring the days of arrival and departure; and a person is who in the United Kingdom for this period in one year of assessment will, *without exception*, be treated as resident. [1]

The six-month period relates to each year of assessment and so it is possible in theory for a visitor to actually spend more than six months in the United Kingdom without being resident, if the period is spread over two years of assessment. This point should be taken with care, because if the visits become regular, even though each one is for a duration which is less than six months in each tax year, it is still possible, taking into account other factors, for the person to be resident. According to Lord McLaren in *Cooper v Cadwalader* [2] this six-month exemption is "one that walks upon two legs". It requires, first, that the party is here for a temporary purpose only, and secondly, that he is here not with a view or intent of establishing a residence. If the argument is lame on one of the legs, then the party does not get the benefit of the exemption, because he must be able to affirm both members of the double proposition.

The interpretation of the first part of the exemption—the meaning of "temporary purpose"—is pertinent to the issue of visits being spread over two years of assessment . In this respect Lord McLaren said [3]:

> . . . temporary purposes mean casual purposes as distinguished from the case of a person who is here in the pursuance of his regular habits of life. Temporary purpose means the opposite of continuous and permanent residence. Nobody ever supposed that you must reside twelve months in the year in order to be liable for Income Tax, and therefore "temporary" does not mean the negation of perpetuity, but means that it is casual or transitory residence, as distinguished from a residence, of which there may be more than one, but which may be habitual or permanent.

The vital words here are "regular habits", "casual" and "transitory". A

---

[1] IR 20, para. 1.2.
[2] [1904] 5 TC 101 at 108–109.
[3] At p109.

person who spends eight months in the United Kingdom spread over two years of assessment may well be stretching those words to their limits, since it is not entirely clear when the visit may be considered to have ceased to be casual or transitory.

With respect to the words "view or intent of establishing his residence" in the second part of the exemption, Lord McLaren said that there seemed to be a recognition of what may be called "a constructive residence as distinguished from actual residence". According to him [1]:

> It is not that you take a house or country place with a view or an intention of establishing a residence, although you may not have had time to become a resident. Still, if you are looking forward to it, apparently that makes you liable to taxation, because in order to get the benefit of the exemption you must say that you have no view and no intention of acquiring a residence there.

What Lord McLaren is saying is that this part of the exemption contains a very subjective element—i.e. did the taxpayer in fact have the view or intention of establishing his residence here?—and if subjectively this is found to be so, then he cannot claim the benefit of s336(1). It therefore seems that the exemption thus granted to people who visit the United Kingdom is fairly limited in scope. Those who visit the United Kingdom for temporary purposes will be well advised to actively seek not to "look forward to" establishing a residence here, and to actively avoid all activities which may be so construed.

If a person is absent from the United Kingdom for the whole of a year of assessment, it is unlikely that he will be resident in that year. This point is illustrated by *Turnbull v Foster.* [2] The taxpayer carried on business for a long time in Madras where he had his residence. His children lived in the family home in the United Kingdom and he had over the years visited them for short periods nearly every year. The taxpayer and his wife were not in the United Kingdom at any time during the year in which the Revenue sought to assess him as a person residing in the United Kingdom. Not surprisingly, the Revenue's attempt failed. The fact that he was never in the country during the year was vital. This fact, if not wholly decisive of the question, is a factor of great importance in the context of an annual tax. [3] It is important to note however that the taxpayer in *Turnbull v Foster* had not previously been ordinarily resident in the United

[1] *Ibid.*
[2] [1904] 6 TC 206.
[3] Per Nicholls J in *Reid v Clark*[1985] 3 WLR 142 at 146.

Kingdom, a fact noted by the court. In the case of a person who has previously been ordinarily resident, other factors may apply to make him resident, even though absent from the United Kingdom throughout the tax year. [1]

### Ordinary Residence in Previous Years

An individual's ordinary residence in the United Kingdom in years prior to a year of assessment in which his residence status is at issue is statutorily relevant only in respect of persons who are Commonwealth citizens and citizens of the Republic of Ireland. The relevant rule is in s334, which provides that, if a Commonwealth citizen or a citizen of the Republic of Ireland who has been ordinarily resident in the United Kingdom leaves the United Kingdom for the purpose only of occasional residence abroad, he shall be assessed and charged to income tax as a person residing in the United Kingdom, notwithstanding such absence. [2]

With respect to the terms used in this rule, the persons who have the status of "Commonwealth citizen" are described in s37 of the British Nationality Act 1981, and we shall discuss the meaning of "ordinary residence" later in this chapter. The other important term, the phrase "occasional residence", has been considered in a number of cases. In *Levene v IRC*[3] a retired businessman who had previously been both resident and ordinarily resident in the United Kingdom went to live abroad. From the date of departure until some time more than five years later, he maintained no fixed place of abode anywhere, but stayed in various hotels, both in this country and abroad. During this time he spent an average of 20 weeks each year in the United Kingdom, his purpose being to obtain medical advice, to visit relatives, to take part in certain Jewish religious observances, and to deal with his income tax affairs. It was held by the House of Lords that the taxpayer originally left the United Kingdom and went to live abroad for occasional residence only, and so was resident in the United Kingdom in the years in question. According to Viscount Sumner[4]:

[1] See below; also *Rogers v IRC* (1 TC 225) in which a master mariner whose wife and family lived in the United Kingdom throughout the year in which he was abroad was taxed as a resident notwithstanding his absence for the whole year, and *Re Young* (1 TC 57).

[2] Cf. para. 2.1 of IR 20 which simply states: "You are *resident and ordinarily resident* in the UK if you usually live in this country and only go abroad for short periods only—for example, on holiday or on business trips." This paragraph says nothing about the person being a Commonwealth citizen or a citizen of the Irish Republic, and therefore its legal status may be doubtful.

[3] [1928] AC 217.

[4] At p227.

The evidence as a whole disclosed that Mr Levene continued to go to and fro during the years in question, leaving at the beginning of winter and coming back in summer, his home thus remaining as before. He changed his sky but not his home. On this I see no error in law in saying of each year that his purpose in leaving the United Kingdom was occasional residence only. The occasion was the approach of an English winter and when with the promise of summer here that occasion passed away back came Mr Levene to attend calls of interest, of friendship and of piety.

In this case, the court could identify an "occasion" which led to the occasional residence abroad—the English winter. In another case, no such occasion was identifiable, and thus the decision went the other way. In *IRC v Combe*[1] the taxpayer, who had been both resident and ordinarily resident in the United Kingdom, left for the purpose of a three-year apprenticeship under a New York employer. The object of his apprenticeship was to qualify him as European Representative of the New York firm, and his employment accordingly made it necessary for him to visit Europe, and especially the United Kingdom from time to time on his employer's business (at times spending almost six months). On these visits he lived in hotels and throughout the three years he had no house and no fixed place of abode in this country. Instead, his business and residential headquarters were permanently in New York throughout the three years. It was held that the taxpayer's departure was not a departure for the purpose of occasional residence abroad and he was not resident in the United Kingdom in the years in question. Lord President Clyde said[2] that "occasional residence" is residence taken up or happening as passing opportunity requires in one case, or admits, in another, and contrasts with the residence, or ordinary residence, of a person who is "resident" or "ordinarily resident" in some place or country.

Lord Sands, concurring, noted that there was a "distinct break" in the nature of the taxpayer's residence when he departed for America.[3] This concept of distinct (or definite) break was applied by Nicholls J in *Reed v Clark*.[4] The taxpayer left the United Kingdom for the USA with the firm intention of living in Los Angeles throughout the relevant year of

---

[1] [1932] 17 TC 405.
[2] At p410.
[3] At p411.
[4] [1985] 3 WLR 142; [1985] STC 323.

assessment but to return to the United Kingdom shortly after the end of that year. He was away for a 13-month period which spanned the whole of the tax year, living for the most part in a house rented for him by a company under his control. Nicholls J held that, considering all the circumstances underlying the taxpayer's departure, including the fact that there was a definite break in the pattern of his life, his departure for the USA was not for occasional residence only, and he was not resident in the United Kingdom in the year in question. He said that the meaning to be given to "occasional residence" was a question of law and that occasional residence was the converse of ordinary residence. According to Nicholls J the taxpayer's journey to America was not made as a matter of "passing opportunity".[1] His business activities had previously taken him, and still took him to America every year, and on that particular trip he had established himself in a way which would make him both resident and ordinarily resident there under the United Kingdom rules. Summing up the matter Nicholls J said[2]:

> . . . it seems to me plain that a British resident's departure abroad for a period of a few weeks or months with the firm intention of returning at the end of the period to live here as before would be likely always to be for the purpose only of occasional residence . . . it seems to me equally plain that the departure of such a resident abroad for a limited period of, say, three years would not necessarily be for the purpose only of "occasional residence" just because from the outset he had a firm intention of returning at the end of the period to live here as before: "not necessarily", because all the facts would have to be considered . . .
> In my view, a year is a long enough period for a person's purpose of living where he does to be capable of having sufficient degree of continuity for it to be properly described as settled. Hence, depending on all the circumstances the foreign country could be the place where for that period he would be ordinarily and not just occasionally resident.

### Regularity of Visits to the United Kindom

The case of *Levene v IRC* (above) shows that where a person makes regular visits to the United Kingdom for periods which are less than six months in any year of assessment, such a person can still be treated as resident even

[1] At p146.
[2] At p157.

if he has no permanent home here. The crucial question is whether the visits are sufficiently regular to be part of his normal life. This point is illustrated even more vividly in *IRC v Lysaght.*[1] The taxpayer, born in England of Irish parents, was a managing director of an English company. After retiring from this post, he was appointed an advisory director to the company. He thereupon sold his house in England and went to live in Ireland, maintaining no definite place of abode in this country. His new position as a consultant to the company brought him to England every month for directors' meetings, on which visits he stayed for about one week, in hotels. The commissioners held that he was resident and ordinarily resident in the United Kingdom in the year in question and this was upheld by the House of Lords. Viscount Sumner noted[2] that it was the shortness of the aggregate time during which Mr Lysaght was in the United Kingdom that constituted the principal point in his favour, but also noted that the question of longer or shorter time, like other questions of degree, is one peculiarly for the commissioners. He did not doubt that the commissioners had understood the word "resident" in its proper legal signification and so applied it. Therefore their decision could not be interfered with.

The result is that an individual may be held resident even if he has no place of abode at all (*Levene v IRC*) or no place of abode in the United Kingdom *(IRC v Lysaght)* if he makes habitual and substantial visits to the United Kingdom. For these purposes, "substantial" means (as per the Revenue code IR 20) that the average annual period(s) of the visits amounts to three months (91 days) or more per tax year (no doubt derived from Mr Lysaght's visits of one week every month amounting to twelve weeks in a year), and "habitual" means that this pattern has been followed for four consecutive years. If it is clear that the person intends to follow this pattern from the beginning, he may be treated as resident from the beginning.[3]

## The Purpose of the Visits to the United Kingdom

Closely connected with the last point is the purpose of the taxpayer's visits to the United Kingdom. If the person is merely in the United Kingdom as a traveller, and not as part of his regular order of life, the visits *per se* will

[1] [1928] All ER 575.
[2] At page 581.
[3] See IR 20, para. 3.3.

probably not be sufficient to make him resident. For example in *IRC v Zorab*[1] the taxpayer was a retired member of the Indian civil service, who in the course of his habitual travels in Europe spent about five months in England each year, the sole purpose being to visit friends. He was held not to be resident by the commissioners, and this was upheld by Rowlatt J. Rowlatt J said[2] that one had to consider not only the time that the taxpayer was here but also the nature of his visit and his connection with this country. In this case the gentleman seemed to be a mere traveller. He was a native of India and had retired from his work there, after which be began to travel extensively in Europe. In these circumstances there was sufficient evidence for the commissioners to hold that he was not resident.

It should be noted however that this test as to the purpose of the taxpayer's visit is not conclusive, since a person may still be resident in the United Kingdom even if he is here for reasons beyond his control. That this is so can be established from the cases. In *IRC v Lysaght* (above) for example, the taxpayer only came to the United Kingdom for the purpose of board meetings, and not for the purpose of living here, but this fact did not help him. The inconclusiveness of volition is further illustrated by *Inchiquin v IRC*.[3] The taxpayer was an Irish peer, who had succeeded to the ancestral titles and estates (including a castle in Ireland) on the death of his father, but who was living in England. On the outbreak of the Second World War in 1939 he was called up for military service and became an officer in the British Army. In 1940, during the course of the war his mother, who was living in the castle in Ireland, died. The prevailing circumstances made it desirable that he should return to Ireland to live in the castle and look after the estate, and in particular to avoid being called an absentee landlord. However his military duties occupied him and he was not relieved until 1942 upon which he took up permanent residence in the castle in Ireland. The commissioners held that he was resident in the years 1940–41 and 1941–42, in spite of the fact that he had always wanted to return to Ireland but was forced to stay here. This decision was upheld by the Court of Appeal. Tucker LJ said[4] that he derived most assistance from the speech of Lord Buckmaster in *Lysaght's* case in which Lord Buckmaster said:

A man might well be compelled to reside here completely against his

---

[1] [1926] 11 TC 289.
[2] At p291.
[3] [1946–50] 31 TC 125.
[4] At 133–134.

will; the exigencies of business often forbid the choice of residence and though a man may make his home elsewhere and stay in this country only because business compels him, yet . . . if the periods for which and the conditions under which he stays are such that they may be regarded as constituting residence, it is open to the commissioners to find that in fact he does so reside.

In this case there was sufficient evidence for the commissioners to decide as they did.

## Place of Abode in the United Kingdom

The availability of accommodation or a place of abode is a factor that often points strongly to residence. However, as we have seen in the context of regular visitors (*Levene* and *Lysaght* above), it is possible for a person to be resident in the United Kingdom even though he has no home or place of abode here. As Lord President Clyde aptly noted in *Reid v IRC*[1]:

Take the case of a homeless tramp, who shelters tonight under a bridge, tomorrow in the greenwood and as the unwelcome occupant of a farm outhouse the night after. He wanders in this way all over the United Kingdom. But will anyone say he does not live in the United Kingdom?—and will anyone regard it as a misuse of language to say he resides in the United Kingdom? In his case there may be no relations with family or friends, no business ties, and none of the ordinary circumstances which create a link between the life of a British subject and the United Kingdom; but, even so, I do not think it could be disputed that he resides in the United Kingdom.

This point was reiterated by Viscount Cave LC in *Levene v IRC*[2]:

. . . where the person sought to be charged has no home or establishment in any country but lives his life in hotels or at the houses of his friends, and if such a man spends the whole of the year in hotels in the United Kingdom, then he is held to reside in this country; for it is not necessary for that purpose that he should continue to live in one

---

[1] [1926] 10 TC at 678.
[2] [1928] AC at 223.

place in this country but only that he should reside in the United Kingdom.

If however a person has a permanent place of abode or accommodation available in the United Kingdom for his use, the Revenue originally took the view that he is resident here for any tax year in which he visits the United Kingdom, however short the visit may be.[1] It appears that this practice was derived from the case of *Cooper v Cadwalader*.[2] The taxpayer in this case was an American barrister who had his ordinary residence in New York and who rented a house in Scotland, with exclusive shooting and sporting rights over the grouse shootings of the property, and fishing rights in the rivers and streams within the bounds of its territory. The house was furnished and was kept up for the taxpayer and placed at his disposal to go to at any time of the year that he chose. He and his valet, whom he brought with him from America, normally resided at this property continuously for a period of about two months each year during the grouse shooting season. He had no place of business in the United Kingdom, and, during his stay here, maintained and kept open his residence in New York so he could return to it at any time. It was held that he was resident in the United Kingdom. According to the Lord President[3] the taxpayer had, in effect, a lease of heritage in Scotland, occupied personally the properties let to him for a considerable portion of each year, and when he was absent in America, these properties were kept in readiness for his return. It was clear that his occupation of the property was not of a casual or temporary character. Rather, it was substantial, and as regards some of its incidents, it was continuous.

The Lord President said[4] that if a person continues to have a residence in the United Kingdom, he is resident there in the sense of the Acts, and that a person may have more than one residence, if he maintains an establishment at each. This statement is the "place of abode" rule, and it may be the source of the Revenue's old rule (although the context in which the statement was made does not suggest that any visit, no matter how brief, will be sufficient). It is important to note here that there was nothing in the statement of the Lord President to suggest that the six-

---

[1] IR 20, para. 2.5 (for persons leaving the United Kingdom permanently); para. 3.3 (for temporary visitors to the United Kingdom—this rule, as far as it relates to temporary visitors, has recently been changed—see ICTA 1988, s336(3)).

[2] [1904] 5 TC 101.

[3] At p105.

[4] At p106.

month rule in s336(1) cannot apply in appropriate cases to negate the rule that he had stated. Indeed such possibility was explored, albeit unsuccessfully, by counsel in *Cooper v Cadwalader*. In response to the argument of counsel that Mr Cadwalader fell within the six-month exemption, the Lord President said[1]:

> This provision appears to be directed to prevent temporary residents for less than six months in one year from being charged in respect of profits received from abroad, but it does not appear to me to apply to a case like the present. I do not think that the Appellant can reasonably maintain that he is in the United Kingdom "for some temporary purpose only, and not with any view or intent of establishing his residence therein," in the sense of the section, as he took [the property in which he had shooting rights] with the view of establishing his residence there during a material part of each year and maintaining his connection with it as tenant during the rest of the years, and he has a residence always ready for him if he should choose to come to it.

What may be deduced from this answer is that, if Mr Cadwalader's visit had been for some temporary purpose only, and if he had never had any intention of establishing his residence in the rented property, s336(1) may have availed him, notwithstanding that he had a place of abode available for his use. This is very far from the Revenue's old stance that any visit will be sufficient to attract a resident status if a person has a place of abode and it is not surprising therefore that the rules governing the relevance of the place of abode were changed.[2] The change relates to those who are in the United Kingdom for temporary purposes only. In this respect, s336(3) provides that the question whether an individual is in the United Kingdom for some temporary purpose only and not with the intention of establishing his residence there shall be decided without regard to any living accommodation available in the United Kingdom for his use.[3] Thus, such persons will not be resident in the United Kingdom simply because they have accommodation available here for their use. However, other factors may still apply to make them resident. The only change in the rule is simply to the effect that the availability of accommodation is in itself no longer a sufficient criterion to make a temporary visitor resident.

[1] *Ibid.*

[2] The changes took effect on 6 April 1993; see ICTA 1988, s336(3).

[3] Compare s9(4) of the TCGA 1992 for similar provisions with respect to capital gains tax.

The situation is thus now much the same as that which was envisaged in *Cooper v Cadwalader* (above)—i.e. the place of abode rule affects those who have some stronger connection with the United Kingdom than the mere availability of accommodation. In *Cooper* it was clear that the taxpayer was not here for "temporary purposes." To summarise the change, the situation is now that an individual will now be non-resident in the United Kingdom if the *only* reason for his having been previously regarded as resident was the availability of accommodation. This seems an eminently sensible approach to the question.

Whether or not a person has a place of abode available for his use is a question of fact, and as *Lowenstein v De Salis*[1] shows, a person does not even have to own or rent the property if it is *de facto* available for his use. In that case a Belgian national, who had his residence in Brussels, visited the United Kingdom each year, and occupied for varying periods property in England, which comprised of a hunting box, together with the hunting stables, garage and gardens, and which belonged to a company of which he was a director and majority shareholder. It was admitted that the taxpayer could, when in the United Kingdom, use the said residence, stables and garage, without obtaining formal permission. In no year was he in this country for up to six months. The main factor that distinguished this from *Cooper v Cadwalader* was that in this case the taxpayer was neither the owner nor the lessee of the property. According to Rowlatt J, it really came to this—whether it is of the essence of the case that a man should be treated as coming here with a view to establishing his residence, and not for a temporary purpose only, that he should have at any rate a proprietary interest, such as a lease or something of that sort, in the house which he occupies when he is here. Rowlatt J held that it was not. He could not see what difference it made. The house was *de facto* available for the taxpayer's occupation whenever he came to this country and that was sufficient. Rowlatt J, concluding the matter, said[2]:

> ... when you are considering a question like residence, you are considering just a bundle of actual facts, and it seems to me that in a case like this you can quite well say that here this man had this house at his disposal, with everything in it or for his convenience, kept going all the year round, although he only wanted it for a short time. Luckily, he was in relation with a Company who were the owners of it, and he

[1] [1926] 10 TC 424.
[2] At pp437–438.

could do that without owning it. It is an accident. It might have been that he could do that with a relation, or a friend, or a philanthropist, or anybody; but in fact there was this house for him; and a lease would not put him in any better position so far as having the house and the availability of it, and the power of coming to it were concerned, so far as I understand the facts. Now I think that it is a case in which you do say you look at the substance of the matter. You do not look at the substance of the matter and say the man is the Company,—that is inaccurate, but you look at the substance of the matter and say: This is the house in which he could reside and did reside. It might have been held that he must not do it any longer, but up to the present time in history there has been no change for the last two or three years. There it is. He has got this house to come to when he likes; he does not own it; he has got no proprietary interest in it, but it is just as good as if he had for the purpose of having it for a residence, and there it is. I am bound to say that I do not think there can be any question upon the facts as clearly found in this case, giving the Appellant the benefit of anything that may be doubtful upon the case ... stated.

Not surprisingly, the fact that *de facto* availability is the crucial point is reiterated in the Revenue's code.[1] However, the Revenue have a lot more to say on the question whether accommodation is available for a person's use. According to the Revenue code, a house which a person owns, and which he lets out on a lease under the terms of which he has no right or permission to stay in it, or which is left empty of furniture, so that it is not in a state to be lived in, will not be treated as being available for his use.[2] Any accommodation rented for use during a temporary stay in the United Kingdom may be ignored if the period of renting is less than two years in the case of furnished accommodation, and one year in the case of unfurnished accommodation.[3] A house owned or rented by one spouse will usually be considered available for the use of the other, and accommodation provided by an employer may be regarded as available in certain circumstances.[4]

Apart from s336(3) ICTA 1988 (availability of a place of abode disregarded for certain purposes in respect of temporary visitors), there is

[1] See IR 20, para. 4.2.
[2] Para. 4.3.
[3] *Ibid.*
[4] Para. 4.2.

another statutory qualification to the place of abode rule. S335(1) ICTA 1988 provides that, where a person works full-time in a trade, profession, vocation, office or employment, and no part of the person's duties are carried on in the United Kingdom, then the question whether he is resident in the United Kingdom shall be determined without regard to any place of abode maintained in the United Kingdom for his use. The Revenue code puts a gloss on this by stating that the place of abode will *not* be ignored where the business of the person concerned has a branch or a place of business in the United Kingdom, and that this is so though he himself does not work here. [1]

With respect to the question whether, for the purposes of this statutory qualification, any part of the duties of an office or employment was performed in the United Kingdom, an allowance is made for "incidental" duties. S335(2) provides that where the duties of an office or employment fall substantially to be performed outside the United Kingdom in any year of assessment, duties performed within the United Kingdom which are merely incidental to the performance the duties performed abroad will be treated as if performed outside the United Kingdom. [2] The question when a duty performed in the United Kingdom can be taken to be "merely incidental" to one which is performed abroad was confronted in *Robson v Dixon*. [3] The taxpayer was employed as a pilot by KLM Airlines, his base being at Schiphol Airport, Amsterdam. He and his wife had their family home in Hertfordshire, meaning that he had a place of abode in the United Kingdom. His duties always commenced in Amsterdam but he would sometimes land at Heathrow en-route to Amsterdam. In the years in question the total number of take-offs and landings made by the taxpayer in all the countries that his flights took him to was 811. Of this number, only 38 took place in the United Kingdom and such stop overs were normally for a duration of some 40 to 60 minutes. It was held that, while the duties performed by the taxpayer in the United Kingdom were small *quantitatively* in comparison with the duties performed by him outside the United Kingdom, they were *qualitatively* of a nature similar to those duties, and were not duties the performance of which was merely incidental to the performance of the duties performed abroad. According to Pennycuick VC [4] the expression "merely incidental to" must be given

---

[1] IR 20, para. 4.4.
[2] See also IR 20, para. 4.4.
[3] [1972] 3 ALL ER 671.
[4] At p677.

effect according to the ordinary meaning of those words. The words are on their ordinary use apt to denote an activity (here the performance of duties) which does not serve any independent purpose but is carried out in order to further some other purpose. He concluded [1]:

> ... the duties performed by the taxpayer, apart from his duties at Schiphol, mainly consisted of taking a plane up at Schiphol, flying it to whatever its destination was and then bringing it down. In the case of the flights from Schiphol to some destination (normally in America) on which there was a stop at England, his duties consisted of taking the plane up at Schiphol, flying it to England, bringing it down at Heathrow or elsewhere, and then taking it up again and flying it again to the next destination, in America. With the best will in the world, I find it impossible to say that the activities carried on in or over England are merely incidental to the performance of the comparable activities carried on in or over Holland or in or over the ultimate destination in America. The activities are precisely co-ordinate, and I cannot see how it can properly be said that the activities in England are in some way incidental to the other activities.

It was said however [2] that a single landing might be disregarded under the *de minimis* rule. Furthermore, landings due to an emergency, such as weather conditions or mechanical trouble, or due to a diversion, might be regarded as incidental to the performance of the duties performed abroad. A situation that presents borderline questions would be one in which "a pilot's normal route did not touch on the United Kingdom but on one or two occasions he landed in the United Kingdom while acting as substitute for some other pilot who was ill". [3]

There exists an argument that this provision in s335(1) speaks only in respect of a place of abode which is *maintained* in the United Kingdom (as opposed to one which is actually *used*), such that if the place of abode is not used at all, then the provision may assist the taxpayer, but that if a person visits that place of abode then the provision will not help him. This type of issue was not raised in *Robson v Dixon* and considering that, if correct, it would by itself alone have been fatal to the taxpayer's case, it seems that the argument is of doubtful force.

---

[1] *Ibid.*
[2] At p677.
[3] Pennycuick VC at p677.

## *The Residence of Partnerships*

S111(2) of the ICTA 1988 provides that, where a trade or profession is carried on by persons in partnership, and any of those persons is chargeable to income tax, the profits, gains, or losses arising from the trade or profession will be computed for income tax purposes as if the partnership were an individual who is resident in the United Kingdom. If any of the partners is not resident in the United Kingdom, then s111 would apply in respect of that person as if the partnership were an individual who is not resident in the United Kingdom. [1]

## *The Residence of Corporations*

Corporations used to be treated as being resident at the location of their control and management. [2] However, the new test for the residence of corporations in s66(1) of the FA 1988 states that any company incorporated in the United Kingdom is resident here with effect 15 March 1988, and the central management and control is no longer taken into account. Transitional provisions existed in Schedule 7 of the FA 1988, for example, providing a five-year period of grace for existing companies.

## **Ordinary Residence**

### *Introduction*

Ordinary residence is of far less importance for the purposes of United Kingdom tax than residence. It is however important in several respects. First, as we have seen above, s334 ICTA 1988 applies to treat Commonwealth citizens and citizens of the Republic of Ireland, who are ordinarily resident in the United Kingdom, and who go abroad for the purposes of occasional residence, as being resident in the United Kingdom during their absence. Secondly, s65(4) and s65(5) ICTA 1988 provide that a Commonwealth citizen or a citizen of the Republic of Ireland who satisfies the Board that he is not ordinarily resident in the United Kingdom is to be taxed on foreign income under Cases IV and V of Schedule D only on income which is remitted here (and not on all income arising). Thirdly, there is a general anti-avoidance provision in

---

[1] S112(1). The section also deals generally with partnerships which are controlled abroad.
[2] *De Beers Consolidated Gold Mines v Howe* [1906] AC 453.

s739(1) of the ICTA 1988 which deals with the transfer of assets by a
person who is ordinarily resident to a person who is not resident or not
domiciled in the United Kingdom. And fourthly, the persons chargeable
to United Kingdom capital gains tax are defined by s2(1) of the Taxation
of Chargeable Gains Act 1992 as persons who are resident or ordinarily
resident in the United Kingdom.

In spite of its importance in the contexts mentioned above, the term
"ordinary residence" is neither defined in statute, nor given a special
technical meaning for tax purposes. The words must bear their natural
and ordinary meaning as words of common usage in the English
language.[1] It is clear from the discussions above that ordinary residence
is not synonymous with residence, that the word "ordinary" qualifies the
word "residence",[2] and that there is thus a need to examine the judicial
definitions. In *Levene v IRC*, Viscount Cave said that ordinary residence
"connotes residence in a place with a degree of continuity and apart from
accidental or temporary absences".[3] In the same case Lord Warrington[4]
defined it as meaning "the way in which a man's life is usually ordered".
In *IRC v Lysaght*[5] Viscount Sumner said that the converse of "ordinarily"
is "extraordinarily", and that part of the regular order of a man's life,
adopted voluntarily and for settled purposes, is not "extraordinary". In
the non-revenue case of *R v Barnet LBC ex parte Shah*[6] Lord Scarman, after
a review of the case law (including *Lysaght* and *Levene*) said:

> Unless, therefore, it can be shown that the statutory framework or the
> legal context in which the words are used requires a different meaning
> ... "ordinarily resident" refers to a man's abode in a particular place
> or country which he has adopted voluntarily and for settled purposes as
> part of the regular order of his life for the time being, whether of short
> or of long duration.

Lord Scarman added[7] that a settled purpose does not require an
intention to stay indefinitely, but that the purpose, while settled, might be
for a limited period only. All that is necessary is that the purpose of living

---

[1] See Lord Scarman in *R v Barnett LBC, ex parte Shah* [1983] 2 AC 309 at 341.
[2] Lord President Clyde in *Reid v IRC* (1926) 10 TC 673 at 678.
[3] [1928] AC 217 at 225.
[4] At p232.
[5] [1928] All ER 575 at 580.
[6] [1983] 2 AC 309 at 343.
[7] At p344.

where one does live has a sufficient degree of continuity to be properly described as "settled". In this context, a specific limited purpose, such as education, can be a settled purpose. However, in spite of the reference to a voluntary adoption of a way of life, volition is no more a necessary ingredient of ordinary residence than it is of residence. Thus, in *Re Mackenzie*[1] for example, a woman who was domiciled in Australia and who came to visit this country and who was detained as a person of unsound mind, was held to be ordinarily resident in the United Kingdom when she died here, still detained, some 50 years later. According to Norton J,[2] "[i]f . . . she was not ordinarily resident in England during the last 52 years of her life, she was not ordinarily resident anywhere else".

This question, like that of residence, is a question of fact, and there are many examples in the cases. The taxpayers in *Levene* and *Lysaght* for example, were held to be ordinarily resident as well as resident. These cases have already been discussed earlier. We will examine two other cases. First, *Reid v IRC*.[3] The taxpayer, a British subject, was in the habit of travelling abroad on the continent of Europe for the greater part of the year, spending only the summer months in the United Kingdom. While abroad, she had no fixed place of abode in this country, staying in hotels both when she was here and when she was abroad. She however had family and business ties here, and her personal belongings, which were not required when she was travelling, were kept in store in London. It was held by the commissioners that she was ordinarily resident in the United Kingdom and this decision was upheld by the Court of Session. Lord President Clyde rejected the suggestion that the meaning of the word "ordinary" is governed wholly or mainly by the test of time or duration. According to him,[4] from the point of view of time, "ordinary" would stand in contrast to "casually". In this case the taxpayer was not a "casual" visitor to her home country. Lord Clyde said he would hesitate to give the word "ordinary" any more precise interpretation than "in the customary course of events".[5]

In response to the argument of counsel that the taxpayer "ordinarily resided" on the continent rather than in this country because she spent nearly three times as much of her life abroad as here, Lord Clyde said that there was nothing impossible in a person ordinarily residing in two

[1] [1941] Ch 69.
[2] At p77.
[3] [1926] 10 TC 673.
[4] At p680.
[5] *Ibid.*

places. Lord Blackburn, concurring, said[1], "[i]t is quite true a man may have more than one ordinary residence; he may have half-a-dozen; and each might be described quite fairly as an ordinary residence." He also noted[2] that a person may be ordinarily resident in the United Kingdom without having any particular house or spot in the United Kingdom which could be described as his "ordinary residence". According to Lord Blackburn, such a person may stay in a different hotel every day of the 365 days in the year. Nobody could say in such situation that the person had an ordinary residence, but everyone would agree in saying that he had been "ordinarily resident" for the whole of the year within the confines of the United Kingdom. That conclusion would be reached entirely from the fact that he had physically resided in the United Kingdom and no other fact, as far as Lord Blackburn could see, is material in construing the expression "ordinarily resident".

The second case that we shall examine is *Miesegaes v IRC*[3]. The taxpayer was a Dutch national. He and his father had originally come to this country as refugees at the beginning of the Second World War. When his father left this country for Switzerland at the end of the war, he remained at boarding school in England. He was at all material times domiciled outside the United Kingdom, and spent his school holidays with his father in Switzerland. It was held that he was ordinarily resident in the United Kingdom. Wynn Parry J at first instance said[4] that the correct test was whether the taxpayer had been here in the ordinary course of his life during his adolescence. The commissioners had applied the test correctly and he could see no justification for interfering with their decision. He was upheld by the Court of Appeal. Pearce LJ, referring to the statement of Lord Buckmaster in *Lysaght v IRC* that volition was immaterial, said[5]:

Lord Buckmaster's remarks as to the exigencies of business seem equally applicable to the exigencies of education. Education is a large, necessary and normal ingredient in the lives of adolescent members of the community, just as work or business is in the lives of its adult members. During the years of youth education plays a definite and dominating part in a boy's ordinary life. In this case the school terms at

[1] At p682.
[2] At p681.
[3] [1957] 37 TC, 493.
[4] At p499.
[5] At p501.

Harrow dictated the main residential pattern of the boy's life. Education is too extensive and universal a phase to justify such descriptions as "unusual" or "extraordinary". It would be as erroneous to endow educational residence with some esoteric quality that must, as a matter of law, remove it from the category of residence, or ordinary residence, as it would be to do so in the case of business residence. The argument based on the institutional or compulsory nature of a boy's life at school is misleading. The compulsion is merely the will of his parents, who voluntarily send him to that school. It would be hazardous, and in my opinion relevant, to investigate whether adolescents are residing voluntarily where their lot is cast and how far they approve of their parents' choice of a home or school. The Appellant's argument might lead to the unreal conclusion that a boy whose parents were in the Far East and who was therefore boarded with a tutor, or at an educational establishment where boys remain all the year round, would not reside anywhere at all. The educational and institutional nature of the residence are, of course, factors to be taken into account; but it would be wrong to hold that such residence cannot be ordinary residence".

The Revenue practice is to treat ordinary residence as being equal to habitual residence [1] (usually for three successive years). A person who is non-resident for a year because he is physically absent from this country for that whole year may still be treated by the Revenue as ordinarily resident, if he was so before that year and comes back to be resident in the next year. [2] It may be that the only case in which an individual would be held to be resident but not ordinarily resident is when he comes from abroad to this country for some temporary purpose but remains for more than 6 months in the tax year. [3]

With respect to students, a person who comes to the United Kingdom for a period of study or education which is expected to last for more than four years will be treated by the Revenue as resident and ordinarily resident from the date of his arrival. [4] If the period of study is not expected to exceed four years, the person may be treated as not ordinarily resident, but the result will depend on whether or not he has

---

[1] IR 20, para. 1.3 ("year after year"); para. 2.1 ("if you usually live in this country"). See also paras. 3.4 to 3.13.

[2] Para. 1.3.

[3] *Ibid.*

[4] IR 20 para. 3.13.

accommodation available here, whether he intends to remain here at the end of his period of education, or whether he proposes to visit the United Kingdom in future years for periods of three months or more per year of assessment. [1] And with respect to other long-term visitors, a person who comes here (whether to work or not) will be treated as ordinarily resident from the date of his arrival if it is clear that he intends to remain here for three years or more. [2]

## Domicile

The domicile of a person is often of much less importance than his residence or ordinary residence. However, it is still important for certain purposes. First, s65(4) and (5) of the ICTA 1988 charge the foreign income of a non-domiciled person on a remittance basis. [3] Secondly s191(1) of the ICTA 1988 defines "foreign emoluments" as the emoluments of a non-domiciled person from an office or employment with an employer who is non-resident (excluding employers in the Republic of Ireland), and thirdly, s6(1) of the Inheritance Tax Act 1984 defines "excluded property" as property situated outside the United Kingdom, of which the person beneficial entitled thereto is domiciled outside the United Kingdom.

Domicile bears its general Conflicts of Laws meaning and detailed discussion can be found in books on Private International Law. [4] It generally refers to a person's permanent home. Everyone must have a domicile and only one. A domicile of origin is acquired at birth and a domicile of choice can be acquired by adults, the requirements being a change of residence to another place and an intention to stay there permanently. The domicile of choice can be abandoned by acquiring another one or by revival of the domicile of origin.

## Citizenship

Citizenship is largely relevant only in respect of Commonwealth citizens or citizens of the Republic of Ireland, and then only in certain clearly defined situations (see, for example, s65 and s334 of the ICTA 1988—

---

[1] *Ibid.*

[2] IR 20, para. 3.8.

[3] Compare s12(1) of the TCGA 1992.

[4] See also IR 20, paras. 5.1 to 5.7, for the Revenue's summary of the position.

both discussed above). Citizenship is determined according to general law. Relevant provisions can be found in the British Nationality Act 1981.

## Self-Check Questions

1. In what circumstances will a person whose home is abroad be treated as resident in the United Kingdom?
2. When is a person's citizenship relevant to his or her residence status?
3. What is the significance of a place of abode in respect of the residence of an individual?
4. Is the question whether a person is in the United Kingdom voluntarily relevant to his or her residence status?
5. What is meant by "ordinary residence" and what is its significance?

## Further Reading

Lyons T, *The Reform of the Law of Domicile*, (1993) BTR 42–51.

Green S, *Domicile and Revenue Law: The Continuing Need for Reform*, (1991) BTR 21–30.

Sheridan D, *The Residence of Companies for Taxation Purposes*, (1990) BTR 78–112.

Oliver JDB, *Some Aspects of the Territorial Scope of Double Tax Treaties*, (1990) BTR 303–312.

Sheridan D, *Private International Law: The Law of Domicile: Observations on the Joint Report*, (1989) BTR 230–240.

Chopin LF, & Granwell AW, *The New Concept of Residence for Federal Income Tax Purposes*, (1985) BTR 62–67 (Discussion on American Law).

Wosner JL, *Ordinary Residence, The Law and Practice*, (1983) BTR 347–352.

Oliver JDB, *Double Tax Treaties in United Kingdom Tax Law*, (1970) BTR 388–405.

# Part Two — Income Tax

# 3
# Income Tax

By comparison to other taxes, income tax is by far the largest source of revenue in the United Kingdom. For example, in 1989 income tax accounted for approximately 26 per cent of the total tax revenue; corporation tax accounted for 11 per cent; and the combined revenue of capital gains tax and inheritance tax accounted for two per cent of the total tax revenue.

It is in the first part of this book that we develop a consideration of the rules and principles that apply to income tax. The problem we initially face is that of seeking to ascertain and present a definition of income. It has often been stated that income tax is a tax on income; but an economist would reply and explain that the flow of revenue from capital is also income. Clearly income tax for our purposes (and for the purposes of the Inland Revenue) does not include income from capital. This calls for a consideration of the distinction between income and capital. Exhaustive and conclusive definitions of income and capital are not provided by the Legislature. There exists a further need to consider the Schedular system and the definitions within that and the roles that the Schedules perform.

## Capital v Income: The Distinction and its Importance

The distinction between an income and a capital item of expenditure or receipt has assumed a lesser importance than it previously enjoyed. Its past importance reflected the absence of a capital gains tax (until its introduction in 1965) and the consequent ability, prior to 1965, to enjoy tax free capital gains. It was eventually conceded that the absence of a capital gains tax presented not only an avenue for tax planning or avoidance, but also supported the possible "injustice" of not taxing those with the ability to pay on the grounds that their income was of a particular type and derived from a particular source (a capital gain).

The introduction of a capital gains tax has not removed the need to recognise the distinction between income and capital—at the very least the distinction is of importance in recognising and advising upon the correct tax principles. The distinction may have practical importance in that the rates applicable to income gains and those applicable to capital gains have not always been the same.[1] For example, capital gains tax enjoyed a maximum rate of 30 per cent for a number of years, whereas income tax rates reached 60 per cent during the same period. Today's assimilation of the rates provides stronger recognition of the often indistinguishable, distinction between income and capital and of the need to tax the latter.[2]

One of the major problems in determining the distinction between income and capital is the absence of precise definitions or determining theories. Judicial comments have confirmed that the question

> ... must depend in large measure upon the particular facts of the particular case[3],

and that

> in many cases it is almost true to say that a spin of a coin would decide the matter almost as satisfactorily as an attempt to find reasons.[4]

Although the good revenue law student should recognise the difficulties in this area, the good student must also possess an awareness of the application of the distinction in relevant case law. We will present a discussion of the more important cases when we consider income receipts and revenue expenditure in Schedule D Cases I and II. For the moment, we will simply highlight the competing theories that have been presented as assisting or explaining the distinctions between capital and income.

## Fixed and Circulating Capital

This theory has enjoyed a great deal of support and involves a recognition that fixed capital is "capital" whereas circulating capital is merely "income". The fixed capital is the structure (permanent or semi-permanent) that generates the income. The income is often represented through

---

[1] Today the rates are the same, except that any capital gain is always to be taxed as the top slice of one's income and thus at any marginal rate of income tax.

[2] It is widely believed that the previous practice of taxing income and capital gains at different rates distorted investment decisions and contributed to the development of a tax avoidance industry.

[3] Per Abbott J, in *Oxford Motors Ltd v Minister of National Revenue* (1959) 18 DLR 712.

[4] Per Greene MR in *IRC v British Salmson Aero Engines Ltd* [1938] 2 KB 482 at 498.

the disposal of the circulating capital items. Those circulating capital items are the creation of the fixed capital.

For example, in *Golden Horse Shoe (New) Ltd v Thorgood*[1], the court was required to decide whether the sale of dumps generated at a Gold Mine was a sale of capital. Romer LJ summarised the issue by stating that:

> . . . the question to be decided in this case is whether the dumps are to be regarded as fixed capital or circulating capital.

In conclusion, the dumps were regarded as circulating capital : their existence and creation was caused by and was an aside to the fixed capital—the mines.

### Fruit of the Tree

In a similar fashion to fixed and circulating capital theory, the "fruit of the tree" theory suggests that the tree represents the capital and the fruit represents income items that are generated by and grow out of and from the capital.

### Accretion to Economic Power

This theory involves a recognition that income is the gain generated out of the application of capital. It has been suggested that the accretion to economic power theory is perhaps a more accurate description of the distinction between income and capital, albeit that the other theories are more frequently cited by the judiciary.

Ultimately the issue is one of fact and, as we shall see in our later discussions, the suggestion that the matter could, as easily and as predictably, be determined by a "spin of a coin" is very close to the truth!

## Sources of Income and the Schedular System

Having ascertained that the funds received are of an income nature, the next stage in determining any tax liability is the need to ascertain whether that type of income is taxable. Some guidance is provided by the legislature through the declaration that certain types of income are non-

---

[1] [1933] All ER 402.

taxable. These include an array of items representing political and policy considerations. For example among the items are : certain social security benefits; war widows pension; redundancy payments; education scholarship and foreign services allowances for civil servants.

Apart from the statutory declared non-taxable incomes, income will be taxable or non-taxable depending upon the application of the doctrine of source and recognition of the schedular system. The schedular system reflects an historical contribution to the UK tax system having been originally developed by Addington during the early 1800s. The schedular system remains today—subject to a number of refinements. The significance of this system is that income in any tax year will not be taxable unless it can be traced to a source identified in a schedule. Thus, for income to be taxable it must be caused, for example, by employment (Schedular E) or trade (Schedule D). Section 1, (TA 1988), supports this conclusion by declaring "Income is taxable if it falls within one or other of the Schedules".

Today's Schedules are as follows:

| | |
|---|---|
| Schedule A | Income from rents and other receipts from land in the UK |
| Schedule C | Income from public revenue |
| Schedule D | |
| Case I | Profits of a trade in UK |
| Case II | Profits of a profession or vocation in UK |
| Case III | Interest, annuities and other annual payments |
| Case IV | Securities out of the UK not charged under Schedule C |
| Case V | Possessions out of the not charged under Schedule C |
| Case VI | Annual profits or gains not falling under Cases I–V and not charged by virtue of any other Schedule |
| Schedule E | |
| Cases I, II and III | Income from offices, employments and pensions. |
| Schedule F | Dividends and distributions by companies. |

*Exclusivity*

Although income tax is one tax its computation must reflect the individual contributions from the Schedules A-F, and the computations within those Schedules. This leads us onto the need to recognise the mutual exclusivity of the Schedules and the rules therein. For example, assessment of income under Schedule E will prevent the assessment of the same income under Schedule D (or vice versa). This was confirmed at an early stage by the House of Lords in *Fry v Salisbury House Estate Ltd.*[1] Here the taxpayer owned a building and let parts of it. The taxpayer was initially assessed under Schedule A on the basis of the building and services and then reassessed for the services under Schedule D. The House of Lords dismissed the reassessment on the grounds that having assessed the rental incomes under Schedule A,

> . . . there is no possibility of subsequently dealing with them under Schedule D.

As between the Cases within the Schedules, it appears that, subject to statutory direction to the contrary, the Inland Revenue may elect under which case to charge income. For example, *in Liverpool and London and Globe Insurance Co v Bennett*[2] a fire and life insurance company was entitled to

> invest money, not immediately required, in such manner as might from time to time be determined.

Using this power the Company invested money in the USA and those investments subsequently yielded interest. The interest was received by the Company abroad but never remitted to the UK (although it did appear on the Company's balance sheet). The Company was assessed under Case 1 of Schedule D (ITA 1842) in respect of the "interest received". The assessment was upheld by the court. The Company had unsuccessfully argued that they ought to be assessed under Case IV only. The advantage of Case IV was that it would only attach to interest from securities abroad if that interest had been received in the UK in the current year. In hearing the case, Lord Shaw of Dunfermline stressed that:

> . . . it is well settled that if a sufficient warrant be found in the statute for taxation under alternative heads the alternative lies with the taxing authority. They have selected Case 1. It appears to me that this selection is . . . founded upon the soundest and most elementary principle of business . . .[3]

[1] [1930] AC 432.
[2] [1913] AC 610.
[3] *Ibid* at 616.

## Doctrine of Source

The Schedular system led to the development of the doctrine of source. The doctrine of source demands that in the current tax year, the source of the income must be an identifiable activity and that activity must be recognised as falling within one of the Schedules. This doctrine has proved problematic when income is identifiable but the source of that income (the activity) is no longer identifiable in the current tax year. For example, in *Bray v Best*[1], a payment in respect of employment that no longer was in existence, nor had it been in existence during the year of assessment, was not taxable. The payment referred to previous employment. Lord Oliver stressed that:

> For an emolument to be chargeable to income tax under Schedule E not only must it be an emolument FROM employment but it must be an emolument FOR the year of assessment in which the charge is sought to be raised.

(This particular payment is now dealt with by statute—but it is still a useful illustration of the requirements of the doctrine of source).

One of the logical developments from the doctrine of source requirements is the development of a residual Schedule or case to catch and sweep-up all sources of income other than those specified in the other Schedules or cases. The provision of a "catch-all" or "sweeping" case would prevent the possible non-taxable income or source (other than those to be declared as exempt by statute). On first impressions Schedule D, Case VI (see later discussion) might be regarded as that residual, catch-all case, but on closer examination its comprehensiveness appears to be incomplete and defective.

## The Tax Unit

Before we examine some of the detailed rules and principles of the various Schedules, we must briefly consider the unit of assessment. In essence, the unit of assessment requires that we make a choice as to how we tax husbands and wives. We may, for example, wish to adopt separate taxation, whereby we treat husbands and wives as if they were single people. Under a system of separate taxation marriage would attract no

[1] [1986] 1 All ER 969.

fiscal incentives or disincentives, nor would there be any disincentives to a married woman seeking and obtaining employment.

An alternative to a system of separate taxation, might be a system of splitting income. This would involve computing the total joint income and splitting (or dividing) that income by two. Tax liability would then be assessed on an individual basis with each partner's taxable income representing their share of the split income. For example, a disproportionate individual income of £20,000 for one partner (husband) and £15,000 for the other partner (wife) would be split to represent taxable income of £17,500 per partner (individual). Under a split system fiscal advantages are apparent where income is unequally earned or if one partner only is working.

Finally, a system of aggregation could apply to the income of husbands and wives. Under the principles of aggregation the income of the husband and wife are summed to represent joint income. Tax liability would then be assessed and determined according to the joint income. For instance, if we use the example above, the assessable income would not be £17,500 per individual but £35,000 per married couple.

Until 1990, the system of aggregation applied in the United Kingdom. Legislation declared that

a woman's income chargeable to tax shall be deemed for income tax purposes to be his [the husband's] income and not to be her income. [1]

The selection of the family unit as the tax unit was not all bad news : the husband became entitled to a married man's personal allowance to help him support his "dependent" wife.

The system of aggregation was subject to much criticism and concern. In the Meade Report, reference was made to the perceptions of dependency as

becoming less and less compatible with modern attitudes to the relationships between men and women. [2]

The Government announced the possibility of change through its Green

---

[1] TA 1988, s279. Repealed by FA 1988, s32 for the year 1990–91 and subsequent years of assessment.

[2] "The Structure and Reform of Direct Taxation": report of a Committee chaired by Professor J E Meade. The Institute of Fiscal Studies (1978) p377.

Paper in 1980 [1], and changes were introduced in the treatment of husbands and wives in the reforms of 1990. These reforms abolished the system of aggregation, and husbands and wives are now subject to individual assessment on their income (both earned and investment income). However, an element of discrimination does remain in that a "married couple's allowance" is available to either the husband or the wife. In practice it is normally attributed to the husband and as such may represent an implicit acceptance of "dependence".

Critics of the 1990 reforms emphasise that the married couple's allowance does little to recognise or assist the needs of the family unit. It is suggested that if the "married couple's allowance" was abolished, then child benefit provision could be doubled. The belief is that a change in that direction would move adequately and effectively represent and assist the needs of the family unit.

Further criticisms of the 1990 reforms are directed at the treatment of investment income. It is now possible for the transfer between husband and wife of investment income profit to reduce tax liability. A higher rate tax partner might transfer his investment income to his wife in order that the income is subject to basic rate liability in her hands (assuming she is a basic rate taxpayer). Some critics believe that investment income ought still (on equitable grounds) remain subject to a system of aggregation.

*Self-Check Questions*

1. Why do we distinguish income gains or profits from capital gains or profits?
2. What is the Schedular system? Why is it important?
3. How do we currently tax husbands and wives? Is this the most appropriate unit of assessment?

---

[1] "The Taxation of Husband and Wife", 1980 Cmnd 8093.

# 4

# Schedule E – Employment Income

Schedule E[1] provides the basis for the taxation of emoluments[2] and income from[3] "offices and employment". Schedule E contains three cases of which Case I is discussed in this chapter. Case I states that

> it applies to any emoluments for any year of assessment in which the person holding the office or employment is resident and ordinarily resident in the United Kingdom.

Case II and Case III involve the need to deal with employment and employment income from overseas.

## Office or Employment?

One of the initial problems to be determined in discussion of the scope of Schedule E is the meaning of "office" or "employment". In the absence of any statutory definition or guidelines, we need to turn to judicial comment and guidance. The accepted meaning, or perhaps the characteristics, of an office appear to be those enumerated by Rowlatt J in *Great Western Railway Co v Bates*[4] and repeated in *Davies v Braithwaite*[5]. Rowlatt J emphasised the non-personal nature of an office, stating that:

> . . . it was something which had an existence independent of the person who filled it. It was something which was held by tenure and title rather than by contract and which continued to exist, though the holders of it might change and it was fulfilled by successive holders.[6]

---

[1] The TA 1988 s19(1) levies income tax under Schedule E.

[2] TA s131—Emoluments include all salaries, fees, wages, perquisites and profits whatsoever.

[3] As we shall discuss later, not all income from employment is caught under Schedule E. Schedule E is concerned with the taxation of income caused by the employment: a distinction that is of vital importance.

[4] [1920] 3 KB 266.

[5] [1931] 2 KB 628.

[6] *Ibid* at 635.

These characteristics of an office were recently approved in *Edwards v Clinch*[1] although the decision in *Edwards v Clinch* is not without difficulty. Mr Clinch had been appointed as inspector at a number of separate public local inquiries. The issue was one of whether Mr Clinch held an "office" at each inquiry or was he merely exercising his profession. The Court concluded that Mr Clinch's appointment at each inquiry was not the appointment to an "office". Having repeated the accepted characteristics of an office, Lord Salmon accepted the words of Ackner LJ[2] that Mr Clinch's appointment was a

> temporary, ad hoc, appointment to a position that did not have an existence of its own, nor any quality of permanency.

This strict adherence to the suggested characteristics of an "office" might result in "few" offices being accepted as such.[3] One wonders to what extent the decision in *Edwards v Clinch* gives effect to the suggestion that the deliberately vague term (office) should be applied according to the ordinary use of language and the dictates of common sense.[4]

It has been suggested that the inclusion of the term "employment" was to extend the scope of Schedule E and might possibly be viewed as a residual category.[5] Today the issue and determination of employment focuses on the distinction between a contract of service and a contract for services. The former is equated with employment.[6] Previous analysis of employment centred on the suggestion that employment "means something analogous" to an office.[7] It is now clear that a person employed by a company is an employee—except where the company and the individual might in fact be treated as the same. Employment lawyers will remind us that a difficulty exists when an employee is seconded to work

---

[1] [1981] 3 All ER 543. Lord Salmon confirmed the meaning of the word "office" is "a subsisting, permanent, substantive position which has an existence independent of the person who fills it."

[2] [1981] Ch 1 at 17–18.

[3] Examples include, a director of a company, an executor and a company auditor.

[4] Lord Wright in *McMillan v Guest* [1942] AC 561 at 566. Cited by Lord Salmon in *Edwards v Clinch*, [1981] 3 All ER 543.

[5] Rowlatt J in *Davies v Braithwaite supra* suggested it was found "convenient" to put "employment" expressly in Schedule E and that is can be viewed as something that was not an "office" and neither earnings from a profession or vocation.

[6] *Andrews v King* [1991] STC 481.

[7] Rowlatt J in *Davies v Braithwaite*, at 635. Also, see Lord Wright in *McMillan v Guest* [1942] AC 561 at 566: The word employment has to be construed with and takes its colour from the word "office".

for another firm. This situation involves a determination of fact and a recognition of tax concessions. [1]

It has been recognised that the exercise of a profession or trade can co-exist with the exercise and engagement of employment. For example, *Mitchell and Eden v Ross* [2] raised the possibility that a consultant radiologist could be in private practice exercising his profession and, in the same year of assessment, receive income from employment with a regional hospital board. The income attributed to the profession (the private practice) would be assessed under Schedule D Case II whereas the employment income would be assessed under Schedule E.

Although the distinction between "office and employment" is assumed to be of little importance [3], the distinction between an office or employment and a "profession" is often a source of concern and importance. [4] In *Davies v Braithwaite* [5] the issue was whether an actress who performed in plays, films and radio productions was exercising a profession in doing so (Schedule D Case II) or merely engaging in contracts of employment (Schedule E). In determining the matter, the court preferred to look at the context of the activities (rather than each isolation activity) and the general arrangements and activities of the taxpayer. By taking such a wide perspective the court was able to conclude that:

> ... where one finds a method of earning a livelihood which does not consist of the obtaining of a post and staying in it, but consists of a series of engagements and moving from one to another—then each of those engagements cannot be considered an employment, but is a mere engagement in the course of exercising a profession ... [6]

In a more recent case, *Fall v Hitchen* [7], the courts were prepared to take a more restrictive approach in concluding that the engagement of a ballet

[1] Extra-statutory concession A37 (1988) declares that fees paid to the individual but accounted for to his firm should not be treated as his taxable income and subject to PAYE.

[2] [1961] 3 All ER 49.

[3] This distinction has been described as being of importance. The example often given is that of the Taxes Act 1988, s291(2) disqualifying an employee but not an officer from holding shares, under the BES scheme, in a connected company.

[4] See later discussion.

[5] *Supra.*

[6] Per Rowlatt J, *supra* 5 at 635. Although Rowlatt J did, rather unhelpfully add: "... every profession and every trade does involve the making of successive engagements and successive contracts and, in one sense of the work, employments ..."

[7] [1973] 1 All ER 368.

dancer involved a contract of employment. This decision is difficult to reconcile with that in *Davies v Braithwaite*. In both instances one would suggest that the nature of the livelihood envisaged and contemplated the entering into of a series of engagement and that each engagement ought not to be viewed in isolation from the nature of the livelihood and from the arrangements and activities of the taxpayer. Perhaps any reconciliation or explanation lies in the apparent change of focus. The focus today appears to involve the analysis of the isolated contract under dispute in an attempt to determine whether that contract—irrespective of other commitments or expectations—was one for services or of service [1]. The emphasis, therefore, appears to be one of determining whether that is a contract of employment rather than consider whether it is in one sense employment but in reality part of the arrangement and exercise of a profession. [2]

Further guidance on the relevance of this distinction can be seen in *Hall v Lorimer* [1993] BTC 473 where Nolan J provided a list of indicators on the issue of employee *versus* self-employed. These included such matters as whether the person performing the services had set up a business-like organisation of his own; the degree of continuity in the relationship between the person performing the services and the person for whom he performs them; how many engagements he performed and whether they were performed mainly for one person or for a number of different people.

## Emoluments

Tax under Schedule E is charged on emoluments from the office or employment. [3] Emoluments are defined as including "all salaries, fees, wages, perquisites and profits whatsoever." [4] Special rules exist to catch benefits in kind and related benefits—those rules are discussed later in this chapter. At this point, discussion will focus on the requirement that the

---

[1] On the basis of such an analysis the conclusion of employment was unavoidable in *Fall v Hitchen*. The contractual details indicated that it was a full-time contract and prohibited the employee from taking on outside activities without the employer's consent.

[2] A further element of explanation can be found in the judgment of Rowlatt J in *Davies v Braithwaite*, where emphasis is placed on the historical background to the introduction of the word "employment" to Schedule E. Rowlatt J appears to suggest that "employment" is a residual category. If the activity is neither an office nor the exercise of a trade or profession, *then* we must turn to "employment" to plug the gap and catch the activity. If that suggestion is accepted, then Rowlatt J's analysis of the activities in *Davies v Braithwaite* would begin and end with "trade or profession".

[3] TA 1988, s19.

[4] TA 1988, s131.

emolument must, for the purposes of Schedule E [1], be from the office or employment. The insistence on "from" or "therefrom" (by reference to the office or employment) is acknowledged to represent a test of causation [2] and demands consideration of the question: when is a fee, salary, reward, etc. received in respect of the employment, or in respect of a personal characteristic or circumstance?

The importance of the test of causation is that is correctly places the focus on the cause and reason for the receipt rather than on the timing or status of the giver. Thus, receipts from non-employers and/or receipts received before or after employment are capable of being treated as caused by the employment and therefore "emoluments" taxable under Schedule E [3]. The often-quoted words of Upjohn J in *Hochstrasser v Mayes* confirms this:

> ... the payment must be made in reference to the services the employee renders by virtue of his office and it must be something in the nature of a reward for services past, present or future. [4]

The facts of *Hochstrasser v Mayes* provide a useful illustration of the causation requirement. Here the employer, ICI Ltd, operated a relocation scheme for its employees whereby ICI Ltd would reimburse any loss suffered on the selling price of the employees house. An employee, Mayes, was required to relocate by ICI Ltd. He did so and sold his house for

---

[1] In accordance with the schedules system, emoluments not caused by and, therefore, not caught under Schedule E might be assessed to tax elsewhere. It has even been suggested that they might be regarded as capital as opposed to income, and conceivably taxable as capital. See *Jarrold v Boustead* [1964] 3 All ER 76.

[2] See Viscount Simmonds in *Hochstrasser v Mayes* [1960] AC 376 at 389: "... the issue turns ... upon whether the fact of employment is the causa causans, or only the sine qua non ...". There is a suggestion that the test is simply one of "emolument" and that in applying such a test we are necessarily establishing that the source is one of employment. See Kerridge 1991 BTR p 313. Perhaps this suggestion does not recognise the distinction between an emolument flowing from employment and an emolument caused by the employment.

See more recently in *Mairs v Haughey* [1993] BTC 339, where it was decided that a payment made to employees to relinquish their contingent rights under a non-statutory redundancy scheme was not taxable because the character of the payment took that of the payment it replaced, namely a redundancy payment. Such a payment was caused through being unemployed rather than being employed!

[3] Practical problems can result from a future sum being received following the termination of employment, or vice versa. The Finance Act 1989 provides some relief by adopting a receipts basis and charging tax by reference to the year of receipt irrespective of the fact that that receipt might not have any source in that year, i.e. the taxpayer is not an employee in that year of receipt and assessment. Objections to the absence of source can be answered by understanding that the tax liability will be by reference to the relevant year of employment.

[4] [1959] Ch 22 at 33.

£350 less than the purchasing price of three years earlier. The Inland Revenue sought to assess the £350 receipt as an emolument under Schedule E—an assessment that failed.

The House of Lords emphasised that the sum of £350 was paid to the taxpayer in respect of his personal situation as a house-owner and not because of or caused by any services given by him. Emphasis was also placed on the "favourable" salary of the employee (the £350 was not a disguised salary payment) and on the fact that the onus is on the Revenue to establish that the reward was for the employees' services. [1]

The fine dividing line between a payment being caused by employment and a payment being caused by some other reason is illustrated in *Hamblett v Godfrey* [2]. Employees at GCHQ who wished to continue in employment following the removal of their rights to belong to a trade union were given £1,000 each in recognition of the withdrawal of those rights. The Court of Appeal agreed with the Revenue that the sum of £1,000 was an emolument caused by their employment and thus assessable to tax under Schedule E. Purchas LJ explained that the approach that the Court should adopt is one of considering the "status of the payment and the context" in which it was made. The status of the payment was one of compensation for loss or rights as an employee. The context was one of employment. Purchas LJ emphasised that:

> . . . if the employment did not exist, there would be no need for the rights in the particular contract in which the taxpayer found herself. [3]

One might respond that the context of the payment in *Hochstrasser v Mayes* was also one of employment. If Mayes had not been in employment with ICI Ltd he would not have been in the situation of the need to relocate albeit on favourable terms. Perhaps the solution, or at least reconciliation, lies in the emphasis and degree placed on the dominant cause of the payment. [4]

In *Hamblett v Godfrey* the rights subject to compensation were stated as being "directly connected with the fact of the taxpayer's employment". That "direct connection" places emphasis on and indicates the dominant

---

[1] Concern has been expressed at the anomaly consequent on this decision. Depending on the nature and manner of provision, housing benefit or contribution may be taxable. For example, the provision of rent free (full or partial) would attract a tax assessment. Similarly mortgage contributions and concessions will attract the attention of an assessment—but contributions in the form of a guarantee against loss or relocation will not (according to the decision in *Hochstrasser v Mayes*)!

[2] [1987] 1 All ER 916.

[3] *Ibid.*

[4] "Apportionment" suggests itself as an equitable, if not practically onerous, solution.

cause of the payment—the employment situation and the employee status. In contrast, the emphasis in *Hochstrasser v Mayes* was placed on the status of house-owner as the dominant reason and cause for the receipt. This type of analysis indicates the fine line and distinctions that are necessary and not all too obvious in this area of law.

The categories of cases selected below are used as a matter of convenience to place and introduce some decisions that illustrate the fine distinctions and degree(s) of emphasis adopted by the courts. The cases also illustrate the breadth of coverage of s19, including payments from non-employees and payments by reference to past, present and future services.[1] It must be appreciated that the distinctions are issues of fact and, in determining fact, the courts will look to the reality of the situation in true *Ramsay* fashion. Thus in *O'Leary v McKinlay*[2] the court looked beyond a trust to the reality of the provision of funds to an employee. Similarly, in *Shilton v Wilmshurst*[3] Southampton paid a £325,000 transfer fee to Nottingham Forest in order to secure the services of Peter Shilton, a well-known professional footballer. Southampton also paid an £80,000 signing-on fee to Shilton.

In addition, Nottingham Forest paid £75,000 to Shilton in order to secure the transfer to Southampton. The reality of the situation was that Nottingham Forest was to receive a net sum of £250,000 (£405,000—£80,000—£75,000) and Shilton was to receive £155,000 (75,000 + £80,000). The final outcome of a series of appeals gave effect to this arithmetic reality—albeit the reasoning did cause some difficulty.[4]

## Examples

*Inducement Payments/Signing-on Fees*

The courts have been required to determine the status of inducement payments paid in return for persuading a person to adopt employment or leave employment. In most cases, the payments are made by the new

[1] It is possible that the scope for the inclusion of payments for past services as emoluments has been limited. Lord Templeman in *Shilton v Wilmshurst* ([1991] STC 88, at 91) indicated that section 19 includes (et al) as emoluments sums paid "as a reward for past services and as an inducement to continue to perform services". Although Lord Templeman stated that the "authorities are consistent" with his analysis, it is not entirely settled that payments for past services must also be an inducement as to future services in order to be treated as an emolument under section 19.

[2] [1991] STC 42.

[3] [1991] STC 88.

[4] Noted by R Kerridge, [1991] BTR at 311.

employer. Although the inducement payments appear to have made in return for an agreement to enter into employment, it has been possible for the courts to conclude that such payments, albeit "flowing" from employment, were not caused by the employment [1]—as different cause might be identifiable, such as the foregoing of some personal advantage or right such as amateur status and rights appertaining to such status.

In *Jarrold v Boustead* [2] the taxpayer received a signing-on fee from Hull Rugby League Club of £3,000. In determining the status of this signing-on fee the Court of Appeal were prepared to look outside the terms of the agreement under which it was paid [3] to conclude that the signing-on fee was not an emolument but an award of compensation to Mr Boustead for relinquishing forever his amateur status and the advantages that flowed from that status. [4] By contrast, in *Riley v Coglan* [5] a sum of £500 paid as a signing-on fee by York Rugby League Club was treated as an emolument from and caused by the employment. The distinction appears to be that in *Riley* the sum was clearly related to the services to be performed : it was repayable if the player failed to serve for the stipulated period (proportionate repayment) and was classified as "a running payment for making himself available to serve the club when required to do so". [6]

In *Pritchard v Arundale* [7], a senior chartered accountant (Mr Arundale) surrendered his accountant and senior partner status, and took up an appointment as a joint managing director of a company. In return Mr Arundale received a full salary and a stake in the business consisting of 4,000 shares. On the issue of whether the transfer of the shares amounted to an "emolument from employment" the court concluded that it did not. Factors influencing this conclusion included (i) the shares were transferred not by Mr Arundale's new employer but by a third party [8]; (ii) under the

---

[1] A distinction drawn by Megarry J.

[2] [1964] 3 All ER 76.

[3] At first instance Pennycuick J held that it was not permissible to look outside the terms of the agreement under which the £3,000 was paid. It is submitted that the Court of Appeal's approach was correct in ignoring expressions of consideration and agreement but focusing on the reality of the payment.

[4] By relinquishing his amateur status, Mr Boustead was barred from playing for or visiting and using the facilities of a rugby union club. Byelaw 24 of the Rugby League provides:

A player who relinquishes his amateur status is permitted to receive a signing-on fee from the club with which he first registers as a professional player. No club shall pay, or offer to pay a signing-on fee to a player who has previously been registered as a professional player with the League.

[5] [1968] 1 All ER 314.

[6] *Ibid*, per Ungoed-Thomas J.

[7] [1972] Ch 229, [1971] 3 All ER 1011.

[8] The third party consisted of the major shareholder of the company. One might suggest that the major shareholder was for all intents and purposes the company—although the decision in *Salomon v Salomon & Co Ltd* [1897] AC 22, illustrates the difficulty in supporting that suggestion.

agreement Mr Arundale was entitled to the transfer of shares "forthwith" (a full six months in advance of entering into employment as a joint managing director)[1]; and (iii) Mr Arundale was to receive a full salary at a commercial rate as an employee.

This analysis was confirmed and followed in *Glantre Engineering v Goodhand*[2] where a £10,000 sum paid to Mr Wells in return for his agreeing to leave a firm of accountants and join another company was held to be an emolument from employment. In this case, Mr Wells received the payment direct from his new employers and it was not regarded as severable from the other benefits to which Mr Wells became entitled under the employment agreement—it was an emolument from that employment agreement and that employment situation. Following an analysis of the arguments that the sum of £10,000 was to compensate Mr Wells for the surrendering of his chartered accountant status (a Jarrold v Boustead attempted analogy), the court remained unconvinced : the loss of status was

> a less important factor than the loss of security that Mr Wells would suffer as a result of leaving the employment of the firm of accountants.[3]

The more recent decision in *Shilton v Wilmshurst*[4] must be added to this discussion. As indicated above, the case involved the transfer of Peter Shilton from Nottingham Forest to Southampton Football Club. Under the transfer arrangement, Southampton were to pay a transfer fee of £325,000 to Nottingham Forest, and a signing-on fee of £80,000 to Peter Shilton. Peter Shilton also demanded and received a fee of £75,000 from Nottingham Forest. The courts were required to determine the status of the £75,000 fee and concluded that it was a fee paid for "being or becoming an employee" and therefore an emolument from employment and taxable irrespective of the fact that it came from Nottingham Forest rather than from Southampton. The decision clearly permits a signing-on fee as taxable even if paid by your ex-employer (cf *Pritchard v Arundale*, above). The difficulty is in determining when a payment made as a signing-on fee will not be

---

[1] It was suggested that the distinction was apparent in that the taxpayer might have died between receiving the shares and entering into the contract of employment. The suggestion was that the shares would still be part of the deceased's estate.

[2] [1983] 1 All ER 542.

[3] See Warner J, *ibid*.

[4] [1991] STC 88.

classed as an emolument from employment. The distinctions adopted in *Pritchard v Arundale* and in *Jarrold v Boustead* remain valid and are a guide in this area. The decision in the *Shilton* case appears to be chipping away at those distinctions (without removing them) and widening the scope of the "emolument" to include payments and signing-on (leaving-fees) fees paid by ex-employers. The decision in the *Shilton* case made fiscal sense when one views the financial and arithmetic reality of the situation.[1] It also makes sense by closing the door on an area of potential in tax planning and evasion—but, what the decision fails to do is provide sufficient guidance on its own limitations; in particular, when we can apply a *Pritchard v Arundale* or *Jarrold v Boustead* analysis in the determination of whether a payment, from a third party in particular, is made in return for one "being or agreeing to become an employee"?

If we search the judicial reasoning in *Shilton v Wilmshurst* we begin to find some, albeit inconclusive, guidance. The Court of Appeal expressed agreement with Morritt J that the emolument from a third party (here an ex-employer) would only be an emolument "from the employment" if that third party could be shown to have an "interest" in the performance of the employment contract.[2] The problem with that analysis was that it gave the wrong result; Nottingham Forest had no interest in the performance of the contract. Nottingham Forest's interest was in the formation of the contract only. Adopting the requirement of "interest" and the distinction between "interest in performance" and an "interest in formation" led the Court of Appeal to the conclusion that the payment of £75,000 was not an "emolument from employment" (arithmetically incorrect!). The House of Lords rejected the Court of Appeal analysis and held the £75,000 to be taxable as an "emolument from employment" (arithmetically correct!).[3] Lord Templeman in rejecting the "interest" requirement, emphasised that it should not and did not matter whether the payment be received from Southampton or from Nottingham Forest; the crucial analysis was whether it was paid for "acting, being or becoming an employee". In determining this we are to include

. . . emoluments which are paid as inducements to enter into contracts of employment and to perform services in the future.[4]

---

[1] See earlier discussion.
[2] [1990] STC 55 at 62.
[3] [1991] STC 88.
[4] *Ibid.*

The use of the word "and" is significant. It, perhaps, sets the boundaries and acts as guidance for later courts. (It might also raise doubts as to the correctness of the *Shilton* case). One might suggest that the requirement of having to show that payment was not only a signing-on fee (or leaving-fee) but also paid on the basis of the "performance of services in the future" (albeit those services might be performed for a new employer) is analogous to the need to establish an "interest" in the employment contract, the interest being one of the "performance of services". If that is so, then we have not, in substance, removed the Court of Appeal's requirement of the need to establish an "interest of performance".

*Rewards and Gifts*

It is possible that rewards and gifts received by employees might be treated as caused other than from the office or employment and therefore they would not be taxable under section 19.[1] Such "gifts", rewards and other payments have been found to have been caused by the desire to recognise and acknowledge achievements[2] or to indicate ones appreciation or goodwill at times of celebration or occasion.[3] The issue is one of fact and degree and is illustrated by the following decisions.

In *Moore v Griffiths*[4], Bobby Moore captained the England football team which won the World Cup in 1966. He then received a bonus of £1,000 from the Football Association. The court decided that this bonus was not taxable as a reward for services; it was of the nature of a testimonial.

---

[1] Although some members of the judiciary and commentators have referred to the testimonial principle, it has been emphasised that the "testimonial principle and the personal gift principle" are not categories to be defined or explained, but merely examples of transactions that do not fall within the taxable category of remuneration for services (per Megarry J in *Pritchard v Arundale* [1972] 47 TC 680 at 686. Megarry J clearly and correctly emphasised that there does not exist a range of categories:
> . . . the question is not one of which of two [or more] straitjackets the transaction best fits, but whether it comes within the statutory language, or else, failing to do so, falls into the undefined residuary class of cases not caught by the Statute . . .

[2] See discussion on *Moore v Griffiths* [1972] 3 All ER 399 and *Seymour v Reed* [1927] AC 554, above. Note also the non-taxable award to a bank employee in recognition of his achievements in his professional examination: *Ball v Johnson* (1971) 47 TC 155.

[3] In *Calvert v Wainwright* [1947] 1 All ER 282, a tip to a taxi driver was held to be taxable. Atkinson J stated that it was a tip ". . . given in the ordinary way as remuneration for services . . .". Atkinson J, further stated that:
> . . . supposing at Christmas, or, when the man is going for a holiday, the hirer says: "You have been very attentive to me, here is a £10 note", he would be making a present, and I should say it would not be assessable because it has been given to the man because of his qualities, his faithfulness, and the way he has stuck to the passenger . . .

[4] [1972] 3 All ER 399.

Brightman J identified six factors that contributed to this conclusion: (i) the payment had not foreseeable element of recurrence; (ii) There was not expectation of award, it came as a surprise to Mr Moore and it was not a contractual right or expectation; (iii) the payment was not made or announced until after the World Cup had been won and the Association had dispensed with the services of the players: (iv) a gift was consistent with the Association's nature and functions of promoting the sport and recognising appropriate achievements; (v) the intention of the giver (the Association) was clearly one of benevolence and not one of employer; (vi) all players, irrespective of the service rendered, received the same award of £1,000—it was not proportionate to services rendered.

By contrast, a proportionate "gift" in *Laidler v Perry* [1] was held to be an emolument from employment. Here an employing company gave each of its 2,300 employees a Christmas "gift" of a £10 voucher. Any employee who had not been with the company for one full year would not receive the full £10 but a proportionately reduced amount. The court concluded that, despite the expression of "gift" and the time of year of its presentation, Christmas, the voucher was an emolument. It did not distinguish between the personal achievements and contributions of the employees (upon qualifying, they would all received a flat rate of £10) but did relate the payment to length of employment.

In *Seymour v Reed* [2] a professional cricketer with Kent County Cricket Club was, under the club regulations, granted a benefit match. The grant of the benefit match was not of right but discretionary. It was the Committee of the County Cricket Club that exercised the discretion in favour of the taxpayer. Following the benefit match, the taxpayer received the gate monies and subscriptions. The Revenue claimed the money was taxable as an emolument from the taxpayer's employment. The court disagreed. The benefit match and monies collected were an appreciation and acknowledgement of the cricketer's contributions and personal qualities. The income was more in the nature of a testimonial to mark appreciation at the end of a professional cricketer's career.

In *Moorhouse v Dooland* [3] the Revenue successfully persuaded the Court that monies and gifts received by a professional cricketer employed by Lancashire Cricket Club were taxable as emoluments from employment. The monies and gifts here consisted of a contractual entitlement to receive

[1]  [1965] 2 All ER 121.
[2]  [1927] AC 554, 11 TC 625.
[3]  [1955] 1 All ER 93, 36 TC 12.

one guinea for every 50 runs scored or six wickets taken, and a right to "collections" for meritorious performance.[1] In concluding that these sums were emoluments from employment, Jenkins LJ identified four issues for consideration: (i) the perceptions of the receiver: did he believe it to be a gift or testimonial, or did he believe it be derived from or caused by his employment?; (ii) was the income part of a contractual entitlement and expectation or was it a purely voluntary payment?; (iii) was the payment of a recurring nature?; (iv) did the circumstances indicate a gift, a payment according to personal needs or qualities?[2]

## Payments for Entering into Restrictive Covenants

Under ICTA 1988, s313, a payment made in respect of an undertaking given by the employee to restrict his activities is deemed to be an emolument. The restriction(s) must be caused by the undertaking as opposed to interest or professional restrictions on the employee or their position.[3] Payments made after 8 June 1988 will be subject to income tax at the appropriate base or higher rate, and the sum paid will be a deductible income expense of the employer. Payments made prior to 8 June 1988 did offer some tax advantages in allowing the employee to enjoy a "grossed up" amount equivalent to basic rate liability : only those employees with higher rate liability would be taxed on the payment received at the appropriate higher rate—lower paid employees (basic rate) would in effect receive a tax free sum!

## Payments Made in Respect of the Variation and/or Termination of Employment

It is necessary to have an awareness of the general principles and of the statutory rules. The general principles attempt to give effect to the issue of causation. They respect the need to consider, as a matter of reality and fact, whether the payment was an emolument caused by the employment in accordance with the requirements of TA 1988, s19. Thus we find that on the matter of payments in respect of the variation and removal of

---

[1] The latter was a right found in the League rules rather than expressly in the contract with Lancashire Council Cricket Club.

[2] These issues can be contrasted with the six factors identified by Brightman J in *Moore v Griffiths* (see discussion, above).

[3] In *Vaughan-Neil v IRC* [1979] 3 All ER 481, a payment made to a barrister for his agreeing not to practice escaped tax. The payment was made upon the barrister taking-up an appointment with a building contractor—inherent in taking-up such employment was a prohibition on a barrister practising at the bar (professional restriction and prohibition).

contractual rights we need to carefully consider the "right" and its context.[1] For example, a payment made in respect of the removal of pension rights was not a payment caused by employment, as required by s19.[2] Strictly speaking the pension is not paid in return for services rendered—albeit it tends to be viewed today as part of the remuneration package!

The need to focus on the exact variation and the focus of the payment or compensation received is illustrated in *Holland v Geoghegan.*[3] In that case the "totting" rights (rights to sell salvaged property) of refuse collectors were terminated. The refuse collectors went on strike and subsequently received a lump sum in respect of terminated rights. The court, however, viewed the lump sum payment as a inducement to return to work and not, primarily, as a payment of compensation. On that basis the lump sum paid was taxable as an emolument from employment.

In *Hunter v Dewhurst*[4] a taxpayer waived his retirement rights under the contract and thereby, continued in his office as director. In return he received £10,000 and agreed to renounce all rights of compensation. The House of Lords held that this sum was not an emolument caused by the office or employment. The House of Lords treated this sum as a payment of compensation for the surrender of retirement rights.

When payments are received in respect of the termination of the employment, *Dale v De Soissons*[5] indicates the danger of including termination rights and payments in the initial contractual terms. Here the contractual terms stipulated that the company would have the right to terminate the contract after only one year. The contract also stated that if the company did exercise their right to terminate after only one year's service, the company would pay a sum in respect of the services and a further sum on the termination. In *Dale v De Soissons*, the company exercised this contractual right and terminated the employment after only one year. The company also paid a sum of £10,000 to the employee, at termination, caused by the employment (albeit paid at termination) because is was part of the employee's rights under the terms and contract of employment.

Finally, as part of the general principles, we must mention the decision

---

[1] See earlier discussion.

[2] See *Tilley v Wales* [1943] 1 All ER 280.

[3] [1972] 3 All ER 333.

[4] [1932] 16 TC 605. There is some concern over the status of the decision in *Hunter v Dewhurst*. In the case, four judges found for the taxpayer (three being in the House of Lords) and five found for the Revenue. In later cases, it has been suggested that *Hunter v Dewhurst* be confined to its special facts. This illustrates the difficulties and uncertainties faced in this area.

[5] [1950] 2 All ER 460.

in *Shilton v Wilmshurst*.[1] The decision of the House of Lords seems to suggest that a payment made (by your employer) at the termination of your employment will be an emolument if paid by reference to the beginning of your employment with another employer (Southampton Football Club).

The relevant statutory principles are to be found in TA 1988, s148. Section 148 is an important residual section in that it applies to payments that are not taxable as emoluments under the general principles. It applies to payments made:

> directly or indirectly in consideration or in consequence of, or otherwise in connection with, the termination of the holding of the office or employment or any change in its functions or emoluments, including any payment in commutation of annual or periodical payments (whether chargeable to tax or not) which would otherwise have been made as aforesaid.

The breadth of coverage of section 148 renders it a useful and attractive residual power—albeit its scope is marginally reduced by provisions found in the TA 1988, s188. For example, a "golden handshake" is caught by section 148 as a payment made "in connection with the termination" of the office or employment; but the whole sum is not taxable. Section 188 allows the first £30,000 of a "golden handshake" to escape tax.[2]

Other exemptions and relief (full or part) found in section 188 include, termination payments made on the death or disablement of the employee and sums paid as part of approved retirement benefit schemes.

## Fringe Benefits ("Benefits in Kind")

In addition to salaries, fees and wages, the term "emoluments" includes benefits in kind[3] (perquisites and profits). The rationale for attempting to include the value of benefits in kind in calculating tax liability was expressed by The Royal Commission on the Taxation of Profits and

---

[1] See earlier discussions.

[2] TA 1988, s188(4); FA 1988, s74(1). Hence in *Shilton v Wilmshurst*, the debate took place in recognition that if the sum paid by Nottingham Forest was not an emolument under the general principles, then it would be caught by section 148 subject to the £30,000 exemption provided by section 188.

[3] An appropriate definition of a benefit in kind can be found in the Final Report of The Royal Commission on the Taxation of Profits and Income, Cmnd 9474 (1055) at para. 208:

... the law includes in its conception of income a benefit having money's worth even though it is only received in kind.

Income as necessary in order to promote equality and equity between taxpayers:

> If advantage can be taken of any weakness in the tax treatment of such benefits, there is an obvious temptation to resort to them as a means of part remuneration. And the harm that results is not merely the absolute loss of revenue: it is unfairness in the distribution of tax as between one taxpayer and another. [1]

The above quote also indicates the importance of not leaving any "gaps" in the taxation of benefits. One assumes that any "gaps" will promote tax planning and tax advantages to the detriment of the equality and equity among taxpayers. Whether the rules on the taxation of fringe benefits achieves or substantially contributes to any desired equal treatment of taxpayers is debatable. [2] The complexity of the rules and principles applying to the taxation of fringe benefits illustrate, or perhaps contribute to, the difficulties in this area. The principles demand that we ask two questions; (i) Is the benefit taxable in the hands of that particular taxpayer? (a "status" and "benefit" issue); (ii) If the benefit is taxable, what is the appropriate value of the benefit? In answering these questions we must consider both common law and statutory rules. Our starting point is consideration of the principle of convertibility.

### Convertibility

This principle was established by the House of Lords in *Tennant v Smith*. [3] At its purest level, this principle states that a benefit is taxable only if the taxpayer is able to convert the benefit into money. Thus in *Tennant v Smith* the provision of free accommodation (valued at £50) to a bank employee was not taxable because it was non-convertible. The bank employee was to act as custodian of the premises and conduct special bank business after bank hours. He was not allowed to sublet the premises nor to use them for any purpose other than the bank's business. It was confirmed that the benefit "is not income unless it can be turned to money". [4]

---

[1] *Ibid.*

[2] See The Royal Commission's Report, *ibid* at para. 211:
... all benefits in kind received in the course of employment and attributable to it are a form of remuneration and should rank as taxable income, since otherwise one taxpayer's income is not equitably balanced against another's.

[3] 1892] AC 150.

[4] Lord Halsbury, *ibid* at 156.

The principle of convertibility has subsequently developed to include the convertible value of benefits that could not be assigned or sold but could be converted into monetary value. For example, in *Heaton v Bell* the taxpayer partook of his employer's car loan scheme. In return for the use of a car, the taxpayer received an amended lower wages (a deduction of just over £2 per week). It is important to appreciate that the employer would enjoy the use of the car but it was an unassignable (to a third party) right. The House of Lords held that the benefit was convertible. It could, at any time, be converted into money by the employee giving notice to his employers that he wished to relinquish his right to use the car and his employers would then be obliged to increase his wages by an amount equal to the amount by which his wages had been reduced by the car loan scheme (£2 per week). [1]

Similarly, in *Abbott v Philbin* [2] a non-assignable share option was convertible in that it could be used to raise monies. Alternatively, the right to exercise the option enabled the taxpayer to obtain shares from the company. Those shares would be property rights of value and freely convertible into money.

It is interesting that in both *Abbott v Philbin* and in *Heaton v Bell*, the benefit was expressed to, or appeared to be, unassignable (directly) to a third party. It is perhaps asking too much of one to accept that both decisions are authorities for allowing the Revenue to ignore expressed or actual restrictions on assignment. In *Tennant v Smith* the court did not appear to look beyond the expressed non-assignability of the benefit as found in the terms of employment and occupation. In *Abbott v Philbin* Lord Radcliffe criticised the "not very precise language" used in *Tennant v Smith*, and suggested that there exist many uncertainties that have yet to be cleared up, including the issue:

> must the inconvertibility arise from the nature of the thing itself, or can it be imposed merely by contractual stipulation? Does it matter that the circumstances are such that conversion into money is a practical, though not a theoretical, impossibility; or, on the other hand, that conversion, though forbidden, is the most probable assumption. [3]

[1] Lord Upjohn dissented explaining that the benefit (the use of the car) could not be turned into money:

> In my opinion, this personal unassignable right for use of the car was not equivalent to money while it continued and that, surely must be the test . . .

[2] [1961] AC 352.

[3] *Ibid*, at 378–9.

The test of convertibility not only determines the taxability or otherwise of the benefit, but it also provides the answer to the question of the "value" of the benefit provided. The value of the benefit provided equals the convertible value at the date of provision. Thus in *Wilkins v Rogerson*[1] an employee who was provided with a suit was assessed on the secondhand value of the suit at the date of provision (the convertible value). The secondhand value was lower than the cost to the employer of providing the benefit but it reflected the value that the employee would expect if he elected to convert the benefit into money.[2]

In *Heaton v Bell* the converted value was of £2 per week—the amount by which the taxpayer's wages would increase if he had elected to withdraw from the car loan scheme and the amended lower wage benefit.

### Statutory Rules

Despite judicial efforts, the convertibility rule remains limited in its scope and, particularly in times of high tax rates, ineffective in controlling and dealing with the growth in fringe benefits.[3] The Legislature has responded to this situation by declaring that certain types of benefit and benefits provided to certain types of employee, will be taxable irrespective of the fact that those benefits would not be convertible under the principle established in *Tennant v Smith*.

### Living Accommodation[4]

Where living accommodation is provided for a person (or to his family) by reason of his employment, its value to him, less anything he pays himself, is taxed under Schedule E.[5] The charge only applies to the provision of

---

[1] [1961] 1 All ER 358.

[2] The suit cost the employer £14 15s to provide, but the taxpayer was attributed as receiving a benefit to the value of £5 only (the secondhand value of the suit).

[3] It has been reported that the use of recognised fringe benefits is far higher in the UK than in any other European country.

The limitations of the principle in *Tennant v Smith* may not have been of concern in 1892 when the standard rate of income tax was only 2.5%: the incentive to substitute income with a fringe benefit was clearly not prominent or strong.

[4] TA 1988, ss145, 146.

[5] Note that this rule does not apply if the accommodation is made subject to a charge to him as income tax elsewhere. For example, if the accommodation is convertible then it will be taxed in accordance with the *Tennant v Smith* principles and not by an application of these statutory rules and valuations.

living accommodation : not to ancillary services such as heating, lighting and furniture (although the provision of such services to "higher paid employees" may be assessable under other statutory provisions). It is also important to establish that the accommodation was provided by reason of the employment. [1]

The assessment is based on the value to the employee of the accommodation provided. The TA 1988, s837 explains that the value to the employer is the annual value, and that the annual value is the rateable value of the property or the rent paid by the employer to provide the accommodation (if the latter presents a higher figure). [2]

An additional charge is imposed an employees who are provided with living accommodation that cost more than £75,000 to provide. [3] The additional charge involves the application of a formula taking into account the actual cost of provision and any rent paid by the employee. [4]

The statutory rules do permit some relief to those who occupy living accommodation provided by their employer in "non-beneficial circumstances". The following classes of non-beneficial occupation and provision will not be chargeable:

(a) where the accommodation is deemed necessary for the proper performance of the employee's duties;
(b) where the employment is one where it is customary to provide living accommodation *and* the accommodation is provided for the better performance of the employment duties;
(c) where the occupation of the premises are part of special security arrangements.

The nature of the employment and the contractual responsibilities will help determine whether it is possible to enjoy the "non-beneficial" occupation exceptions. For example, it is probable that hotel staff will

---

[1] In practice, if the accommodation is provided by your employer it is deemed to have been provided by reason of your employment.

[2] Section 837 initially provides that the annual value is a "fictitious rent" equating to that which might reasonably be expected to be obtained on a yearly letting if the tenant undertook to pay rates and taxes and the landlord undertook to pay for repairs and insurance.

In practice, it is the rateable value rather than the value of the "fictitious rent" that is used for assessment purposes.

[3] TA 1988, s146. (Introduced by FA 1983, s21).

[4] The formula provides:

[(cost of providing accommodation) minus £75,000 x official rate of interest] minus any excess rent paid by the employee.

enjoy exception (a). Similarly, in *Tennant v Smith* the obligation to occupy the premises was related to the performance of contractual duties. The requirements in situation (b) of "customary" and "better performance" might present an additional burden. "Customary" will demand an examination of "industry wide" practices and an examination of the history and length of those practices. [1] This burden can be balanced against the requirement in exception (a) to show that the occupation was "necessary" for "proper performance" rather than merely promoting "better performance".

### Vouchers and Credit-Tokens

If an employee receives a voucher or credit token that can be exchanged for goods and/or services, he will be taxed on the cost of provision, i.e. the amount that it cost the employer to provide the voucher or token. [2] Prior to the introduction of legislation covering this area, the convertibility principle would have caught many vouchers and, possibly, credit tokens. [3] Problems did occur with the growing use of non-convertible credit-tokens, such as credit-cards and non-transferable season tickets. Here the voucher or token remained in the physical possession of the employee and, although it may have been used to acquire goods or services, it remained non-converted: under today's legislation, convertibility is irrelevant and the credit token or voucher will be taxable on the value of "the cost of provision."

### Special Statutory Provisions Applying Only to Directors and "Higher Paid Employees"

In 1948 special rules were introduced to tax certain benefits provided to directors and higher paid employees that were not "otherwise chargeable to tax." In other words, these benefits will be taxable even though they are not convertible within the principle of *Tennant v Smith*. The relevant rules can now be found in the TA 1988, Part V, Chapter II and Schedules 6 and 7. The statutory rules began life in 1948 as an attempt to control the

---

[1] See *Vertigan v Brady* [1988] STC 91.

[2] TA 1988, s141, 142 and 144. Note, TA 1988 ss143, 144—if a voucher is exchangeable for cash, the exchange value of the voucher is chargeable under the PAYE Scheme.

[3] The "convertibility" principle did develop to recognise an element of the cost of provision or, more accurately, the debts incurred by the employer in providing the benefit. For example, in *Nicholl v Austin* (1935) 19 TC 531 a company paid an employee's debts and the court held that the benefits provided were convertible into a sum equating with the costs to the employer of providing those benefits (the cost of settling those debts).

tax avoidance benefits provided through the use of expense account provisions. Today the rules apply to a wider range of benefits and attempt to provide some recognition of the practice of providing remuneration and benefit packages. The main specific benefits which are chargeable to income tax by the TA 1988, Part V, Chapter II are : (a) expense allowances, (b) benefits in general, (c) beneficial loan arrangements, (d) expenses connected with living accommodation, (e) cars and petrol, and (f) scholarships.

It is important to appreciate that this legislation only applies to (a) directors and employees with emoluments of £8,500 or more, per annum[1] and (b) directors with emoluments of less than £8,500, except where those directors work full-time in the company and control less than five per cent of the company.[2] In computing the employees emoluments for the purposes of the £8,500 threshold level, it is assumed that the rules in TA 1988, ss153 and 154 are applicable and sums computed on the basis of ss153 and 154 are included within the initial computation of the employees' emolument level. Such sums will later be ignored if the initial emolument level does not reach the £8,500 threshold level.

## *Payments for Expenses and Allowances*[3]

Any sum paid to an employee, by reason of his employment, in respect of expenses is treated as income of that employee or director. This includes expense allowances and the reimbursement of expenses. The expenses are caught under this provision unless "otherwise chargeable to tax". Furthermore genuine expenses[4] are deductible and are not treated as emoluments.

## *Benefits in General*[5]

TA 1988, s154 requires that certain benefits provided to directors or higher paid employees are to be treated as emoluments from their office or employment. The benefits caught by s154 include sums spent on or in

---

[1] The FA 1989, s53, explains that employees earning over £8,500 are no longer to be described as higher paid. We shall continue to use the term as one of convenience.

[2] "Directors" need not be formally appointed as "directors" in order to be caught by the legislation (TA 1988, s168).

The 5% requirement relates to 5% of ordinary share capital or distribution rights and satisfies the statutory requirement of "material interest" (TA 1988, s167).

[3] TA 1988, s153.

[4] To be deductible, expenses must satisfy the tests laid down in TA 1988 ss198, 201 and 203.

[5] TA 1988, s154.

connection with the provision of (a) accommodation, other than living accommodation, (b) entertainment, (c) domestic of other services, and (d) other benefits and facilities "of whatsoever nature". Note the potential breadth and extent of application of the final category of "benefit".

Section 154 applies only to benefits provided by reason of the employment[1], and it does not apply to income excluded from tax by some other provision[2]. Section 154 does not apply to sums chargeable under the general principle of convertibility under *Tennant v Smith*. Those sums represent sums "otherwise chargeable to tax" although any non-convertible excess amounts will be assessed for liability under s154. Section 154 applies to the "provision" of benefits irrespective of whether those benefits were requested, used, or that the "provision" was greater in cost than an alternative or self-provision. So, for example, in *Rendell v Went*[3] a taxpayer was assessed on the cost of a benefit of legal expenses provided by his employers. The cost of that benefit was £641. The employee's objection that his own provision of such services would only have cost £60 was ignored as irrelevant under the wording of section 154.

*Rendell v Went* illustrates that the charge on the benefit provided is upon the "cost of the benefit". The cost of the benefit demands that we recognise the expenses "incurred by the employer in or in connection with" securing the provision of the benefits. Thus in *Rendell v Went* the cost of the benefit provided was the full cost to the employer of £641.

Assessing the cost of the provision of an in-house service, such as reduced rate or free travel to airline employees, has proved difficult and might possibly lead to absurd results. The obvious (and perhaps logical) solution would be to follow the approach of most other OECD countries and insert market-value as the cost of provision. Another sensible choice would be to use the "marginal cost" of the provision as the relevant employer's cost. Unfortunately, the legislation appears to indicate that the appropriate cost is the "actual cost" of provision.

The actual cost must include

---

[1] Provision for an employee *or* for members of his family or household, by his employer, are deemed to be made by reason of the employment.

[2] TA 1988, s155 contains many exemptions from the s154 charge. These include:
—the provision of accommodation and supplies used at the employee's place of work and used solely for work purposes;
—canteen meals provided for the staff generally;
—expenses incurred in the provision of any pension, annuity or other like benefit for the director or employees and their families upon the employee's death or retirement;
—medical insurance and treatment for foreign visits.

[3] [1964] 2 All ER 464.

a proper proportion of any expenses relating partly to the benefit and partly to other matters.

Thus in *Pepper v Hart*[1] employees of Malvern College had taken the benefit of a scheme whereby their sons were educated at the school at one-fifth of the fees normally charged. The employees submitted that the cost of the benefit should be the marginal cost, and that in this instance, the marginal cost of the boys' education represented some additional expenditure on items such as food, laundry and stationery. It was clear that the presence of the boys did not increase the other expenses of running the school: staff salaries, insurance, heating and maintenance of buildings, maintenance of grounds, remuneration of administrative and other staff, and so on. Nor would the absence of the boys have reduced these "other expenses". Unanimously the Court of Appeal rejected the submissions of the taxpayers. Nicholls LJ explained[2] that the

> statutory formula is concerned with one specific calculation: the amount of the expense incurred by the employer in providing the benefit.

Applying that calculation it was clear that each place in the school cost the school as much as every other place. Thus the expense incurred by the school in providing the benefits to the assistant school masters and bursar must include a proper portion of the general running expenses of the school; that portion represents the statutory requirement of including

> a proper proportion of any expenses relating partly to the benefit and partly to other matters.

The taxpayers were properly assessed on the full cost rather than the marginal cost of the benefit; Nicholls LJ admitted[3] that the necessary rateable apportionment of the relevant expenses would produce a figure close to the amount of the ordinary school fees—thus removing the benefit!

Initial academic and press response suggest that this decision may have adverse and absurd effects on existing fringe-benefit concessions.[4] The

---

[1] [1990] STC 786.

[2] *Ibid* at 791.

[3] *Ibid* at 788.

[4] For an initial response see J Dyson, [1990] BTR 122 and D Wright, the *Sunday Times*, 18 November 1990, at 11.

suggestion is that employees may be assessed on a cost basis that may exceed the cost of the benefit to non-employees. For example, airline staff occupying otherwise empty seats on an aircraft amounts to very little in marginal costs but amounts to an excessive amount if the cost is to include an apportionment of full costs. [1]

An appeal by the taxpayers to the House of Lords was successful. The taxpayers' were charged on the marginal cost of provision. The House of Lord's decision is important in a wider context in the pronouncements made on the issue of statutory interpretation and the use of supplementary material, including the use of Hansard. On the less important issue of the value to be attributed to the benefit provided there appear to be two approaches. In the minority, Lord Mackay LC insisted that once the benefit to be taxed has been identified, one must then consider whether that benefit was received as of right or as result of the exercise of the provider's discretion [1992] STC 898 at 901). If it was as a result of the exercise of discretion, then the surplus (marginal) costs of exercising that discretion and providing, in this case the surplus school places, must be the cost of provision.

Lord Browne-Wilkinson (representing the majority) expressed disagreement with the approach of Lord Mackay on the ground that the distinction proposed was "not reflected in the parliamentary proceedings". Lord Browne-Wilkinson preferred the approach of accepting that the relevant statutory provisions were ambiguous and thus, he referred to the debate in Hansard and in particular to the responses given by the, then, Financial Secretary to the Treasury, which made it clear that the absurd consequence of apportioning total costs to those enjoying an in-house provision or benefit was never intended. Nor was it intended that market-price should apply (an original provision that was withdrawn during debate). Lord Browne-Wilkinson concluded that parliamentary debate reveals that the value of the benefit provided (in-house) was intended to be and should represent and reflect the marginal costs of provision. Commenting on the difficulties that a reference to Hansard and parliamentary debate might cause, Lord Brown-Wilkinson suggested that he did not believe that the practical difficulties arising from this approach to statutory interpretation were

> . . . sufficient to outweigh the basic need for the courts to give effect to the words enacted by Parliament in the sense that they were intended by Parliament to hear . . . [2]

---

[1] [1992] STC 898.
[2] [1992] STC 898 at 921.

The Legislature has been able to predict and make provision in other potentially difficult areas. For example, where the provided (the benefit) remains the property of the employer, the employee is taxed on the "annual value" of the asset, plus any other expenses of provision excluding acquisition and production costs. [1] The "annual value" for the provision of land is its rateable value. For other assets, the annual value is 20% of their market value at the time that it is first provided by the employer. [2] If the ownership of the asset is subsequently transferred to the employee the employee may be charged on the value of the item when he first received it less any annual value charges that may have been applied. [3] This is an anti-avoidance provision preventing the abuse of the normal rule [4] of market value at the date of transfer in circumstances of depreciating assets.

If the expense incurred by the employer is partly to provide a benefit to the employee and partly for some other identifiable purpose, section 156 allows "apportionment" to take place. The employee is only taxed on the proper proportion of the expense and the benefit. For example, in *Westcott v Bryan* [5] a managing director was required by his employers to live in a large house, close to the Potteries in Staffordshire. The managing Director would have preferred to have lived in London and would have preferred a much smaller property. His employers were concerned over the need to entertain clients and the convenience of the location. The employers paid most of the running costs of the house. The court held that the taxpayer was to be assessed on only a proportion of the running costs provided by his employers. The money spent by his employers was partly for the taxpayer's benefit and partly for the benefit of others. [6]

## *Living Accommodation (Ancillary Services)* [7]

The general rules in TA 1988 s145 covering the provision of living accommodation are supplemented in the case of directors and higher paid employees to facilitate the taxation of services provided with the

---

[1] TA 1988, s156(4).

[2] TA 1988, s156(5).

[3] TA 1988, s156(4).

[4] TA 1988, s156(3).

[5] [1969] 3 All ER 564.

[6] It is significant that in *Rendell v West* [1964] 2 All ER 464, apportionment of the legal fees was not allowed on the grounds that "no part of the money was spent on something that did not benefit the taxpayer". The taxpayer enjoyed all the money in that it was all spent to cover his legal fees.

[7] TA 1988, s163.

accommodation (such as furniture, heating, telephone, etc). The "general benefits" provisions in section 154 will normally attach to the provision of "ancillary services". However, where those ancillary services are provided in relation to non-beneficial occupation some relief is provided in section 163. Section 163 provides that in instances of non-beneficial occupation the provision of sums in respect of heating, lighting, cleaning, repairs, furniture, etc, must not exceed ten per cent of the emoluments of the employment—a maximum charge for the provision of those services and benefits.

### *Low Interest Loans* [1]

If the employer provides the employee with a low interest or interest free loan, the employee is taxed on the cash equivalent of that loan. The cash equivalent represents a computation of the benefit received by calculating the difference between the amount of interest that would have been paid at an official rate and any interest actually paid.

Some relief is provided in that a *de minimis* exception applies [2] and loans for "qualifying purposes" are excluded. A "qualifying purpose" is one that is generally recognised as deductible from total income. For example, loans to purchase one's main residence are eligible for interest relief under the general law (although a £30,000 limit applies).

Should the employer release or write-off (whole or in part) the amount due, a charge will be imposed on the amount so released or written-off (the benefit provided). This will also apply to the release or writing-off of loans made for a qualifying purpose. [3]

### *Cars and Fuel* [4]

If an employee is provided with the use of a car, that benefit may be

[1] TA 1988, s160 and Schedule. 7.

[2] TA 1988, s161 (currently a "cash equivalent" of £300).

[3] A benefit has been provided in that the outstanding amount of the loan (and interest) are no longer repayable.

[4] TA 1988, ss157 and 158. On 30 July 1992, the Inland Revenue issued a Consultative Document, "Company Cars—Reform of Income Tax Treatment".

The Document contains the broad aims of (1) ensuring that the tax charged is a fair reflection of the benefit received; (2) avoiding distortions in the car market; (3) minimising incentives to drive less fuel efficient cars; (4) keeping administrative costs to a minimum.

The central proposal is that the car cash equivalents should be based on a percentage of the price of the car supplied. No charges are proposed to the apportionment rules or to the "business deductions" rules.

Although the general aim of "neutrality" is accepted, some critics have suggested that the proposals fall short of satisfying the declared aims, and that the proposals fail to recognise that the majority of taxable, except where that car is a "pool car". A "pool car" is a car that is genuinely available to more than one employee; is not regularly garaged at an employee's house; and any provide use is purely incidental to its business use. [1] In all other cases, the provision of the car will be a taxable benefit. The value of the benefit provided is represented by a cash equivalent fixed by statute. Some concerns have developed as to whether the statutory regime adequately taxes the private value of the "company car" and some changes have been introduced to try to reflect concerns. Provided below is an outline of both the "old" regime and the "new" rules.

### *"Old" Regime*

Under the "old" regime a declared cash equivalent is reduced by 50 per cent if the car is used preponderantly for business travel (at least 18,000 miles per annum). Conversely, if business travel is below 2,500 miles per annum the cash equivalent is increased by 50 per cent—the personal benefits exceed the car's business utility. [2]

If the employer also provides the employee with free petrol for private motoring, a statutory scale of charges similarly applies. The scale and charge is reduced by 50 per cent if business mileage exceeds 18,000, *BUT*, the charge is not increased if business mileage is less than 2,500 miles per annum.

### *"New" rules*

The "old" rules have been changed with effect from 6 April 1994. The new rules will tax cars on a cash equivalent of 35 per cent of the price of the car based on the full cost (i.e. car price including VAT and cost of any accessories and delivery) with a one-third reduction for 2,500 plus business miles and a reduction of two-thirds for over 18,000 business miles per annum. A further reduction of one-third may be made if the car is four years old or more at the end of the year (section 157, Schedule 6).

Relief still remains for pool cars. Similarly the "related benefit" of fuel for private use still raises a tax charge (section 158).

---

company cars are work cars—figures reveal that less than 8% of "company cars" travel less than 2,500 business miles per annum whereas over 26% travel 18,000 plus, business miles per annum (see K Paterson [1992] BTR 368).

[1] TA 1988, S159.

[2] TA 1988, s168(5); TA 1988, s157 and Schedule 6.

*Scholarships* [1]

If a member of a director's or higher-paid employee's family receives a scholarship (directly or indirectly) from the employer, the director or higher-paid employee will be taxed on the value of the scholarship. Some relief is available in that the charge can be avoided if it is shown that the scholarship was from a trust or similar scheme and that such payments do not represent more than 25 per cent of payments made from that fund in that year.

*Mobile Phones* [2]

Although aspects of the provision of a mobile phone might be caught under section 156, the Finance Act 1991 introduced a scale charge of £200 whenever a mobile phone is provided and is available for private use.

## Deductible Expenses

The rules and principles in the deductibility of expenses have been described as "notoriously narrow in their application" and "notoriously rigid, narrow and restricted in their operation". [3] Certainly when one compares the deductibility rules in Schedule E with the Schedule D taxpayer, the Schedule E employee does appear to be at a disadvantage. The Schedule D taxpayer enjoys a deductibility test of wider application.

It is normal to draw a distinction between (a) expenses connected with travelling, and (b) other expenses. The TA 1988, 198(1) explains that the Schedule E taxpayer can only deduct travel expenses if the taxpayer is

> necessarily obliged to incur those expenses in the performance of the duties of the office or employment.

The application of section 198 involves the application of two tests:

1. Was the taxpayer *necessarily* obliged to incur those expenses?
2. Were the expenses necessarily incurred in the *performance* of the taxpayer's duties?

---

[1] TA 1988, s165.

[2] TA 1988, S159A added by FA 1991, s30(2).

[3] See the Final Report of the Royal Commission on Taxation of Profits and Income. Cmnd 9474 (1955). The Report also reveals opinion that the "existing rule drew the line as fairly as could be expected of any general rule and that no other form of wording would be an improvement upon it".

The test of "necessary" travel expenses appears to be an objective test demanding consideration of whether the class of employee (or potential employee) would necessarily incur those travel expenses as part of his or her duties [1]. In some instances, the class of employee might be so small as to demand an assessment of whether it was necessary for an individual to incur those expenses as part of his or her duties. In *Ricketts v Colquhoun* [2] the class of employee (or potential employee) was wide and could have included those who lived in the Portsmouth area where the work was to be undertaken rather than in London. The taxpayer's decision to reside in London was a personal decision and his travel expenses from London to Portsmouth were not necessarily incurred as a consequence of his employment or office in Portsmouth. By contrast in *Taylor v Provan* [3] the class of potential employee was very narrow; it consisted of the need to acquire the services of one particular individual. The question of whether he would necessarily have to incur travel expenses from Canada to London in the performance of his duties became a personal question and was answered in the affirmative: the employers could only employ him and must accept his decision on residence.

The second part of the section 198 test demands consideration of whether the travel expenses were incurred in the performance of the duties of employment. It seems that the application of this part of the test invites the following *general* rules:

1. The costs of travelling to work from home are not deductible on the grounds that the travel does not involve the "performance of your duties": your duties commence when you arrive at work, not on your way to work.
2. The costs of travelling from one place of employment to a place of different employment are not deductible. Once again you are not travelling in the course of your employment: you are travelling from one employment to another employment.
3. In contrast to (2) above, if you are travelling from one place of employment to another place of the *same* employment, it is likely that you are travelling in the performance of your duties. In such a case, it is likely that any expenses incurred will be deductible as necessarily incurred in the performance of your duties (provided, of course, that the employee is obliged to travel within the same employment).

---

[1] See *Ricketts v Colquhoun* [1926] AC 1, ". . . the expense had to be one which each and every occupant of the particular office was necessarily obliged to incur".

[2] *Ibid.*

[3] [1974] 1 All ER 1201.

4. It is possible that the employee's "home" can be classed as a point where work commences (a place of work) and travel between that point to another point of the same work will be deductible, as a continuation of those duties.

The following decisions indicate the complexity of the above rules and of the distinctions adopted.

### *Ricketts v Colquohoun* [1]

This involved a barrister who resided in London. His earnings from the bar were assessable under Schedule D, Case II. The barrister also took up an appointment as Recorder of Portsmouth (Schedule E appointment). The barrister sought to deduct the costs of travelling from his home in London to Portsmouth. His claim failed. The costs of travel were not necessarily incurred. As explained above, he could have elected to have lived in Portsmouth. Nor were the costs incurred in the performance of his duties: his duties as Recorder did not commence until he reached the office in Portsmouth—when travelling to that office he was travelling to his employment, and not in the course of that employment.

### *Owen v Pook* [2]

The taxpayer, a medical practitioner, worked as a general practitioner at his home in Fishguard. The taxpayer also held a part-time appointment as an obstetrician and anaesthetist at Haverfordwest, 15 miles from Fishguard. The part-time appointments included stand-by duties. These duties required the taxpayer to be accessible by telephone and he often gave advice by phone. The costs of travelling between the taxpayer's home in Fishguard and the hospital in Haverfordwest were deductible. Lord Guest explained that the taxpayer had, in contrast to *Ricketts v Colquhoun*, two places where the duties were performed. Dr Owen's duties commenced at the moment he was first contacted by the hospital authorities. He took responsibility for a patient as soon as he received a telephone call. He often advised treatment by telephone:

> . . . there were thus two places where his duty is performed, the hospital and his telephone in his consulting room. If he was performing his

[1] [1926] AC 1.
[2] [1969] 2 All ER 1.

duties at both places, then it is difficult to see why, on the journey between the two places, he was not equally performing his duties . . .

## Taylor v Provan [1]

The taxpayer was appointed as a director of an English Brewery Company. The taxpayer was resident in Canada but was appointed by the English Company because of his very special knowledge and skills on matters of amalgamation and merger within the brewing industry. The taxpayer completed most of his work in Canada but frequently made visits to England. He did not receive any remuneration for the work completed, but he did receive income to cover the travel expenses to England. The House of Lords held by a majority of 3:2 that the expenses were an allowable deduction. The reasoning of the majority is not altogether settled and certain. Lord Morris and Lord Salmon appear to accept that the taxpayer was travelling between two places of the same employment and was thus travelling in the course of, and in the performance of, his duties of employment. More controversially, Lord Reid in his search for the ratio of *Owen v Pook* appeared to accept that the expenses were deductible on the grounds of "necessity". [2] If the latter is the sole reasoning of Lord Reid and of *Owen v Pook*, then it fails to recognise the dual requirements of "necessity" and "performance" of section 198— unless the latter requirement was implicitly accepted as present on the facts presented in both cases.

One of the more interesting concerns expressed by Lord Reid was the danger of adopting a test on the ground of one's home being regarded as a place of work. Lord Reid expressed concern that the majority in *Owen v Pook* did not intend to

> decide that in all cases where the employee's contract requires him to work at home he is entitled to deduct travelling expenses between his home and his other place of work. Plainly that would open the door widely for evasion of the rule. There must be something more. [3]

It has been suggested that the emphasis should not be upon where the work started (is your home a place of work?) but on when the work started. [4] If the emphasis is then placed on the issue of *when* duties will be

[1] [1974] 1 All ER 1201.
[2] [1974] 1 All ER 1201, at 1207.
[3] *Ibid.*
[4] BUKTG, p209.

deemed to have commenced any necessary travelling will be in the performance of those duties.

Finally, it is generally accepted that if travel expenses are allowable then any incidental expenses of the travel will also be allowed.[1]

### Other Expenses

Expenses, other than travel expenses, are deductible if they are "wholly, exclusively and necessarily incurred in the performance of duties".[2] As a matter of convenience this test can be broken down into three parts.

### 1. Performance of Duties

As with travel expenses, other expenses are only deductible if those expenses are incurred in the performance of your duties. This requirement excludes expenses incurred in enabling an employee to acquire qualifications or training to facilitate later performance or performance at a different level of employment—preparation costs. For example, in *Lupton v Potts*[3] a solicitor's clerk was not allowed to deduct the expenses of Law Society Examination fees, partly on the ground that the fees and the examinations were not part of the performance of his duties—they were part of preparation costs for new duties. Similarly, a schoolteacher in *Humbles v Brooks*[4] was not allowed to deduct the costs of a weekend course in history on the grounds that he was not performing his duties by attending the course merely getting background information.

### 2. Necessarily Incurred

As explained above, the test of whether an expense is necessarily incurred is an objective test based upon the question of "whether the duties could be performed without incurring that expense".[5] Thus, we ignore the personal attributes of the individual employee, and look to the attributes a reasonable class of employees and the requirements of the employment.

---

[1] The normal example is the allowance for airline pilots and staff. See *Nolder v Walters* (1930), 15STC 380.

[2] TA 1988, s198(1).

[3] [1969] 3 All ER 1083.

[4] [1962] 40 TC 500.

[5] *Brown v Bullock* (1961) 40 TC 1, per Donovan LJ, "The test is not whether the employer imposes the expense but whether the duties do, in the sense that, irrespective of what the employer may prescribe, the duties cannot be performed without incurring the particular outlay."

For example, one employee with defective eyesight could not recover the costs of glasses on the ground that the expense would not necessarily have ben incurred by the employment: the objective test would raise the issue of the reasonable class of employee, including many good-sighted persons. [1] Similarly in *Lupton v Potts*, above, Plowman J explained that the duties of the taxpayer under the contrast of employment were perfectly capable of being performed without incurring the expense of Law Society Examination fees. In *Humbles v Brooks*, the course fee was not deductible, the court explained that he was not "necessarily obliged" to attend the weekend course. Finally, in *Brown v Bullock* [2] a bank manager was not allowed to deduct the costs of a club membership as membership of that club was not necessary for the performance of his duties; although it was admitted that membership might assist the manager in developing "local contacts".

### 3. Wholly and Exclusively

The test of "wholly and exclusively" is not totally objective. We need to consider whether the individual derives any personal, private, benefit or advantage from the expenditure. Thus, for example, in *Brown v Bullock* the bank manager would obtain the private benefits of "club membership". The test of wholly and exclusively does, however, permit some private benefit provided that the sole object of the expenditure was incurred in performance of the employee's duties and that any private benefit was an unintended but inescapable incidental result or effect of that expenditure: a test that is very difficult to satisfy. For example, in *Ward v Dunn* [3] a taxpayer claimed an allowance in respect of clothing worn for work purposes. The claim failed. Walton J explained that the expenditure on the clothing was not wholly for the purposes of his employment.

> . . . when Mr Dunn purchases a suit he purchases it, maybe partly with a view to going round the sites [his employment] but, at any rate, partly with a view to wearing it in the ordinary course as one wears clothing for comfort and for covering one's nakedness [intended private benefit] . . . [4]

[1] *Roskams v Bennett* (1950) 32 TC 129.
[2] *Supra*, 2.
[3] [1979] STC 178.
[4] Walton J did appear to suggest that the matter would be very different if the clothes that Mr Dunn wore were special clothing worn only at, and for, places of work rather than clothing that could be used for ordinary wear.

The requirement of "wholly and exclusively" is not without relief in that apportionment appears to be available in appropriate instances. For example, where a telephone is used partly for business calls the taxpayer can deduct the expenses of those business calls as they are "wholly and exclusively" intended for business purposes: costs of private calls are obviously not deductible. Any telephone rental charges are not deductible because the intention of the rental agreement and expenses is a dual intention of business and private use.[1]

## Entertainment Expenses

Legislation has been introduced to supplement the section 198 requirements in relation to entertainment expenses. The Taxes Act 1988, section 577 prohibits the deduction of entertainment expenses subject to a number of exceptions including a *de minimis* exception of £10 per annum. However, should an employee receive an entertainment allowance, s577 allows the employee to escape liability on that part of the expenditure that satisfies the requirements of section 198 that the expenditure was

> wholly, exclusively and necessarily incurred in the performance of duties.

## Self-Check Questions

1. What is an "office"?
2. Distinguish employment from a trade or professsion.
3. What are emoluments? How do we determine whether a "gift" from a third party is or is not an emolument?
4. Why should we seek to tax fringe benefits?
5. What is the test of convertibility?
6. When is the provision of living accommodation a non-taxable fringe benefit?
7. When are an employee's travel expenses deductible?
8. Explain the following decisions:
   (i)   *Hunter v Dewhurst*
   (ii)  *Shilton v Wilmshurst*
   (iii) *Pepper v Hart*
   (iv)  *Owen v Pook.*

---

[1] *Lucas v Cattell* (1972) 48 TC 353.

**Further Reading**

Olowofoyeku AA, *In the Performance of Duties: Fact, Law, or Both?* (1996) BTR 28.

Ward J, *What Can it Matter? Why Should it Matter? The Taxation of Offices*, (1989) BTR 281–301.

Bandal S, *The Legacy of Tennant v Smith*, (1984) BTR 333–43.

Kerridge R, *Emoluments and Causation—Hochstrasser Investigated*, (1982) BTR 272–91.

Smith PF, *Travelling Expenses*, (1977) BTR 290–301.

# 5

# Schedule D-Cases I and II: income from trade, profession or vocation

Tax is charged under Schedule D Case I on the "annual profits or gains" of a *trade* carried on in the United Kingdom or elsewhere.[1] Case II charges income tax on the "annual profits or gains" of a *profession* or *vocation*.[2]

## Trade

An insufficient statutory definition of trade exists. The definition merely states what trade might include without being exhaustive as to the items and activities of a trade.

Section 832 (TA 1988) provides that trade includes *every trade, manufacture, adventure or concern in the nature of trade*. Perhaps the usefulness of this "definition" is the implicit suggestion that trade can include an isolated act (an "adventure") as opposed to the need to demonstrate continuity and repetition. The difficulty of providing a definition of trade is illustrated by the uncertain and reluctant nature of judicial comment in this area. For example, trade has been defined as

> commonly used to denote operations of a commercial character by which the trader provides to customers for reward some kind of goods or services.[3]

> ... trade must be bilateral—you must trade with someone.[4]

And, perhaps most illuminating,

[1] TA 1988, section 18. The term "elsewhere" is redundant in that the House of Lords has declared that Case I does not apply to a trade carried on wholly outside the United Kingdom (*Colquhoun v Brooks* 1889).

[2] Note that although section 18 refers to "profits or gains", "gains" do not include capital gains. The charges raised under Schedule D apply only to income gains.

[3] Lord Reid in *Ransom v Higgs* [1974] 3 All ER 949 at 955.

[4] Lord Wilberforce, *ibid* at 964.

Try as you will, the word "trade" is one of those common English words which do not lend themselves readily to a definition but which all of us think we understand well enough. We can recognise a trade when we see it . . . [1]

In the latter case, Lord Denning suggested that we should try to identify the characteristics of trade and measure any transaction against these characteristics. This is sound advice for any student of revenue law. The ability to identify and apply the characteristics of trade will undoubtedly be rewarded. Assistance in performing this task is given through the "badges of trade". Before we turn to consider those badges, it is important to appreciate that the question of whether there is a trade or not, is a question of fact. This means that the courts will only interfere with the decision of the commissioners if the decision and findings are inconsistent or the facts are such that "no person acting judicially and properly" could have come to the same decision. [2]

## The Badges of Trade

The (Radcliffe) Royal Commission on the Taxation of Profits and Income in 1954 (Cmnd 9474) identified "six badges of trade".

*1. Subject Matter*

If the subject matter of the transaction is such that the purchaser cannot possibly regard it as an investment or for his own personal use or pleasure, then the subject matter will point to the activity being a trading activity. For example in *Rutledge v IRC*[3] the taxpayer bought one million rolls of toilet paper for £1,000 and subsequently sold the lot at a profit. It was held that this was an adventure in the nature of a trade. Although it was a one-off transaction, it could still be an adventure in the nature of trade and, as was pointed out the

purchase of such a vast quantity of toilet paper was for no other conceivable purpose than for re-sale at a profit.

[1] Lord Denning in *J P Harrison (Watford) Ltd v Griffiths* [1963] AC 1.
[2] *Edwards v Bairstow and Harrison* [1955] 3 All ER 48.
[3] [1929] 14 TC 490.

## 2. *Period of Ownership*

The Radcliffe Commission suggested that property that is meant to be dealt in (stock-in-trade or trade property) is realised within a short time after acquisition. It has been suggested that this is not a very compelling "badge", and even the Radcliffe Commission admitted that "there are many exceptions to this universal rule". Normally, investment items (capital assets) require an intention to hold onto an item for a long period.

*Rutledge v IRC* can also be used to support and illustrate this badge. The rolls of toilet paper were bought and disposed of within a short period of time.

## 3. *Frequency of Transactions*

Although we have noted that an isolated transaction might amount to trading, repetitions of the same type of transaction provide an even stronger indication of "trading". It is possible for the courts to retrospectively categorise an activity as "trading" by examining subsequent, similar, acts. For example in *Leach v Pogson*[1] the taxpayer had started a driving school which he then sold to a company that he had incorporated. He then repeated this activity by buying and selling a further 30 driving schools over successive years. The taxpayer disputed the claim that his first purchase and sale of a driving school was a trading activity. The courts held that the character of the first transaction could be determined by reference to later transactions. The purchase and sale of the first driving school was therefore held to be a trading activity.

## 4. *Supplementary Work*

If supplementary work takes place to render the subject matter more marketable, or if an organisational structure is brought into being to assist in the promotion and disposal of the subject matter, then that supplementary activity is indicative of "trading". For example, in *Martin v Lowry*[2] a taxpayer purchased 44 million yards of aircraft linen. In order to facilitate its disposal he created a business structure, including the appointment of sales staff and the rental of premises.

[1] [1962] 40 TC 585.
[2] [1927] AC 312.

This supplementary activity of creating a business structure to facilitate disposal of the linen was a strong indication of "trading".

Similarly, in *Cape Brandy Syndicate v IRC*[1], wine merchants bought brandy and then proceeded to "blend" it before resale. This supplementary act of "blending" was an indication of "trade".

### 5. *Circumstances of Realisation*

This "badge" is essentially a negative badge. The circumstances for realisation might point to reasons of disposal other than for trading profit or gain. In *West v Phillips*[2] a builder purchased houses with the intention to let them as an investment. When faced with rent controls, high taxation and the cost of repairs, he quickly changed his mind and sold the houses. The court held that the purpose of the sale of the houses was not trade, but simply a disposal of an investment in response to external influences.

### 6. *Motive*

An intention to trade and to make a profit is not essential to the finding of a trade: your activities might objectively demonstrate the characteristics of trade despite your declared motives. However, evidence of an intention to make a "quick profit" is an indication of trading. In *IRC v Reinhold*[3] the taxpayer purchased four houses and sold them three years later at a profit. Although the taxpayer admitted an intention to make a profit (not a "quick profit" on the facts) the court concluded that the profit was not a trading profit. Lord Keith explained that

> the intention to resell some day at a profit is not *per se* sufficient to support a conclusion of trading

and other factors must be present.

*IRC v Reinhold* should be contrasted with the decision in *Wisdom v Chamberlain*[4]. Norman Wisdom bought silver bullion as a hedge against devaluation and subsequently sold the bullion at a profit. The

---

[1] [1921] 2 KB 403.
[2] [1958] 38 TC 203.
[3] [1953] 34 TC 389.
[4] [1969] 1 All ER 332.

Court of Appeal held that this profit was a trading profit. Harman LJ declared that:

> ... [if the activity] is not an adventure in the nature of trade I do not really know what it is. The whole object of the transaction was to make a profit. ...

Perhaps the contrast between the treatment of "motive" in the *Reinhold* case and in the *Wisdom* case confirms the uncertainty and unpredictability of what is and what is not a trade. It should be repeated that the issue is one of fact and the badges of trade are non-exhaustive characteristics of trade. Perhaps Lord Denning was correct in suggesting that we all know trade when we see it, but we have great difficulty in defining it—or even agreeing on what we see!

## Mutual Trading

We have noted the suggestion that trade must be bilateral or reciprocal—you must trade with someone. The principle that no man can trade with himself has led to the recognition of tax free surpluses of mutual associations. To obtain recognition as a mutual association, or recognition of your mutual trading, the situation must be such that an identifiable class of persons (members) contribute to funds and enjoy and participate in the surplus—there must be complete identity between the contributors and participators. [1]

Two points must be noted in relation to mutual trading.

1. If a mutual association trades with outsiders (non-contributors) then any surplus from those dealings will be trading profits and thus taxable. For example, in *Carlisle and Silloth Golf Club v Smith* [2] although the annual subscriptions received from members were not taxable because those members were also participators; the green fees from non-members were taxable as trading income. As non-members they were not entitled to participate in profits or surpluses—there was no "mutuality".
2. It has been suggested that the "mutuality" and, in particular, the participation, must be genuine. For example, in *Fletcher v Jamaican*

---

[1] See Lord MacMillan in *Municipal Mutual Insurance Ltd v Hills* (1932) 16 TC 430 at 448.
[2] [1913] 3 KB 75.

*Commissioner of Income Tax*[1], hotel owners paid subscription fees to a members' club as part of an arrangement to allow the hotel guest access to some private bathing areas. The Privy Council declared that no "mutuality" was present. Lord Wilberforce suggested that "mutuality" ought to require a reasonable relationship between what a member contributes and what he is entitled to receive from the fund. In the present case it was clear that such a relationship was not "reasonable". The hotel owners were required to contribute much more and were entitled to much less than the other members in the club. It was an unreasonable and disproportionate "participation".

## Illegal Trading

The issue of whether proceeds from criminal activities (illegal trading profits) are taxable has long been debated and is still uncertain. It is interesting to note that the court does not necessarily view the taxing of proceeds of illegal activities as the State participating in unlawful gains. Rowlatt J explained that the State would merely be taxing a man according to his resources[2]: a reflection of the equity that he who can pay should pay tax—perhaps!

A recent example of a tax assessment of the earnings of an illegal trade involved the assessment of earnings for a six-year period of prostitution. In *IRC v Aken*[3] Lindi St Clair appealed against the assessment alleging that the proceeds were derived from illegal acts and should not therefore be taxable. The Court of Appeal disagreed and upheld the assessments.

## Profits

Although tax under Cases I and II of Schedule D is stated to be charged on the "annual profits or gains"[4] of the trade, profession or vocation, there is no statutory definition of "annual profits or gains". Judicial comment explains that profit is the

> difference between the price received on a sale and the cost of what is sold[5]

[1] [1972] AC 414.
[2] *Mann v Nash* [1932] 1 KB 752.
[3] [1990] STC 497.
[4] TA 1988, section 18.
[5] Sir George Jessel MR, *Erichsen v Last* (1881) 8 QBD 414.

and that

> profits and gains must be ascertained on ordinary principles of commercial trading. [1]

This was confirmed by the Committee on the Taxation of Trading Profits when it reported the need to compute a balance of a profit and loss account[2]. The Committee also suggested that it was settled that profits should be computed in accordance with established commercial accountancy principles[3]—although Lord Denning has more recently confirmed that the courts are not absolutely bound by accountancy principles and practice.[4]

At a very general level it is normal to compute the value of receipts and to deduct allowable expenditure. There is also a need to consider the valuation and transfer of stock-in-trade.

## Receipts

Receipts normally represent the income received as a consequence of the goods and/or services provided. These income receipts represent your fee or sales income. The need to include income receipts only has invited discussion on the distinction between *capital* receipts and *income* receipts. Capital receipts are to be assessed under capital gains tax principles and not income tax principles. The distinction was of paramount importance pre-1965 when capital receipts and gains were able to avoid a tax change. Today, the distinction is still important—despite the assimilation of rates—often because of the rules on allowances and deductions. We have identified and discussed at an earlier stage the various theories presented to explain and support the distinction. It is sufficient for us to repeat that the issue is one of fact and that the court will only overturn the findings of the Commissioners in instances of inconsistency or unreasonableness. There are many many cases where the distinction has been questioned. It is easier to consider a selection of those cases under sub-headings, albeit that the sub-headings have no significance in themselves; they merely provide categories of convenience.

---

[1] Lord Halsbury LC, *Gresham Life Assurance Society v Styles* [1892] AC 309.

[2] Cmd 8189 (1951).

[3] *Ibid*. The Committee suggested this was "settled" following the House of Lords decision in *Usher's Wiltshire Brewery Ltd v Bruce* [1915] AC 433.

[4] *Heather v PE Consulting Group* [1973] Ch 189.

*Compensation Payments*

Many cases could be included under the head of "compensation payments". They frequently involve a trader receiving a sum of money to compensate for breach of contract or for some other loss. If the sum received is in return for the premature termination or for the breach of contract one might reasonably assume that the receipt is of an income nature; after all, businesses sell their goods and services by entering into contracts. Unfortunately the matter is not as simple as first appears.

It is possible that the contract in question was so important to the business that it might be regarded as a capital asset and receipts from that item would be of a capital nature.

For a contract to be so regarded it appears that it must be more than a profit-earning contract: the contract must provide, or substantially contribute to the provision of, the profit earning apparatus of the trade.

In *Van den Berghs Ltd v Clark*[1] an English company entered into an agreement with a Dutch company to regulate competition between them. The agreement detailed prices and areas of supply of the product margarine. It also provided for a sharing of profits and management arrangement. A dispute arose and the contract was eventually terminated on the understanding that the Dutch company would pay £450,000 to the English company as compensation for the termination of the contract.

The House of Lords examined the contractual arrangements and concluded that the contract was a capital asset and thus the £450,000 was a capital receipt. The court explained that the contract was more than a contract for the disposal of products.

> The cancelled agreements related to the whole structure of the Appellants profit making apparatus.

The contract

> formed part of the fixed framework within which the circulating capital operated. It provided the means of making profits.

In *Kelsall Parsons & Co v IRC*[2], manufacturers' agents held a number of contracts for several manufacturers. These agents would arrange, under these contracts, to sell the manufacturers' products in return for a

[1] [1935] 19 TC 390.
[2] [1938] 21 TC 608.

commission fee. One of the agency contracts was terminated by one of the manufacturers and the agents received compensation amounting to £1,500. The court held that the £1,500 was an income receipt from trading. The loss of one agency contract did not affect the profit-making apparatus of the business. Such contracts were not part of the fixed framework of the agent's business, but part of its normal variable elements of trade [1]—agents normally deal in contracts!

An interesting illustration of the dependency on interpretation is to be found in *Burmah Steamship v IRC* [2] where the late delivery of a steamship resulted in the payment of a sum of money as compensation for the breach of contract (the late delivery) and for loss of profits attributed to the loss of trade suffered because of the late delivery of the steamship. The compensation payment was treated as an income receipt but could so easily have been regarded as a reduction in the purchase price of a capital item (a capital loss/receipt)—in reality the sum of money was offset against the purchase price of the steamship!

### Restriction of Activities

A sum of money might be received in return for forgoing or giving up business and trade opportunity or activity. If the activity or opportunity results in a substantial restriction in or removal of the profit-making apparatus (the "tree") then any monies received in return will be capital sums. Conversely, the activity or opportunity surrendered might simply be a trading or profit opportunity (the "fruit") and the monies received will represent income or trading receipts.

In *Higgs v Olivier* [3], Laurence Olivier starred in the film, Henry V, and received a sum of £15,000 in return for agreeing that he would not, for a period of 18 months,

> appear as an actor in or act as producer or director of any film to be made anywhere by any other company.

The Court of Appeal held that the sum of £15,000 was a capital receipt for a substantial restriction on the professional activities of the taxpayer.

---

[1] There is some suggestion that because the contract is question only had one year to run, that it could not be regarded as providing the degree of continuity or permanence required of a capital asset.

[2] [193] 16 TC 67.

[3] [1952] 1 Ch 311.

By contrast in *White v G and M Davies*[1] a farmer received an EC subsidy for agreeing not to sell milk products and to restrict his dairy farming activities. The court held that the subsidy represented trade income. It was a sum received for agreeing to work (trade) in a particular way. One might also suggest that there was no substantial restriction on the farmer's activities. He could still farm the land, albeit not wholly for dairy farming purposes.

In *Thompson v Magnesium Elektron Ltd*[2] the taxpayers used chlorine in the production of magnesium. They were also able to produce caustic soda, a by-product of the use of chlorine. ICI then agreed to supply chlorine to the taxpayer at below market price in return for the taxpayer agreeing not to produce its own chlorine and caustic soda. ICI also paid a sum to the taxpayer to reflect the loss of caustic soda sales that the taxpayer was likely to suffer. ICI wished to protect its own market position in the production and sales of caustic soda. The court held that the monies received by the taxpayer were trading income representing the loss of trade profit on the sale of caustic soda.

### Sale of Information or "Know How"

Statute has been introduced to deal with this type of receipt. Previously case law had suggested that if a trader disposed of a patent or know-how the sum received would be trade income unless the disposal was part of the disposal of a business interest and assets in a distinct area, normally a foreign county.

The latter disposal would be one of capital (in part).[3] TA 1988 ss530-1 now provides that the receipts from the sale of know-how will be treated as trade income unless the sale is consequent on the sale of the business entity when it will then be treated as a capital receipt—although even here the taxpayer can elect to treat the sum received as an income receipt.

## Valuation of Trading Stock

In addition to income receipts, a trader will need to take into account expenses and the purchase of and remainder of trading stock (or work-in-progress) when computing his "annual profits or gains". The importance of trading stock is reflected in the need to carefully consider its value. It is

---

[1] [1979] STC 415.
[2] [1944] 1 All ER 126.
[3] See *Evans Medical Supplies Ltd v Moriarty* [1957] 3 All ER 718.

normal to add to income the value of remaining trading stock, otherwise the receipts could be expended to purchase such stock and the taxpayer would enjoy deductible expenses without taking into account the value of the asset in the trading stock—taxable profits would be artificially reduced! Similarly the same trading stock would be entered as expense in the accounts in the following year in order to avoid the danger of the same assets suffering double taxation. Needless to say at the end of the day it is important to appreciate the principles of valuation—if not the reasons why!

The general principle on the valuation of stock is that stock must be valued at the lower of its cost price and market value. [1] However, this general principle is subject to exceptions.

### Valuation of Trading Stock on Discontinuance

On the discontinuance of a trade, TA 1988 s100 provides that the value of trading stock must be entered in as market value not cost price irrespective of which is the lower. However, the rule in s100 will not apply if the stock is sold to another UK trader and is to appear in his trading accounts.

### The Rule in Sharkey v Wernher [2]

This rule provides that where a trader disposes of trading stock otherwise than in the course of a trade (eg a personal gift), the disposal is deemed to be at market value and should be entered as such in his accounts. *Sharkey v Wernher* involved Lady Wernher transferring five horses from her business of a stud farm for her own personal enjoyment of horse racing. In accordance with accounting practice, the transfer was entered into her accounts at cost price, thereby cancelling the initial entry of cost price of the stock-in-trade.

The insertion of cost price would mean that the business would be in a no-gain, no-loss situation. The initial expense of "cost" would be offset by the credit of a transfer at "cost". The Revenue successfully claimed that "cost price" was not the correct figure for such a transfer; "market value" was "better economics" and would present a "fairer measure of assessable profit". [3] On that basis it was declared that a transfer, other than in the course of trade, would be deemed to be a transfer at market value.

---

[1]  *IRC v Cock Russell & Co Ltd* [1949] 2 All ER 889.
[2]  [1955] 3 All ER 493.
[3]  Lord Radcliffe, *ibid* at 506.

The decision and the rule in *Sharkey v Wernher* have not been accepted without criticism. It has been suggested that the reasoning in the case conflicts with established principles of mutuality, with the existence of TA 1988, s770, and with the principle that one should be taxed on what one receives not on what one could or might have received.[1] Further criticism and concern can be directed at the rule in *Sharkey v Wernher* when one tries to ascertain the limits or parameters of the rule.

The first limit or parameter to note is that the rule is limited to Schedule D and perhaps even to Case I in Schedule D. Thus it would be possible to confer benefits on oneself in relation to activities within other Schedules (perhaps rent free accommodation in Schedule A) without fear of *Sharkey v Wernher* attributing market value to that transfer. The suggestion that the rule in *Sharkey v Wernher* might be confined to Case I of Schedule D is a consequence of the decision in *Mason v Innes*.[2]

Hammond Innes had written a book called "The Doomed Oasis" and had incurred and deducted travelling expenses in obtaining background material used in the writing and the production of the book. Hammond Innes then assigned the copyright to his father by way of a gift. The market value of the copyright was around £15,000.

The Revenue sought to rely on the rule in *Sharkey v Wernher* and tax the market value of the copyright as a receipt of Hammond Innes' profession. The Court of Appeal disagreed. They held that the rule in *Sharkey v Wernher* did not apply emphasising that the nature of a profession and the nature of a trade were very different—essentially one did have stock-in-trade or work-in-progress and one did not. Lady Zia Wernher did deal in the sale of horses whereas Hammond Innes did not deal in the sale of copyrights.

The Court also emphasised that in *Sharkey v Wernher* the accounts were presented on an earnings basis whereas in *Mason v Innes* the accounts were presented on a cash basis. At the end of the day Hammond Innes was able to enjoy the benefits of the deductible expenses in relation to the production of "The Doomed Oasis" and to confer the benefits of future sales to his father.

---

[1] See Butterworths UK Tax Guide 1992–93 at 328. Note that the final criticism might be misplaced in that the principle of not interfering with trading and transaction presumes a genuine trading intention whereas the rule in *Sharkey v Wernher* concerns non-commercial and non-trading intentions.

For further comment on the decision see Potter [1964] BTR 438.

[2] [1967] 2 All ER 926.

We said at the beginning that *Mason v Innes* might signal that the rule in *Sharkey v Wernher* is not applicable to Case II of Schedule D. Much depends upon how one interprets the reasoning in *Mason v Innes*. It could be possible to say that the discussion of the different nature of a "profession" and a "trade" is sufficient to indicate that *Mason v Innes* was suggesting that *Sharkey v Wernher* has no role to play because of the different nature of a profession—yet it could equally play a role there because, despite the absence of a recognised stock-in-trade, many professionals provide services that could confer personal benefits and those benefits could be valued at standard market rates.[1] Such a task might not be as difficult as we are lead or encouraged to believe.

An alternative perception of the reasoning and the decision in *Mason v Innes* focuses upon the manner and method of presentation of accounts. One could view *Sharkey v Wernher* as simply establishing that the correct manner of presentation of transfers "other than for trading purposes" when accounts are presented on an earnings basis is to enter market value—thus the accounting practice at that date was tested and declared wrong.

On that interpretation *Sharkey v Wernher* was not saying anything with regard to the correct accountancy and presentation rules and practice for accounts presented on a cash basis as in *Mason v Innes*. The court in *Mason v Innes* was correct therefore in refusing to regard itself bound by the decision in *Sharkey v Wernher*. The concern with such an analysis is whether we are paying true respect to the overriding determination and taxation of "annual profits or gains". In relation to that overriding task the manner of the presentation of accounts ought to be irrelevant in sofar as they accurately reflect the "annual profits or gains".

A further limitation of the rule in *Sharkey v Wernher* is that it will not apply to a genuine commercial transaction, even if that genuine commercial or trading transaction represents a "bad bargain" in terms of a sale at below market value. For example in *Jacgilden (Weston Hall) Ltd v Castle*[2] a bona fide trading transaction involved the sale of an "option" on a property for £72,000 when its market value was approximately £150,000. Although this sale might be regarded as a bad decision, market value would not be substituted because of the genuineness and bona fide nature of the sale.

---

[1] For example the accountant might agree to provide bookkeeping services to his family or friends for no fee or a nominal fee—albeit he may face difficulties in respect of professional rules and etiquette.

[2] [1969] 3 All ER 1110.

*Transfer Pricing (TA 1988, s770)*

This provides that where a sale or other transaction (including the grants and transfers of rights, interests or licences) takes place between associated bodies, and that sale is at an undervalue or overvalue and consequently confers tax benefits, the Revenue can substitute market value for the transfer price.

Bodies are "associated" if one controls the other or both are controlled by the same third party. The aim of s770 is to control transfers between associated companies when one is resident outside the UK. Such a situation may invite favourable transfers. For example, in the absence of s770, a UK resident company could transfer (sale) at undervalue (perhaps creating a deductible loss) to its associated non-UK resident company who would, in UK terms, enjoy an enhanced tax free gain. TA 1988 s770 should prevent such a deliberately planned occurrence.

## Deductable Expenses

So far, in our quest to compute "annual profits or gains" we have considered receipts and trading stock. The next item for consideration is that of deductible expenses. Deductible expenses are allowed by implication. The term "profits or gains" infers the need to deduct the cost of earning that "profit or gain". Similarly, TA 1988, s74 lists a number of prohibited deductions, thereby suggesting that other deductions are permissible.

In determining our deductible expenses there are three main considerations that we must address:

(i)   the expense must be of an income and not a capital nature;
(ii)  the expense must be incurred wholly and exclusively for the purpose of the trade, profession and vocation; and
(iii) the particular expense must not be prohibited by statute.

*Income or Capital Expense?*

This requirement invites the same distinction and discussion that took place when considering the need to take into account only income receipts and not capital receipts. The same difficulties exist when trying to categorise the nature of the expenditure and perhaps Lord Greene's suggestion[1] that the "spin of a coin" could satisfactorily substitute the search for reasoning is equally applicable here. In examining judicial comment in this area one can trace a history of appearance of a variety of tests—or perhaps merely a range of approaches to the one test of whether the expenditure is of a capital or revenue nature. Early cases refer to the distinction between fixed and circulating assets and allow, as a revenue cost, the costs of circulating assets.[2]

Guidance here would come from accountancy principles and practice in terms of identifying and representing assets as current or circulating assets. Circulating assets are those assets that would circulate or flow through the business with a degree of frequency with the intention of contributing to and earning profit, eg trading stock. Permanent or semi-permanent investment items, such as plant and machinery, would normally be treated as capital assets and expenditure on them would not generally (excluding any Capital Allowance Schemes) be deductible.

A second test or approach can be ascertained from the statement of Lord Cave in *British Insulated and Helsby Cables Ltd v Atherton* that if expenditure is made to

> bring into existence an asset or an advantage for the enduring benefit of a trade

that expenditure ought to be regarded as capital expenditure and therefore it is not deductible within the general principles of deductibility. This "enduring benefit" test enables the court to consider the nature and effects of the expenditure and of the asset, outside the traditional accountancy practice of categorisation and balance sheet representation of fixed and current assets. It also enables the court to deal with the realistic effects of the expenditure.[3] For example, in *Mitchell v B W Noble Ltd*[4] a company was able to deduct a sum of money paid to a director to induce him to resign. It was for the enduring benefit of the company to get rid of the director in circumstances that would avoid undesirable publicity and damage to their goodwill.

A third test or approach, demands an examination of the nature of the

---

[1] Per Greene MR [1938] 2 KB 482 at 498 cited earlier, in Income Tax, Capital v Income Ch 3.

[2] See *Ammonia Soda Co v Chamberlain* [1918] 1 Ch 266; *Golden Horseshoe (New) Ltd v Thorgood* [1934] 1 KB 548.

[3] The enduring benefit test is not without its critics because of the ability to find an "enduring benefit" from non-capital items.

[4] 1 KB 719.

asset and an examination of the nature of the expenditure on that asset. The existence of this approach was confirmed by the House of Lords in *Tucker v Granada Motorway Services Ltd*[1] where the nature of expenditure on a particular asset was classed as capital expenditure and was not deductible. The asset in question was a lease. Expenditure on that asset might have been of a capital nature, i.e. acquisition of this capital asset, or merely expenditure of a revenue nature concerning, for example, not the acquisition but the safe keeping, security and review of the lease. In this particular instance, the House of Lords concluded that payment for release and variation of terms of the lease was expenditure of a capital nature. Similarly, in *Pitt v Castle Hill Warehousing Co Ltd*[2] expenditure on an asset, a road, was held to be capital expenditure. The expenditure on the road was expenditure on its construction whereas if the expenditure on the same asset had been for its maintenance and upkeep such expenditure might conceivably have been classed as revenue expenditure and deductible. The whole basis of this third approach or test is that, unlike the fixed *versus* circulating capital test, the item of expenditure is not categorised and fixed exclusively by the nature and category of the asset.

For example, we have seen that in *Pitt v Castle Hill Warehousing Co Ltd* expenditure on the same asset might be revenue or capital nature depending on the nature of the expenditure in relation to the asset. The same fixed asset might invite both capital and revenue expenditure. One might suggest that this third test has elements of a merging of tests one and two. We need to identify the asset and its nature (fixed or circulating) and then we consider the nature of the expenditure on that asset, presumably considering whether it brings into the business an enduring benefit or advantage. Thus in the *Pitt* case, the expenditure on the construction of the road to facilitate access to an industrial site without disturbing residents brought in an enduring asset and a benefit and advantage in terms of public relations and goodwill!

Once again we are tempted to conclude with Lord Greene's suggestion that the matter might be determined by a "spin of a coin". Equally we could suggest that the matter is one of common sense. Both the Court of Appeal and the House of Lords have suggested that the distinction is one of common sense and reality. Unfortunately in applying that common sense and reality the Court of Appeal and the House of Lords reached

[1] [1979] 2 All ER 801.
[2] [1974] 3 All ER 146.

different conclusions as to the status of the expenditure in *Lawson v Johnson Matthey plc.*[1] The expenditure in this case consisted of a £50 million injection by a parent company (Johnson Matthey plc) into one of its wholly-owned subsidiaries, Johnson Matthey Bankers Limited (JMB). This cash injection was part of a scheme to facilitate the disposal of the wholly-owned subsidiary to the Bank of England. The Bank of England was not willing to buy the (worthless) shares of JMB unless, immediately prior to the purchase and transfer of the shares and the company, Johnson Matthey plc would inject the £50 million. This Johnson Matthey plc was willing to do in order to facilitate the disposal and avoid the insolvent liquidation of JMB. If Johnson Matthey plc had held onto JMB, JMB would have faced insolvency with severe ramifications for the goodwill and trading implications for the rest of the companies in the Johnson Matthey group. There was even a suggestion that it might lead to a closure of Johnson Matthey plc itself.

The General Commissioners took the view that the £50 million payment by Johnson Matthey plc was of a revenue and not capital nature because its purpose was

to preserve the trade of Johnson Matthey plc from collapse.[2]

The Commissioners further noted that the link between the £50 million expenditure and the subsequent transfer of shares to the Bank of England did not operate to convert the £50 million into expenditure of a capital nature. On appeal, the High Court expressed disagreement with the General Commissioners, and declared that the nature of the expenditure must be determined objectively and that its determination must recognise the nature of what it could achieve.[3]

Such an analysis would facilitate the recognition of the achieved disposal of the shares and business of the subsidiary, JMB. That recognition would objectively indicate the expenditure to be of a capital nature; being part of the disposal of a capital asset. On appeal to the Court of Appeal, the Court reviewed the long history of judicial comment in this area, noting that the "enduring benefit" test of Viscount Cave has been undermined by later judicial comment and opinion. The Court noted the absence of any definitive test for the determination of the

---

[1] [1991] STC 259 (CA); [1992] STC 466 (HL).
[2] [1990] STC 149.
[3] [1990] STC 160.

revenue versus capital issue. Consequently the Court of Appeal decided to follow the "common sense" approach [1], and concluded that:

> ... (i) JMB was a capital asset to the taxpayer company; (ii) the taxpayer company disposed of JMB to the Bank; (iii) the only terms on which the Bank was willing to acquire JMB was on payment of the £50m by the taxpayer company to JMB.
>
> The position was, in reality, the same as if the Bank had said: "We will take over JMB if you pay us £50m". Whichever way it was done, the payment seems to me to be a payment by the taxpayer company to enable it to get rid of a capital asset. ... In my view the common sense of the matter is that the £50m was capital expenditure. ... [2]

The House of Lords acknowledged the absence of any definitive test in this area and sought also to apply an approach of common sense and reality. [3] In applying a common sense and reality approach the House of Lords disagreed with the "realism" of the Court of Appeal and concluded that

> the payment of £50m did not bring an asset into existence and did not procure an advantage for the enduring benefit of the trade. It was paid solely to enable the taxpayer company to be able to continue in business

and therefore, it was revenue expenditure and deductible. Lord Goff referred to the Court of Appeal's analysis as

> ... attractive. But on reflection I have come to the conclusion that it is too narrowly based, and ignores the reality of the situation. [4]

The "reality" that Lord Goff acknowledged was that the £50m was not paid for the divestiture of shares, but as a contribution to part of a scheme to remain and continue in business—it was a revenue payment.

---

[1] [1991] STC 259 at 264. The Common Sense approach was advocated by Lord Reid in *Strick (Inspector of Taxes) v Regent Oil Co Ltd* [1966] AC 295 at 313.

[2] *Ibid*, at 265.

[3] [1992] 2 All ER 647. See Lord Templeman's support (at p651) of Lord Macmillans dictum in *Van der Berghs Ltd v Clark (Inspector of Taxes)* [1935] AC 431 that "... no infallible criterion emerges ...".

[4] *Ibid* at 657.

*The Expenditure Must Have Been Incurred "wholly and exclusively" for Business Purposes (TA 1888 s74 (a))*

The term "wholly" refers to the amount or extent of expenditure, whereas the term "exclusively" refers to the object or purpose of the expenditure. A strict application of this requirement means that the sole reason or purpose of the expenditure must be that of a business purpose. If, at the time of incurring the expenditure, the taxpayer had, wholly or partly, some other purpose such as a personal, private benefit, then the whole expenditure will be incurred for a dual purpose and will be disallowed. This strict rule must be qualified in instances of unintended but incidental benefit, and in instances of apportionment. In instances of unintended but incidental benefit, the rule was explained by Romer LJ in *Bentleys, Stokes & Lowless v Beeson* as demanding that the sole purpose must be a business purpose and not some other purpose; but that

> . . . if, in truth, the sole object is business promotion, the expenditure is not disqualified because the nature of the activity necessarily involves some other result, or the attainment or furtherance of some other objective, since the latter result or objective is necessarily inherent in the act. [1]

Thus it appears that an inherent or unintended incidental personal or other benefit will not detract from the sole business purpose and the deductibility of the expenditure. This has more recently been confirmed by Lord Brightman in *Mallalieu v Drummond* [2]. Lord Brightman explained that expenditure made exclusively to serve the purpose of the business, may confer a private advantage but that that private advantage will "not necessarily preclude the exclusivity of the business purpose". Emphasis must be placed on the purpose of the expenditure at time of its incurrence—that purpose must be a business purpose albeit it may also confer some unintended private benefits!

This apparently pragmatic and one might suggest sensible approach or rule was not entirely apparent in the House of Lord's decision in *Mallalieu v Drummond* [3]. The case involved a lady barrister who sought to deduct the cost of clothes bought for wear in court. The clothes were of a type demanded by court etiquette and it was clear that when the clothes were

---

[1] [1952] 2 All ER 82 at 85.
[2] [1983] STC 665.
[3] *Ibid*

purchased the motive or object was exclusively the need to comply with court etiquette. The House of Lords dismissed the claim to deduct the cost of the clothes on the grounds that they were purchased for a dual purpose. Lord Brightman admitted that Miss Mallalieu's only conscious motive when buying the clothes may have been her professional and business requirements but stated:

> . . . I reject the notion that the object of a taxpayer is inevitably limited to the particular conscious motive in mind at the moment of expenditure. Of course the motive of which the taxpayer is conscious is of vital significance, but it is not inevitably the only object which the commissioners are entitled to find to exist. . . .

The "other object" that the commissioners were found to be entitled to assume was in existence at the time of purchase was the personal object of the clothing needs of a human being, including the needs of warmth and decency and the need of clothes to wear during the journey to work!

This rather harsh application of the "dual purpose" rule added the possibility of the courts deciding on your subconscious motives at the time of purchase. It may be explained partly by the "policy" considerations intimated by Lord Brightman of the benefits of Schedule D allowing the self-employed to maintain a wardrobe of clothes at the expense of the general taxpayer—a clearly inequitable benefit. Further, the decision is not all doom and gloom for those who must incur expenditure on business clothing. Lord Brightman went on to explain that the question is always one of fact and degree.

He cited the example of a self-employed waiter who would need to wear "tails" as an essential part of the equipment of his trade. In such an instance Lord Brightman suggested that

> it would be open to the commissioners to allow the expense of their upkeep on the basis that the money was spent exclusively to serve the purpose of the business.

The problem caused by the issue being one of fact and degree is the uncertainty and unpredictability of the rule and its application. On that basis most students would be advised to note the rule and its distinction from the unintended but inevitable private benefit and seek to consider the application of both principles to the same set of facts on the grounds of the uncertainty of the extent of "degree" required by Lord Brightman.

## Apportionment

We mentioned earlier that the "wholly and exclusively" rule must be qualified in instances of apportionment. If the expenditure incurred can be divided to represent (i) expenditure that was wholly and exclusively incurred for business purposes, and (ii) expenditure that was incurred for, wholly or partly, a non-business purpose, the Revenue may accept apportionment of that expenditure. For example, the use of a room in one's home for business purposes may permit the apportionment of heating, lighting and other expenses of maintaining the house. Similarly, in *Copeman v Flood*[1] the court allowed the apportionment of the costs of a salary when it was clear that only part of it represented a genuine salary expense.

Strictly speaking "apportionment" demands a clear, identifiable demarcation between expenditure incurred "wholly and exclusively" for business purposes, and expenditure incurred for other reasons or purposes. In practice, such a precise demarcation and apportionment is difficult to establish and, contrary to the strict approach of the House of Lords in *Mallalieu*, the Revenue is generous in its practice of negotiating and agreeing apportionment.

## Expenditure Prohibited or Qualified by Statute

We mentioned earlier that one of the reasons why expenditure could be deducted was by implication from the wording of TA 1988, s74. Section 74 contains a list of expenses which are stated not to be deductible— hence other expenses ought to be deductible. For example, section 74 includes the following items.

## Domestic Expenditure

Section 74(b) provides that no sum may be deducted in respect of

> any disbursements or expenses of maintenance of the parties, their families or establishments, or any sums expended for the trade, profession or vocation.

Thus, for example, when a taxpayer severed a tendon in one of his fingers

---

[1] [1941] 1 KB 202.

he sought to deduct the costs of an operation on the basis of his profession as a guitarist. The court refused to allow the expense on the grounds that it was expenditure to support, in part, his hobby of playing the guitar. On that basis it was a sum expended for some "other domestic or private purpose distinct from the purposes of the profession". It is important to appreciate that the taxpayer played the guitar both as a hobby and as a profession. [1]

## Rent

Section 74(c) prohibits the deduction of rent for "any dwelling house or domestic offices or any part thereof". Except that s74(c) does allow the apportionment and deduction of that part that is used for business purposes—such as a room in an individual's private house.

## Repairs and Improvements

Section 74(g) prohibits the deduction of sums spent on improvements (capital expenditure) whereas, by implication, s74(d) permits the deduction of sums spent on repairs and alterations (income expenditure) of assets for business purposes. The distinction between repair and improvement (or renewal) is often a fine distinction and not easy to recognise. [2] A variety of approaches have been suggested and, at times, applied by the courts. One of the more attractive approaches is to consider whether the final result produces an increase in value of the asset. For example, expenditure on the same asset, a railway line, may result in an improvement (via an increase in its value) or merely a repair. In *Rhodesia Railways Ltd v Bechwanaland Protectorate IT Collector* [3] expenditure on the replacement of rails was deductible as a repair constituting the restoring of worn track to its normal condition. Whereas in *Highland Railway Co v IRC* [4] the replacement of old track and rail was not deductible because it represented an improvement: the new rail was of a superior kind and represented an increase in the value of the railway line.

Another, perhaps less satisfactory approach, stems from the much quoted statement of Buckley LJ in *Lurcott v Wakely and Wheeler* [5], that:

[1] *Prince v Mapp* [1970] 1 All ER 519.

[2] Perhaps this "difficulty" accounts for the Revenue practice of allowing the cost of replacing machinery and plant as a revenue expense.

[3] [1933] AC 368.

[4] [1889] 2 TC 585.

[5] [1911] 1 KB 905.

. . . repair is restoration by renewal or replacement of subsidiary parts of a whole. Renewal, as distinguished from repair, is reconstruction of the entirety, meaning by the entirety not necessarily the whole but substantially the whole subject matter under discussion.

The criticism of this approach is the need to be able to ascertain and identify a "part" and the "entirety'. In some instances, this might prove to be difficult or at least uncertain. In *O'Grady v Bullcroft Main Collieries Ltd*[1] a chimney was replaced with a new one and the court did not allow the company to deduct the costs of building the new chimney on the grounds that it was not "part" of the factory but an "entirety". By contrast, in *Samuel Jones & Co (Devondale) Ltd v IRC*[2] the costs of replacing a chimney at a factory were allowed on the ground that the factory was an "entirety" and the chimney was only "part" of the entirety. Perhaps, the consideration of whether there was an increase in value, and thus an improvement through the replacement and rebuild would have been a better approach. It is clear that at the end of the day the distinction between works of repair and works of improvement is a question of fact.

One interesting application of this distinction can be found in the apparently anti-avoidance approach to "reduced costs" of purchase. Generally, if the acquisition costs of an asset are reduced to reflect the works that are needed to put the asset into a usable state, actual and subsequent costs of those works are not deductible. The works and costs represent capital expenditure—they are part of the costs of acquiring a "usable" asset. In *Law Shipping Co Ltd v IRC*[3], the shipping company bought a ship (at a reduced price) and subsequently were required to spend monies on repairs to enable the ship to pass a Lloyd's survey and to be in a recognised "usable" condition. The court rejected claims that these costs should be deductible as repair costs. The court explained that

. . . when the purchasers started trade with the ship, the capital they required was not limited to the price paid to acquire her, but included the cost of the arrears of repairs which their predecessors had allowed to accumulate. . . .

By contrast, in *Odeon Associated Theatres Ltd v Jones*[4] a sum of money spent

---

[1] [1932] 17 TC 93.
[2] [1951] 32 TC 513.
[3] [1924] 12 TC 621.
[4] [1972] 2 WLR 331.

on completing repairs to a cinema that had recently been purchased was allowed as a deductible expense. The cinema was purchased in a state of disrepair because repairs had been impossible to complete owing to war-time restrictions.

> Nevertheless, the cinema at the date of its acquisition was a fully effective profit-earning asset, and the price which Odeon paid for it had not been diminished to obtain licences to carry them out (per Salmon LJ).

This analysis, together with its consistency with accounting practice, enabled the courts to view the expenditure as merely repair costs of a capital asset rather than as part of the acquisition costs of a capital asset.

## Damages and Losses

Section 74(e) prohibits the deduction of

> any loss connected with or arising out of the trade, profession or vocation. [1]

Perhaps the easiest way of conceptualising the loss referred to by section 74(e) is to picture that the loss must be occasioned or suffered as a consequence of pursuing profit through the exercise of the trade, profession or vocation: the loss must come to you in your professional or trade capacity and not in any other capacity. For example, in *Strong & Co of Romsey Ltd v Woodifield* [2], the taxpayers carried on the business of brewers and innkeepers. Part of their hotel (a chimney) collapsed and injured a guest. The taxpayer's paid compensation to the injured guest and then sought to deduct that payment as a "loss" arising out of the trade. The House of Lords held that the "loss" was not deductible—it did not arise out of the trade of the taxpayer (the provision of accommodation, food and drink) but arose out of their position as property owners (a separate and distinct capacity). [3]

[1] The "loss" referred to here is not that of an overall trading loss computed in accordance with accountancy practice, taking account of the trader's performance, expenses and receipts over the relevant period or year.

[2] [1906] AC 448.

[3] The speech delivered by Lord Davey was distinct in that it did not focus on the issue of "loss" (section 74(e)). Lord Davey appeared to support his conclusion by a consideration of the general requirement that the expense (loss, in this instance) must be "wholly and exclusively incurred for the

In practice a wide range of losses have been allowed, even through it is not always possible to agree on or perceive the link between the loss and the carrying on of or capacity of the trade, profession or vocation.[1] The solution might lie in recognising the significance of the degree of the expenditure and the degree of the link to the pursuit of the trade, profession or vocation. For example, in *Curtis v J & G Oldfield*[2], petty thefts by employees were treated as deductible losses, whereas a £15,000 misappropriation by a company director in *Bamford v ATA Advertising Ltd*[3] was disallowed. The former was an incident of the company's trading activities, the latter was not.

## Bad Debts

Section 74(j) prohibits deductions in respect of

> any debts, except bad debts proved to be such, and doubtful debts to the extent that they are respectively estimated to be bad.

It is clear under section 74(j) that a general accounts provision or general reserve against future bad debts is not deductible. Similarly if a bad debt that has been claimed and deducted under section 74(j) is subsequently repaid (wholly or in part), the sums received will be treated as trading receipts in the year of receipt.

purpose of the business". In a rather famous dictum, Lord Davey said:

> It is not enough that the disbursement is made in the course or arises out of or is connected with the trade or is made out of the profits of the trade. It must be made for the purpose of earning profits.

Some authors have suggested that this apparent gloss on the general requirement of "wholly and exclusively" has introduced a further requirement or hurdle in the pursuit to enjoy deductible expenses. It is debatable as to whether a "further requirement" has been introduced. In *Strong & Co of Romsey v Woodifield*, Lord Davey's reasoning was clearly in the minority (in terms of its source, if not its substance). The majority of the Lords reached the same conclusion through an analysis of the capacity in which the loss was occasioned (section 74(e)). Similarly there is little substance in later cases to support the "additional" or "further requirement" rather than an application of the section 74(e) requirements. At the end of the day, it is probably of little significance in practice which approach is adopted. The application of the general requirement in section 74(a) or the specific requirements in section 74(e) can be consistently applied to achieve the desired distinction and result.

[1] Examples include:

—damages for libel published in the course of publishing a newspaper,

—damages for the wrongful dismissal of an employee,

—legal expenses,

—advertising expenses,

—sponsorship expenses.

[2] [1925] 94 LJKB 655.

[3] [1972] 3 All ER 535.

## Illustrations of Deductible Expenditure

Apart from the specific expenditure items dealt with in section 74, and the general requirements of distinguishing revenue from capital expenditure, certain specific types of expenditure are often included in assessment and examination questions. Below is a list and discussion of the more frequently examined items and types of expenditure in this area.

### Medical Expenses

Medical expenses could normally be dismissed under section 74(b) as "sums expended for domestic or private purposes". This is so even though part of the purpose of the expenditure was a trade purpose. In *Murgatroyd v Evans-Jackson*[1] the taxpayer was treated in a private nursing home and sought to deduct 60 per cent of the cost of the treatment. His choice of a private nursing home was to enjoy the use of a private room from which he could continue to conduct his business. His claim failed. The expenditure had a dual purpose—or at least, it was expenditure for domestic or private purposes (his health).

### Gifts and Entertainment Expenses

By contrast to the decision in *Bentley, Stokes and Lowless v Beeson*[2], statute now produces a general rule that business entertainment expenses and gifts are no longer deductible (TA 1988, s577). However, there are exceptions to this general prohibition:

(a) expenses incurred in the entertainment of bona fide members of staff are deductible, provided that the provision is not incidental to the provision of entertainment for others;
(b) in relation to gifts, a *de minimis* principle of £10 per donee per year of assessment applies;
(c) expenses incurred in the provision of small gifts carrying conspicuous advertisements are allowed (eg calendars, diaries, pens, etc);
(d) expenses incurred in the entertainment of overseas customers are no longer deductible except where those expenses were incurred under a contract made before 15 March 1988;
(e) expenses incurred in providing "anything which it is his trade to

---

[1] [1967] 1 All ER 881.
[2] [1952] 2 All ER 82.

provide" either gratuitously with the object of advertising or for payment, are deductible. This exception would include the provision and gift of theatre tickets by a theatre owner, or books by a publisher. It is normal for theatre owners to provide complimentary tickets or for publishers to provide complimentary copies of new books—particularly for review purposes.

### Travel

It appears that the cost of travelling from your home to your place of business is not deductible, essentially because it is not expense incurred in the course of the trade, profession or vocation because the trade, profession or vocation does not commence until your reach your place of business. Similarly, the cost of travelling from your place of business to your home is not deductible on the ground that it is expenditure of a dual purpose or dual nature. You are not travelling "wholly and exclusively" in the course of your trade, profession or vocation, but partly (if not exclusively) for the private purpose of travelling to one's home. These propositions are supported by the decisions in *Sargent v Barnes*[1] and *Newsom v Robertson*[2]. In *Sargent v Barnes*, a dentist sought to deduct the cost of travelling from his home to a dental laboratory and then on to his surgery. On the return journey he would once again travel from his surgery on to the dental laboratory and then on to his place of residence. The court concluded that the expenditure was not incurred "wholly and exclusively" for business purposes. Oliver J explained that the taxpayer incurred the expenditure:

> . . . if not exclusively then at least in part, for the purpose of enabling the taxpayer to get from his private residence to the surgery where his profession was carried out.

Commenting upon the intermediate destination of and stop at the dental laboratory, Oliver J added that the fact that the travel and the journey enabled the dentist to call at the dental laboratory to

> carry out an activity exclusively referable to the business did not convert the dual purpose of the travel into a single purpose.

[1] [1978] 2 All ER 737.
[2] [1953] Ch.7.

The taxpayer was still (partly) travelling for his own private purpose.

In *Newsom v Robertson*, a barrister worked partly at home (in the country) and partly in his chambers in London. He sought to deduct the costs of travel between his home and his chambers. Once again his claim was disallowed, essentially because the costs of travel were not wholly and exclusively incurred for business purposes. His home was not his base or exclusive base of operations; he also resided there for his own personal and private benefits and purpose. Travel to and from his own home must have been partly for his private benefit and purpose.

By contrast in *Horton v Young*[1], the taxpayer, a self-employed bricklayer, was allowed to deduct the cost of travelling between his home and various building sites where he worked for short durations. In this case the taxpayer's home, where he kept his tools and did his office work, was held to be his base of operations. When travelling between this base of operations to the various building sites he was travelling wholly and exclusively for business purposes and in the course of his business. His business activities, his trade, commenced at his base of operations and was continued at the various building sites.[2]

On the basis of *Horton v Young* it has been suggested that the expenses of travelling between the barrister's chambers and the court in *Newsom v Robertson* would be allowed. The taxpayer (barrister) would then be travelling wholly and exclusively for the purpose of and in the course of his business—he would be travelling between "bases of operations". However, should he travel between the court and his chambers (or vice versa) on his intended and deliberate journey home, he might find the expenses disallowed on the application of the dual purpose found in *Sargent v Barnes*. Alternatively, the expenditure may be disallowed on the Brightman J's classification of the taxpayer's home probably falling outside the "normal area of his work".[3]

The decision in *Horton v Young* also raises the possibility of categorising one's home as a "base of operations" and enabling travel from that base to other bases of work as deductible. It has been suggested that despite the

---

[1] [1972] Ch 157.

[2] It is interesting to note that Brightman J did suggest a possible restriction in terms of ascertaining his "normal area of work". Should the taxpayer's home be situated outside that "normal area" then travel to and from that home would not be in the course of business and, consequently, would be disallowed.

[3] *Ibid*. On the facts of *Newsom v Robertson*, the "normal area of his work" might conceivably have been deemed to have been London (the location of his chambers) and the travel to home in the country would clearly have been outside that "normal area" and thus disallowed.

fact that the taxpayer in *Newsom v Robertson* did complete some of his work at home and maintained a study for that purpose, he did not do enough to convert his home into his "base of operations". With respect, one doubts whether the taxpayer in *Newsom v Robertson* would ever have succeeded in assuming his home or his study at home to be his base of operations—unless he "lived over his shop"[1]. If one examines the speeches in *Horton v Young* it is clear that it is the nature of the office, trade or profession, rather than the nature of the taxpayer's premises that determines the issue. Further, the nature of the taxpayers trade must not facilitate a permanent external (to one's home) base of operations:

> ... where a person has no fixed place or places at which he carries on his trade or profession but moves continually from one place to another, at each of which he consecutively exercises his trade or profession on a purely temporary basis and then departs, his trade or profession being in that sense of an itinerant nature, the travelling expenses of the person between his home and the places where from time to time he happens to be exercising his trade ...[2]

will be allowed.

## Conference Attendance and Expenses

The attendance at a conference will normally involve travel, accommodation, subsistence and possibly conference fee expenses. Of the general requirements, the requirement that the expenditure be incurred "wholly and exclusively" for business purposes appears to be prominent here. In *Bowden v Russell and Russell*[3], a solicitor attended conferences in Washington and Ottawa. His wife accompanied him on these visits. Although he did put forward genuine business reasons to support his choice of conference, he also admitted an intention to enjoy, together with his wife, the social and holiday opportunities presented by the visits to Washington and Ottawa. The conference and travel expenses were disallowed on the grounds of the taxpayer's dual purpose—the expenses were not wholly and exclusively incurred for business purposes.

By contrast in *Edwards v Warmsley, Henshall & Co*[4], a partner in a firm

[1] Salmon LJ, did suggest the inseparable location of home and "shop" (or business) ought to ensure that travel expenses were wholly and exclusively incurred for business purposes. Ibid

[2] Brightman J, [1971] 2 All ER 351 at 356.

[3] [1965] 2 All ER 258.

[4] [1968] 1 All ER 1089.

of accountants represented the practice at an international conference in New York. The exclusive purpose in incurring the expenses of attending this conference was business and, as a consequence, the expenses were deductible.

It is important to appreciate at this point the illustration of the medical consultant, provided by Lord Brightman in *Mallalieu v Drummond*[1]. Lord Brightman was carefully seeking to illustrate and confirm the distinction between *object* and *effect*.

An expenditure may be made exclusively to serve the purposes of the business, but it may have a private advantage. The existence of that private advantage does not necessarily preclude the exclusivity of the business purpose. For example, a medical consultant has a friend in the South of France who is also his patient. He flies to the South of France for a week, staying in the home of his friend and attending professionally upon him. He seeks to recover the costs of his air fare. The question of fact will be whether the journey was undertaken solely to serve the purposes of the medical practice. This will be judged in the light of the taxpayer's object in making the journey. The question will be answered by considering whether the stay in the South of France was a reason, however subordinate, for undertaking the journey, or was not a reason but only the effect. If a week's stay on the Riviera was not an object of the consultant, if the consultant's only object was to attend upon his patient, his stay on the Riviera was an unavoidable effect of the expenditure on the journey and the expenditure lies outside the prohibition in section 130.[2]

Thus, it appears that the taxpayer in *Edwards v Warmsley, Henshall & Co*, having incurred the expense with the proper business purpose, might seek on his arrival in New York to indulge in the personal benefits and opportunities of visiting New York. The latter might be regarded as an incidental effect of the exclusive business purpose!

Finally, the decision and the distinctions adopted in *Watkis v Ashford Sparkes & Harwood*[3] provide an interesting treatment of the costs of food, drink and accommodation. The relevant facts of this case involved a firm of solicitors who wished to deduct (i) the costs of lunchtime and evening meals incurred by the solicitors during business meetings held at

[1] [1983] STC 665.
[2] *Ibid.*
[3] [1985] STC 451.

lunchtime and in the evening – during those meeting, and throughout the meals, the solicitors would discuss the firm's business; and (ii) the cost of overnight accommodation, drinks and meals – these expenses were incurred as part of the attendance of the solicitors at the firm's annual conference. It was held that expenses in category (i) were not deductible, but all the expenses incurred in category (ii) were deductible. Norse J explained that the expenses of the meals in category (i) were expenses of a dual purpose; they served their private needs and purposes

> Just as Miss Mallalieu needed to wear clothes not only when she was in court but also when she was not, so did the taxpayers need food and drink irrespective of whether they were engaged on a business activity or not. [1]

Norse J further explained that the cost of food, drink and accommodation at the annual conference stood on a different footing. It could not necessarily be said to have been expenditure which

> met the needs of the partners as human beings . . . they did not need it . . . they had their own homes where they could have spent the night.

Thus the whole expenditure at the conference (food, drink and accommodation) was deductible as expenditure incurred wholly and exclusively for business purposes. [2]

### Partnerships

Partnerships are not legal persons. The profits and expenses belong to the individual partners. The logical consequence of the partnerships lack of legal personality is that one must look to the individual partners rather than the firm's intentions when considering the purpose of the expenditure incurred by the firm. For example, in *MacKinlay v Arthur Young McClelland Moores & Co* [3] a partnership (the "firm") sought to deduct expenditure incurred by the firm in providing a substantial contribution toward the removal expenses of two of the partners. The partners had moved at the firm's request. The Court of Appeal had suggested that

---

[1] *Ibid*, at 468.

[2] It is interesting to note that, with regard to the costs of the food and drink, Norse J emphasised that "reasonable amounts, are usually allowed in full. I have no reason to think that that practice does not correctly represent the law". (*Ibid* at 469).

[3] [1989] STC 898.

these expenses were deductible because they were incurred by the firm "wholly and exclusively" for business purposes. [1] Slade J suggested that

it is the collective purpose of this notionally distinct entity which has to be ascertained.

On appeal, the House of Lords disagreed with the reasoning of the Court of Appeal. [2] The House confirmed that in ascertaining the purpose of the expenditure one must look to the intentions and motives of the individual partners. In this particular case, the expenditure had a dual purpose, including the provision of personal and private benefits to the partners as householders. Accordingly the expenditure was disallowed as not being incurred "wholly and exclusively" for business purposes.

## The Basis of Assessment

The normal basis of assessment under Schedule D is known as the preceding year basis. In practice this means that the owner of a business is normally assessed for each year of assessment ending 5 April on the profits of his accounting year ending in the year preceding the year of assessment; for example, if he makes up his accounts to December 31 in each year he will be assessed for the year 1991 – 92 (ending April 5 1992) on the profits of the account ending 31 December 1990. Exceptions to this preceding year basis of assessment apply to the opening years of the business and to the closing years of the business.

The choice and application of the "normal basis" of assessment has frequently been a course of debate and concern. [3] In the 1991 Budget speech it was announced that a consultative document on the rules that apply and the basis of assessment would be forthcoming. The document, "A simpler system for taxing the self-employed: Proposals for the reform of the administrative arrangements for taxing the self-employed and the basis of assessment", was published on 14 August 1991. As the title of the document suggests, the broad aim is to make the system of assessment

[1] [1988] STC 116.

[2] *Supra.*

[3] Prior to the introduction of the present "preceding year" basis, a rather complicated system of assessing the average profits of the three accounts years preceding the year of assessment existed. The present preceding year basis was introduced in 1927–28 (Finance Act 1926) following the recommendations of the Royal Commission on Income Tax, 1920.

It is interesting to note that both the Radcliffe Committee, Cmnd 9474, (1955) and the Report of the Committee on the Taxation of Trading Profits, Cmnd 8189 (1951) concluded that a true "current year" basis of assessment of profits under Schedule D could not be achieved.

"easier and cheaper to administer and to reduce dealings between the Inland Revenue and the taxpayer". Two options for changing the basis of assessment are proposed : (1) current year basis, and (2) accounting period basis.

Under the current year basis of assessment, tax would be broadly paid on the amounts received in the current year, that is in respect of the profits from the accounts ending in the same year rather than the preceding year. However, the "preceding year" still has a relevant role. The current year basis proposal requires that interim payments are made on 1 January and on 1 July (before actual profits are known) with an adjustment following the computation of actual profits, on 1 January of the following year. In order to agree and calculate the "interim payments", profits and performance in the preceding year will be the basis for calculation.

The advantages of the current year basis, include the fact that the taxpayer (following the 1 January adjustment) is to pay tax on actual performance. The current year basis also removes the complex "opening and closing year" rules.

The accounting period basis is an attempt to follow corporation tax rules of demanding a return of income in respect of a stated accounting period. However, unlike corporation tax, payments are to be made either (i) by two instalments, 9 and 15 months after the start of the accounting periods, each equal to 50 per cent of the final liability for the last period; or (ii) one payment, twelve months after the start of the accounting period.

This attempt to bring the basis of assessment in line with that operated in relation to companies, provides a contribution to the declared aim of "neutrality". The proposals represent an attempt to bring the basis of assessment for all businesses "into line", so that

> the form of business vehicle chosen would be irrelevant from a tax perspective.

Initial response to these proposals suggests that the detail will not achieve the state aims, and that further consultation and clarifications is needed. [1]

In the March 1993 Budget, the Chancellor announced further developments, including the introduction of a self-assessment system. The Chancellor also explained that the preceding year basis of taxation was

> one of the least attractive features of our present tax system

[1] See A J Shipwright, [1992] BTR 12.

and declared that he proposed a "major simplification" through the introduction of a current year basis of assessment and taxation of the self-employed.

## Trading Losses

*Introduction*

A trading loss will arise if, in the relevant accounting period, the computation of "profits" reveals that expenditure and allowances (including adjustments to stock) exceeds receipts. If a loss is computed the taxpayer will need to consider whether any relief is available. [1] That some relief should be available has long been acknowledged [2], but the form of the relief has caused some debate. The debate has focused on the issues of (i) whether relief should be confined to allowing the taxpayer to carry forward any loss to set against the future profits of the same trade or business only; (ii) whether the relief suggested in (i) should be limited in time, perhaps for six years only; (iii) whether the taxpayer should enjoy the ability to carry forward the loss to set against his future profits or income from whatever source; and (iv) whether the taxpayer ought to be able to roll back the loss suffered and set it off against previous years trading profits—with or without a time limit.

Following the enactment and development of earlier legislation, provisions now exist (TA 1988, ss380 – 401) to facilitate loss relief in the form of (i), (iii) and (iv) above. Loss relief started life as the ability to set-off trading loss against current trading profit enjoyed by the same taxpayer in distinct and separate trades. [3] This was developed to provide the ability to set off a trading loss against other income (from whatever source) of the same period. Eventually, we reached the situation where business or trade loss could be carried forward to be set-off against trade profits of the same business or trade. [4] This ability to carry forward was also developed and

---

[1] Exceptionally, the Schedule E employee might suffer a loss. In such a case relief is also available under TA 1988, s380.

[2] For example, see the Final Report of the Royal Commission on the Taxation of Profits and Income, Cmd 9474 (1955) at para 486 when it explained that any suggestion that a relief for loss should not be available was a "plainly" unacceptable suggestion.

The same Committee did, however, refer to the development of "loss" provisions under Schedule D as a "comparatively recent growth".

[3]

[4] This was originally subject to a six year limitation period—until the limitation period was removed by the Income Tax Act 1952.

applied to the ability to set-off against "general income" from whatever source.

The issue of whether a taxpayer ought to be allowed to carry back loss, caused concern. In 1951 it was stated that "objections of principle can be raised" against any suggestion of carry back.

It would introduce a novel proposition into income tax if tax admittedly due for a particular year and correctly representing the taxpayer's capacity to pay for that year could be reclaimed by reference to circumstances arising in a later year.[1]

In 1955 it was confirmed that it would be "theoretically unreasonable" to allow losses to be carried back and set-off against profits of past years.[2]

Despite the theoretical objections, both Committees strongly objected to any general ability to carry back losses, on practical grounds. It was stated that complicated provisions would be necessary in order to facilitate and achieve "carry back" and that it would cause additional work to the Inland Revenue and to the taxpayer and his advisers.

However, one exception and permitted area of carry back, was deemed necessary to facilitate the circumstances where, during the last year of the businesses operation, the business and the taxpayer suffer a substantial loss with no corresponding general income against which that loss might be set. There is therefore a need to provide an avenue of relief for such a loss. That avenue of relief is now to be found in section 388, TA 1988.

Before we proceed to examine the details of today's provisions dealing with loss relief, it is important to appreciate that there is an overlap between some of the provisions with an accompanying choice as to which provision and relief the taxpayer may enjoy.[3]

*The Details (ss380—401)*

*(i) Relief under TA 1988, S380*

Section 380 allows the taxpayer to carry across loss from his trading activities to be set off against his general income in that year of assessment. Relief must first be applied to earned income (being income of a "corresponding class") and then to investment or unearned income.

---

[1] Report of the Committee on the Taxation of Trading Profits, Cmd 8189 (1951) at para. 80.
[2] *Supra* n2.
[3] See *Butt v Haxby* [1983] STC 239.

Any unrelieved losses can be carried forward for one year provided that the business continues for all or part of that year. There is also the possibility, since 1991, to elect to set any unrelieved losses against any chargeable gains tax realised in that year. In making such an election, the taxpayer will not enjoy any capital gains tax annual exemption. [1]

Two main restrictions apply to the use of section 380. First, the taxpayer must make a specific written election in each year that he wishes to enjoy the application of section 380. This election must be within a two year period from the end of the relevant year of assessment. Second, relief is only available if the business was genuine, ie the loss-making business was run on a commercial basis with a reasonable expectation of profit. [2]

### (ii) Relief under TA 1988, S385

Section 385 allows the taxpayer to carry forward any unrelieved loss of his trade, profession or vocation and set that loss against the first available profits of the same trade, profession or vocation without time limit. In carrying forward the unrelieved loss, it can be set-off against any income received by the business which has already been taxed at source; such as dividend or interest payments. In doing so, a repayment claim may be made.

The overriding restriction imposed on section 385, is the requirement that the taxpayer carries on the trade, profession or vocation. Any discontinuance of the activity will remove the relief, except in the following circumstances.

1. Any technical discontinuance of a partnership through the retirement of one of the partners shall be ignored. The continuing partners will be entitled to carry forward a share of the loss [3].
2. If the taxpayer transfers his business to a company in return for a transfer of shares, the taxpayer can carry forward the loss to set off against income derived by him from the company—for example, earned income from a service contract with the company, or unearned income in the form of a return on his shares (dividends). [4]

Note that relief under section 385 will automatically apply unless the taxpayer makes a specific election to enjoy the benefits under section 380.

[1] FA 1991, s72.
[2] TA 1988, s384.
[3] TA 1988, s113.
[4] TA 1988, s386.

If the latter is chosen, then any unrelieved loss remaining after the application of section 380 will be dealt with, automatically, under section 385.

### (iii) Relief under TA 1988, S381

Section 381 allows losses sustained in the first year of the business, or in any of the next three years of assessment, to be carried back and set-off against general income for the three years before that in which the loss was sustained. The loss must be first set against the earlier year against earned income before unearned income.

Section 381 is only available to individuals (partners, sole traders) but not to limited companies. The individual must make a specific election within two years from the end of the year of assessment in which the loss is sustained.

### (iv) Relief under TA 1988, S388

Section 388 allows a "terminal loss" to be carried back and set-off against the profits for a period of three years preceding the one in which the trade ends. As the phrase "terminal loss" indicates, a carry back under section 388 only applies where the trade, profession or vocation has been permanently discontinued. Once again, relief under section 388 will require a re-assessment of tax liability. Relief must be first given against a later rather than an earlier year of assessment.

### (v) Relief under TA 1988, S386

If a business, a sole trader or partnership, is "sold" (either through incorporation or take over) to a limited company, any loss sustained by the business in its final year cannot be carried forward to the company. Instead, section 386 allows the former proprietor of the business to set-off any loss against any future income that he receives from the Company (salary, dividends, etc) provided that in the relevant year of assessment he own shares in the company and the company continues to trade. It will be normal for the proprietor to hold shares that are received as part of the consideration for the transfer of his business to the company.

As an alternative to section 386, the proprietor could use the carry back provisions of section 388. Or, in a more complex situation, section 386 will assist in providing relief for any unabsorbed losses under section 388.

*Self-Check Questions*

1. What is the meaning of trade? How useful are the "badges of trade"?
2. How do you determine whether business expenses are deductible?
3. When will (i) travel expenses; and (ii) conference expenses be deductible?
4. List three statutory prohibited expenses.
5. When and in what circumstances can a trading loss be carried forward?
6. Explain the significance of the following cases:
   (i) *Sharkey v Wernher*
   (ii) *Mallalieu v Drummond.*

## Further Reading

Saunders J, *The Role of Intention in Identifying Trade or Business Income: The United Kingdom and Canadian Approaches*, (1990) BTR 169–89.

Grout V, *"Wholly and Exclusively" and Duality of Purpose Pts I & II*, (1979) BTR 44–49; 96–111.

De M Carey, D *Trade—The Elusive Concept*, (1972) BTR 6–14.

Olowofoyeku AA, *In the Performance of Duties; Fact, Law or Both?* (1996) BTR 28

# 6

# Capital Allowances

## Introduction

In the post-war period in particular, businesses have received tax incentives in an attempt by the government to encourage the acquisition of and investment in capital assets such as plant, machinery and industrial buildings. The tax incentives have taken the form of an allowance to be set-off against the annual profits of the business. Normally, the acquisition costs of the capital asset would only be taken into account on the assets "disposal" under the capital gains tax regime—a large and unnecessary wait. Relying on the capital gains tax regime to accommodate the costs of expenditure would probably result in a disincentive effect with little investment taking place in the development and updating of business machinery and premises. A lack of investment would have consequent adverse effects on the economy.

The "allowance" received under the capital allowances scheme has varied from a 100 per cent initial allowance to a reduced percentage writing down allowance only. The latter demanded more patience and planning from the businesses and would not offer immediate tax consequences and benefits.

It became increasingly apparent that the capital allowance system was subject to abuse: businesses would invest in unnecessary or unproductive capital simply to enjoy the tax deductions attributable to those investments. This abuse (and suspected abuse) caused the Government to review the system and announce a three-stage reform of the capital allowances system. The (then) Chancellor of the Exchequer, Mr Nigel Lawson, explained that

> too much of British investment had been made because the tax allowances made it look profitable rather than because it would be truly productive.

In order to encourage

investment decisions based on future market assessments, not future tax assessments

Mr Lawson announced a three-stage reform as follows:

> In the case of plant and machinery . . . the first year allowance will be reduced from 100 per cent to 75 per cent for all such expenditure incurred after today [13 March 1984], and to 50 per cent for expenditure incurred after 31 March next year. After 31 March 1986 there will be no first year allowances, and all expenditure on plant and machinery will qualify for annual allowances on a 25 per cent reducing balance basis. . . .

> . . . For industrial building, I propose that the initial allowance should fall from 75 per cent to 50 per cent from tonight, and be further reduced to 25 per cent from 31 March next year. After 31 March 1986 the initial allowance will be abolished, and expenditure will be written off on an annual 4 per cent straight line basis. . . . [1]

The full details of these changes can be found in the Capital Allowances Act 1990. Before we look at those details, we must first consider the meaning of industrial building and plant and machinery.

## Industrial Buildings

Industrial buildings are defined in the 1990 Act. [2] The definition is complex but worthy of discussion. In essence the definition attempts to equate "industrial" with manufacture and production, but not distribution activities. However, if the storage and distribution of goods is for the purpose of the business, then the building and its use will be classed as "industrial". [3]

Also excluded from the definition of "industrial" is the use of a building as a dwelling, retail shop, hotel, office or showroom. [4]

---

[1] March 13, 1984. Hansard, HC, Vol 56, Cols 295–296. Mr Lawson still believed that the much amended and reduced capital allowance system would still be more generous than a system of commercial depreciation.

*Note* that an initial allowance has been retained in respect of industrial buildings in particular circumstances, such as Capital expenditure on the construction of a building in an enterprise zone.

[2] See s18, CCA 1990.

[3] See *Saxone Lilley and Skinner (Holdings) Ltd v IRC* [1967] 1 All ER 756.

[4] CCA 1990, s18 (4).

Apportionment is allowed to facilitate part qualifying and part non-qualifying use. Apportionment is subject to a very generous allowance of total costs where the non-qualifying use is insignificant—representing not more than 25 per cent of the total construction costs of the building. [1]

Finally, it is important to appreciate that where an initial allowance still remains, it is only available to the person who incurs the cost of the building; writing down and balancing allowances are available to those who enjoy a relevant interest. A relevant interest means that the person who incurs the expenditure must have an interest in the property at the time of the expenditure. [2] For example, a leaseholder or freeholder who incurs capital expenditure on improvement would be able to enjoy the allowance. Their position as freeholder or leaseholder represents an interest in the property.

## Plant and Machinery

"Plant" and "machinery" are not defined by legislation. Their meanings must be determined by the courts and must depend on the particular facts of the case. Judicial guidance on this matter contains many contradictions and difficulties. The best advice is to focus on the facts of the case and to consider

> ... whether it can really be supposed that Parliament desired to encourage a particular expenditure out of, in effect, taxpayers' money and ... ultimately, in extreme cases, to say that this is too much to stomach. . . . [3]

The real difficulty in understanding and distinguishing "plant" involves the need to distinguish "premises and setting" from "plant", in a manner that facilitates the recognition of plant as an integral part of the carrying-on of the business. Such a recognition of the integral nature of plant has appeared in judicial comments as the "functional", "business" or "amenity" test. Some even refer to a very broad "premises" test to support the need for a distinction. The *dicta* of Lindley LJ in *Yarmouth v France* is often cited as the basis for the adopted distinctions:

---

[1] Ibid, at s18(7).

[2] Ibid at s20.

[3] Per Lord Wilberforce in *IRC v Scottish and Newcastle Breweries Ltd* [1982] STC 296.

It was suggested that this was destined to become known as the "nausea test". See [1983] BTR 54 at 55.

... in its ordinary sense [plant] ... includes whatever apparatus is used by a business man for carrying on his business—not his stock-in-trade which he buys or makes for sale; but all goods and chattels, fixed or moveable, live or dead, which he keeps for permanent employment in his business.[1]

It appears that we ought to accept (with some caution) that "plant" is not stock-in-trade nor business premises—unless those business premises perform the function of and represent "plant" (integral to the business).

The following cases might be of interest in illustrating the distinctions and the difficulties in this area:

The case of *IRC v Scottish and Newcastle Breweries Ltd*[2] included a claim for costs of metal structures (seagulls in flight) incurred by the owners of a hotel. The purpose of the purchase and erection of these metal structures was to contribute to the creation of an "ambience" or "atmosphere" in the hotel. The court accepted that the metal structures were plant. The court emphasised that the seagulls performed a functional role in that the

creation of ambience or atmosphere was an important function of the trade of successful hoteliers and publicans.

It was also stated that the metal structures were not part of the

setting in which they did their business—but, the setting offered to customers for them to resort to and enjoy, and hence plant.[3]

In *IRC v Barclay Curle & Co Ltd*[4], expenditure was incurred on the excavation and concrete work in the construction of a dry dock. The House of Lords accepted that this represented expenditure on plant. Lord Reid explained that although the dry dock was a structure or premises, it was also plant:

The only reason why a structure should also be plant ... is that it fulfils the function of plant in the trader's operations. ...[5]

---

[1] [1887] 19 QBD 647 at 658.
[2] *Supra* n3.
[3] This case inspired the advice that one should "always re-decorate one's walls and ceilings with loose chattels". [1983] BTR 54 at 56.
[4] [1969] 1 WLR 675.
[5] *Ibid* at 679.

Similarly in *Cooke (Inspector of Taxes) v Beach Station Caravans Ltd*,[1] the "structures" of a swimming pool and a paddling pool in a caravan park were held to be plant. Megarry J emphasised that they were not premises in the sense of "where it's at" (the location of the business activity). They were apparatus in that they were part of the means whereby the trade of a caravan park was carried on.

In *J Lyons & Co Ltd v A-G*[2], the purchase and erection of lamps in a tea shop were not plant in that they performed a general function of the provision of light and not a specific trade function in relation to the particular needs and conduct of that trade.

In *Wimpy International Ltd v Warland*[3], Wimpy failed in its claim that expenditure on such items as shop fronts, floors, suspended ceilings, lights and wall finishes represented expenditure on plant. The court emphasised that

> the fact that different things might perform the same functions of creating atmosphere was irrelevant: what matters is that one thing may function as part of the premises and the other as plant.

Thus it was concluded that

> ... something which becomes part of the premises instead of merely embellishing them, was not plant, except in the rare case where the premises are themselves plant.[4]

## Capital Allowances: the Details

A consolidated Act, the Capital Allowances Act 1990, provides the details of the allowances and charges for the chargeable periods ending after 5 April 1990.

## Plant and Machinery

The details allow this capital allowance to be claimed by Schedule D Case I and II taxpayers and Schedule E taxpayers. It is also available in relation to furnished holiday lettings under Schedule D Case VI and, where the

[1] [1974] STC 402.
[2] [1944] Ch 281.
[3] [1989] STC 273.
[4] *Supra* at 279, per Fox LJ.

plant and machinery is used in the maintenance or management of premises, to a general landlord under Schedule A or Schedule D Case VI.

In respect of the Schedule D taxpayer, the expenditure must be incurred wholly and exclusively for the purposes of the trade, although apportionment is expressly stated as available in circumstances of dual purpose.[1] The Schedule E taxpayer is required to establish that the expenditure on the plant and machinery took place because its provision was "necessary" in the performance of the duties of the Schedule E taxpayer.[2] This additional requirement of the Schedule E taxpayer can, once again, prove excessively onerous.[3]

To accord with accountancy practice, there have been some major changes in relation to the determination of the date when the expenditure is deemed to have been incurred. The expenditure is now deemed to have been incurred on the date on which the obligation to pay becomes unconditional.[4] It is important to appreciate that this change will recognise the situation where an obligation to pay becomes unconditional even though the sum does not have to be paid until a later date. Exceptions apply if the date of payment falls four months after the obligation to pay has become unconditional—the due date of payment will then be used in this instance.

Having determined the date of incurrence, we need to consider next the tax period in which the allowance may be claimed.[5] For the corporation tax payer, the relevant period is the incurrence within the appropriate accounting year. Similarly, the Schedule E taxpayer's relevant period is the year of assessment. For those who adopt a preceding year basis under Schedule D, it normally means a delay in the enjoyment of the allowance or claim in accordance with the application of this basis of assessment.

If, having applied the allowance or change to the annual profits of the trade, profession or employment, there remains a surplus of allowance or charge, the surplus can be rolled forward to be set against future profits[6] or against general income.[7]

---

[1] CAA 1990, s79.

[2] CAA, 1990, s27(2)(a)—although this requirement is not to apply in relation to the purchase of a motor vehicle (s27(2A)—(2E)).

[3] See *White v Higginbotham* [1983] STC 143—where the provision of a projector to a vicar was not "necessarily" incurred for the performance of his duties.

[4] CAA 1990, 159(3). The previous rule used the "date" when the expenditure became payable (CAA 1968, s82).

[5] CAA 1990, s160.

[6] CAA 1990, s140.

[7] TA 1988, ss382, 383.

## The Allowance

Previously a first year allowance together with a writing-down allowance was permitted. We noted in the introduction the concern that was caused by the possible abuse of, in particular, the first year allowance—hence its removal. First year allowances are not available for expenditure incurred after 31 March 1986.

The writing-down allowance has been retained and this allows the taxpayer to progressively write-off the cost of the plant and machinery.

### (i) The Basic Allowance

This consists of an allowance of 25 per cent (on a reducing balance basis) of the "qualifying expenditure" (expenditure minus any other allowances) on the plant and machinery. The allowance will apply once the expenditure has been incurred, irrespective of whether the asset is in use, on assets wholly and exclusively purchased for the purposes of the trade, profession or vocation. Apportionment of the allowance on terms that are just and reasonable is permitted to recognise non-business purpose and use. [1]

### (ii) Pooling

It is normal for a trade to acquire a number of items of plant and machinery. It then becomes convenient, and possible, to create a "pool" of plant and machinery. The writing-down allowance of 25 per cent will then be applied to the value of the "pool" rather than the value of individual items. [2]

### (iii) Disposal

If an item of plant or machinery is disposed of, provision must be made to ensure that the disposal consideration or value is taken into account. [3] It is most important that the allowance enjoyed by the business equate with the actual cost to the business of that item of plant or machinery.

"Disposal" is given a wide meaning to include a disposal by sale; a

---

[1] CAA 1990, s79.

[2] CAA 1990, s24. Note that more detailed rules demand that certain assets must be pooled separately or that certain assets may not be pooled. For example, see CCA 1990, ss31, 34, 37 and 41.

[3] CAA 1990, s26.

disposal by extinction (destruction) and a disposal through the loss of possession ("loss" or theft). [1] Sale consideration, insurance monies or deemed market value will represent the sum that must be taken into account.

### (iv) Balancing Allowances and Charges

No writing-down allowance is available in the year that the business ceases or terminates. Proceeds from the sale of the plant and machinery are deducted from the qualifying expenditure in the pool (or individual items if non-pooled). If a surplus of "qualifying expenditure" remains, that surplus will be converted into a "balancing allowance" to be deducted from the taxpayer's profits and income. Conversely, if the proceeds of sale of the plant and machinery exceed the qualifying expenditure, the excess is treated as a balancing charge and becomes a taxable receipt of the business—this process is known as the "clawback" of capital allowances.

### (v) Short-life Assets [2]

It is possible for the taxpayer to elect that certain short-life assets should not join a general pool of plant and machinery. It is also possible to enjoy a pool of short-life assets. A short-life asset is one that is expected to be disposed of within five years. Any election in relation to those assets must be made within two years from the date of their acquisition.

The purpose of this permitted de-pooling election is to enable the taxpayer to realise the balancing allowance on short-life assets at an earlier time than would normally be available. If those assets were part of a general pool, it normally results in 80 per cent of the cost being written-off over eight years.

## Industrial Buildings

Capital allowances are available for the construction or purchase of an industrial building. The base allowance is a writing-down allowance at a rate of four per cent of the cost price of the industrial building. [3] This four per cent allowance is available for each year the taxpayer uses the

---

[1] CAA 1990, s24.
[2] See details in CCA 1990, s37.
[3] CCA 1990, s3.

building for industrial purposes up to a maximum of 25 years. The entire expenditure is deemed to have been written-off after 25 years.

A balancing allowance or charge will arise if the building or interest in the building is sold (or if it is demolished, destroyed or relevant use ceases) within the 25 year period.[1] The balancing allowance or charge is computed involving a comparison of the disposal expenditure with the outstanding qualifying expenditure. It is important to appreciate that a balancing charge will not recover more than the allowances given, thus an excessive disposal consideration will give rise to the potential of capital gains tax.

The purchaser of a secondhand industrial building, may also be entitled to a writing-down allowance.[2] This entitlement depends on the sale to the purchaser falling within the 25 year period. That purchaser will then be entitled to an allowance (not confined to the four per cent rate) based upon the residue of expenditure. The residue of expenditure represents any unrelieved expenditure of the vendor plus any balancing charge (or minus a balancing allowance).

Special rules apply to (i) hotel buildings and extensions[3]; and (ii) Enterprise Zones[4]. Although hotels do not technically fall within the definition of industrial buildings, specific provisions have been introduced to permit expenditure on the construction or improvement of "qualifying hotels" to be written-off on an annual writing-down allowance of four per cent.

In order to stimulate development in declared Enterprise Zones, 100 per cent initial allowances are available for capital expenditure on industrial buildings, hotels and commercial buildings. The 100 per cent initial allowance is not mandatory : an election can be made to enjoy a reduced percentage initial allowance with the balance being written-off annually at 25 per cent of the cost on a straight line method of provision.

## Other Allowances

Other specific items and areas of expenditure are eligible for capital allowances and charges. These include expenditure incurred on the construction, wholly or partly, of agricultural or forestry buildings[5]; expenditure incurred on the construction of property for letting as assured

---

[1] CAA 1990, s4.
[2] CAA 1990, s10.
[3] CAA 1990, s7.
[4] CAA 1990, ss1 and 6.
[5] CAA 1990, Part V.

tenancies [1]; capital expenditure on scientific research [2]; and expenditure incurred in the acquisition of patents and "know-how". [3]

## Assessment of the Changes and Reform

We mentioned at the beginning of this chapter, that Mr Nigel Lawson sought reform of the capital allowance system in a direction that would encourage a balanced approach to investment. He, and others, were concerned that the "old" system of capital allowance was far too generous and had resulted in low-yielding, and even loss-making, investment at the expense of jobs. There is now some concern that the reforms may have swung the pendulum too far: that there is no longer sufficient encouragement for investment. During the 1990s there have been various campaigns seeking a more generous treatment of investment. These have included campaigns by the CBF, and by employers' federations in engineering, motor manufacturing and in metal trades. They have been supported in their campaigning by the results of academic papers and research. For example, Devereux concluded that the new system of capital allowances acts as a disincentive to real investment. [4]

It is certainly a difficult task to develop and arrange a system of capital allowances that provides the required balance of sufficient incentives for good investment. Although in the March Budget of 1993, the Chancellor did provide some good news for businesses, the issue of capital allowances and incentives for investment was once again a cause of criticism. The Chancellor announced a number of peripheral and limited changes to capital allowance details. [5] The failure to directly address or consider the possible extension and increase of capital allowances was described as "one by omission". [6]

It also drew the following comments from industry:

We were disappointed that little emphasis was placed on improving investment in high technology. This Budget fell short of directly

[1] CAA 1990, Part III.

[2] CAA 1990, Part VII.

[3] TA 1988, ss 520–528.

[4] M Devereux. "Corporation Tax: The Effect of 1984 Reforms on the Incentive to Invest", (1988) *Fiscal Studies*, 9(1), 62.

[5] Those changes relate to the ability of a connected person to elect to treat the sale of industrial buildings as having taken place at their tax written-down value.

[6] *Financial Times*, March 17, 1993 at p24.

encouraging UK companies to invest and to meet the anticipated recovery. [1]

And,

This Budget does nothing to bring about the massive switch from consumption to investment which is essential for lasting recovery. [2]

The debate is certain to continue!

*Self-Check Questions*

1. What are capital allowances? Why are they important?
2. What is an industrial building? When will premises constitute plant?
3. What are "pooling provisions"? What is a "clawback" of capital allowances?
4. Explain the concept of a writing-down allowance?

---

[1] Spokesperson for the Machine Tool Technologies Association. Reported in *Financial Times*, March 17 1993.

[2] Mr Neil Johnson, Director-General of the Engineering Employers' Federation. Reported in *Financial Times*, March 17 1993.

# 7

# Schedule D Case VI

Schedule D Case VI is declared to apply to

> any annual profits or gains not falling under any other case of Schedule D, and not charged by virtue of Schedule A, C or E.[1]

This is the general or sweeping-up provision of the schedular system (see earlier discussion of the doctrine of source). Case VI also catches matters specifically declared by statue to be placed within Case VI—these include profit and gains from furnished lettings; securities transactions; post-cessation receipts; and the transfers of assets abroad.

It is the general (or sweeping-up) aspects of Case VI that are of interest. An examination of judicial comments and application of Case VI reveals that it is neither as wide nor as all-embracing as it initially appears. The first restriction on Case VI is that it applies to income receipts only (not capital gains or profits). Thus in *Scott v Ricketts*[2] the Court of Appeal declared that a payment to an estate agent for the agent agreeing to forgo claims in a development scheme was a capital sum and therefore not caught or taxable under Case VI. Similarly in *Earl Haig's Trustee v IRC*[3] a trustee owned some diaries and the copyright attached to those diaries. The trustees permitted the use of the diaries in the production of a bibliography and received a sum of money for doing so. The Court of Appeal held that the sum of money received was as a consequence of a realisation (in part) of a capital asset (the diaries and copyright). The money was not income and was not therefore assessable under Case VI.

A second limitation on the scope of Case VI emanates from the words "profits or gains".[4] The term "profits or gains" is used elsewhere in

---

[1] TA 1988, s18 (It is also a residual provision to those sums not caught by Schedule F, TA 1988 s20).

[2] [1967] 2 All ER 1009.

[3] [1939] 22 TC 725.

[4] The term "annual" does not imply that the profit or gain must recur, simply that the "profit or gain" must fall within and be assessed in a year of assessment.

Schedule D and the implication is that the words must be consistent in their meaning and application and that the activities that present or create the profit or gain must be analogous. Technically the requirement is that the "profit and gains" are of the same kind (*ejusdem generis*) as "profit and gains" taxed elsewhere under Schedule D. This requirement has invited the conclusion that the profit or gain must be derived from an activity analogous to an "adventure in the nature of a trade or profession"[1]. This means that Case VI will usually apply to casual earnings (normally from the performance of services) but not gifts[2] nor betting winnings and receipts. For example, in *Hobbs v Hussey*[3] a solicitor's clerk wrote and published his memoirs in the *People* newspaper. This was not the clerk's profession or trade, merely a "casual" activity. The clerk also assigned the copyright of the article to the newspaper. The court held that the payment received by the clerk was in return for the performance of "casual" services and therefore assessable under Case VI. Although the performance of the services also involved the sale of property (the copyright), Lawrence J emphasised that the essence of the performance was the revenue nature of the receipt which was "the fruit of the individual's capacity" derived from but was not "the capital itself".

In some instances the distinction between an "adventure in the nature of trade" (Schedule D Case I) and an analogous activity (Schedule D Case VI) is difficult to determine. For example, in *Jones v Leeming*[4] the taxpayer was party to a scheme whereby he participated in the acquisition and sale of rubber estates for a profit. The House of Lords concluded that the profit was not assessable under Case VI because it was not a profit within Schedule D. At an earlier stage the Court of Appeal had pointed out the difficulty (if not illogical approach) of the *ejusdem generis* application. Lawrence LJ suggested that if an isolated transaction such as this is not an adventure in the nature of a trade (Case I) then it is difficult to conclude that it is a transaction *ejusdem generis* with such a transaction (Case VI):

> . . . All the elements which would go to make such a transaction an adventure in the nature of trade in my opinion would be required to make it a transaction *ejusdem generis* with such an adventure.

---

[1] This analogy is necessary because "profits and gains" are related in Schedule D Cases I and II to "adventures in the nature of a trade or profession". The *ejusdem generis* approach demands such an analogy and application.

[2] In *Scott v Ricketts* [1967] 2 All ER 1009, Lord Denning MR confirmed that "profits and gains" does not include gratuitous payments.

[3] [1942] 1 KB 491.

[4] [1930] AC 415.

The logical conclusion would be that Case VI is redundant in that *ejusdem generis* activities must demonstrate the characteristics of trade and would therefore be "trade" and assessable under Case I. Perhaps a more generous approach to the interpretation of Case VI is required— especially if it is to adequately perform a role as a "sweeping-up" provision.

*Self-Check Questions*

1. What is the purpose of Schedule D Case VI? What types of activities are caught by Case VI?
2. How effective is Schedule D Case VI as a sweeping-up provision?

# 8

# The Taxation of Pure Income Profit

## Introduction

The uncertainties of life in modern societies often lead the astute to endeavour to lay aside some money, either to save for the proverbial "rainy day" or to provide some security in respect of inevitable retirement. In such cases it often makes sense to keep the money not in current banking accounts, which return no profit but rather attract charges, but, for the security conscious, in interest yielding building society/bank accounts or government treasury bills; or, for the more adventurous and daring, in various high profit investments. Whichever way the money is kept, it will or may yield some financial return. This will normally be pure profit (in the sense that the financial return is, in its entirety, a profit), or investment income, and, inevitably, there will be income tax implications. This chapter is concerned with the principles that govern the taxation of such "pure profit", or investment income.

The principal charging provision for income tax purposes is s18(3) of the ICTA 1988 which charges tax under Case III of Schedule D in respect of:

1. any interest of money, whether yearly or otherwise, or any annuity or other annual payment, whether such payment is payable within or out of the United Kingdom . . . but not including any payment chargeable under Schedule A;
2. all discounts;
3. income from securities which is payable out of the public revenue of the United Kingdom or Northern Ireland.

For the purposes of corporation tax, s18(3A) provides for a different charge under Case III. In this respect, the subsection charges tax under Case III in respect of:

1. profits and gains which, as profits and gains arising from loan

relationships, are to be treated as chargeable under this Case by virtue of Chapter II of Part IV of the FA 1996[1];
2. any annuity or other annual payment which
   (i) is payable . . . in respect of anything other than a loan relationship and
   (ii) is not a payment chargeable under Schedule A;
3. any discount arising otherwise than in respect of a loan relationship.

The discussions in this chapter will focus mainly on annuities and other annual payments, while interest and discounts are examined in outline only.

## Interest of Money

### Definition

As is typical of the Taxes Act, the statutory definition of "interest" is not particularly illuminating. S832(1) of the ICTA 1988 provides that interest "means both annual or yearly interest and interest other than annual or yearly interest". This strange definition still leaves us with the question "what *is* interest?" Rowlatt J answered the question in *Bennett v Ogston*[2], saying that interest is a "payment by time for the use of money". In *Re Euro Hotel (Belgravia) Ltd*,[3] Megarry J referred with approval to a definition given by Rand J of the Supreme Court of Canada in *Reference Re Saskatchewan Farm Security Act 1944, Section 6*, that, "interest is, in general terms, the return or consideration or compensation for the use or retention by one person of a sum of money belonging to, in a colloquial sense, or owed to, another".

The essence of interest is that it is a payment which becomes due because the creditor has not had his money at the due date.[4] It may be regarded either as representing the profit which the creditor might have made if he had had the use of his money, or the loss that he suffered because he did not have that use. The general idea is that the creditor is entitled to compensation for the deprivation.[5] Megarry J in *Re Euro Hotel (Belgravia) Ltd*[6] summed up the nature of interest thus:

[1] Case V of Schedule D does not include tax in respect of any income falling under this provision.
[2] 15 TC 374 at 379.
[3] [1975] 3 All ER 1075 at 1084.
[4] Lord Wright in *Riches v Westminster Bank Ltd.* [1947] 1 All ER 469 at 472.
[5] Lord Wright, *ibid.*
[6] [1975] 3 All ER 1075 at 1084.

It seems to me that running through the cases there is the concept that as a general rule two requirements must be satisfied for a payment to amount to interest, and a fortiori to amount to "interest of money". First, there must be a sum of money by reference to which the payment which is said to be interest is to be ascertained . . . Secondly, those sums of money must be sums that are due to the person entitled to the alleged interest; . . . I do not, of course, say that in every case these two requirements are exhaustive, or that they are inescapable. Thus I do not see why payments should not be "interest of money" if A lends money to B and stipulates that the interest should be paid not to him but to X: yet for the ordinary case I think that they suffice.

### Tax on Interest

The general scheme of Schedule D Case III is the deduction of income tax at source by the payer under s348 and s349 (concerning which we shall say more later), so that the payee or recipient receives the sums net of tax. By virtue of s348(1) and s349(1), payments of interest are excluded from these deduction rules. Thus the general rule is that interest is to be paid gross, and the recipient will be assessed directly under Case III. There are exceptions however. S 349 (2) requires the payer to deduct the amount of income tax (at the lower rate – see sections 1A, 3, and 4) from any payment, and account for such deduction to the revenue, where the payment is a payment of yearly interest chargeable under Schedule D Case III, paid, (a) by a company (excluding building societies) or local authority, otherwise than in a fiduciary or representative capacity (i.e. paid on their own behalf); or, (b) by or on behalf of a mixed partnership (i.e. one having a company in it); or, (c) to any person whose usual place of abode is not in the United Kingdom.

Because the deduction requirement under s349(2) applies to "yearly" interest, a distinction is drawn between "short" interest which is always paid gross, and yearly interest. This issue was addressed by the Court of Appeal in *Cairns v McDiarmid*.[1] According to Kerr LJ[2],

. . . the authorities show that the answer depends on the true intention of the parties. A bank loan for a fixed period of less than a year does not carry "yearly" (or annual) interest merely because the rate of

[1]  56 TC 556; [1983] STC 178.
[2]  56 TC at p582.

interest is expressed as a percentage by reference to the period of a year . . . On the other hand, a loan on a mortgage which is nominally repayable after six months and which carries interest at a rate per annum will qualify as carrying annual interest because the true intention of the parties is that it should be a long-term loan, beyond a year and indeed probably over many years.

Sir John Donaldson MR concurred, saying [1];

It is well settled that the difference between what is annual and what is short interest depends upon the intention of the parties . . . because it is possible to have a short term and indeed a very short term investment, e.g. over-night deposits, and such an investment does not involve any annual interest, regardless of whether the interest is calculated at an annual rate. On the facts found by the Commissioners, the loan to Mr Cairns was never intended to last for more than a few days, albeit the was entitled to postpone repayment for two years. In fact, as was always intended, his liability was discharged within the week . . .

S349(3) provides exceptions to the deduction requirements of s349(2). This would in some cases mean that the payment of interest is to be gross, and, in some other cases, special deduction rules apply. The exceptions apply in the following situations:

(a) Interest payable on an advance from a bank, if at the time when the interest is paid the person beneficially entitled to the interest is within the charge to corporation tax as respects the interest (i.e. interest which is paid to a bank by a customer who has borrowed money from the bank, if the bank would be liable to corporation tax in respect of the interest). This type of interest is always paid gross.
(b) Interest paid by a bank in the ordinary course of its business. Note in this respect s480A which applies to interest paid by a "deposit taker" requiring a deduction of tax at source in certain situations (e.g., if the payee is an individual who is resident in the United Kingdom) [2].
(c) A payment to which s124 applies (interest on quoted Eurobonds).
(d) A payment to which s369 applies (mortgage interest payable under deduction of tax).

---

[1] 56 TC at p. 581.
[2] See s481 for definitions and requirements.

(e) Payments which are "relevant payments" for the purposes of Chapter VIIA of Part IV (paying and collecting agents).
(f) Cases to which the deduction rules under s480A apply.
(g) Cases to which the deduction rules under s480A would apply, but for s480B.
(h) Cases to which the deduction rules under s480A would apply, but for s481(5)(k).

*Discounts*

Most people who have shopped for goods at some time have been given a "discount"—in the form of reduced prices—by their vendors. This is a common usage of the word "discount" but this, and other popular usages of the term, are not necessarily the type of discount taxable under Schedule D Case III. As Rowlatt J said in *Brown v National Provident Institution*[1];

> ... it is clear that it is not every difference in amount between a sum payable in future of the same sum represented by cash down which is an annual profit or gain by way of discount even though popularly the word "discount" may be used to describe it ... [T]he difference between the cash and the credit prices of an article bought is commonly described as discount for ready money allowed by the seller but it is not taxable as income under case 3.

For the purposes of Schedule D Case III, Fox LJ in *Ditchfield v Sharp*[2] referred with approval to the dictionary definition of "discount":

> ... a deduction ... made for payment before it is due, of a bill of account ... the deduction made from the amount of a bill of exchange or promissory note by one who gives value for it before it is due".

The receiver of the bill is the one who gives the discount. According to Lord Sumner in *Brown v National Provident Institution*[3] there are two economic elements present in discounts: "one the value of the usufruct forgone, as measured by interim interest, and the other the risk that the money will never be repaid at all".

[1] [1919] 2 KB 497 at 506.
[2] [1983] STC 590 at 593.
[3] [1921] 8 TC 57 at 96.

One of the most common forms of discount is government Treasury Bills, where the public purchase bills for less than the redemption value (in effect lending the government money for a period) and redeem the bill on maturity for its redemption value. What is taxed is the difference between what was given for the bill and what was finally received on the bill's maturity.

In cases of loans, since there is no general rule that any sum which a lender receives over and above the amount which he lends ought to be treated as income, [1] the question often arises whether an amount received by a lender in excess of the loan represents a discount, or a premium, i.e. a sum payable on the return of money lent, in excess of the loan, but which is not interest because it is not paid by reference to time (e.g., a fixed sum of £500 payable on any loan above £25,000). [2] In *Lomax v Peter Dixon* [3], it was held that where no interest is payable as such, the transaction will normally, if not always, be a discount (this will also apply where the interest is inadequate). Where a proper rate of interest is charged, the extra sum demanded in addition will be a premium.

## Annuities and Other Annual Payments

*Introduction*

The term "annuity" generally refers to income which is payable year by year. It was more particularly described by Watson B in *Foley v Fletcher* [4] when he said that an annuity means

> where an income is purchased with a sum of money, and the capital has gone and has ceased to exist, the principal having been converted into an annuity.

This statement obviously refers to purchased annuities but some annuities are not purchased, e.g., annuities under a will or trust.

The precise boundary between annuities and what is described as "other annual payments" is yet to be fixed, but this of itself is of no serious consequence as similar principles apply to both types of payment. All

---

[1] Per Lord Greene MR in *Lomax v Peter Dixon* (1943) 25 TC 353 at 363.
[2] Premiums are normally capital in nature.
[3] [1943] 25 TC 353.
[4] [1858] 157 E.R. 678 at 684.

annuities are annual payments but not vice versa. Since it is not possible to give a precise definition of "other annual payments", we must examine the characteristics which a payment must have in order to fall into this category.

## Characteristics of "Annual Payments"

The characteristics of an annual payment were listed by Jenkins LJ in *IRC v Whitworth Park Coal Co. Ltd*[1]:

1. The *ejusdem generis* rule applies—i.e. not all recurrent payments are "annual payments" for the purposes of Schedule D Case III. The payment must be *ejusdem generis* with (i.e. of the same type as) the specific instances given in the shape of interest of money and annuities[2]. Most of the other characteristics to be discussed are actually reflections of this requirement.

2. A binding obligation is required. Voluntary payments cannot be annual payments—at best, they will be gifts. In order to be an annual payment a payment must fall to be made under a legally enforceable obligation, as distinct from mere voluntary payments.[3] The essence of annual payments is that the payer is thereby alienating a slice of his income. So if the payments are not made under a binding legal obligation, the payer can hardly be said to have alienated any part of his income. The income is still his, to do with it as he likes. Thus for example, dividends paid by a company are not annual payments since there is no obligation to pay them and their distribution depends in every instance upon a declaration by the company.[4]

   For the purposes of the required obligation, a will, a contract, or a deed of covenant will suffice. Furthermore, according to Jenkins LJ, the fact that the obligation to pay is imposed by an order of court and does not arise by virtue of a contract does not exclude the payment from Case III. Thus a court order will also suffice.

3. Recurrence: like interest and annuities, the payment must possess the essential quality of recurrence implied by the description "annual".[5]

---

[1] [1958] 2 All ER 91 at 102–104.

[2] Jenkins LJ, referring to Hamilton J in *Hill v Gregory* (1912) 6 TC 39 at 47; see also Watson B in *Foley v Fletcher* (1858) 157 E.R. at 685.

[3] Jenkins LJ, referring to Lord Sterndale MR in *Smith v Smith* [1923] P. 191 at 197.

[4] Per Viscount Simon in *Canadian Eagle Oil Co. Ltd v R.* [1945] 2 All ER 499 at 504.

[5] See also Lord Maugham in *Moss Empires Ltd v IRC* [1937] AC 785 at 795.

This requirement has been given a broad interpretation in the authorities. Thus Warrington LJ said in *Smith v Smith*[1] that the fact that a payment is to be made weekly does not prevent it from being annual, provided that the weekly payments may continue beyond the year.[2] Furthermore, according to Lord Macmillan in *Moss Empires Ltd. v IRC*[3] the fact that payments are contingent and variable in amount does not affect the character of the payments as annual payments. Therefore the element of recurrence is satisfied if the payment is capable of being recurrent[4], even if it never recurs in fact.[5] In *Moss Empires* itself, the taxpayer company, by agreement, undertook to another company, to make available to that company a sufficient sum to enable it to pay certain dividends, if its profits fell below a certain level. In each of the five years covered by the agreement, the taxpayers were called upon to make payments under their obligation. The payments thus made by the taxpayer varied significantly from year to year. It was held that the payments were annual payments even though they were contingent and variable.

4. Pure income profit—it is necessary for the payments to be pure income profit in the hands of the recipient. According to Lord Radcliffe in *Whitworth Park Coal Co. v IRC*[6], it is inconsistent with the scheme of deduction of source that Case III of Schedule D should contain payments that are gross in the hands of the recipient and which are not his pure income; and according to Lord Guest in *Campbell v IRC*[7], it is well settled that tax cannot be deducted by the payer in respect of payments which in the hands of the recipients are gross receipts for advice or services or goods supplied which merely form an element in discovering what the profits of the recipients are. Thus to be an annual payment for the purposes of Case III, a sum must be of such a nature that it is taxable in its entirety. There are some "annual" payments which, by their very nature and quality, cannot possibly be treated as the pure profit income of the recipient

---

[1] [1923] P. 191 at 201.

[2] Cf. Lord Sterndale MR (at page 196)—an obligation which cannot exceed twelve months cannot create an annual payment.

[3] [1937] AC 785 at 793.

[4] Lord Maugham in *Moss Empires* (at page 795).

[5] See Lord Greene MR in *Asher v London Film Productions Ltd.* [1944] KB 133 at 140—"You can have an annual payment . . . even though it happens by some accident or other to fall due in one year only".

[6] 38 TC 531 at 575.

[7] [1970] AC 77 at 107.

(the proper response to them being to treat them as an element to be taken into account in discovering what the profits of the recipient are) or which themselves contain payments of such nature. Such payments will not fall within Case III.[1] What then is the correct test for determining which payments are pure income profit in the hands of the recipient? Lord Donovan provided the answer in *Campbell v IRC*[2].

One must determine, in the light of all the relevant facts, whether the payment is a taxable receipt in the hands of the recipient without any deduction for expense or the like. Whether it is, in other words, "pure income" or "pure profit income" in his hands, as these expressions have been used in the decided cases. If so it will be an annual payment under Case III. If, on the other hand, it is simply gross revenue in the recipient's hands, out of which a taxable income will emerge only after his outgoings have been deducted, then the payment is not such an annual payment.

This test shows for example that a trading receipt will not be an annual payment. The point is illustrated by *Howe v IRC*[3]. The taxpayer had paid some premiums in respect of his life policies to a life insurance company which he claimed to deduct in computing his total income for super tax purposes. It was held that such deduction was not allowable. The payments were not pure income in the hands of the insurance company, since they would only be trading receipts, to be taxed in its hands only after deducting allowable expenditure. According to Scrutton LJ[4]:

It is not all payments made every year from which income tax can be deducted. For instance, if a man agrees to pay a motor garage £500 a year for five years for the hire of and upkeep of a car, no one suggests that the person paying can deduct income tax from each yearly payment. So also, if he contracted with a butcher for an annual sum to supply all his meat for a year. The annual instalment would not be subject to tax as a whole in the hands of the payee, but only that part of it which was profits.

For the same reason that trading receipts cannot be annual payments

---

[1] See generally, Lord Greene MR in *re Hanbury; Comiskey v Hanbury* (1939) 38 TC 588 at 590.
[2] [1970] AC 77 at 112.
[3] [1919] 2 KB 336.
[4] At p352.

within Case III—the need to deduct expenses before arriving at a profit figure—receipts of a person's profession will not be annual payments. [1]

The principle with respect to trading and professional receipts is clear enough. What is not so straightforward is the response to the proposition that, when a payment is made subject to a counter-stipulation, or in return for consideration, then it is not pure profit in the hands of the person who is subject to the counter-stipulation or who has to give the consideration. This proposition has some support in the cases. In *IRC v National Book League* [2] the League was in receipt of covenanted payments from its members, who then obtained access to its facilities and services. In deciding whether the covenanted payments were, in these circumstance, pure income profit in the League's hands, Lord Evershed MR said [3] that the question was, "looking at the substance and reality of the matter can it be said that those who entered into these covenants have paid the sums covenanted without conditions or counter stipulations"? In this case the question was answered in the negative, and it therefore followed that the payments under the covenants were not pure income profit. Similarly, in *Taw and Torridge Festival Society Ltd. v IRC* [4], the society received payments under deeds of covenant, offering seats at reduced rates for all concerts, recitals, ballets and plays, as a privilege to the covenantors. Wynn-Parry J held that *IRC v National Book League* applied, that he was, on the facts of this case, unable to apply the *de minimis* rule to ignore the counter stipulation, and that the payments under the covenants were not pure income profit. A more recent example is *Essex County Council v Ellam.* [5] The council arranged for S's son to attend a special school. The school normally looked to local authorities to pay the fees of any child on the usual termly basis, leaving it to the authorities to make any appropriate arrangements for the child's parents to reimburse or contribute to the fees for the child's terms. S then signed an agreement to reimburse the council any amount paid in respect of the fees of his son. Later S executed a deed of covenant to make payments to the council in respect of the said fees. A claim that the payments under the covenant were pure income profit was rejected. Dillon LJ said [6] that it was impossible to regard the payments by S under

---

[1] See *Jones v Wright* (1927) 13 TC 221—solicitor trustee charging for his services under a charging clause.

[2] [1957] Ch 488.

[3] At p503.

[4] [1959] 38 TC 603.

[5] [1989] STC 317.

[6] At p322.

the deed as pure income of the council without regard to the obligation which the council undertook to pay the fees of S's son. One goes to cancel the other. He said however [1] that the payments would clearly have been the pure income of the council if they had not been earmarked as they were for the particular purpose for which they were earmarked.

In spite of cases like this, however, it is now well established that the question whether or not there existed some counter stipulation or whether consideration was given, is not decisive. It was Lord Donovan who said in *Campbell v IRC* [2]:

> ... one cannot resolve the problem whether a payment is an annual payment within Case III simply by asking the questions "Must the payee give or do something in return?" or "Did the payer make some counter stipulation or receive some counter benefit?"; or "Was it pure bounty on his part?" ...

According to Lord Donovan the question is not whether there was a counter stipulation in respect of a payment but simply whether any sum can be claimed as an expense of earning the payment. In the same case Viscount Dilhorne explained further [3]:

> ... the fact that there is consideration for the promise to pay, whether or not in the form of a condition or counter-stipulation, does not necessarily exclude the annual payment from the scope of [Case III]. If however, the consideration or counter-stipulation relates to the provision of goods or services and so deprives the payments of the character of "pure income profit", it will have that effect.

Apart from these *dicta,* the proposition that the presence of consideration or counter stipulations is not necessarily fatal to a payment being pure income also has support in direct decisions. In *Delage v Nugget Polish Co Ltd* [4] the defendants became entitled, by virtue of an agreement with the plaintiffs, to use a trade secret for the making of "blacking". This was to be in return for payments, for a period of 40 years, of an annual sum of money calculated as a percentage of the gross receipts on the sale of the

---

[1] At p325.
[2] [1970] AC 77 at 112.
[3] At p98.
[4] [1905] 92 LT 682.

said blacking, and brown polish. It was held that the payments under the agreement were annual payments.[1] Furthermore, annuitants under purchased annuity schemes do give consideration (cash) for the annuities that they receive, but these are still within Case III.

Nevertheless, the effect of a counter-stipulation or the provision of consideration cannot always be predicted with certainty. This creates problems for bodies which need to attract funding by donations/deeds of covenant, and which may need to provide some incentive (in the form of benefits) to attract such funds. In this respect statute has now stepped in to assist certain charities in this situation. If the sole or main purpose of a charity is the preservation of property, or the conservation of wildlife, for the public benefit, such a charity is permitted by s59 FA 1989 to provide consideration (in the form of viewing rights) to persons from whom it receives annual payments. With respect to charitable trusts, Lord Hodson said in *Campbell v IRC*[2] that where the money is paid for the benefit of a charitable trust, and it confers an "incidental benefit" outside the purpose of the trust, the incidental benefit will not disqualify the money so paid as an annual payment for the purposes of Case III.

In addition to the aforementioned characteristics of annual payments outlined by Jenkins LJ in *IRC v Whitworth Park Coal Co Ltd* two other factors emerge from the cases.

First, the payment must "have the character of income in the hands of the recipient".[3] What this means is that the payment must be of an income (and not capital) nature. This is clear from the requirement that it be pure income profit. It is however not always easy to distinguish an income payment from a capital payment or from a payment which represents part income and part capital. This is especially so where a sum of money is being paid in instalments in circumstances in which it is possible to identify an asset in respect of which the payments are made.

One thing is clear however. Where payments represent instalments for the purchase price of a capital asset they will be capital instalments and not annual payments[4]. Thus in *IRC v Ramsay*[5] where the taxpayer agreed to buy a dental practice for £15,000, of which £5000 was to be

---

[1] See also *Asher v London Film Productions Ltd* [1944] KB 133.

[2] [1970] AC at 104.

[3] Per Viscount Dilhorne in *Campbell v IRC* [1970] AC at 95.

[4] See for example Channell B in *Foley v Fletcher*—"I am of opinion that the words ... annual payments do not include those payments which are in respect of the purchase money of an estate, and are in the nature of capital and not of income" (1858) 157 ER at 686.

[5] 20 TC 79.

paid at once, the balance being paid by ten yearly instalments, it was held that the instalments were capital payments, and not annual payments. Note however that if a payment is part income and part capital it can be dissected. In *Vestey v IRC*,[1] shares worth £2 million were sold for £5.5 million, to be paid in 125 yearly instalments of £44,000. The £5.5 million was stated to be without interest. It was held that the amounts of the instalments should be dissected into capital and interest. Also, in *Secretary of State for India v Scoble*[2] where the East India company brought a railway, paying by instalments (described as "annuities") over forty six years, the instalments were dissected into capital and interest.

Secondly, the payment must "form part of the income of the recipient".[3] This is a different matter from the income/capital discussion above. It is concerned with whether the payment is really the income of the recipient or of someone else. In *Campbell v IRC* itself, a charity received sums under a deed of covenant, which sums it was then obliged to pay to another party. The payments were held not to be annual payments. According to Lord Guest[4]:

> There must be a transfer of title to the income. If *unico contextu* with the alleged transfer there is a contract to pay it back on the purchase of the business, then there is no transfer of title to the income and, therefore, no annual payment.

## Deduction of Tax at Source

*Introduction*

As has been noted earlier, the scheme of Schedule D Case III is the deduction of income tax by the payer before making the payment. The rationale for such deductions was given by Lord Guest in *Campbell v IRC*[5];

> For the purposes of income tax the payer is regarded as having parted with that part of his income which by covenant or contract he pays

---

[1] [1962] Ch 861.
[2] [1903] AC 299.
[3] Viscount Dilhorne in *Campbell v IRC* [1970] AC at 95.
[4] At p105.
[5] [1970] AC at 108.

away. The income that he pays away is that of the payee and so he is entitled to deduct tax on paying it.

The machinery for the deduction is contained within ss348 and 349 ICTA 1988. Both sections apply to different types of payment and the consequences attendant upon their application are significantly different—all we will say about this now is that s348 is far more beneficial to the taxpayer than s349.

First, we need to identify the types of payment to which each of the sections applies. S348 applies

> where any annuity or other annual payment charged with tax under Case III of Schedule D, not being interest, is paid *wholly* out of profits or gains brought into charge to income tax. [1]

The section extends to certain royalties paid wholly out of profits or gains brought into charge to income tax. [2] On the other hand s349 applies where the payments are "not payable or not wholly payable out of profits or gains brought into charge to income tax". [3] Hereafter, we will refer to the phrase "profits or gains brought into charge to income tax" as "taxed income", and to profits or gains which do not fall within that description as "untaxed income".

If s348 applies only in respect of payments made wholly out of taxed income and s349 applies in respect of payments not so made, the question then arises as to how the source of any particular payment is to be decided. The first point to note here is that the mere fact that accounts are kept in some particular way ought not to alter the rights of the Revenue, and ought not to militate against the rights of the taxpayer, [4] i.e. the particular form adopted by a taxpayer in his accounts should neither assist nor injure him.

The question of how the source of a payment is to be determined was answered by Lord Wilberforce in *IRC v Plummer* [5]:

> The general rule, in the case of an individual at least, is that what is significant when one is considering the application of the statutory rule,

---

[1] See s348(1) (emphasis added).
[2] S348(2).
[3] See s349(1).
[4] Per Lord Hanworth MR in *Central London Railway Co v IRC*, 20 TC 102 at 134.
[5] [1980] AC 896 at 909.

is not the actual source out of which the money is paid, nor even the way in which the taxpayer for his own purposes keeps his accounts, if indeed he keeps any, but the status of a notional account between himself and the revenue. He is entitled, in respect of any tax year, to set down on one side his taxed income and on the other the amount of the annual payments he has made and if the latter is equal to or less than the former, to claim the benefit of [s348].

What this statement means is simply that if the payer has income out of which the annual payment could have been made, s348 applies rather than s349, even if the payment is actually made out of capital. All that we are concerned with is whether the payer had sufficient taxed income to cover the payment, and not, for example, whether he made the payment straight out of his salary or out of funds borrowed from Australia.

Example:

Launcelot is a barrister who earns at least £100,000 every year from his profession. He has an obligation under a covenant to make payments of £2,000 every month to his favourite charity for the next six years. Last year, he made a cash purchase of some farmland at an auction, and so was a little short of cash. He had to sell some of his shares on the stock market in order to meet his obligations under the covenant.

Although Launcelot's payments for last year were actually made out of the proceeds of the sale of the shares, and not out of his earnings as a barrister, they will still be covered by s348. He earned enough from his profession (at least £100,000) to cover his obligations under the covenant (£24,000) and the fact that the payment was in real life made from another source is irrelevant.

If, however, the payer has deliberately restricted himself for other legal reasons to pay out of capital, then the general rule stated by Lord Wilberforce is overridden and s349 will apply. The point was made by Romer LJ in *Central London Railway Co v IRC*[1] that although the form in which accounts are kept is not conclusive, yet it may be that a particular form has been adopted for the purpose of definitely deciding and recording the fact that a decision has been made, that a certain payment is to be made out of capital. Such a form of account, which debits the

[1]  20 TC 102 at 140.

payment to capital, may have been adopted for the purpose of making it clear that revenue is set free for other purposes. This point is illustrated by *Chancery Lane Safe Deposit and Officers Co Ltd v IRC.*[1] The company borrowed some money to finance building works. On the advice of its auditors, the company, in order to give a fair view of its affairs, charged part of the interest payments on the loans to capital (the company's taxable profits exceeded the amount of the interest payments and so it could have paid out of taxable profits). The Revenue claimed that the interest payments were paid out of capital and not out of profits or gains brought into charge to tax. The company on the other hand claimed that the allocations to capital were mere bookkeeping entries irrelevant for tax purposes, and that the interest payments were made out of profits brought into charge to income tax.

It was held by a majority of the House of Lords (Lords Reid and Upjohn dissenting) that the payments must be treated as having been made out of capital. There was a deliberate choosing of attribution to capital rather than to revenue. It was not a matter of method of domestic bookkeeping. The accounts merely evidenced the fact that a decision was taken, was acted upon, and was maintained. The company's definite attribution precluded an entirely inconsistent attribution for tax purposes. The following extract from the speech of Lord Morris of Borth-y-Gest[2] is enlightening:

> If a company makes and adheres to a decision that a payment should be out of capital and orders all its affairs on that basis, it would be strange if it could assert that the payment should be deemed to be one payable out of profits or gains. An attribution of a yearly payment to profits or gains brought into charge to tax can only be in reference to the year in which the payment is made. If a payment is attributed to capital, the practical result follows that the sum available or carried forward as available for distribution by way of dividends is increased. If a sum is so carried forward it does not, of course, follow that distribution by way of dividends will take place, nor does it follow that, if there are dividends, there will be deductions of tax. It would seem incongruous, however, if a company, having decided (which means the same as "definitely" decided) to charge a payment to capital and having regulated its proceedings on that basis, could say that the

[1] 43 TC 83.
[2] At p115.

payment was not to be deemed to be charged to capital. This does not mean that in any ordinary case a company, in seeking *vis-a-vis* the Revenue to make an attribution of an annual payment, is fettered merely because of some form of entry that it has made in books or accounts. It merely means that what was in fact and in reality a payment out of capital cannot be paraded in the guise of a payment out of revenue. That would be more than departing from documents or accounts: it would be departing from fact: it would be a distortion of history.

The gist of this decision is that a deliberate decision to pay out of capital, which has practical consequences in the real world, or which affects the interests of persons other than the decision maker, cannot thereafter be interpreted differently. If Mr X decides to make a particular payment out of his savings, or from proceeds of the sale of his car, that is his own business (as long as his taxed income is sufficient to cover his liability to make annual payments in the relevant year). The method so chosen may just have been the most convenient means of making the payment at that particular time—a case of simple domestic bookkeeping, and he has not committed himself, for any defined period, to keep on making the payments in that fashion. The same result will ensue if the managing director of X Ltd decided to make this month's royalty payment from the proceeds of a sale of equipment, simply because the cash was available there and then. That is again a case of domestic bookkeeping. If however the same X Ltd passed a resolution to make all future payments of particular royalties by realising investments, this, because of all the consequences that will invariably flow therefrom, may lead to a different result, and X Ltd may not be able to claim that the payments are from income. As Lord Morris noted in the *Chancery Lane* case [1], a payment cannot in one and the same year be debited to capital, with the result that the dividend fund is enhanced, and also notionally be treated as debited to revenue so as to enable tax which is deducted to be retained.

That would require the sum in one year to render two incompatible and inconsistent services. The money must speak either as a payment out of capital or as a payment out of income.

We now go on to examine the effects of the application, first, of s348, and secondly, that of s349.

[1] 43 TC at p117.

*Payments under s348*

When s348 applies, the payer is entitled (but not obliged) to deduct and retain out of the payment income tax at the basic rate (s348(1)(b)); the recipient shall allow such deduction to be made, and the payer shall be discharged of his obligation to make the payment (s348(1)(c)). This in effect means that the payment is deductible in the hands of the payer. As has been noted earlier, the payment is an alienated slice of the payer's income, and since it represents the income of someone else (i.e. the recipient) and not of the payer, it follows that the payer is not liable to tax on that slice of income.

Example:

Natalia covenants to pay a gross sum of £1,000 every year to "Save the Elephant", a registered charity. Assuming a basic rate of 23%, if s348 applies, Natalia is entitled to deduct tax of £230 and to pay the balance of £770 to the charity.

The annual payment is part of the recipient's total income in the year when the payment becomes due and if the deduction is made, the recipient is treated as having received the gross sum, and as having paid tax on it at basic rate (s348(1)(d)). Thus in the example above, "Save the Elephant" will be treated as having received £1,000, and having paid tax of £230 on that sum.

If the recipient is only a basic rate tax payer then there is nothing more to be done in respect of the payment. If, on the other hand, the recipient is a higher rate tax payer then he has to pay the difference between the tax paid at basic rate and that which would have been due at the higher rate. If the recipient's marginal rate is zero (e.g., charities, and individuals who either have no income or whose income fall below the personal allowance) then a refund of tax can be claimed from the Revenue.

*Payments Under s349*

"When s349 applies, the payer is obliged to deduct the amount of income tax from the payment (s349(1)). Where only part of the payment was not made out of taxed income, the tax, in effect, only has to be deducted from that part. Furthermore, the person by or through whom the payment was made, is obliged to deliver an account of the payment to the inspector, and is liable to tax at the applicable rate on the whole of the payment, or on so much of it as it is not made out of tax income (s

350(1)). The applicable rate is that which is specified in s4 (i.e. the lower rate in respect of interest, and the basic rate in other cases). Obviously if the payer has deducted the tax as required, all that is left for him to do is to pay it to the Revenue.

## Payments Without Deduction of Tax

We have just discussed the requirement for deduction of tax under s349. What if the parties wish to dispense with the deduction of tax? This section examines the various ways in which such a wish may possibly be achieved.

### 1. Agreements for Non-deduction

One obvious method of implementing a wish to dispense with the deduction of tax is for the parties to enter into an agreement to that effect. However, an obstacle to this course of action exists in s106(2) TMA 1970, which provides that every agreement for the payment of interest, rent or other annual payment in full without allowing deduction of income tax shall be void. A number of points should be noted with respect to this provision. First, the provision applies only to agreements. It does not for example apply to trustees. In *Re Goodson's Settlement*[1] the settlor directed trustees to pay annuities to his wife, and directed that the annuities should be enjoyed free of income tax. It was held that the settlor did not by the settlement create any agreement with the trustees or anybody else. Thus the provisions of (what is now) s106(2) TMA 1970 did not apply (see below however, for the effect of a "free of tax" stipulation). Secondly, the provision invalidates only the part of the agreement relating to non-deduction of tax and not the whole agreement. It follows that where there is such a provision in an agreement, the payer is still entitled, or obliged to deduct tax depending on whether s348 or s349 applies.[2]

### 2. The Use of Formulae

The provisions of s106(2) TMA 1970 can be circumvented by the use of certain formulae. If the parties wish to ensure that a fixed sum is paid each year to the recipient irrespective of fluctuations in tax rates, such a wish

---

[1] [1943] Ch 101.
[2] See Scrutton J in *Blount v Blount* [1916] 1 KB 230 at 237–238.

can be implemented by the means of the common formula—to pay such sum as after the deduction of income tax at the basic rate for the time being in force will leave x amount. Such a formula was approved in *Booth v Booth*[1] as not being contrary to s106(2). All it means is that the amount so specified is net of income tax. The payer is thus left with the responsibility for handling the tax affairs in respect of the gross sum. However, while circumventing s106(2) TMA 1970, this is only a partial solution to the problem of non-deduction of tax. The recipient is relieved of the responsibility of bothering about tax deductions, but the payer is not. In fact, the payer is in a situation which is not much different from what it would have been if the formula had not been used at all.

### Payments "Free of Tax"

It is actually possible to stipulate that a payment be made "free of tax". A provision to pay £x "free of tax" does not fall foul of s106(2) because of the decision of the House of Lords in *Ferguson v IRC*[2] that the effect of such a provision is an undertaking to pay such sum as after deduction of income tax leaves £x. In *Ferguson*, a husband and wife entered into a deed of separation whereby the husband agreed to pay the wife the sum of £35 free of income tax. During the relevant periods, the husband lived abroad and had no UK income and thus the Revenue sought to tax the wife on the £35. It was held that the sum had already borne tax because the agreement was to pay a gross sum which, after deduction of tax, leaves £35, and that therefore the tax sought was not claimable.

A "free of tax" stipulation attracts a number of consequences. Generally, it operates to ensure that the recipient in any event ends up with the specified amount, no more and no less. Thus if the recipient obtains any repayment of tax from the Revenue, he is obliged to return such repayment to the payer. This is the rule in *Re Pettit*.[3] In this case a testator provided an annuity "free of tax" by his will. The sums were paid wholly out of taxed income, and the annuitant received some repayment from the Revenue. It was held that the annuitant must return a proportion of that repayment to the trustees as the annuity bore to the annuitant's total income. A further consequence is that if the recipient is liable to higher rate tax, the payer is obliged to satisfy this liability too. This is the rule in *Re Reckitt*.[4]

[1] [1922] 1 KB 66.
[2] [1970] AC 412.
[3] [1902] 2 Ch 765.
[4] [1932] 2 Ch 144.

The result is that the obligation of the payer varies with the marginal rate of the payee and this can present some accounting problems. Apart from this fact, just as with the case of the use of formulae (above), a "free of tax" stipulation does not actually provide a solution to the non-deduction problem. While it relieves the recipient of all responsibility for tax, it imposes on the payer a far higher burden than he would normally have had to bear. As such, except this is precisely what the parties want, such a provision is counter-productive. The inevitable conclusion therefore is that there is no practical way of implementing a non-deduction of tax.

## Failure to Deduct Tax

### *The Payer and the Recipient*

In cases of a failure by the payer to deduct the tax which he is entitled or obliged to deduct there is no obligation on the recipient to refund the over payment—at least as long as the payer failed to make the deduction under a mistake of law (e.g. thinking that no deduction is necessary because the recipient is a charity). An action will not lie against the recipient for recovery of the sum, and the payer is not entitled to withhold later payments. [1] Where the payment is one of a series within the same tax year, and some instalments remain to be paid, the payer may not make good his loss by making the deduction from one of the later payments. [2]

Exception may be made, where the failure to deduct was due to a mistake fact, in which case recovery is possible[3] (e.g. where the mistake is one of calculation); and where the applicable rate of tax increases after the payment, the excess can be recovered. (s821 ICTA 198.)

### *The Parties and the Revenue*

The first point to note here is that there is no penalty for non-deduction. If the payment is made under s348, failure to deduct tax will not generally be of any concern to the Revenue, since they will have got the tax already, or will still get it (in both cases, from the payer). However, since any deduction which is made is to be treated as income tax paid by the

---

[1] *Re Hatch* [1919] 1 Ch 351; *Warren v Warren* [1895] 72 LT 628.
[2] *Johnson v Johnson* [1946] 1 All ER 573 (explaining *Taylor v Taylor*, [1937] 3 All ER 571).
[3] *Turvey v Dentons* [1953] 1 QB 218.

recipient (s348(1)(d)), it follows that, in cases of non-deduction, no tax can be treated as having been paid. The Revenue take the view that the recipient cannot make a repayment claim, but give concessionary relief in respect of maintenance payments. [1]

If the payment is made under s349 the Revenue will simply assess the payer, who in any case is liable under s350(1), to the appropriate tax on the payment. The result is that the payer has nothing to gain by not deducting the tax.

### The 1988 Rules

The Finance Act 1988 introduced new rules in respect of the income tax treatment of annual payments, the effect of which is to take most of them out of the tax system. The relevant provision is now in s347A, ICTA 1988, which provides that any annual payment made after 14 March 1988 *by an individual*, which would otherwise have fallen within Case III of Schedule D, shall not be a charge on the payer's income, that no deduction can be made on account of the payment, and that the payment is not the income of the recipient or of any other person. This means that, as a general rule, new arrangements for annual payments (e.g. covenants) by individuals have no income tax consequences whatsoever. Thus, for example, the covenants which parents used to make in favour of their children who were attending university will no longer be effective as a means of getting the Revenue to "subsidise" university education.

This is the general rule, but s347A(2) provides exceptions for payments of interest, covenanted payments to charity, payments made for bona fide commercial reasons in connection with an individual's trade, profession or vocation etc. (e.g. partnership retirement annuities), and payments which fall within s125(1) (i.e. purchased annuities paid wholly or partly out of capital). Payments made in pursuance of an existing obligation were exempted from this rule by s36(3) FA 1988. "Existing obligation" for these purposes is defined by s36(4), and generally refers to obligations incurred before 15 March 1988. However, Schedule 17, para. 4(1), FA 1995 provides;

> Section 347A of the Taxes Act 1988 (annual payments not a charge on the income of the payer) applies to a payment which is treated by virtue of Chapter IA of Part XV of the Taxes Act 1988 as income of the payer notwithstanding that it is made in pursuance of an obligation

---

[1] Under ESC A52. This concession is now classified obsolescent.

which is an existing obligation within the meaning of section 36(3) of the Finance Act 1988.

What this means is that payments which are treated as the income of the settlor under the anti-avoidance rules of part XV (see below) now fall within the exclusions in s347A. Generally, an annual payment will be ineffective for tax purposes under part XV, and the payments will be treated as the income of the payer (s660A) unless the income arises from property in which the settlor has no interest (see exceptions in s660A(8) and s660A (9). By this token, even covenants entered into before 15 March 1988 would seem now to be ineffective unless they fall within an exception to the s660A provisions. The result is that the only exceptions now are those within s347A itself, and those excluded from the operation of s660A—basically, covenanted payments to charities, etc. and, perhaps, capital settlements.

Note that the 1988 rules apply only to payments made by individuals (references to an individual in s347A(2) include references to a Scottish partnership in which at least one partner is an individual[1]). Thus payments made by other entities, such as companies or trusts, and payments under wills, are not affected, and are still subject to the normal Case III provisions.

## Anti-Avoidance Provisions

A discussion of the taxation of pure income profit will not be complete without a mention of the anti-avoidance provisions contained in Part XV ICTA 1988, and which generally apply in respect of "settlements". Annual payments within Case III will generally come within the scope of these provisions because of the wide meaning given to "settlement". S660(G)(1) defines a settlement as including any disposition, trust, covenant, agreement or arrangement, or transfer of assets. Most annual payments are made under trusts, covenants, or agreements, and any payment not made under these will definitely be made under an "arrangement" or a "disposition". The Part XV provisions are discussed in more detail in the next chapter. However, it is useful to note here the general principle in s 660A(1) to the effect that (with certain exceptions) any income arising under a settlement during the life of the settlor will be treated as the income of the settlor unless the settlor has no interest in the property from which the income arises.

[1] See s347A(6).

*Self-Check Questions*

1. In what circumstances will a payment of interest be subject to deduction of tax by the payer?
2. What is the difference between a discount and a premium?
3. What is the effect of the presence of a counter-stipulation or consideration on the question whether a payment is pure income profit?
4. What are the differences between the deduction rules in s348 and s349 ICTA 1988?
5. What is the effect of a stipulation that annual payments be made "free of tax"?

## Further Reading

Wosner J, *The Meaning of Annual Payment—I*, (1989) BTR 265–270.
Robson RH, *The Meaning of Annual Payment—II*, (1989) BTR 270–276.
Stebbings C, *The Taxation of Mortgage Interest at Source in the Nineteenth Century*, (1989) BTR 348–358.
Stopforth D, *Charitable Covenants by Individuals—a History of the Background to their Tax Treatment and their Cost to the Exchequer*, (1986) BTR 101–116.

# 9

# Taxation of Trusts and Settlements

## Introduction

Individuals, partnerships and corporations are generally taxable on their income, whether arising from employments, trades, or investments. The taxation of the income arising or accruing to these persons or entities are covered in various sections of this book. There remains, however, yet another entity which is capable of making profits and receiving income. This entity is the trust.

Trusts can often serve as convenient mechanisms for splitting, accumulating, or distributing income. The planning opportunities inherent in this method of handling income are evident. For example, a taxpayer with income-yielding properties may settle the property with a direction to the trustees to accumulate the income arising therefrom. On one view of the matter, tax could be saved—the income accrues to the trustees and therefore the settlor will not be liable to tax on it. Since it does not "really" belong to the trustees, they might also not be liable to tax on it. The income will accumulate tax-free, until one day, when it has been capitalised, it will be distributed free of income tax to one or more beneficiaries. In another scenario, an individual with a high marginal rate may settle income or income-producing assets on trust for beneficiaries who are not taxpayers or who have lower marginal rates. This would not only take advantage of the beneficiaries' lower rates, it would also take advantage of their personal reliefs.

Not surprisingly, this state of affairs is largely a dream because, under the UK tax system, trustees are "persons", trusts are taxable entities in their own right, just like individuals and corporations, and the income accruing to trustees is taxable in their hands. Lest this be seen as presenting another opportunity for total avoidance of UK tax (e.g. by appointing foreign trustees), although any income arising from the trust property would normally accrue to the trustees only, it is not the rule that the trustees alone are to attract the attention of the tax collector.

According to Viscount Cave LC in *Williams v Singer*[1], such a principle would lead to "strange" results. Rejecting the principle, he said

> If the legal ownership alone is to be considered, a beneficial owner in moderate circumstances may lose his right to exemption or abatement by reason of the fact that he has wealthy trustees, or a wealthy beneficiary may escape Super-tax by appointing a number of trustees in less affluent circumstances. Indeed . . . a beneficiary domiciled in this country may altogether avoid the tax on his foreign income spent abroad by the simple expedient of appointing one or more foreign trustees.[2]

Thus, the taxation of the income accruing to trustees falls into a three-tier system. In some cases, income tax is charged on the trustee. In cases where a trustee is made chargeable with the tax, the statutes recognise the fact that he is a trustee for others, and he is taxed on behalf of his beneficiaries, who will accordingly be entitled to any exemption or abatement which the income tax statutes allow.[3] In other instances, the tax is charged on the beneficiary, who will normally be given credit for any tax already borne by the trustees in respect of the income that is to be taxed. Finally, in certain situations (see the anti-avoidance rules in respect of "settlements" below), tax is charged on the settlor.

Trust law is generally thought to be complex, and the law relating to the taxation of income from trusts and settlements is not seen as any less complex. Recent years have witnessed moves to simplify the applicable rules (particularly those relating to the taxation of "settlements"), but these have probably not gone far enough. The discussion that follows attempts to present the principles in a clear and accessible way.

## Trust

The word "trust" is not defined in the Taxes Act. Since it does not appear to have any special meaning for tax purposes, its plain and ordinary meaning under the general law would suffice. Trust law texts are often shy of giving a definition and perhaps it is impossible to produce a universally acceptable and all encompassing definition. Thus, we will not attempt to

---

[1] [1921] 1 AC 65; 7 TC 387.
[2] 7 TC at 411.
[3] See Viscount Cave LC in *Williams v Singer* 7 TC at 411—412.

give such a definition here. We can however take as a starting point one of the definitions in the Concise Oxford English Dictionary, which defines trust as *inter alia*: "A confidence placed in a person by making that person the nominal owner of property to be used for another's benefit." [1]

This is one aspect of the matter. In another respect, the trust could be seen as the entity in which the property is placed, or, the vehicle whereby the person in whom the confidence is placed is able to become the nominal owner of the property in question.

## Trustee

There is also no definition of "trustee" for income tax purposes. Again, this word is not a term of art and does not generally have any special meaning or tax purposes. [2] The Concise Oxford English Dictionary defines trustee as: "A person or member of a board given control or powers of administration of property in trust with a legal obligation to administer it solely for the purposes specified." [3]

In *Williams v Singer* [4] Lord Phillimore said

> The very essence of the position of a trustee is that he is a person who at law has all the rights of an owner, but who has nevertheless the obligation, which he has undertaken by accepting the trust, of using his powers as legal owner for the benefit of some person not himself or some object not his own.

## The Charge on Trustees

There is no specific provision in the Taxes Act which charges trustees to income tax on income accruing to them. However, the Act does contain specific provisions charging people who receive income. Thus, s21(1) of the ICTA 1988 provides that income tax under Schedule A shall be charged on and paid by the persons receiving or entitled to the income.

---

[1] 9th Ed., 1995, p1498.

[2] See however s69(1) TCGA 1992 which provides that the trustees of a settlement shall be treated as being ": . . a single and continuing body of persons (distinct from the persons who may from time to time be the trustees) . . ."

[3] 9th Ed., 1995, p1498.

[4] 7 TC 387 at 416.

Since it is the trustees who are normally in receipt of trust income, such provisions apply to charge them to income tax in respect of the income which they have received. The principle that trustees are charged only by virtue of the fact that they receive income is exemplified in the speech of Viscount Cave LC in *Williams v Singer*, where he said

> ... if the Income Tax Acts are examined, it will be found that the person charged with the tax is neither the trustee nor the beneficiary as such, but the person in actual receipt and control of the income which it is sought to reach. The object of the Acts is to secure for the State a proportion of the profits chargeable, and this end is attained (speaking generally) by the simple and effective expedient of taxing the profits where they are found. If the beneficiary receives them he is liable to be assessed upon them. If the trustee receives and controls them he is primarily so liable. [1]

The point was reiterated in *Reid's Trustees v IRC*[2] where trustees were held assessable under Schedule D because they received the income. The Lord President (Lord Clyde)[3] rejected the argument that the only "person" to whom income could arise or accrue within the meaning of the Act is a person who is beneficially entitled to the income in his own right. In his view, trustees are the proper persons to be assessed in all cases in which the income of the trust estate *received by them, or to which they are entitled,* is not tax-deducted at source; and, in the case of income of the trust estate which is tax-deducted at source, they could not be heard to ask repayment of the tax on the plea that the income did not arise or accrue to them but to others, whether such others were income-beneficiaries or capital-beneficiaries. [4]

## The Scope of the Charge

It has been seen that trustees are charged on behalf of their beneficiaries.[5] This means that their personal circumstances are not relevant to the charges on them in their capacities as trustees. There are a number of points to note in this respect, which are discussed immediately below.

[1] 7 TC at 411.
[2] 14 TC 512.
[3] At p523.
[4] At p524 (emphasis added).
[5] Viscount Cave LC in *Williams v Singer* (7 TC at pp411–412).

## Individuals

Although trustees in their official capacities are "persons", they are not "individuals". This has certain consequences. First, because personal reliefs are generally available only to individuals, the trustees cannot claim any personal reliefs [1], although they may claim reliefs available to "persons" (e.g. loss relief) and they may claim deductible expenses in respect of a trade carried on by the trust. Secondly, the trustees are not charged at the lower rate because this applies only to individuals. [2] Thirdly, the trustees are not liable to higher rate tax because, by virtue of s1(2)(b) ICTA 1988, this rate of tax is charged only on individuals. This particular point makes trusts still appear to be profitable devices for tax planning by high income earners whereby they may dump their income-producing assets in trusts, and leave the income thereof to accumulate. The attractiveness of this has been reduced by the introduction of a different rate of tax (the "rate applicable to trusts") in respect of certain types of trust (see below).

## Trust Expenses

In calculating the taxable income of the trust for basic rate tax purposes, no deduction can be made for trust expenses of administration. In *Aikin v MacDonald's Trustees* [3] the trustees had an interest in certain tea estates in India. They received remittances representing profits from those estates. This income was subject to charge under Schedule D Case V and the trustees sought to deduct certain expenses incurred in this country in connection with the management of the trust. The Lord President, rejecting the claim, said

> It seems to me that all the authorised deductions and charges occur at an earlier stage than that at which these expenses have been incurred. When the net sum was placed in the hands of the trustees, it had passed through all the vicissitudes which entitled anyone to make deductions.

[1] See for example Lord Johnston in *Fry v Shiels* (1914) 6 TC 583 at 588:
I think that the question before us is solved at once when one observes that Section 19, which gives this relief commences not with the usual words, "Any person" which may be held to include not merely a plurality of persons but a body, whether trustees or a corporation, regular or irregular, but that the word "individual" is used; and I think it is used with a clear intention, and that intention is one which squares with the object of the provision. That object I conceive to be to relieve a man who by his own exertions and his own daily work makes an Income.

[2] See s1(2)(aa) ICTA 1988.
[3] [1894] 3 TC 306.

It had come home, and was in their hands for them to apply to their uses. The fact that their uses are trust uses does not seem to me to make any difference in the present question . . . It seems to me that the expenses which are authorised to be deducted are expenses excluded by the terms of the present claim, because the words of the present claim are quite explicit that these expenses have been incurred in this country in connexion with the management of the trust, and they are not expenses at all specifically relating to the investment in question, except in this sense, that the income of the investment in question constitutes the bulk of the trust estate. [1]

The *ratio* of this decision is that the deduction sought was not permissible under Schedule D because it had not (as required by the Schedule D deduction rules) been incurred wholly and exclusively in earning the profit in question, but had rather been incurred after the income was earned. According to Lord Adam [2], the expenses looked very much like sums "expended in any domestic or private purposes, as distinct from the purposes of the manufacture, adventure, or concern". Lord McLaren said [3] that the only kind of deductions allowed is expenditure incurred in earning the profits, and, "that there is no deduction under any circumstances allowable for expenditure incurred in managing profits which have been already earned and reduced into money pounds, shillings, and pence". Lord Kinnear said [4] that this was not a deduction of money laid out or expended for the purpose of the trade or concern at all, but merely a deduction from the cost of distributing net income after it had come into this country.

However, even though the case did not purport to lay down any general principle in respect of trust expenses of administration generally, its practical effect is that such expenses will not ever be deductible for basic rate tax purposes, simply because they could never be expenses of earning the relevant income.

### Trustees not Receiving Income

The principle that trustees are charged tax simply because they receive income seems to have the corollary that, if the trustees do not receive the income, but the income rather accrues directly to a beneficiary, the

[1] At p308.
[2] At 308–309. Compare Lord McLaren at p309.
[3] At p309.
[4] At p310.

trustees are not liable to income tax. The authority for this proposition is *Williams v Singer*[1]. In this case, the trustees were resident in the United Kingdom but the trust income in question was derived from shares in an American company. The trustees were the registered owners of the shares, and they gave instructions to the Bank of British North America, in New York, to collect and receive the dividends on the shares and to credit them to the account of the beneficiary at the said bank in New York. No part of the dividends was at any time remitted to, or received in, this country and the beneficiary was at all material times resident and domiciled outside the United Kingdom. Since the beneficiary (being non-domiciled and not having remitted any income to the United Kingdom) could not be taxed on the income, the Revenue sought to tax the trustees. The Revenue relied on the first general rule in s100 of the Income Tax Act 1842 which, like s21(1) of the ICTA 1988, charged tax on the persons "receiving or entitled unto" such profits, and argued that, since the income in the case "accrued" to the trustees as the legal holders of the investments, and the trustees were the persons legally entitled "to receive" the income, they were the persons chargeable under the Act. The Revenue claimed that they were entitled to look to those trustees for the tax and were neither bound nor entitled to look beyond the legal ownership. It was held that the trustees were not liable to tax on the income, because they had received no part of it. Viscount Cave LC said[2] that the trustees, who had directed the trust income to be paid to the beneficiaries, and who had themselves received no part of it, were not assessable to tax in respect of such income. Lord Phillimore said[3] that the trustees in this case merely existed in order to preserve the settlement. Their duty so long as the beneficiary remained alive was to see that the dividends reached her. Although they in law were entitled to the dividends, the person "entitled" within the meaning of the relevant statutory provisions, and the person to whom they "belonged" within the meaning of the provisions was the beneficiary. This case indicates that the person "entitled" to receive income is not necessarily the person in whom the legal title vests.

In cases in which a trustee has directed income to be forwarded directly to a beneficiary or to an agent of the beneficiary, the only duty imposed upon the trustee is in s76 TMA 1970. S76(1) TMA 1970 requires the trustee to make a return of the name, address and profits of the person to whom the payment was directed to be made.

[1] [1921] 1 AC 65; 7 TC at 387.
[2] 7 TC, at p412.
[3] At p418.

*The "Rate Applicable to Trusts"*

As seen earlier, because trustees (not being "individuals") are not liable to higher rate tax, trusts provide planning opportunities for those in higher income brackets, whereby income-producing assets could be settled, the income taxed at the trustee's (basic) rate, left to accumulate, and finally be distributed as capital. The attraction of such planning has been reduced (but not eliminated) by the imposition of a special tax rate on the income of certain trusts. This special rate is known as the "rate applicable to trusts". [1] S686(1A) of the ICTA 1988 (as amended by s54(3) of the FA 1997) provides that the rate applicable to trusts, in relation to any year of assessment for which income tax is charged, shall be 34 per cent or such other rate as Parliament may determine.

The rate applicable to trusts currently in force still amounts to a few percent below the higher rate of tax. This means that it may still be profitable for people with high incomes who possess income-yielding properties to settle such properties on trusts which will attract the rate applicable to trusts.

S686(2) specifies the situation in which the rate applicable to trusts applies. The first condition is that the trust income is income which is to be accumulated or which is payable at the discretion of the trustees or any other person (whether or not the trustees have the power to accumulate the income). [2] The second condition is that the income is not, before being distributed, either the income of any person other than the trustees, or treated as the income of a settlor for any of the purposes of the Income Tax Acts. [3] In short, the rate applicable to trusts applies to accumulation and discretionary trusts in circumstances wherein the income, while remaining with the trustees, is treated only as that of the trustees. Exception is made in respect of income arising under trusts established for charitable purposes only, and to income from investments, deposits or property held for the purposes of certain specified retirement benefit schemes and personal pension schemes. [4] The revenue expenses of the trustees are deductible for the purposes of the rate applicable to trusts. [5]

---

[1] Another special rate, known as "The Schedule F Trust Rate" similarly applies in respect of income which is Schedule F – type income. This rate is effective in relation to distributions made on or after 6 April 1999. See FA (no.2) 1997, S32.

[2] S686(2)(a).

[3] S686(2)(c).

[4] S686(2)(c).

[5] S686(2)(d).

It has been seen that one of the conditions for the rate applicable to trusts is that the trust income is income which is to be accumulated or which is payable at the discretion of the trustees. For these purposes, it is not necessary for the trustees to be under a duty to accumulate. It suffices that they have a power to accumulate the income. In *IRC v Berrill*[1] the trustees of a settlement were directed to hold the income for the settlor's son. The trustees had an overriding power, during the beneficiary's life, or for 21 years, whichever was the shorter, to accumulate the whole or part of the trust income and to hold such accumulations as an accretion to capital. The trustees having exercised the power to accumulate, the Revenue assessed them to tax at the additional rate (now the rate applicable to trusts). The taxpayers argued that the language of s686(2) which describes the income arising to trustees which is to be subject to additional rate tax, is wholly inapt to include income arising to trustees to which a beneficiary is entitled subject to a power of accumulation, because the opening words of paragraph (a), "income which is to be accumulated", are apt to describe only income which trustees are under a positive duty to accumulate. They also argued that the words "before being distributed" in paragraph (b) were apt to exclude and must have been intended to exclude from subsection (2) a trust under which income when it arises to trustees is income to which a beneficiary is entitled subject to the exercise of a power to accumulate it. They contended that the relevant contrast was between income which, when it arises, is income to which a beneficiary is entitled (albeit subject to a power to accumulate it) and income which will become the income of a beneficiary only when it is distributed in pursuance of some discretion vested in the trustees or in some other person. Vinelott J, whilst of the view that the argument was "formidable"[2] held that the trustees were indeed assessable at the additional rate. According to him,[3] the words "income ... which is payable at the discretion of the trustees" were as easily applied to income which trustees have power to withhold from a beneficiary entitled in default of the exercise of the power, as they were to income which they have power to apply or which they are bound to apply pursuant to a mandatory discretionary trust. He said that while it is true that the words "whether or not the trustees have power to accumulate it" do not fit naturally the case where the discretion consists of a power to withhold

---

[1] [1981] 55 TC 429; [1981] STC 784.
[2] 55 TC at 441.
[3] At p443.

income by accumulating it, that inelegance of expression did not afford a ground for departing from what appeared to be the plain intention of the legislature. He accepted the Revenue's argument that the purpose of subsection (2)(a) is to describe in general terms the income to which subsection (2) is intended to apply, and that subsection (2)(b), (c) and (d) are particular savings or exceptions from that general description. [1]

The rate applicable to trusts also applies in situations where infant beneficiaries have contingent interests and s31 Trustee Act 1925 applies, whereby the trustees may apply the income for their maintenance. Finally, the trustees of a discretionary trust may be subject to a further charge to tax under s687 when they make a distribution of income to a beneficiary. This charge will arise where the rate of income tax is higher in the year of distribution than it was in the year when the income arose to the trustees. The section applies where in any year of assessment trustees make a payment to any person "in the exercise of a discretion" (whether the discretion is exercisable by them or by another person) in circumstances wherein the income is, by virtue of the payment only, the income of the recipient for all the purposes of the Income Tax Acts, or is treated as the income of the settlor by s660B. [2] By virtue of s687(2), the amount paid will be treated as a net amount corresponding to a gross amount from which tax has been deducted at the rate applicable to trusts for the year in which the payment is made. The tax which is deemed to have been deducted will be treated as tax paid by the recipient (or where appropriate, by the settlor), and will be treated as income tax assessable on the trustees. The trustees will be entitled to credit for the tax already borne by them at the time when the income arose, and to some other specified deductions. [3] Obviously, if there is no difference between the tax rates applicable in the year in which the income arose and those applicable in the year in which the payment was made, the section would have no real bite. Thus it is only of real importance when tax rates are increasing.

## The Charge on Beneficiaries

Trust income which has accrued to trustees would normally have suffered tax either by deduction at source before payment to the trustees, or in the hands of the trustees. Thereafter, either there will be beneficiaries entitled

[1] *Ibid.*
[2] S687(1).
[3] See generally, s687(3).

to the income, or the trustees will exercise a discretion to accumulate, or distribute the income among beneficiaries. The taxability of a beneficiary depends on whether or not he or she has a vested right in the trust income.

## Vested Rights

Income to which a beneficiary is entitled forms part of his total income, whether or not he receives it from the trustee. This is because the income "belongs" to the beneficiary, not to the trustee. The leading case is *Baker v Archer-Shee*.[1] In this case, Lady Archer-Shee had a life interest, under her father's will, in a trust estate held by trustees in the United States. The trust fund consisted of foreign stocks and shares. The dividends, as they accrued, were placed to the credit of Lady Archer-Shee's bank account in New York and were not remitted to this country. The question was whether these dividends fell to be assessed as part of the income of her husband, who was resident in the United Kingdom. It was held that, since Lady Archer-Shee was entitled to the trust income during her life, her husband was rightly assessed whether the income was remitted here or not. According to Lord Wrenbury[2], the question is not what the trustees had thought proper to hand over and had handed over (which is a question of fact) but what, under her father's will, Lady Archer-Shee was entitled to (which is a question of law). Even though the trustees had a first charge upon the trust funds for their costs, charges and expenses, the fund still belonged to the beneficiary. Lord Carson concurring, said

> In my opinion upon the construction of the will of [Lady Archer-Shee's father] once the residue had become specifically ascertained, the Respondent's wife was sole beneficial owner of the interest and dividends of all the securities, stocks and shares forming part of the trust fund therein settled and was entitled to receive and did receive such interest and dividends. This, I think, follows from the decision of this House in *Williams v Singer* . . . and in my opinion the Master of the Rolls correctly stated the law when he said "that when you are considering sums which are placed in the hands of trustees for the purpose of paying income to beneficiaries, for the purposes of the Income Tax Acts you may eliminate the trustees. The income is the income of the beneficiaries; the income does not belong to the trustees".[3]

[1]  11 TC 749; [1927] AC 844.
[2]  11 TC at 778-779.
[3]  11 TC 749 at p782.

The principle established here is that a beneficiary who is entitled to trust income is taxable on it in the year in which it arises, because it is his income. Thus there is liability even on undistributed income. The rate applicable to trusts will not apply even if income is accumulated because the income "before distribution" belongs to someone other than the trustees, i.e. the beneficiary.

The rule established in *Baker v Archer-Shee* applies only where two conditions are fulfilled. First, that the beneficiary has a vested interest, and, secondly, that the beneficiary's interest is not liable to be divested, i.e. it is indefeasible. The rule will not apply where the beneficiary's interest is contingent, or where the interest can be divested. This latter principle is illustrated by *Cornwell v Barry*[1] in which funds were held in trust for settlor's grandchildren then living, or born during the eight year life of the settlement, for their, his or her absolute use and benefit. During the period, there was only one child. A claim was made in respect of personal reliefs and allowances on behalf of the child, on the ground that, as he was the only child living, the trustee was required during those years to hold the income as and when received upon trust for the child absolutely. It was held that the child's interest, if vested, was liable to be divested. His interest was defeasible because more children could have been born during those eight years, and thus the claim failed. Harman J said[2] that any child either in existence when the deed was made or coming into existence during the eight years thereafter was an object of the trust. He rejected the argument of the taxpayer that, so long as there is only one child who fulfills any of those qualifications, he is entitled to the whole income as and when received, and it is indefeasibly his. This, according to Harman J, would be an entirely mistaken view of the trust, because

> ... [t]he Trustee is to look not only at the child in existence but any child who may come into existence, and during the eight years he is not bound, as I see it, to make any application of the money at all. He would if he were a reasonable man, but he is not bound to. It is quite true that the trust is for the absolute use and benefit of these children, but it is in such shares and in such manner as the Trustee thinks fit. Consequently, he has the eight years in which to make up his mind. He may during that time divide it into shares or give it all to one or other of the objects of the trust, and even if at any time during the eight years

---

[1] [1955] 36 TC 268.
[2] At p274.

there were no object of the trust, he would still, in my view, have to hold the money in case, before the end of the period, an object should come into being. Consequently, though it may well be, and I think is, the fact that [the child] being in existence had got a vested interest in this money, it was an interest which was liable to be divested if another object of the trust came into existence during the eight years. It is not until the end of this time that you could say: The class is closed; the object is achieved; and the money, if there be any unapplied, vests absolutely in any of the persons who were objects of the trust, and whether then dead or then living matters not. [1]

### Grossing Up

The income to which the beneficiary is entitled would have suffered tax in the trustee's hands. In order to ascertain the amount which will enter into computation for the beneficiary's total income, the income would fall to be grossed up in order to reflect basic rate tax paid by the trustees. Depending on the beneficiary's circumstances, he may either be liable to higher rate tax on the trust income, or be entitled to a refund. The formula for grossing up the income is as follows:

$$\frac{\text{Payment}}{1} \times \frac{100}{100 - \text{Rate of Tax}}$$

The gross amount will, however, not necessarily be the same as the income accruing to the trustees. This is due to the decision of the Court of Session in *Macfarlane v IRC*[2] where it was held that although trust expenses are not deductible in the trustees' hands in computing the trustee's income they are deductible in the trustees' hands in computing the beneficiary's income. In this case the taxpayer had made a claim to the Revenue for repayment of income tax on the basis that the whole of the income of the trust estates was his income, without any deduction in either case in respect of the expenses of management of the estates (i.e. that he was liable to income tax in respect of the part of the income of the trust estate which was expended upon the administration of the trust, so as to yield a higher repayment of tax). The Revenue argued that the taxpayer's income was only the net income remaining after deduction of

---

[1] *Ibid.* See also *Stanley v IRC*, 26 TC 12; [1944] 1 All ER 230.
[2] [1929] 14 TC 532.

the expenses of management of the trust estates. The Revenue's argument was upheld. Lord Sands said[1] that the primary aspect of the matter was not one of abatement or exemption but of initial liability. He said that the argument of the taxpayer involved the contention that he was liable to income tax in respect of income which he did not handle and could not under any arrangement handle, which was not expended under any authority conferred by him, and over the expenditure of which he had no control. Lord Blackburn said[2] that, on the true construction of the trust deed, the income to which the beneficiary was entitled was no more than the amount of the income of the trust funds which may be available after the expenses of the trust had been paid.[3]

Thus a beneficiary is worse off because he ends up with a lower tax credit, as the following example shows.

The trustees receive income amounting to £100. They incur £20 expenses in managing the trust. Since this £20 is not deductible in their hands in computing their own tax liability, they pay tax on the full £100. Assuming a basic rate of 23 per cent, they pay £23 in tax, and have £77 left for distribution. Because the £20 is deductible in their hands in computing the beneficiary's income, they deduct it, and have £57 left for distribution to the beneficiary. This amount is grossed up at the basic rate;

$$57 \times \frac{100}{77} = £74.02$$

The tax credit is: £74.02−£57 = £17.02

Since the total income coming into the trust has suffered £23 in tax, a tax credit of just £17.02 leaves the taxpayer out of pocket.

## Annuities

Where the beneficiary is entitled to an annuity under a trust, he is not entitled to the trust income as it arises, and the rule in *Baker v Archer-Shee* does not apply. The annuity will fall to be taxed under Case III of Schedule D. The Finance Act 1988 provisions, which render annual

---

[1] At p540.
[2] *Ibid.*
[3] See also *Elizabeth Murray v IRC*, 11 TC 133.

payments by individuals ineffective, do not apply to take the payments out of the tax scheme because the trustees are not "individuals".

## No Vested Rights

Typical cases in which beneficiaries do not have vested interests in trust income involve discretionary and accumulation trusts. A beneficiary under a discretionary or accumulation trust cannot be taxed unless he receives the income, since he is not entitled to anything. If and when a payment is made to the beneficiary, the income would fall to be classified as an annual payment under Schedule D Case III.

## Contingent Rights: Trustee Act 1925, Section 31

Where beneficiaries have contingent rights to income, the rule in *Baker v Archer-Shee* cannot apply simply because the contingency which will entitle them to income may never happen. This will be the case where s31 of the Trustee Act 1925 applies. S31 relates to trusts for infant beneficiaries. In subsection (1), it provides that, where any property is held by trustees in trust for any person, whether that person's interest is vested or contingent, the trustees may (at their sole discretion), during the infancy of such person, pay or apply the whole or part of the income produced by the trust property for his maintenance, education or benefit. The trustees have the discretion regardless of whether any other fund exists for the same purpose, and regardless of whether there is any person bound by law to provide for the infant beneficiary's maintenance or education. [1] The trustees are obliged by s31(2) to accumulate the residue of the income during the beneficiary's infancy. The power to apply the income for the infant's education, maintenance or benefit is subject to any prior interests or charges affecting the settled property. [2] The effect of s31 of the Trustee Act 1925 is to convert all trusts in which an infant has an interest (which interest is not dependent on that of an adult) into an accumulation and maintenance trust in the sense that any income which is not spent on the maintenance or education of the infant must be accumulated.

If the beneficiary, on attaining the age of 18, does not have a vested interest in the income, the trustees are directed to pay the income from the trust property and the income from any accretions thereto to the beneficiary, until he dies, or his interest fails, or he attains a vested interest

[1] Trustee Act 1925, s31(1)(a) and s31(1)(b).
[2] S31(1).

in the income.[1] This means that if a beneficiary only had a contingent interest during his infancy, he will, on attaining the age of 18, be entitled only to the income from the accretions and not to the accretions themselves. On the other hand, if the beneficiary attains the age of 18 years or marries under that age, and the beneficiary had a vested interest in the income until either event, then the trustees are to hold all accumulations in trust for that beneficiary absolutely.[2] The same principle applies where, on attaining the age of 18 or on marriage below that age, the beneficiary becomes entitled to the settled property from which the income arises.[3] In any other case (for example where a beneficiary dies below 18 years), the trustees must hold the accumulations as an accretion to the capital of the settled property.

A number of things follow from these provisions. First, even in cases where an infant beneficiary has a vested interest in trust income, he will not be liable to income tax on any undistributed income. The income is not his own because, although he has a vested interest, his right to receive income is contingent or subject to being divested if he fails to attain majority. This is because, by virtue of s31(2), the accumulations will be added to capital in that event, and will not go to his estate. If he eventually reaches 18 and the accumulations are paid to him, they will by then have become capital in nature. The leading case is *Stanley v IRC*.[4] In this case an infant had vested interests in certain estates under his father's will. The trustees accumulated the surplus income which was not applied for his maintenance, and when he attained majority, he became absolutely entitled to those accumulations. The Revenue sought to tax him for the years of his infancy. The real question concerned the precise interest in surplus income which an infant having a vested interest enjoys during his infancy by virtue of the provisions in s31. The Revenue's contention was that the infant had a vested interest in the surplus income as it accrued and that there was nothing in s31 which deprived him of that interest during infancy. Rather, all that the section did was to divest him of his title to the accumulations of surplus income if he died before attaining his majority. In other words, an infant has a vested interest in the accumulations, which interest is defeasible in the event of his dying before majority. The Court of Appeal rejected these arguments and held that the income was not the infant's income at the time that he should have been assessed to tax on it. The reason for this was that by s31 of the Trustee Act

---

[1] S31(1)(ii).
[2] S31(2)(i)(a).
[3] S31(2)(i)(b).
[4] [1944] 26 TC 12; [1944] 1 All ER 230.

1925, if he had not attained majority, the accumulations would never have been his, but would have been added to capital which would go to the remainderman. Lord Greene MR said:

> The infant does not during infancy enjoy the surplus income. It is not his in any real sense. The title to it is held in suspense to await the event and if he dies under [the age of 18] his interest in it (whether or not it be truly described as a vested interest) is destroyed. He is in fact for all practical purposes in precisely the same position if his interest in surplus income were contingent. If he attains [the age of 18] he takes the accumulations, if he dies under [the age of 18] he does not . . . We are disposed to think that the effect of the Section is better described not as leaving the interest of the infant as a vested interest subject to defeasance, but as engrafting upon the vested interest originally conferred on the infant by the settlement or other disposition a qualifying trust of a special nature which confers on the infant a title to the accumulations if and only if he attains [the age of 18] or marries. The words in Subsection (2)(i)(a), if "his interest . . . during his infancy or until his marriage is a vested interest", and the corresponding words in Subsection (2)(ii), "notwithstanding that such person had a vested interest in such income", appear to us to refer to the nature of the interest conferred upon the infant by the settlement or other disposition, and not to affirm that the interest of the infant in the surplus income remains a vested interest notwithstanding the alteration in his rights effected by the Section. If this view is right, the interest of the Appellant in the surplus income during his minority was a contingent. [1]

Thus, the effect of s31 of the Trustee Act 1925 is to make the infant's interest in the surplus income accruing during his infancy a contingent interest only—it prevents an infant from having an indefeasible vested interest in the income of the trust fund (i.e. until something is paid, nothing is an infant's income, no matter what his interest is in the trust property). However, if an infant who does not have a vested interest in the settled property receives income from the trustees, or if amounts are applied for his education, maintenance or benefit, then the infant becomes liable to tax on those payments. S687 will apply, and the amount of the payment (grossed up at the rate applicable to trusts) will enter into the computation of his total income.

[1] At p19.

In cases wherein a beneficiary has an interest in income, which interest is contingent upon his attaining an age in excess of 18 (e.g. "to S when he is 30 years old"), s31(1)(ii) provides that the trustees should pay the income (from the trust fund and from the accretions to the fund) to him on attaining 18. This means that, on attaining majority, the beneficiary obtains an indefeasible vested right in the income and he will be liable to tax in respect of that income whether or not he receives it. This is illustrated by *IRC v Hamilton-Russell*.[1] The trustees in this case were directed to hold funds and income for the beneficiary upon his attaining 21. The beneficiary attained 21 in 1928, became the sole beneficiary under the settlement and thereupon became entitled to call for the transfer of all the trust funds and the accumulations thereof to himself. He did not do so, but allowed the trustees to receive the income from the trust fund and the accumulation fund, and to continue investing the income, until early in 1939. The beneficiary's executors argued that, although as the sole beneficiary under those trusts he could have legally determined them, he did not in fact do so. Consequently the income did not become his, but was accumulated under the trusts, and turned into capital before the trusts were determined. The Court of Appeal however held that the income belonged to the beneficiary from the time he attained 21 and was assessable to income tax. Luxmoore LJ said[2] that the trust became unenforceable as soon as the specified event occurred. The trustees could at any time after the happening of that event, even though asked by the beneficiary to continue the accumulations, have refused to do so, and, in the same way, the beneficiary could, contrary to the wishes of the trustees, have insisted on a transfer to himself of the whole of the trust funds. According to Luxmoore LJ, the reason why the trusts then became unenforceable and ineffective was because the funds were "at home" and belonged solely to the beneficiary for his own absolute use and benefit. The capital and income were his and no one else was interested in them: if the income was left in the hands of the trustees, and they invested it, they only did so by the sufferance of the beneficiary whose income it was.

## Payments Out of Capital

The general rule in respect of payments out of capital is that, when trust income has been capitalised, it retains that character when paid out to the beneficiaries, and is not liable to income tax. However, where the trustees

[1] [1943] 25 TC 200; [1943] 1 All ER 474.
[2] 25 TC at p208.

have to pay an annuity, with power to supplement the payments with payment out of capital, the situation may be different, and payments made out of capital in such cases may be income in the recipient's hands. The principle is that the situation depends on the rights of the recipient, not the source of the payments. In *Brodie's Will Trustees v IRC*[1] the testator directed the trustees to pay the income from certain trust property to his widow during her life. He wished that the payments would not be less than £4,000 per annum and therefore directed that, should trust income be deficient in any year to pay up to this sum, recourse should be had to capital to make up the deficiency. During a number of tax years, the trustees made payments to the widow of varying amounts out of the capital of the estate, in order to make up that sum each year. It was held that the payments were income in the hands of the widow and were taxable under Case III of Schedule D, even though they were paid out of capital. Finlay J said[2]

> . . . if payments out of capital are made, and made in such a form that they come into the hands of the beneficiaries as income, it seems to me that they are income, and not the less income because the source from which they came was in the hand, not of the person receiving them, but in the hands of somebody else, capital.

Finlay J said[3] that, if the capital belonged to the beneficiary or if he was beneficially entitled to both the income and capital of the trust, then the payments out of capital would have been capital in his hands. In *Cunard's Trustees v IRC*[4] trustees held a fund on trust to pay the income thereof to the testatrix's sister. The will further provided that, if in any year the income of the trust fund was insufficient to enable the sister to live at the testatrix's residence in the same degree of comfort as during the testatrix's lifetime, the trustees were empowered to resort to the capital of the testatrix's residuary estate to make up any deficiency in the trust income. The trustees paid sums out of capital to the sister in two years of assessment. The Court of Appeal held that the payments were income in the hands of the beneficiary. Lord Green MR said[5] that the sister's title to the income arose when the trustees exercised their discretion in her

---

[1]  17 TC 432.
[2]  At p439.
[3]  17 TC 432 at 439.
[4]  [1945] 27 TC 122; [1946] 1 All ER 159.
[5]  27 TC at p132.

favour and not before, and that at that moment a new source of income came into existence. The fact that they were made out of capital was irrelevant. The payments were to be made "by way of addition to the income" in order to enable the sister to live in the same degree of comfort as before. The testatrix was in fact providing for a defined standard of life for her sister, that provision being made in part out of income and in part (at the discretion of the trustees) out of capital. According to Lord Greene MR, the purpose of the payments was an income purpose and nothing else [1] and the payments were therefore income.

This type of reasoning led the Revenue to argue in *Stevenson v Wishart* [2] that any payment out of capital, which is made for an income purpose, is income in the beneficiary's hands. In this case, properties were transferred by the settlor into discretionary trusts on behalf of (*inter alia*) his mother-in-law (Mrs H). The trustees made a series of payments totalling £109,000 out of the capital of the fund to meet Mrs H's medical and nursing home expenses before her death. The Revenue claimed that the payments, being recurrent sums paid out of capital for the maintenance of a beneficiary, were for an "income purpose" and therefore constituted the income of the beneficiary for tax purposes. The argument was rejected. The Court of Appeal held that, although payments by trustees out of capital could be income in the beneficiary's hands, it was not sufficient that the payments were either periodic, for educational purposes, or for personal maintenance. The payments involved in this case, although recurrent, were of substantial amounts that were outside normal income resources, did not create an income interest, and were of capital nature. Fox LJ said

> ... there is nothing in the present case which indicates that the payments were of an income nature except their recurrence. I do not think that is sufficient. The trustees were disposing of capital in exercise of a power over capital. They did not create a recurring interest in property. If, in exercise of a power over capital, they chose to make at their discretion regular payments of capital to deal with the specific problems of [Mrs H's] last years rather than release a single sum to her of a large amount that does not seem to me to create an income interest. Their power was to capital what they appointed remained capital. [3]

[1] At p133.
[2] [1987] 59 TC 720; [1987] STC 266; [1987] 1 WLR 1204.
[3] At p765.

It is thus clear that neither regularity nor recurrence is a conclusive factor, and the courts have to look at the whole set of circumstances.

## Settlements

*Introduction*

We have seen earlier in our discussions about trusts the planning opportunities which are presented by the devices of trusts and covenants. A person who wishes or who is obliged to provide another person with an income, or with a source of income may do so in one of many ways. First he may simply transfer the sum of money, either in a lump sum or periodically, and without any legal formalities. This is a simple transfer of assets. Each such transfer is entirely voluntary and is in law nothing more than a mere gift. Secondly, he may execute a deed or other type of legal instrument transferring part of his income. This may be referred to as an income settlement—it enables the donor to retain the source from which the income flows (the tree), while giving away the income itself (the fruit). While the execution of the instrument transferring the money may have been voluntary, a legal obligation may arise under the instrument, and the payments thereunder may be legally due. Thirdly, he may transfer income-producing capital assets to trustees to pay the income generated thereby for the benefit of the objects. This is known as a capital settlement, because the donor gives away the capital out of which the income is to be made (the tree—and by the same token, the fruit which it produces). The first method (voluntary gifts) would not normally be tax efficient, and would in most cases attract no income tax consequences. Little planning can be achieved in this way. On the other hand, income and capital settlements inherently contain tax planning opportunities, especially for those in large income brackets. Income or capital may be settled for one's children or grandchildren (who one would normally be obliged to maintain) to take advantage of their personal reliefs and/or low tax rates, and to reduce one's total income from high tax brackets to lower ones.

The tax system's response to the planning opportunities has been two-fold. First, to introduce a different rate of tax (the rate applicable to trusts) for certain types of trusts (see above) and, secondly, to introduce anti-avoidance legislation in Part XV of the ICTA 1988, in respect of arrangements described as "settlements". All three methods of parting with one's income or property described above may well fall within the scope of these anti-avoidance provisions. The Finance Act 1988 has rendered new income settlements largely ineffective by disallowing the deduction of annual payments made by individuals, and so the real choice now for new arrangements is whether or not to settle capital. The discussion that follows analyses the anti-avoidance principles relating to the taxation of settlements.

### "Settlement"

S660(G)(1) ICTA 1988 defines settlement to include any disposition, trust, covenant, agreement, arrangement, or transfer of assets. This is a very wide definition, which would cover almost all types of transaction that a person may engage in—including the type of voluntary gifts referred to above. A number of cases provide illustrations. In *Thomas v Marshall*[1] a father opened Post Office Savings Bank accounts for his children, and transferred certain sums into those accounts by way of absolute and unconditional gifts. He also gave each child £1,000 in three percent defence bonds. The interest on the bank accounts and on the bonds were treated by the Revenue as his income for tax purposes. The taxpayer, while conceding that each of the relevant gifts might be described as a transfer of assets, if the phrase were to be given its ordinary meaning, argued that, since the word "settlement" was the only word used in the charging provision, it was "the dominant word", and a transaction does not come within the provision unless it was "something in the nature of a settlement". Thus, a transaction which might ordinarily be described as a transfer of assets did not come within the section unless, either it was accompanied by some restraint on alienation, such as would subject the transferee to some action at law or in equity if be attempted to alienate the subject of the gift, or, the income and the capital of the subject of the gift were given to different persons, or, the legal title and the equitable interest in the subject of the gift were conferred on different persons. The House of Lords however held that there was nothing in the context which should lead the courts to give the words "transfer of assets" any meaning other than that which they ordinarily bore, or to infuse into them some flavour of the meaning ordinarily given to the word "settlement".[2] Thus, the absolute gifts to the children were settlements. Similarly, in *Hoods-Barrs v IRC*[3] the taxpayer transferred a block of shares to each of his two infant

[1] [1953] 34 TC 178; [1953] AC 543.
[2] See Lord Morton of Henryton at p202.
[3] 27 TC 385.

and unmarried daughters. It was held that these, as transfers of assets, were settlements and that he was liable to tax on the dividends. The argument that the phrase "transfer of assets" cannot include an absolute gift by a parent to a child was rejected by the Court of Appeal.

These cases illustrate the width of the definition given to the word "settlement" and the willingness of the courts to give certain words in the definition (particularly "transfer of assets") their ordinary (and wide) meanings. It has even been held that transfers of money can be settlements if made under compulsion (e.g. under a court order).[1] However, according to Nourse J in *IRC v Levy*[2], it has long been recognised that Parliament cannot have intended the definition of "settlement" to extend as widely as a literal reading of it might suggest. Thus, the courts have imposed a limitation on the meaning of settlement. This judicial gloss on the statutory words takes the form of a requirement of "bounty" in a transaction in order for it to constitute a settlement. This requirement was laid down by the House of Lords in *IRC v Plummer*[3]. In this case, a charity paid £2,480 to the taxpayer in return for a covenant by the taxpayer to pay it a sum of £500 each year for five years. The purpose of the scheme was to enable the taxpayer to deduct the payments and so reduce his total income for surtax purposes. The Revenue claimed that, far from being annual payments, the scheme was a settlement and the payments remained the income of the taxpayer. It was held that, because the transaction contained no element of bounty, it was not a settlement.[4] Lord Wilberforce said:

> [I]t can, I think, fairly be seen that all of these provisions [in Part XV], have a common character. They are designed to bring within the net of taxation dispositions of various kinds, in favour of a settlor's spouse, or children, or of charities, cases, in popular terminology, in which a taxpayer gives away a portion of his income, or of his assets, to such persons, or for such periods, or subject to such conditions, that Parliament considers it right to continue to treat such income, or income of the assets, as still the settlor's income. These sections, in other words, though drafted in wide, and increasingly wider language, are nevertheless dealing with a limited field—one far narrower than the field of the totality of dispositions, or arrangements, or agreements,

[1] See *Yates v Starkey* 32 TC 28; *Harvey v Sivyer* (1985) 58 TC 569.

[2] [1982] 56 TC 68 at 86.

[3] [1979] 54 TC 1; [1980] AC 896.

[4] Note that the effect of this decision has now been reversed with respect to reverse annuity schemes (see ICTA 1988 s125).

which a man may make in the course of his life. Is there then any common description which can be applied to this? The courts which, inevitably, have had to face this problem, have selected the element of "bounty" as a necessary common characteristic of all the "settlements" which Parliament has in mind. The decisions are tentative, but all point in this direction. [1]

Similarly, in *IRC v Levy*, [2] where the taxpayer made an interest-free loan to a company of which he was the sole beneficial shareholder, it was held that there was no settlement as there was no element of bounty (even though the company got something—the use of the money—for nothing). Nourse J said:

> Before a disposition, trust, covenant, agreement or arrangement can be a settlement within [s660(G)(1)] it must contain an element of bounty. For that purpose a derivative bounty of the kind conferred by the exercise of a special power of appointment may be enough. On the other hand, a commercial transaction devoid of any element of bounty is not within the definition. The absence of any correlative obligation on the part of him who is on the receiving end of the transaction may be material, but is not conclusive in determining whether it contains an element of bounty or not. [3]

The decisions on "bounty" are not necessarily inconsistent with those which held payments made under compulsion to be settlements. Cases such as *Yates v Starkey (supra)* and *Harvey v Sivyer (supra)* involved payments by parents to their own children under court orders. Nourse J suggested in *Harvey v Sivyer* [4] that it may well be that the natural relationship between parent and young child is one of such deep affection and concern that there must always be an element of bounty by the parent, even where the provision is on the face of things made under compulsion.

### *"Settlor"*

S660(G)(1) provides that a settlor is any person by whom the settlement was made. S660(G)(2) further provides that a person shall be deemed to have made a settlement if he has made or entered into it directly or

---

[1] 54 TC at p43.
[2] [1982] 56 TC 68; [1982] STC 442.
[3] 56 TC at p87.
[4] 58 TC at 577.

indirectly and, in particular, if he has provided or undertaken to provide funds directly or indirectly for the purpose of the settlement or has made with any person a reciprocal arrangement for that other person to make or enter into the settlement. The word "purpose" in this definition does not import any mental element, as *IRC v Mills*[1] shows. The taxpayer in this case was an actress. When she was 14 years old, her father, in order to make sure that her earnings were "legally protected", incorporated a company and settled the shares on trust for her absolutely on attaining the age of 25. She then signed a service contract with the company giving it the right to her exclusive services for five years at a salary of £400 a year. The bulk of the company's profits in respect of her films was distributed to the trustees as dividends. The trustees accumulated the income. It was held that the incorporation of the company, the issue and settlement of the shares therein, and the service agreement, were an arrangement which constituted a settlement. The taxpayer was the settlor, since it was her services that provided the company with funds from which to pay dividends to the trust—she had thereby indirectly provided income for the purposes of the settlement. Viscount Dilhorne said:

> I do not agree with Lord Denning M.R. that the word "purpose" in this section connotes a mental element or with Buckley L.J. that there must be a motivating intention. I do not myself think that it assists to consider whether the question he posed is to be answered objectively or subjectively. I do not consider it incumbent, in order to establish that a person is a settlor as having provided funds for the purpose of a settlement, to show that there was any element of mens rea. Where it is shown that funds have been provided for a settlement a very strong inference is to be drawn that they were provided for that purpose, an inference which will be rebutted if it is established that they were provided for another purpose.[2]

It is possible to have more than one settlor for a settlement. For example, in *IRC v Mills* the taxpayer's father was also a settlor because he had made the settlement.[3] However, where there is more than one settlor, then s660E(1) provides that the provisions shall apply to each settlor as if he were the only settlor, whereby references to property comprised in a

---

[1] [1975] 49 TC 367; [1975] AC 38.

[2] At p408.

[3] See Viscount Dilhorne at p409.

settlement would only include property originating from that settlor[1], and references to income arising under the settlement would include only income originating from that settlor.[2]

### The Basic Charge

S660A(1) provides that income arising under a settlement during the life of the settlor shall be treated for all purposes of the Income Tax Acts as the income of the settlor and not as the income of any other person, unless the income arises from property in which the settlor has no interest. From this basic charge, s660A(9) excludes income consisting of annual payments made by an individual for bona fide commercial reasons in connection with his trade, profession or vocation, and covenanted payments to charity (as defined by s347A(7)). By virtue of s660C(1), the tax charged under this Chapter will be charged under Schedule D Case VI. The settlor is entitled to the same deductions and reliefs as he would have if the income taxed here had been received by him (s660C(2)). The income is treated (subject to s833(3)) as the highest part of the settlor's income (s660C(3)). The settlor is entitled to reclaim tax paid under this provision from the trustee or any other person to whom the income is payable (s660D(1)). Where there are two or more settlors, s660E provides for apportionments to be made.

### Retaining Interest

We have seen that the general charge under Part XV does not apply in respect of income arising from property in which the settlor has no interest. In what circumstances does a person retain an interest in property for these purposes? S660A(2) provides (subject to the rest of the section) that, a settlor shall be regarded as having interest in property, if that property, or any derived property is, or will, or may become payable to or applicable for the benefit of the settlor or the settlor's spouse in any circumstances whatsoever. "Derived property" is defined by s660A(10) as being, in relation to any property, income from that property or any other property directly or indirectly representing proceeds of, or of income from, that property or income therefrom.

However, there are some permitted interests and, by virtue of s660A(4),

---

[1]  s660E(2)(a).
[2]  s660E(2)(b).

the settlor will not be regarded as having an interest in property if the property can only be payable to or applied for the benefit of the settlor or the settlor's spouse in the event of

1. the bankruptcy of any person who is or may become beneficially entitled to the property or any derived property, or
2. an assignment of or charge on the property or any derived property being made or given by some such person, or
3. in the case of a marriage settlement, the death of both parties to the marriage and of all or any of the children of the marriage, or
4. the death of a child of the settlor who had become beneficially entitled to the property or any derived property at an age not exceeding 25.

S660A(5) also provides another exception—that, a settlor will not be regarded as having an interest in property if and so long as some person is alive and under the age of 25, during whose life the property concerned or any derived property cannot be payable to the settlor or the settlor's spouse, except in the event of that person becoming bankrupt or assigning or charging his interest in the property or any derived property.

For these purposes, the "spouse" of the settlor does not include a person to whom the settlor is not married but who he may later marry. [1] The term also does not include a spouse from whom the settlor is separated, under a court order, or under a separation agreement, or in such circumstances that the separation is likely to be permanent. [2] Finally, it does not include the widow or widower of the settlor. [3]

### Gifts Between Spouses

We have referred earlier to the suggestion of Nourse J in *Harvey v Sivyer* that the natural relationship between parent and young child is one of such deep affection and concern that there must always be an element of bounty by the parent. It may well be thought that the same goes for the natural relationship between spouses. In order to prevent the situation which may otherwise arise that gifts between spouses will be treated as settlements, these anti-avoidance provisions provide some relief for transfers of property between married couples. S660A(6) provides that the

[1] S660(3)(a).
[2] S660(3)(b).
[3] S660(3)(c).

reference in s660A(1) to a settlement does not include an outright gift by one spouse to the other, of the property from which the income arises, unless either the gift does not carry a right to the whole of that income, or the property given is wholly or substantially a right to income. "Outright gift" is defined by exclusion. For these purposes, a gift is not an outright gift if it is subject to conditions, or if the property given or any derived property is or will or may become payable to or applicable for the benefit of the donor in any circumstances whatsoever. S660A(7) also excludes from the scope of the meaning of settlement an irrevocable allocation of pension rights by one spouse to another in accordance with the terms of a relevant statutory scheme, and s660A(8) excludes income arising under a settlement made by one party to a marriage by way of provision for the other, either after the dissolution of the marriage, or while they are separated under an order of a court, or under a separation agreement or in such circumstances that the separation is likely to be permanent.

### Unmarried Minor Children of the Settlor (s660B)

The lenient treatment given to spouses does not extend to unmarried young children of the settlor. Thus, there is a residual charge in respect of income paid to an unmarried minor child of the settlor during the settlor's life. Where the income arising under a settlement has not been treated as the settlor's income under s660A, and it is then paid to an unmarried minor child of the settlor during the settlor's life, the income so paid is treated for all the purposes of the Income Tax Acts as the income of the settlor and not as the income of any other person.[1] An exemption is provided in s660B(5) in respect of income paid to a child in a year in which the aggregate amount paid to that child does not exceed £100.

For the purposes of this residual charge, "child" is defined to include a step child and an illegitimate child.[2] "Minor" means a person under the age of 18, and references to "payments" include payments in money or money's worth.[3]

The provision is widened to cover possible payments out of capital (in cases where trust income has been accumulated), for which purpose s660B(2) provides that, where income arising under a settlement is retained or accumulated by the trustees, any payment whatsoever made thereafter by virtue or in consequence of the settlement to an unmarried

[1]  s660B(1).
[2]  s660B(6)(a)
[3]  s660B(6)(c)

minor child of the settlor shall be treated as a payment of income to the extent that there is available retained or accumulated income. For this purpose s660B(3) deems that there is available retained or accumulated income if the aggregate of the income which has arisen under the settlement since it was made is more than the aggregate of any income so arising, which has been

1. treated as the income of the settlor or a beneficiary, or
2. paid (whether as income or capital) to or for the benefit of a beneficiary other than an unmarried minor child of the settlor, or
3. applied in defraying any of the trustees' expenses which were properly chargeable to income, or would have so been but for any express provision of the trust.

### Capital Sums Paid to the Settlor (s677)

S677(1) provides that any capital sum paid to the settlor by the trustees of a settlement shall be treated as the settlor's income, to the extent that it falls within the amount of available income of the year of payment and up to the next ten years. Any sum which is treated as the settlor's income under this section is grossed up at the rate applicable to trusts [1] in order to ascertain the amount that would enter into the calculation of his total income. Tax is charged under Schedule D Case VI, and credit is given for tax at the rate applicable to trusts, or the tax charged on the grossed up sum, whichever is less. [2] The provisions apply equally to capital sums received by the settlor from a body corporate connected with the settlement. [3]

By s677(9), "capital sum" means any sum paid by way of loan or repayment of a loan, and any other sum paid otherwise than as income, which is not paid for full consideration in money or money's worth. The definition excludes sums which could not have become payable except in one of the events mentioned in s673(3), but a sum paid to the settlor includes sums paid to the settlor's spouse, or to the settlor or the settlor's spouse jointly with another person. [4] Also included within the scope of sums paid to the settlor are sums paid by the trustees to a third party at the settlor's direction, or by virtue of assignment by the settlor of his right to receive it, if the assignment was on or after 6 April 1981; and, any sum

[1]  S677(6)
[2]  S677(7).
[3]  s678.
[4]  S677(9)(b).

which is otherwise paid or applied by the trustees for the benefit of the settlor.

For the purposes of s677(1), s677(2) provides that, "available income", in respect of a capital sum paid in a year, is the aggregate of the income arising in the year and the income of previous years, to the extent that such income has not been distributed. Thus the concept is linked to income which the trustees have accumulated. Certain deductions from these sums are available in arriving at the amount of available income— for example sums which have already been treated as the income of the settlor for tax purposes, and an amount equal to tax at the rate applicable to trusts on the aggregate of undistributed income which has already been treated as the settlor's income. [1]

Where the capital sum paid to the settlor was by way of a loan, and he repays the whole of the loan, no part of it shall be treated as his income for any year subsequent to the year of repayment. [2]

The moral of the anti-avoidance provisions is that the settlor should create a capital settlement in which he has completely divested himself of all interest in the settled property. He should also ensure that neither himself, nor his spouse, nor any of his unmarried infant children can or do receive any money from the trustees of that settlement.

### *Self-Check Questions*

1. In what circumstances will the rate applicable to trusts apply?
2. What is the significance of the rule in *Baker v Archer-Shee*?
3. Discuss the effect of s31 of the Trustee Act 1925 on the taxation of a beneficiary.
4. In what circumstances will payments out of capital be income in a beneficiary's hands?
5. What is a "settlement" for the purposes of Part XV ICTA 1988?
6. Discuss the various heads of charge under Part XV ICTA 1988.

## **Further Reading**

Stopforth D, *The First Attack on Settlements Used for Income Tax Avoidance*, (1991) BTR 86–103.
Stopforth D, *Settlements and the Avoidance of Tax on Income—the Period to 1920*, (1990) BTR 225–250.

[1] See generally, s677(2).
[2] S677(4).

# Part Three — Capital Gains Tax

# 10

# Chargeable Persons and Activities

## Introduction

From the introduction of direct taxation in the late 18th century until 1962, profits or gains of a capital nature fell largely outside the direct taxation schemes. The "all or nothing" principle governing the taxation of a particular gain, depending on whether it was a gain of an income nature, or a capital gain, meant that the question whether a particular payment was income or capital in the hands of the recipient was of paramount importance. If the payment was of an income nature it was taxable in its entirety (with due allowance for various statutory reliefs) at what used to be very high rates. If, on the other hand, the payment was of a capital nature, no part of it was taxable. This understandably encouraged a thriving tax avoidance industry, and led to artificial attempts to convert what in a straightforward transaction would have been income, into capital.

However, the feeling eventually began to take root that there was no sound reason why capital profits should not be taxed. Apart from the argument that the absence of a tax on capital gains contributes to the course of inflation, [1] there was the view that the question whether a particular profit should be taxed at all should not depend on whether it happened to have been labelled income or capital (especially when the assignment of such label was sometimes a "spin of a coin" affair). A profit is a profit, regardless of its nature, and if one type of profit were to be taxed, the same should apply to other types. A simple example suffices. Let us suppose that X and Y each had a sum of £500,000 to invest. X sets up a business with his money, or puts it into high interest accounts. The profits of either option would attract tax. Suppose that Y, on the other hand, buys a nice country estate with his money, lives in it for a few years, and then sells it at a huge profit. This profit, being capital in nature, would escape tax. To anyone who was not already indoctrinated on the

[1] See for example, The Royal Commission on the Taxation of Profits and Income, 1955 Cmd. 9474, para. 104 (the Commission did not endorse this argument).

"income/capital" divide, this result might seem rather odd. [1] Apart from this type of scenario, there was the point that, most people, poor and rich, earned some sort of income, and were taxed on it, while only the rich and propertied classes were likely to engage in large capital transactions yielding capital profits. Therefore the exemption of capital profits from direct taxation was unfair, as it was just a disguised means of protecting the rich. [2]

Eventually, a limited scheme was introduced in 1962, in which short-term capital gains were taxed as income under Schedule D case VII. [3] Soon afterward, capital gains tax (CGT) was introduced (by the Finance Act 1965) to tax all capital gains other than short-term capital gains. According to Purchas LJ in *Kirby v Thom EMI Plc* [4], the purpose of the tax was

> to provide that part of the wealth gained or, according to how one views it, the protection afforded against erosion by inflation as a result of appreciation in the value of assets without any effort on the part of the owner should be taxed so as to divert part of the gain achieved, or loss avoided, to the benefit of the Crown.

True to the principle that "tax is much more easily opposed, ridiculed and guyed than it is proposed, imposed or justified" [5] capital gains tax attracted the criticism of impeding the movement of capital, hindering economic growth, penalising savings and inhibiting personal endeavour. [6] These criticisms obviously did not lead to the abandonment of the tax, although the charge on short-term capital gains under Schedule D case VII was finally abolished in 1971. In 1979, the Capital Gains Tax Act consolidated the capital gains tax legislation not relating exclusively to companies, and in 1992, the Taxation of Chargeable Gains Act (TCGA) consolidated all the capital gains tax legislation. The TCGA 1992 is now the basic legislation for capital gains tax and, unless otherwise stated, all references to statutory provisions in the following discussions are references to this Act.

---

[1] Note that, even today, Y would still escape tax—not because his profit was capital, but because of the relief given in respect of an individual's only or main residence.

[2] See generally, the Memorandum of Dissent to the Royal Commission's report, para. 35.

[3] The Royal Commission on the Taxation of Profits and Income recommended against taxing capital gains as income (1955 Cmd. 9474, paras. 94–108).

[4] [1988] 2 All ER 947 at 957.

[5] H.H. Monroe: *Intolerable Inquisition? Reflections on the Law of Tax*, 18 (1981) Stevens & Sons, London.

[6] R.A. Toby: *The Theory and Practice of Income Tax*, 71 (1978) Sweet & Maxwell, London.

## The Scope of the Charge

S1 of the TCGA 1992 provides that tax shall be charged under the Act in respect of capital gains, that is to say, chargeable gains, accruing to a person on the disposal of assets. Within this phrase is encapsulated all the prerequisites for a charge to capital gains tax, namely:

1. a chargeable person
2. an asset
3. a disposal of the asset by the chargeable person
4. a chargeable gain derived from such disposal. [1]

The discussion that follows will examine the law relating to the taxation of chargeable capital gains under these four broad headings.

## Chargeable Persons

*General*

As seen above, s1(1) charges tax on capital gains accruing to a person on the disposal of assets. The use of the word "person" rather than "individual" here is to be noted. This indicates that capital gains are taxed not only in respect of individuals but also in respect of other legal persons, for example trustees and personal representatives. Companies are not subject to capital gains tax, but their chargeable gains (computed on normal capital gains tax principles) [2] are subject to corporation tax, at the usual corporation tax rates (s1(2)). An unincorporated association is a "person" for capital gains tax purposes. Accordingly it is an entity of assessment and is liable to tax on its chargeable gains. [3]

With respect to the question whether a particular person is a "chargeable person" for capital gains tax purposes, s2(1) TCGA 1992 provides that a person shall be chargeable to capital gains tax in respect of chargeable gains accruing to him in a year of assessment during any part

---

[1] Compare Purchas LJ in *Kirby v Thorn EMI Plc* ([1988] 2 All ER 947 at 958)—"A chargeable gain, therefore, imports the following elements: (1) the acquisition of the asset; (2) an increase in the capital value of the asset whilst in the ownership of the person to be charged; (3) a disposal of the asset giving rise to a realisation of the gain which has accrued during the period of ownership".

[2] See s8.

[3] *Frampton v IRC* [1985] STC 186 (Peter Gibson J).

of which he is resident in the United Kingdom, or during which he is ordinarily resident in the United Kingdom. This means that, unlike income tax in which the connecting factor that brings a person within the scope of United Kingdom tax is residence, as far as capital gains tax is concerned ordinary residence is also such a connecting factor.

Residence and ordinary residence have the same meaning as in the Income Tax Acts (see s9(1)), and in this respect the six-month rule of residence is similarly applicable here. S9(3) provides that an individual who is in the United Kingdom for some temporary purpose only and not with a view to establishing his residence there will be charged to capital gains tax only if he is in the United Kingdom for more than six months in the relevant tax year. Concessionary relief is available in respect of the dates of commencement and cessation of residence. ESC D2 provides that a person who is treated as resident in the United Kingdom for any year of assessment from the date of his arrival here, but who has not been regarded at any time during the 36 months immediately preceding such arrival as resident or ordinarily resident here, will be charged to CGT only in respect of the chargeable gains accruing to him from disposals made after his arrival in the United Kingdom. The concession also provides that when a person leaves the United Kingdom and is treated on his departure as not resident and not ordinarily resident in the United Kingdom, he will not be charged to CGT on gains accruing to him from disposals made after the date of his departure. This concession does not extend to gains on the disposal of United Kingdom assets used for the purposes of a United Kingdom trade, profession or vocation carried on by a person through a branch or agency, at any time between the date of his departure from the United Kingdom and the end of the year of assessment during which such departure took place.

## Branch or Agency

Where a person is neither resident nor ordinarily resident in the United Kingdom, but he carries on a trade in the UK through a branch or agency, he will be chargeable to capital gains tax on gains accruing on the disposal of assets *situated in the UK*, used at, or before the time when the capital gain accrued, in or for the purposes of the trade, or used or held for the purposes of the branch or agency (s10(1)). For this purpose "branch or agency" means any factorship, agency, receivership, branch or management, but the term does not include general agents and brokers (s10(6)).

*Non-Domiciled Persons*

An individual who is resident or ordinarily resident but not domiciled in the United Kingdom is only chargeable on gains accruing on the disposal of *foreign assets* on a remittance basis, i.e. only on sums received in the United Kingdom (s12(1)). For the purposes of this provision, s12(2) provides that there shall be treated as received in the United Kingdom in respect of any gain, all amounts paid, used, or enjoyed in, or in any manner or form transmitted or brought into the United Kingdom. The subsection furthermore provides that the elaborate provisions of s65 (6)—(9) of the ICTA 1988 on the question of when a person is deemed to have received a sum of money in the United Kingdom apply here as well. Those provisions, applied in the context of capital gains tax, would mean that the following will be taken as sums received in the United Kingdom:

1. Any sum applied outside the United Kingdom by a person resident or ordinarily resident in the United Kingdom, in or towards the satisfaction of:
    (a) any debt for money lent to him in the United Kingdom or for interest on money so lent, [1]
    (b) any debt for money lent to him outside the United Kingdom and received in or brought into the United Kingdom, [2]
    (c) any debt incurred for satisfying in whole or in part a debt falling within paragraph (a) or (b) above. [3]
2. Money borrowed abroad by a person who is ordinarily resident in the United Kingdom, which the person then receives or brings into the United Kingdom, in cases in which the debt for that money is wholly or partly satisfied before it was brought into or received in the United Kingdom. [4]

## Assets

*What is an Asset?*

It has been seen that capital gains tax is chargeable on a gain accruing on a disposal of assets. The term "assets" is defined by s21(1) as all forms of property, whether situated in the UK or not, including:

[1] S65(6)(a) ICTA 1988.
[2] S65(6)(b) ICTA 1988.
[3] S65(6)(c) ICTA 1988.
[4] S65(7) ICTA 1988. See also subsections (8) and (9) of s65.

(a) options, debts and incorporeal property generally, and
(b) any currency other than sterling, and
(c) any form of property created by the person disposing of it [e.g. paintings, copyrights], or otherwise coming to be owned without being acquired [e.g., goodwill, and property which is found].

It is clear from the wide definition that the term extends far beyond merely physical property, and that it possesses a meaning for capital gains tax purposes which is different from its usage in colloquial terms. A number of cases illustrate the way in which intangible property may constitute assets for capital gains tax purposes. In *O'Brien (HMIT) v Benson's Hosiery (Holdings) Ltd*[1], the sales director of the taxpayer company, who was employed under a seven-year service agreement, obtained a release from the agreement when it had about five years left to run, in consideration of a payment of £50,000 to the company. It was held that the employer's rights under the service agreement were an asset for capital gains tax purposes, even though contracts of personal service were not assignable. Lord Russell said[2]:

It was contended for the taxpayer that the rights of an employer under a contract of service were not "property" or an "asset" of the employer because they cannot be turned to account by transfer or assignment to another. But in my opinion this contention supposes a restricted view of the scheme of the imposition of the capital gains tax which the statutory language does not permit. If, as here, the employer is able to extract from the employee a substantial sum as a term of releasing him from his obligations to serve, the rights of the employer appear to me to bear quite sufficiently the mark of an asset of the employer, something which he can turn to account, notwithstanding that his ability to turn it to account is by a type of disposal limited by the nature of the asset.

*Marren (HMIT) v Ingles*[3] is another illustrative case. The taxpayer sold shares in a private company in consideration of an immediate payment of £750 per share, plus the right to receive a further payment if the market value of the shares on flotation of the company exceeded £750. When the

---

[1] [1980] AC 562.
[2] At p573.
[3] [1980] 3 All ER 95; STC 500; applied in *Marson (HMIT) v Marriage*[1980]STC 177—a right to future payment under an agreement was a chose in action and therefore a chargeable asset.

flotation took place, the taxpayer received a further £2,825 per share. It was held that the contingent right to further payment was an asset and, because a capital sum was derived from it, there was a disposal of that asset and a capital gains tax liability.

Still on intangible property, a technical point arose in *Zim Properties Ltd. v Procter (HMIT)*[1] concerning whether an intangible right had to be capable of being described as "property" in order for it to be an asset. The taxpayer company had brought an action in negligence against its solicitors. The action had eventually been compromised, and a sum of £69,000 had been paid to the taxpayer in compensation. Warner J, after "considerable hesitation", came to the conclusion that even if the right to sue the solicitor was not a form of "property" it was nonetheless an asset for capital gains tax purposes. This was based on the decision of the House of Lords in *O'Brien v Benson's Hosiery (Holdings) Ltd (supra)*, the *ratio* of which, Warner J felt, was that the rights in that case were assets because they could be turned to account. He said that the House of Lords in *O'Brien* treated as virtually irrelevant the use of the word "property" in what is now s21(1). Warner J then concluded[2] that it would be inconsistent with the decision on *O'Brien* "to hold that a right to bring an action to seek to enforce a claim that was not frivolous or vexatious, which right could be turned to account by negotiating a compromise yielding a substantial capital sum, could not be an 'asset' within the meaning of that term in the capital gains tax legislation". He accepted that not every right to a payment is an asset for capital gains tax purposes.[3] One example of a right that would not be an asset was the right of a seller of property to payment of its price. The relevant asset, then, is the property itself. What this showed however was "no more than that the interpretation of the capital gains tax legislation requires, as does the interpretation of any legislation, the exercise of common sense, rather than just the brute application of verbal formulae".[4]

Thus, an intangible right must be capable of being turned into pecuniary account, and if it is a right of action, then the claim must not be frivolous or vexatious. Furthermore, in order for a "right" to be an asset,

---

[1] [1985] STC 90.

[2] At p106.

[3] At p108.

[4] *Ibid.* For other examples see *Welbeck Securities Ltd. v Powlson (HMIT)* [1987] STC 468 (an option to acquire an interest in a property development); *Golding (HMIT) v Kaufman* [1985] STC 152 (a "put" option).

it must be legally enforceable and capable of being owned. This principle is illustrated by *Kirby (HMIT) v Thorn EMI Plc.*[1] Thorn EMI Plc (Thorn) agreed to sell three subsidiaries to an American company, General Electric. Thorn, in consideration of a capital sum, entered into a restrictive covenant that no company in the Thorn group would engage in the trade carried on by the three subsidiaries, for a period of five years. The Revenue argued that the right to engage in a commercial activity was an asset, and thus, the payment for restricting the commercial activities was liable to capital gains tax. The Court of Appeal disagreed, and held that the right of freedom to trade and compete in the market place was not an asset for capital gains tax purposes. According to Nicholls LJ[2]:

> ... the liberty or freedom to trade, enjoyed by everyone, is not a form of "property" within the meaning of [s21]. This liberty, or freedom, is a "right" if that word is given a very wide meaning, as when we speak of a person's "rights" in a free society. But in [s.21] the words used are "assets" and "property". "Property" is not a term of art, but takes its meaning from its context and from its collocation in the documents of Acts of Parliament in which it is found and from the mischief with which the Act or document is intended to deal ... The context in the instant case is a taxing Act which is concerned with assets and with disposals and acquisitions, gains and losses. I can see no reason to doubt that in [s.21] "property" bears the meaning of that which is capable of being owned, in the normal legal sense, and that it does not bear the extended meaning that would be needed if it were to include a person's freedom to trade.

However, the Court of Appeal held that the sum was taxable as a capital sum derived from Thorn's goodwill. Even though Thorn itself was not carrying on the trades of the three companies, it could have goodwill in respect of those trades. The company had received payment for agreeing not to exploit that goodwill for a period, and as the question of goodwill had not been canvassed before the commissioners, the case would be remitted to them for further consideration of evidence and arguments on it.

---

[1] [1988] 2 All ER 947; [1987] STC 621.
[2] At page 627.

*Types of Assets*

*Non-chargeable Assets*

Assets are either chargeable or non-chargeable and, unless otherwise specifically stated, all assets are chargeable. Some specifically identified non-chargeable assets are:

1. s263: motor cars—these are described as mechanically propelled road vehicles constructed or adapted for the carriage of passengers, except vehicles of a type not commonly used as a private vehicle and unsuitable to be so used;
2. s204(1): the rights of an insurer under a policy of insurance;
3. s45(1): tangible movable property (chattels) which are wasting assets, subject to certain exceptions;
4. s251(1): debts, except debts on a security.

No chargeable gain or allowable loss accrues on the disposal of non-chargeable assets.

*Pooled Assets*

Generally, assets are treated as individuals and distinct items. However, some items are pooled. For example, s104(1) and Schedule 2 paragraph 4(3) state that any number of quoted securities of the same class, held by one person in one capacity, shall be regarded as indistinguishable parts of a single asset (referred to as a "holding"). This asset grows on the occasions on which additional securities of the same class are acquired and diminishes when some of the securities in the class are disposed of. Generally, the word "securities" means:

1. any shares or securities of a company, and
2. any other assets, where they are of a nature to be dealt in without identifying the particular assets disposed of or acquired (s104(3)).

Shares or securities of a company will not be treated as being of the same class unless they are so treated by the practice of a recognised stock exchange or would be so treated if dealt with on a recognised stock exchange.

## Disposals

A charge to capital gains tax arises when an asset is disposed of. Apart from express provisions, there cannot be a disposal unless the disponor had an asset of which he could dispose, since according to Nicholls LJ in *Kirby (HMIT) v Thorn EMI plc*, [1] the Act presupposes that, "immediately prior to the disposal, there was an asset, and that the disponor owned it". Although disposals are central to the theme of the capital gains tax legislation, the term is not defined in the Act. However, there have been some relevant *dicta*. In *Kirby (HMIT) v Thorn EMI plc* [2] for example, Nicholls LJ said that what is envisaged by the term is a transfer of an asset (i.e. of ownership of an asset) as widely defined, by one person to another; and in *Welbeck Securities Ltd v Powlson (HMIT)* [3] Slade LJ accepted the submission that the word "disposal', as used in section 1 itself is not apt to include the mere release of an option, which is accompanied by no corresponding acquisition of the right in question, but has the effect of extinguishing it. [4]

There are several types of disposal known to the capital gains tax regime. For example, there may be actual disposals, deemed disposals, total disposals (disposing of all interests in an asset), part disposals (disposing of some interests in an asset while retaining other interests, or creating a new interest in the asset by the disposal), and disposals of part (disposing of all interests in a part of the asset—e.g. by selling half of it). An actual disposal is one which has taken place in fact. Most disposals for capital gains tax purposes will be of this nature. However, there are some situations where no disposal may have taken place in fact, but the legislation nevertheless deems one to have occurred. We first examine here the general concept of deemed disposals. Part disposals are discussed later in this chapter.

## Deemed Proposals

*Introduction*

When a statute requires that something be deemed to have happened, one is required to implement a fiction. The capital gains tax legislation contains many instances of deemed disposals, and it is therefore helpful to

[1] [1988] 2 All ER 947 at 951.
[2] Above, at page 951.
[3] [1987] STC 468 at 473.
[4] However, such a release in return for payment will be a deemed disposal under s22(1).

make some general observations about the proper approach to deeming provisions. With respect to deeming provisions in general, Lord Asquith said in *East End Dwellings Co Ltd v Finsbury Borough Council*[1]

> If you are bidden to treat an imaginary state of affairs as real you must surely, unless prohibited from doing so, also imagine as real the consequences and incidents which, if the putative state of affairs had in fact existed, must inevitably have flowed or accompanied it ... The statute says that you must imagine a certain state of affairs; it does not say that having done so, you must cause or permit your imagination to boggle when it comes to the inevitable corollaries of that state of affairs[2].

With particular reference to deeming provisions in taxing statutes, Nourse J said in *IRC v Metrolands (Property Finance) Ltd*[3]:

> When considering the extent to which a deeming provision should be applied, the court is entitled and bound to ascertain for what purposes and between what persons the statutory fiction is to be resorted to ... it will not always be clear what those purposes are ... If the application of the provision would lead to an unjust, anomalous or absurd result then, unless its application would clearly be within the purpose of the fiction, it should not be applied. If on the other hand, its application would not lead to any such result then, unless that would clearly be outside the purposes of the fiction, it should be applied.

And, finally, Peter Gibson J said in *Marshall (HMIT) v Kerr*:

> But I do not read the authorities as requiring in the case of a deeming provision the abandonment of what is sometimes called the golden rule of construction, that is to say that in construing a statute the grammatical and ordinary sense of the words is to be adhered to, unless that would lead to some absurdity or some inconsistency, in which case the grammatical and ordinary sense of the words may be modified so as to avoid that absurdity and inconsistency but no further.[4]

---

[1] [1952] AC 109 at 132–133.
[2] Compare Peter Gibson J in *Marshall (HMIT) v Kerr* [1993] BTC 194 at 200.
[3] [1981] 1 WLR 637 at 646.
[4] [1993] BTC 194 at 199.

With these observations in mind we will now examine the various incidents of deemed disposals in the capital gains tax legislation.

## Capital Sums

S22(1) provides that there is a disposal of assets by their owner where any capital sum is derived from the assets, notwithstanding that no asset is acquired by the person paying the capital sum. [1] In *Marren (HMIT) v Ingles* [2] the House of Lords considered the meaning of the words "notwithstanding that no asset is acquired by the person paying the capital sum". The taxpayer argued that they introduced a condition of a limiting character, with the result that, if an asset is acquired, the subsection does not apply. Slade J at first instance accepted this contention, but the House of Lords disagreed. Lord Wilberforce said [3]:

> In my understanding they are evidently words not of limitation but of extension, the purpose of which is to apply the subsection (so as to establish a "disposal") to cases to which it would not otherwise apply and in which a "disposal" would not naturally be thought to exist. In other words they mean, in my opinion, "whether or not an asset is acquired". . . .

The charge in s22(1) fastens on the receipt of a capital sum derived from an asset, including an asset which then becomes destroyed, or which has previously been destroyed, or which has ceased to exist as a distinct asset and which cannot therefore be said to have been disposed of in the ordinary sense of the word. [4]

There are several examples of the general operation of this provision and we will examine some of them in outline.

1. In *O'Brien (HMIT) v Benson's Hosiery, (supra)* the company derived a capital sum from releasing an employee from his service agreement, and this was a disposal of the company's rights under the agreement.
2. In *Marren (HMIT) v Ingles, (supra)* the taxpayer derived a capital sum

---

[1] The term "capital sum" in this section means any money or money's worth which is not excluded from the consideration taken into account in the computation of the gain (s22(3)).

[2] [1980] 3 All ER 95.

[3] At p98.

[4] See Vinelott J in *Golding (HMIT) v Kaufman* [1985] STC 152 at 162–163.

from his right to receive payment, and was taxable although the payer acquired no asset.

3. In *Zim Properties v Procter (HMIT)*, *(supra)* the company received a sum in compromise of a negligence claim against its solicitors.

4. In *Davenport (HMIT) v Chilver*[1], a right to compensation in respect of expropriated property in the USSR, conferred by the Foreign Compensation (Union of Soviet Socialist Republics) Order 1969 was an asset, and the compensation payment itself was a capital sum derived from that asset, resulting in a deemed disposal thereof.

A number of examples involve options. In *Welbeck Securities Ltd v Powlson (HMIT)*[2] the company had been paid £2m for agreeing to release and abandon an option to acquire an interest in a property development in the City of London. It was held that the company had derived a capital sum from an asset (the option) and had therefore disposed of the asset, making a chargeable gain. The date of the disposal was the date when the capital sum has received. *Golding (HMIT) v Kaufman*[3] involved a taxpayer who had options entitling him to require a company to purchase his shareholding in another company. The taxpayer was paid £5,000 in consideration for his abandonment of the options. The question arose whether this was a capital sum derived from an asset, and thus a disposal liable to capital gains tax. Another question that arose in the case was whether the taxpayer had "abandoned" the options for the purposes of a provision which stated that the abandonment of an option by a person shall not constitute a disposal of an asset by that person (see s144(4)). Vinelott J held that the £5,000 was taxable as a capital sum derived from an asset. He also held that the effect of the provision referred to above (s144(1)) was to qualify the operation of s24(1) (thereby restricting losses). It does not operate to qualify s22(1), and thus the charge still attached.

Apart from the generality of the provisions however, s22(1) also provides particular instances of situations to which it relates:

(a) capital sums received by way of compensation for any kind of damage or injury to assets or for the loss, destruction or dissipation of assets, or for any depreciation or risk of depreciation of an asset;

(b) capital sums received under an insurance policy with respect to the

---

[1] [1983] STC 426.
[2] [1987] STC 468.
[3] [1985] STC 152.

risk of any kind of damage or injury to, or the loss or depreciation of, assets;

(c) capital sums received in return for forfeiture or surrender of rights, or for refraining form exercising rights. There are several examples of this particular situation in the cases, many of which we have discussed above (e.g. *O'Brien (HMIT) v Benson's Hosiery*);

(d) capital sums received as consideration for use or exploitation of assets (e.g. for the right to exploit a copyright).

## *Causation*

A vital factor in the principle which treats the derivation of a capital sum from an asset as a disposal is causation. If the capital sum concerned is caused by something other than the asset, then it is not "derived from" the asset. Thus in *Drummond (HMIT) v Brown*,[1] a payment of statutory compensation for the termination of a lease was not derived from the lease, but from the statute. It followed that it was not a capital sum derived from an asset and neither was it (on the facts of the case) compensation for the loss of an asset (because the lease had come to an end by the effluxion of time and the taxpayer was not entitled to security of tenure). Fox LJ said[2] that the payment was simply a sum which Parliament said should be paid.[3] It was therefore not chargeable.

It is to be noted however that there is no general principle that compensation awarded by statute is outside s22(1).[4] One must look in each case to see whether the capital sum is "derived" from the asset, or from something else. When examining the issue of causation the important thing to look for is the *real*, rather than the *immediate*, source of the capital sum.[5] It thus follows that the fact that the immediate source of a capital sum is a statutory provision does not necessarily mean that the sum is not derived from an asset. This principle can be seen in *Pennine Raceway Ltd v Kirklees Metropolitan Council (no. 2)*.[6] The company had obtained a licence from the owner of an airfield to use the field for the purposes of drag motor racing. The drag racing was covered by existing

[1] [1984] STC 321.

[2] At p324.

[3] See also *Davis (HMIT) v Powell*([1977] STC 32) where it was held that compensation paid to a tenant under s.34(1) of the Agricultural Holdings Act 1948 was not derived from an asset (the lease). It was simply a sum which Parliament said shall be paid.

[4] Per Croom-Johnson LJ in *Pennine Raceway Ltd. v Kirklees Metropolitan Council (no. 2)* [1989] BTC 42 at 51; [1989] STC 122.

[5] *Ibid.*, referring with approval to Warner J in *Zim Properties Ltd. v Procter* [1985] STC 90 at 107.

[6] [1989] BTC 42.

planning permission with respect to the field. Permission to use the field for drag racing was subsequently revoked by Kirklees Metropolitan Council, the revocation being confirmed by the Secretary of State for the Environment. The company then made an application for planning permission but was refused. The company later received compensation under s164 of the Town and Country Planning Act 1971, for loss of income and other costs incurred as a result of the revocation of the original planning permission. The question was whether the compensation received was a capital sum derived from an asset under s22(1). The Court of Appeal held that it was.

Croom-Johnson LJ said[1] that, first, the payment would be a capital sum received by way of compensation for (i) any kind of damage or injury to the asset, or (ii) any depreciation of the asset. Even if there had been no damage or injury to the licence which (as a licence) was still in existence although useless, it could not be said that there had not been a depreciation of the licence, which had granted to the company "sole rights to promote motor and motor cycle events on the Airfield". Counsel had submitted that the payment was simply compensation payable by the council under the statutory requirement laid down by the Town and Country Planning Act 1971, and was derived from the statutory obligation, not from any event in s22(1). In response to this submission, Croom-Johnson LJ adopted the approach of Warner J in *Zim Properties Ltd. v Procter* (referred to above)—it would be a mistake to say that the asset from which a capital sum is derived must always be the asset that constitutes its immediate source. One has to look for the real source. Croom-Johnson LJ concluded[2]:

> In the present case Pennine had an asset, which was the licence, and that licence depreciated in value when the planning permission was revoked. For that depreciation they are entitled to a capital sum by way of compensation, and their right to the compensation is given by the Town and Country Planning Act 1971, s164(1) because their asset . . . has sustained loss or damage which is directly attributable to the revocation of the permission. It is clear that the capital sum is "derived" from the asset.

Stuart-Smith LJ[3] rejected the submission of counsel that the capital sum had to be consideration for a bargain:

[1] [1989] BTC 42 at 50.
[2] At p51.
[3] At p57.

But it is perfectly clear that both para. (a) and (b) envisage capital sums that do not result from any bargain. Compensation is normally awarded by a court or other Tribunal. Sums received under a policy of insurance are not paid in consideration of the loss or damage to the asset in the sense that there is any bargain for the disposal in that way.

Another question of vital importance was raised in *Pennine*. This concerned whether or not the general words of s22(1) (i.e. "a capital sum . . . derived from assets") govern the particular words of paragraphs (a) to (d). Two views were to be found in the case law. First, Nourse J in *Davenport (HMIT) v Chilver*[1] had held that the particular words in paragraphs (a) to (d) stood on their own feet. They were to be construed independently of the opening general words, and if necessary, they were to prevail over the general words. On the other hand, Warner J in *Zim Properties Ltd v Procter (HMIT)*[2] held that paragraphs (a) to (d) were particular instances of the application of the principle enacted by the general words. Consequently, a case cannot come within any of those paragraphs if it cannot come within the general words.

While holding that the issue did not arise for decision in the present case, two members of the court expressed preferences. Stuart-Smith LJ[3] was content to assume that the narrower construction favoured by Warner J in *Zim Properties Ltd v Procter* was correct. Ralph Gibson LJ[4] on the other hand was inclined to agree with Nourse J in *Davenport v Chilver*.

This divergence of opinion, both at first instance, and in the Court of Appeal, leaves the situation confused. However, when the actual wording of s22(1) is examined it is, with all respect to Nourse J and Ralph Gibson LJ, difficult to see how the words in paragraphs. (a) to (d) can stand on their own feet. After the general words "where any capital sum is derived from assets" the words immediately preceding paragraphs. (a) to (d) are "and this subsection applies in particular to . . . ". This indicates that the subsequent words are meant to be particular instances of those preceding that statement. This is in consonance with the *ejusdem generis* rule—where general words are followed by particular words, the particular words ought to be taken as limited in scope to matters of the same kind as the general words. Thus it seems that the approach of Warner J in *Zim Properties v Procter* is to be preferred.

[1] [1983] STC 426 at 439.
[2] [1985] STC 90 at 106.
[3] [1989] BTC at 56.
[4] [1989] BTC at 54.

*Value Shifting*

S29 treats certain types of transactions as disposals of asset, notwithstanding that no consideration passes, and, in such cases, also treats the consideration or added consideration that could have been obtained if the parties were dealing at arm's length as the market value of the asset:

(a) s29(2): where a person having control of a company exercises his control so that value passes out of his shares in the company or out of his rights over the company and passes into other shares in, or rights over the company, there is a disposal of the shares or the rights out of which the value passes. This provision also applies in cases where the value passes out of shares of a person connected with the person who has control of the company, in the way described above.

(b) s29(4): where after a transaction which results in the owner of the land or any other property becoming the lessee thereof, there is any adjustment of the rights and liabilities under the lease, in a manner which is favourable to the lessor, this is treated as a disposal by the lessee (i.e. the owner), of an interest in the property.

(c) s29(5): where a person extinguishes or abrogates in whole or in part, any right or restriction held by him over an asset, this is a disposal of the right or restriction.

*Satisfaction of Debt*

S251(2) provides that the satisfaction of a debt or part thereof shall be treated as a disposal of the debt by the creditor at the time when the debt is satisfied. Note however that with the exception of debts on securities, debts are not chargeable assets (s251(1)).

*Appropriation of Stock-in-trade*

Where a person appropriates an asset which was not originally acquired as trading stock into his trading stock, this will be treated as a disposal of the asset for its market value, if a chargeable gain or allowable loss would have accrued to him on its disposal for its market value (s161(1)). However, by virtue of s161(3), a trader who is taxable under Case I of Schedule D can elect to have the market value of the asset computed for income tax purposes, as being reduced by the amount of the chargeable gain, or increased by the amount of the allowable loss that would have accrued on this deemed disposal. The effect of this is to convert what would have been an immediate liability to capital gains tax into a deferred income tax liability.

Example:

> Vladimir bought an asset at a cost of £100. He appropriated this asset into his trading stock when it was worth £150. This will normally be treated as a disposal of the asset for a consideration of £150 under s161(1), leading to a gain of £50.
>
> If Vladimir makes an election under s161(3), he will be treated for income tax purposes as having acquired the asset as part of his trading stock at a price of £100 (instead of its current market value of £150). When he eventually sells it as part of his trading stock, the profit on the sale will reflect the £50 gain which the asset was carrying at the time of its appropriation into trading stock.

### Termination of Life Interest in Possession

When a person entitled to an interest in possession in settled property dies, the assets forming part of the settled property, and which still remain in the settlement, will be deemed to have been disposed of and immediately re-acquired by the trustee at its market value (s72(1)). However, no chargeable gain accrues on this disposal.

### Beneficiary Becoming Absolutely Entitled Against Trustee

S71(1) provides that when a person becomes absolutely entitled to any settled property as against the trustee, all the assets forming part of the settled property to which he becomes entitled will be deemed to be have been disposed of by the trustee, and immediately reacquired by him in his capacity as trustee, at market value. Such assets are deemed to be vested in the beneficiary, the acts of trustee are deemed to be on the behalf of the beneficiary (s60(1)). Transfers between them are therefore disregarded accordingly.

### Assets Lost or Destroyed

The occasion of the entire loss, destruction, dissipation or extinction of an asset constitutes a disposal of the asset, whether or not compensation is received in respect of it (s24(1)). If any compensation or insurance payment is received for such loss or destruction, and this is applied for the purposes of replacing the asset within one year of receipt or such longer period as the inspector may allow, the taxpayer can "roll over" [1] any gain on the old asset onto the new asset (s23(4)). For the purposes of this provision the fact that an asset has ceased to be of any value does not indicate that it has been "dissipated" or "lost". [2]

### Assets Becoming of Negligible Value

S24(2) provides that, where the owner of an asset which has become of negligible value makes a claim to that effect, the owner will be deemed to have sold and immediately re-acquired the asset for the amount specified in the claim. This means that the owner of the asset will have incurred an allowable loss. S 24(2)(a) indicates that the time of the deemed disposal is the time when the claim was made, or, if certain conditions are fulfilled, any earlier time specified in the claim. The strict view used to be that the period of this notional disposal is the date on which the inspector was satisfied that the asset had become of negligible value. However, in *Williams (HMIT) v Bullivant* [3] Vinelott J preferred the view relating the notional disposal back to the date when the owner made the claim—a view which (with some exceptions) has now been given statutory effect.

The timing of the notional disposal is important because of the fact that losses can only be carried forward. Thus since the application of the provision will invariably lead to a loss, the claim should be made as early as possible. *Williams (HMIT) v Bullivant* itself is illustrative of the point. The taxpayers owned shares which, by the end of February 1974, had become of negligible value. They only made a claim in 1978. In the meantime, the taxpayers had made chargeable gains back in 1974. It was held that the notional disposal (and losses) could not be related back to any time before the claim was made. Thus they could not set the notional loss against the gains made in 1974.

While the principle that the disposal is deemed to take place when the claim was made is better than that which deemed it to take place when the inspector became satisfied, it could itself lead to problems. These

---

[1] Roll over relief is a mechanism whereby liability to capital gains tax is deferred. We will look at this in more detail in the chapter on disposal consideration.

[2] Nicholls J in *Larner v Warrington (HMIT)* [1985] STC 442 at 449–450.

[3] [1983] STC 107.

problems were highlighted in *Larner v Warrington (HMIT)*[1], in which Nicholls J applied the *Williams v Bullivant* test, but with apparent misgivings. His reservations are poignant:

> I have to confess that on the basis of [*Williams v Bullivant*], that on the inspector allowing the claim [s24(2)] takes effect as if the claimant had sold the asset when the claim was made and not on the happening of the event giving rise to the claim, [s24(2)] does seem to me to be capable of working considerable hardship to taxpayers. If a chargeable gain accrues to a taxpayer in a year of assessment and within the same year an asset of his becomes of negligible value, one might have expected that on the latter fact being satisfactorily established following a claim duly made under the subsection, the loss on the notional sale could have been deducted from that chargeable gain even though the claim was not actually made before the close of the year of assessment. As it is, a well-advised taxpayer by making his claim within that year will be able to obtain an advantage of which the less well-informed taxpayer, as a matter of strict law, may be deprived. I say "as a matter of strict law" because that is the effect of the decision in *Williams (Inspector of Taxes) v Bullivant*. In practice the Revenue tempers the wind to the shorn lamb by permitting retrospection for a period of two years. But the existence of this extra-statutory concession serves to underline the unattractive consequences which in law may flow from [s24(2)] as construed in *Williams (Inspector of Taxes) v Bullivant*. Of course, the loss arising from the notional sale can be deducted from any gains accruing not only in the year of assessment in which the claim is made but also in subsequent years. But this will provide cold comfort indeed to a taxpayer ... who has no such gains and is unlikely to have any such gains in the forseeable future.

Nicholls J referred in the passage quoted to the Revenue tempering "the wind to the shorn lamb" by permitting retrospection. This concessionary relief was contained in ESC D28 in the following terms:

> Where an asset has become of negligible value [TCGA 1992, s24(2)] allows the owner to claim to be treated as though the asset had been sold and immediately reacquired at the specified value. If the claim is accepted, this will normally give rise to an allowable loss.
>
> In strictness [s24(2)] requires the deemed sale and reacquisition to be

---

[1] [1985] STC 442, at 449.

treated as taking place when the claim is made. In practice the Inland Revenue are prepared to accept that a claim by the owner to be treated as having sold and reacquired the asset at a particular date may be made not later than 24 months after the end of the tax year (or accounting period in the case of a company) in which that date fell, provided that the asset is of negligible value both when the claim is made and at that earlier date (whether or not it had first become of negligible value before that earlier date).

This has now been given statutory effect in s24(2)(b). This subsection allows an earlier time to be specified in the claim, if the asset had become of negligible value at that earlier time, and, (for CGT purposes) if that earlier time is not more than two years before the beginning of the year of assessment in which the claim is made, or, (for corporation tax purposes) if that earlier time is on or after the first day of the earliest accounting period ending not more than two years before the time of the claim.

### Assets Held on 6 April 1965

Schedule 2 paragraph 17(1) provides that, on an election by the person making the disposal, assets held by him on 6 April 1965 will be deemed to have been sold and immediately reacquired by him at market value on that date. The rules applicable to assets held on 6 April 1965 are discussed in more detail below

### Assets Held on 31 March 1982

S35(2) provides, with respect to disposals on or after 6 April 1988, that assets held on 31 March 1982 will be deemed to have been sold and immediately reacquired by their owner at their market value on that date. This provision and the exceptions thereto are discussed in more detail below.

### Charities

S256(2) provides that if property which is held on charitable trusts ceases to be so held, the trustees shall be treated as having disposed of it and immediately reacquired it at the market value, and any gain on the disposal will be treated as not accruing to a charity.

## Part Disposals

*Introduction*

S21(2)(a) provides that references to a disposal of an asset include reference to a part disposal of an asset. The term "part disposal" is defined by s21(2)(b). It includes situations where:

(i)   an interest or right in or over the asset is created by the disposal;
(ii)  an interest or right subsists before the disposal;
(iii) on a disposal, any description of the property derived from the asset remains undisposed of.

A part disposal of an asset is treated as a disposal of the asset, not as a disposal of part of the asset[1]. Examples of part disposals are the grant of an easement over land, and the creation of a leasehold interest. In both of these examples an interest over the asset is created by the disposal, and some description of property derived from the asset (namely, that part which is retained by the owner—e.g. the freehold) would remain undisposed of.

Part disposals always lead to apportionments. The disposal consideration is not apportioned since it only relates to the part disposed of, but in order to determine the gain attributable to the part disposal, the aquisition cost and other allowable expenditure will be apportioned (s42(1)). The formula for such apportionment is given by s42(2):

$$\frac{A}{A+B} \times C$$

Where
A = the value or consideration for the disposal
B = the market value of the undisposed part
C = the total allowable expenditure on the asset

The amount arrived at, that is the expenditure which is attributable to the part that has been diagnosed of, is deducted from the disposal consideration to arrive at the amount of the gain that is chargeable. The remainder will be the amount of allowable expenditure which is attributable to the undisposed property. Any expenditure which, on the

[1] Sir John Vinelott in *Watton (HMIT) v Tippett* [1996] BTC 25 at 32.

facts, is wholly attributable to the part which has been disposed of is not apportioned (s42(4)).

Example:

Sharm bought some freehold property for £100,000. She soon after spent £25,000 on improvements. One year later, she granted an easement over the property to a local company in return for a payment of £5,000. As a result of the easement, the property is now worth £110,000.

The allowable expenditure on this part disposal would be:

$$\frac{£5,000}{£5,000+£110,000} \times £125,000 = £5,434.78$$

Thus the allowable expenditure attributable to the part disposal (the easement) amounts to £5,434.78.

Assuming that the indexation allowance is nil the gain/loss would be:

$$£5,000 - £5,434.78 = £-434.78$$

This indicates that the transaction of granting the easement has resulted in Sharm incurring a capital gains *loss* of £434.78.

The expenditure which is attributable to the part of the property which remains undisposed of after the easement (the freehold) would be:

$$£125,000 - £5,434.78 = £119,565.22$$

## Leases

The payment of a premium on the grant of a lease is a part disposal of the freehold or other asset out of which the lease is granted (Schedule 8 paragraph 2(1)). In applying the provisions of s42 (above) to this part disposal, the property which remains undisposed of includes a right to any rent or other payments, other than a premium, payable under the lease. Such a right falls to be valued as at the time of the part disposal (Schedule 8 paragraph 2(2)).

As part disposals, leases are subject to a special regime under Schedule 8. By Schedule 8 paragraph 5(1) premiums which have been taxed under s34 of the ICTA 1988 are exempt from capital gains tax.

*Small Part Disposals of Land*

Special provisions apply to small part disposals of land. S242(1) applies to a transfer of land forming part of a holding of land, where the consideration for the transfer does not exceed one-fifth of the market value of the holding immediately before the transfer, and the transfer is not one which is treated by s58 (husband and wife) or s171(1) (transfers within a group) as giving rise to neither a gain nor a loss. S242(3) provides further requirements, that the consideration for the relevant transfer should not exceed £20,000, and that the consideration for all disposals of the land made by the transferor in the relevant year should not exceed £20,000.

If these conditions are satisfied, s242(2) provides (subject to timing requirements in s242(2A)) that, if the transferor so elects, the transfer will not be treated as a disposal, but the consideration for it will be deducted from the allowable expenditure attributable to the whole holding when the holding is subsequently disposed of. This means that the tax is deferred until the future disposal of the holding.

## Death and Capital Gains Tax

*Introduction*

S62(1)(a) provides that the assets of which a deceased person was competent to dispose should be deemed to be acquired on his death by the personal representatives, or any other person on whom they devolve, at their market value on the date of death. However, s62(1))b) provides that these assets shall not be deemed to be disposed of by the deceased at his death, meaning that there is an acquisition with no disposal, and no CGT liability. The death extinguishes all accrued capital gains. The assets which a deceased person was competent to dispose of are defined by s62(10) as those of his assets which he could, if of full age and capacity, have disposed of by will.

*Sale of Assets by Personal Representatives*

As seen above, by s62(1)(a), the personal representatives of a deceased person acquire the deceased's assets at their market value on death. When they dispose of the assets (otherwise than to legatees) they may be liable to CGT on gains accruing since the date of death. For these purposes s62(3) provides that "personal representatives" shall be treated as a single and continuing body of persons (distinct from the persons who may from time to time fill the posts), and that body shall be treated as having the deceased's residence, ordinary residence and domicile at the date of death. Thus, if the deceased was not resident and not ordinarily resident in the United Kingdom at death, there will be no CGT liability on personal representatives, even if they are resident.

Where CGT is due, s65(1) provides that it may be assessed and charged on and in the name of any one or more of the personal representatives. The personal representatives are not to be treated as an individual (s65(2)) and thus they will only be liable to basic rate tax (s4(1) and (2)). However, personal representatives are entitled to a full annual exemption for the year of death, and the next two years (s3(7)).

## Disposals to Legatees

S62(4) provides that, on a person acquiring an asset as legatee, no chargeable gain shall accrue to the personal representatives, and the legatee shall be treated as if the personal representatives' acquisition of the asset had been his own. This means that the legatee is treated as having acquired the asset at the time when the personal representatives acquired it (the date of the deceased's death), and that legatee's base cost for CGT purposes is the market value of the asset at the date of the deceased's death. Similar provisions apply in respect of instruments of variation. S62(6) applies where, within the period of two years after a person's death, any of the dispositions (however effected) of the property of which he was competent to dispose are varied, or the benefit conferred by any of those dispositions is disclaimed. Such variation must be made by an instrument in writing made by the persons or any of the persons who benefit or who would benefit under the dispositions. If these conditions are fulfilled, and the persons making the instrument so elect, the variation or disclaimer shall not constitute a disposal, and the provisions of s62 shall apply as if the variation had been made by the deceased, or as the case may be, as if the disclaimed benefit had never been conferred.[1]

Harman J (at first instance) said in *Marshall (HMIT) v Kerr*[2] that this

---

[1] According to Lord Browne-Wilkinson in *Marshall (HMIT) v Kerr* ([1994] BTC 258 at 270) this consequence operates only for the purposes of the section and does not directly apply to any other section.

[2] [1991]BTC 438 at 449; STC 686 (decision reversed by the Court of Appeal, but restored by the House of Lords ([1994] BTC 258)).

subsection applies as if the variations were effected by the deceased so that the legatee taking them, and the personal representatives assenting to their vesting, are to be treated as if the deceased by his will had made the provisions which is in the instrument of variation. This sufficiently takes out of any tax net and any computations differences in value between the date of death and the date of the instrument. The main consequences are that the legatee's acquisition date is the date of death, and the value at which the legatee acquired the asset is the value of the asset at the date of death. [1] Lord Browne-Wilkinson in the House of Lords said [2] that the interests of a beneficiary which in fact arise under the dispositions made by the instrument of variation ("the varied beneficiary") are to be treated as though they were contained in the will of the deceased. Thus, assets which the deceased was competent to dispose of at the death, which are not sold in due course of administration, but which are vested in the varied beneficiary, are deemed to have been acquired by the varied beneficiary as legatee under the will. However, Lord Browne-Wilkinson stressed [3] that not *all* assets vested in the varied beneficiary are to be deemed to have been acquired from the deceased, and that such deemed only applies to assets of which the deceased was competent to dispose at his death. According to him, other assets, whether cash representing the proceeds of sales made by the personal representatives or property purchased by the personal representatives in the course of administration, fall to be treated as though the varied beneficiary's acquisition was the personal representative's acquisition, that is as being made at the time, and from the person from whom the personal representatives in fact acquired such cash or property in the course of administration. He said that there was nothing in [s62(6)] which requires one to assume that *all* the assets vested in the varied beneficiary as "legatee" are to be treated as acquired from the deceased at the date of death. [4] Lord Browne-Wilkinson said that still less was there anything which requires one to ignore the process of administration of the estate. He concluded the matter thus:

> Assets acquired by the personal representatives after the death are not deemed to have been acquired by them (and hence by the varied

---

[1] See also Peter Gibson J in the Court of Appeal ([1993] BTC 194 at 200–201).
[2] [1994] BTC at p270.
[3] At p271.
[4] *Ibid* (emphasis supplied).

beneficiary as legatee) at any time or cost or from any preson other than the time, cost and person at which, and from whom, they were in fact acquired. For the purposes of calculating the capital gains tax liability of the varied beneficiary on any future disposal by him of such assets, the acts done by the personal representatives in the course of administration remain relevant and indeed decisive. I cannot therefore see any ground for holding that, once assets are vested in the varied beneficiary, the effect of [subsection (6)] is retrospectively to wipe out the process of administration and deem all the assets vested in the varied beneficiary as having been acquired by him at the date of death from the deceased.[1]

"Legatee" is defined by s64(2) as including any person taking under a testamentary disposition (e.g. a will) or an intestacy or partial intestacy, whether he takes beneficially or as trustee. A person taking a gift by way of *donatio mortis causa* is treated as a legatee, and his acquisition is treated as made at the time of the donor's death, but s62(5) exempts from CGT gifts made by way of *donatio mortis causa.*

By virtue of s64(1), a legatee is entitled to deduct the cost of transferring assets to him by the personal representatives in computing his gains for CGT purposes.

## Settled Property

*Definition*

S68 defines settled property as property held in trust, other than property to which s60 applies. S97(7) stipulates that "settlement" and "settlor" have the same meaning as under s660G(1) & (2) of the ICTA 1988. According to s660(G)(1) of the ICTA 1988, "settlement" includes any disposition, trust, covenant, agreement or arrangement or transfer of assets, and "settlor", in relation to a settlement, means any person by whom the settlement was made. By virtue of s660(G)(2) a person is deemed to have made a settlement if he has made or entered into the settlement directly or indirectly, and, in particular, if he has provided or undertaken to provide funds directly or indirectly for the purposes of the settlement, or has made with any other person a reciprocal arrangement for that other person to make or enter into the settlement. S97(7) TCGA 1992 further provides

[1] At pp271–272.

that "settlor" includes, in the case of a settlement arising under a will or intestacy, the testator or intestate, and that "settled property" shall be construed accordingly.

S60 relates to nominees and bare trustees. S60(1) provides that assets held for another as nominee or bare trustee (i.e. for a person absolutely entitled as against the trustee) are treated as if they are vested in the person for whom the assets are held, that is the beneficiary. In such a case, the acts of the nominee or trustee in relation to those assets are treated as the act of the beneficiary.

### Trustees

S69(1) provides that the trustees of a settlement shall be treated as a single and continuing body of persons, and that body shall be treated as being resident and ordinarily resident in the United Kingdom *unless*:

1. the general administration of the trust is ordinarily carried on outside the UK, and
2. the trustees, or a majority of them, for the time being are not resident or ordinarily resident in the UK.

*Note* that trustees in that capacity are, by s286(3), connected with:

1. the settlor,
2. any person who is connected with the settlor, and
3. a body corporate connected with the settlement.

### Disposals

With particular respect to settlements a number of activities are disposals for the purposes of CGT. The discussion that follows examines the instances and CGT consequences of actual and deemed disposals relating to settlements.

### Creation of the Settlement

A creation of a settlement will usually involve an actual disposal of assets by the settlor. By s70, a gift into a settlement is also treated as a disposal of the entire property thereby becoming settled property, notwithstanding that the transferor has some interest as a beneficiary under the settlement, and notwithstanding that he is a trustee, or the sole trustee, of the settlement. For these purposes the term "gift" is to be taken according to its ordinary meaning—a voluntary transfer of property to the trustees, without any corresponding consideration from the trustees.[1] However the term "gift in settlement" seems to be related to the beneficial interests created, not to the legal transfer of title. This is also to be taken in accordance with its ordinary meaning.[2] The creation of a settlement will be subject to a market value consideration under s17 (i.e. the assets will be deemed to have been disposed of for a consideration equal to their market value). If the assets are chargeable, a gain or a loss will result.

### Actual Disposals by Trustees

If trustees sell assets (to unconnected persons) this will attract the normal CGT consequences.

### Exit Charge (Assets Leaving the Settlement)

By virtue of s71(1), where a person becomes absolutely entitled to any settled property as against the trustee, all the assets forming part of the settled property to which he becomes so entitled are deemed to have been disposed of and immediately reacquired by the trustee as a bare trustee (s60(1)) for a consideration equal to the market value. The implications of this are:

1. there is a charge to CGT imposed on the trustees on the gain accruing on the assets during their period of ownership;
2. the subsequent acts of the trustee in relation to the property are attributed to the beneficiary by s60(1).

In this respect, the words "absolutely entitled against the trustee" do not presuppose that the beneficiary has to be *beneficially* entitled to the property. In *Hoare Trustees v Gardner (HMIT)*[3] Brightman J said that if "absolutely entitled" is confined to absolutely entitled in a beneficial sense, then the words "as against the trustee" are meaningless, because they add nothing to the expression. An absolute beneficial owner of property held in trust is absolutely entitled as against the whole world, and not merely as

---

[1] See Buckley LJ in *Berry v Warnett (HMIT)*[1980] STC 631 at 644–647—approved by Lord Roskill in the House of Lords ([1982] STC 396 at 401);

[2] Lord Wilberforce in *Berry v Warnett (HMIT)*[1982] STC 396 at 399.

[3] [1978] STC 89 at 108.

against his trustee: he cannot have absolute beneficial ownership as against some persons and not others. According to Brightman J, the description of a person as being "absolutely entitled as against the trustee" carries the implication that the expression is being used in the sense that that person is not necessarily absolutely entitled as against everyone else. Brightman J gave the following examples:

> If property is held by T, the trustee, in trust for L for life with remainder to R, R, if living at L's death, would then be absolutely entitled to that property as against T. If R were dead, one would think that R's executor would similarly be absolutely entitled to that property as against T, even if the executor is not beneficially entitled. If R's estate is fully administered and there has been an assent in favour of the trustees of R's will, one would think that the trustees of R's will had become absolutely entitled to the property as against T or as against R's executor, as the case might be. If R, in the lifetime of L, assigned his remainder interest to X, on L's death X would become absolutely entitled to the property as against T. The answer should be the same whether X is a person who became beneficially entitled by virtue of the assignment or whether he is the trustee of some new settlement. The absolute entitlement of the propositus as against T, the trustee, would appear to be reasonably clear in those cases as a matter of simple language. There is no particular reason to equate absolute entitlement with beneficial ownership in such cases, but rather with the ability to give a good discharge. [1]

Where a person becomes absolutely entitled on the death of a person entitled to an interest in possession in the settled property, s73(1) provides that no chargeable gain shall accrue on the disposal. For example, if trust property is held in the following terms–"To A for life, and then to B"—on A's death, B becomes absolutely entitled to the settled property. He takes the assets at their market value on A's death, but no CGT is payable by the trustees.

Note that for the purposes of the exit charge, it is possible for persons acting in their capacity as trustees of a new settlement to become absolutely entitled to assets against themselves as trustees of an existing settlement. [2] With regard to the timing of when a person can be treated as having become absolutely entitled as against the trustee, Blackburne J

---

[1] *Ibid.*

[2] Hoffman J in *Swires (HMIT) v Renton* [1991] BTC 362 at 371; STC 490.

held in *Figg v Clarke (HMIT)*[1] that, where a person suffered an injury disabling him from having further issue, the impossibility of his having more children should be ignored, and his children became absolutely entitled against the trustees at the date of his death, and not at the date of the injury.

### Termination of Life Interests

By s72(1), if an interest in possession terminates on the death of the person entitled thereto, and the property continues to be settled property, the trustees are deemed to have disposed of, and immediately re-acquired the assets at market value, but no chargeable gain shall accrue on the disposal. The effect of this is to re-base the assets to their market value on the death.

### Disposals of Interests by Beneficiaries

S76(1) provides that no chargeable gain arises to a beneficiary where he disposes of an interest under a settlement, provided that he or someone before him did not acquire his interest for a consideration in money or money's worth (other than another interest under the settlement).

## Timing of Disposals

The timing of a particular disposal depends much on the type of disposal, and on whether or not it is a deemed disposal. Some general principles apply.

### Capital Sums

S22(2) provides that when a capital sum is derived from an asset under s22(1), the time of the disposal shall be the time when the capital sum was received.

### Contracts

S28(1) provides, subject to s22(2) above, that, when an asset is disposed of and acquired under a contract, the time at which the disposal and acquisition is made is the time when the contract is made, and not, if

[1] [1997] BTC 157.

different, the time at which the asset is conveyed or transferred. However, s28(2) provides that, where the contract is conditional, the time of the disposal/acquisition is the time when that the condition is satisfied.

### Hire-Purchase Transactions

By virtue of s27, a hire-purchase transaction will treated as an entire disposal of the asset which is the subject matter of the transaction at the beginning of the period for which the hire-purchaser obtains the use and enjoyment of the asset. The section extends to any transaction whereby the use and enjoyment of an asset is passed, but the transfer of the title and consideration is deferred. This provision is illustrated by *Lyon (HMIT) v Pettigrew.* [1] Certain taxis, together with their licences to ply for hire, were sold under contracts providing that the purchase price was payable in instalments spread over 150 weeks. The contracts also provided that the consideration for the licences was to be severed from the consideration for the sale of the taxis, with the property in the taxis passing immediately to the purchaser, and the property in the licences passing when all instalments had been paid. The taxpayer contended that the contracts were conditional and that the time of disposal was the time when all the instalments are paid. It was held that the contracts were not conditional, that the licences could not be severed from the taxis, and that (what is now) s27 applied. Thus, the time of the disposal was when the purchaser first obtained the use of the taxis. Walton J said: [2]

> The words "contract is conditional" have traditionally, I think, been used to cover really only two types of case. One is a "subject to contract" contract, where there is really no contract at all anyway, and the other is where all the liabilities under the contract are conditional on a certain event. It would, for example, be possible for a hotelier to make a booking with a tour operator conditionally on the next Olympic Games being held in London. Then, until it had been decided that the next Olympic Games were going to be held in London, there would be no effective contract: the whole contract would be conditional, the whole liabilities and duties between the parties would only arise when the condition was fulfilled. But it is quite clear that the present contract is not in the slightest like that.

[1] [1985] STC 369.
[2] At p380.

With respect to the present contract Walton J said that, if there be only one contract, he could not see how the postponement of the carrying out of one part of one contract until the fulfillment of the consideration by the other party could in any way be properly described as a "condition" of the contract, as distinct from a perfectly ordinary part or term of the contract.

## Tax Rates

The normal rate of CGT is equal to the basic rate of income tax for the relevant year (s4(1)). Where an *individual* has no income for a year of assessment, or where his total income for the year is less than the lower rate limit, then the individual is chargeable at the lower rate to the extent that the sum of his income and chargeable gains fall within the lower rate limit (s 4(1A) & (1B)). If an individual is a higher rate tax payer he is charged to CGT at the higher rate (s4(2)). If the taxpayer is a basic rate tax payer, but his chargeable gains exceed the unused part of his income tax basic rate band, CGT on the excess is charged at the higher rate (s4(3)).

By virtue of s5, trustees of discretionary and accumulation trusts are liable to CGT at the rate applicable to trusts for the relevant year.

*Self-Check Questions*

1. What is meant by an "asset" for CGT purposes?
2. Who is a chargeable person?
3. Discuss the principle of causation in the context of deemed disposals, and capital sums derived from assets.
4. What are part disposals, and what are the principle which govern the CGT treatment of part disposals?
5. What are the CGT consequences of death?

## Further Reading

Kerridge K, *Capital Gains Tax—What Next?*, (1990) BTR 68–72.
Bracewell-Milnes B, *The Meade Report and the Taxation of Capital*, (1979) BTR 25–43.

# 11

# Disposal Consideration

## Introduction

We have thus far examined three of the four main questions relevant to the capital gains tax charge, namely, what constitutes a chargeable person, what constitutes an asset, and what constitutes a disposal of an asset. The final question concerns what constitutes a chargeable gain. This will involve detailed examination of the principles applicable to the calculation of a chargeable gain or allowable loss. The rest of our discussions on capital gains tax will be devoted to this question. Broadly speaking, a capital gains tax gain or loss is (due allowance being made for all exemptions and reliefs) computed by deducting allowable expenditure on an asset from the consideration received for its disposal. This chapter is concerned with the matters that are taken into account in arriving the at the amount which a person is taken to have received in return for the disposal of an asset.

In general, the value or consideration for a disposal is the actual value or consideration that passed between the disponor and the disponee. There are potential problems here however. First, there are times when no real consideration passes at all. In this type of case the parties would, if left to themselves, be able to manufacture losses or very low profits at will. Secondly, in some cases in which some consideration actually passes, the consideration is either far below the market value of the asset, or much higher than such market value. Furthermore, there are cases in which consideration is given which cannot be valued, such as love and affection or friendship. Finally, there are those cases in which there is no disposal in the real world, but which fall within the instances of statutory deemed disposals, and for which a value has to be fixed as the consideration for the disposal.

In cases where real consideration passes in a bargain at arm's length there is no need for statutory intervention. In the other situations outlined above the statute has to intervene to counter the obvious planning opportunities. Thus there are various provisions adjusting the disposal consideration (if any). In some instances, a market value is substituted, and in others the disposal is treated as having been for a no-gain/no-loss consideration.

## Market Value

*Transaction's Not At Arm's Length: Section 17*

S17(1)(a) provides that a person's acquisition or disposal of an asset shall be deemed to be for a consideration equal to the market value of the asset where he acquires or disposes of the asset otherwise than by way of a bargain at arm's length—particularly, where the acquisition or disposal is:

(a) a gift
(b) a transfer into a settlement by a settlor
(c) a distribution from a company in respect of its shares.

The typical situations in which this rule will apply concern gifts [1] and transfers at an undervalue. There are however a number of other situations in which it has been applied. In *Davenport (HMIT) v Chilver* [2] for example, Nourse J held that, a right to compensation, conferred by a statutory instrument, on a taxpayer who had nothing beforehand, was an asset acquired by the taxpayer otherwise than by way of a bargain made at arm's length. The right was therefore to be deemed to have been acquired by the taxpayer for a consideration equal to its market value. The argument that in this case the market value must be the actual amount received, giving rise to neither a gain nor a loss, seemed to appeal to Nourse J, who then suggested [3] that the proper course would be for the Crown to proceed on the footing that there had been neither a gain nor a loss in the value of the taxpayer's right during the material period. [4]

This market value rule was also applied in *Zim Properties Ltd v Procter (HMIT)* [5] where Warner J held that the taxpayer's right to bring an

---

[1] See e.g. *Turner v Follett (HMIT)* [1973] STC 148—gifts by the taxpayer to his children were treated as disposals at market value.

[2] [1983] STC 426.

[3] At p442.

[4] Nourse J said however that, if asked to do, so he would remit the case to the commissioners to calculate the market value.

[5] [1985] STC 90, discussed in chapter 9.

action against its solicitors for negligence was an asset acquired at the time of the solicitors' allegedly negligent act. Such an acquisition was not by way of a bargain at arm's length, and thus the right must be deemed to have been acquired for a consideration equal to its market value, if any.

S17(1)(b) extends this market value rule to situations in which a person acquires or disposes of an asset wholly or partly for a consideration that cannot be valued. The effect of this provision is illustrated by *Fielder (HMIT) v Vedlynn Ltd.*[1] The taxpayer company sold some shares in some of its subsidiaries in return for a sum (which was acknowledged to be the market value of the shares), and some guarantees by the purchaser, that the subsidiaries of the taxpayer into which it was buying would discharge their obligations to the taxpayer. The special commissioner decided that, although the guarantees formed part of the consideration for the sale of the shares they did not add any monetary value to the sums that had been paid. Harman J, dismissing the Revenue's appeal from the decision of the special commissioner, said[2]:

> The consideration was in part the guarantee by [the purchaser]. It seems to be that . . . one would certainly require some prima facie case that the guarantees had a separate monetary value, or were capable of having such value, perhaps because one could find a market in which a comparable guarantee had been sold or some accustomed way of dealing in guarantees so they could be said to be capable of valuation. If that is not so a consideration has passed which cannot be valued and it falls clearly within [s17(1)(b)]. Therefore one is thrown back on the market value of the assets (the shares). It is agreed that the shares passed at full market value at the cash price. Upon that basis again it seems to me that the special commissioner was entitled to reach the conclusion he did.

## Connected Persons: Section 18

S18(2) treats transactions between connected persons as transactions other than by way of a bargain at arm's length. This means that the market value rule of s17 automatically applies.

---

[1] [1992] BTC 347.
[2] At p361.

S286 deals with the meaning of "connected persons", as follows.

## Individuals

By virtue of s286(2), an individual is connected with:

(a) His or her spouse—thus where in divorce proceedings property is transferred by a husband to his wife under a consent order, this is to be taken as a disposal by the husband at market value.[1] Note that, although husbands and wives are connected with each other, ss17 and 18 do not apply to them if they are living together. S58 instead applies roll over relief, to ensure a "no gain/no loss" situation. On the other hand where the husband and wife are not living together, tax is chargeable.[2]

(b) His/her relatives—a relative is defined in s286(8) as a brother, sister, ancestor or lineal descendant, and their spouses.

(c) His/her spouse's relatives, and their spouses.

## Trustees

S286(3) provides that a trustee is connected (in his capacity as trustee) with the settlor, anyone connected with the settlor, and with any body corporate connected with the settlement.

## Partners

S286(4) provides that, except for acquisitions and disposals of partnership assets pursuant to bona fide commercial arrangements, partners are connected with each other, and with each other's spouses and relatives.

## Companies

By virtue of s286(6) a company is connected with another person if it is controlled by that person, either alone, or in conjunction with persons who are connected with him.

---

[1] *Apsden (HMIT) v Hildesley* [1982] STC 206.

[2] *Apsden (HMIT) v Hildesley, supra.*

*Value Shifting*

This has been discussed in the preceding chapter in our examination of deemed disposals.

*Appropriations To and From Trading Stock*

This has also been discussed earlier.

*Market Value—Definition*

S272(1) provides that "market value", in relation to an asset, means the price which that asset might reasonably be expected to fetch on a sale on the open market. No reduction can be made on this price on the basis of any assumption that the whole of the assets are to be sold at the same time (s272(2)). It may be that, in some situations in which some consideration had actually been given and in which there is no other evidence as to the market value, the consideration that actually passed will be taken as the best evidence of market value, [1] particularly where the so-called market value is wholly hypothetical. [2]

## No Gain/No Loss (Hold/Roll Over Relief)

*Introduction*

In a number of situations the statute provides for a disposal or acquisition to be valued at a consideration which will ensure that neither a gain nor a loss accrues to the disponor. The provisions usually achieve this result by implementing what is known as "roll over" relief. This, in effect, is a means of deferring the tax which is due on a gain until the occurrence of some event which does not attract the relief. The usual mechanism is by treating the gain as not accruing until the conditions for the relief no longer exist. Practically, roll over relief involves reducing both the consideration which the disponor is to be treated as having received, and

---

[1] See Sir John Vinelott in *Whitehouse v Ellam (HMIT)* [1995] BTC 284 at 290.
[2] Sir John Vinelott said in *Whitehouse v Ellam (HMIT), ibid*—"I do not see how any other method of valuation can possibly have had the result of displacing what was actually received in favour some wholly hypothetical value . . .".

(sometimes) the acquisition cost of the disponee [1], by the amount of the chargeable gain that would otherwise have accrued to the disponor. This would then result in a situation where the disponor has made neither a gain nor a loss and is not taxable on the transaction. The corollary of this is that the disponee (who may sometimes be the same person as the disponor) has acquired the asset for a reduced cost, and his profit figure will be correspondingly higher when he eventually disposes of the asset.

We will now go on to examine some of the more important instances of no gain/no loss.

## Husband and Wife

S58(1) provides that, if in any year in which they are living together, a husband and wife dispose of assets to one another, the transaction will be treated as if the asset was acquired for such consideration as would secure that neither a gain nor a loss would accrue to the disponor. By virtue of s58(2)(a) this provision does not apply if the asset, before disposal, formed part of the trading stock of the disponor, or if it was acquired as trading stock by the disponee. S58(2)(b) also excepts any disposal by way of *donatio mortis causa* from the operation of the provision.

Concerning the question when a husband and wife will be taken as living together, s288(3) stipulates that the matter shall be construed in accordance with s282 of the ICTA 1988. According to s282 ICTA 1988, a husband and wife shall be treated as living together unless they are separated under an order of a court of competent jurisdiction, or by deed of separation, or they are in fact separated in such circumstances that the separation is likely to be permanent.

## Gifts to Charity

S257(1) and (2) provide, in respect of gifts to charities (and certain other national bodies listed in Schedule 3 of the Inheritance Tax Act 1984) that, if the disposal is not one to which s 151A(1) applies (venture capital trusts), the disposal and acquisition shall be treated as being for such a consideration as would ensure that neither a gain nor a loss accrues. When the charity later disposes of the asset, the acquisition of the person who made the gift to it is treated as its own acquisition.

---

[1] Sometimes only the disponor is involved in the disposal and acquisition.

*Replacement of Lost or Destroyed Assets*

S23(4) applies if an asset is lost or destroyed, and the insurance compensation received in respect of such loss or destruction is applied for the purpose of replacing the asset within one year of receipt, or such longer period as the inspector may allow. On a claim by the owner, he will be treated as having disposed of the old asset for a consideration which will secure that neither a gain nor a loss accrues to him, and as having acquired the new asset for a consideration reduced by the held over gain.

Where a building is destroyed or irreparably damaged, and a capital sum received by way of compensation for the destruction or damage (or under an insurance policy in respect thereof) is wholly or partly applied in constructing or otherwise acquiring a replacement building elsewhere, both the original and the replacement buildings shall, for the purposes of a claim under s23(4), be treated as distinct assets separate from the land on which they stand, and the old building shall be treated as lost or destroyed (s 23(6)). All necessary apportionments of any consideration or expenditure will be made in such manner as is just and reasonable (s23(7)).

*Replacement of Business Assets*

S152(1) provides roll over relief in cases wherein the consideration received for the disposal of assets or of an interest in assets ("the old assets") used solely, throughout the period of ownership, for the purposes of a person's trade, is applied in acquiring other assets or interests in other assets ("the new assets"), which on acquisition are taken into use solely for the purposes of the trade. In such cases, if the trader makes a claim with respect to the consideration which has been so applied, he will be treated as having disposed of the old assets for a no gain/no loss consideration. The acquisition cost of the new assets will then be reduced by the amount by which the actual consideration exceeds the "no gain/no loss" value (the held over gain). These provisions do not affect the treatment of the other parties to the transactions involving the old and the new assets.

Where there is a part disposal of a single asset which was acquired for an unapportioned consideration, it cannot be said that the part disposal is a disposal of "old assets", or that the retained part constitutes "new assets", or, that the consideration arising from the part disposal was applied in the acquisition of "other assets". [1] Thus, roll over relief will not

[1] Sir John Vinelott in *Watton (HMIT) v Tippett* [1996] BTC 25.

apply in such cases. This is because a part disposal of an asset is to be treated as a disposal of the asset, not as a disposal of part of the asset (for example, the grant of a lease of a house is a part disposal of the house but not a disposal of part of the house). [1] However, a part disposal of an asset may involve a disposal of a severable part. If, for example, a taxpayer were to buy from the same vendor two adjacent properties under two separate but contemporaneous contracts, there would be no reason in principle why the sale of one should not be treated as the sale of old assets, and why the retained part should not be treated as new assets for the purposes of s152. [2] According to Sir John Vinelott in *Watton (HMIT) v Tippett* [3] the description of assets as "old" and "new" is functional and not temporal, and it may be that the result would be the same if the two properties were acquired under the same contract and at a time when they were not physically separated, provided that they could be treated as separate assets and, that the consideration was apportioned between them at the time of sale. [4]

For the purposes of roll over relief on replacement of business assets, when the proceeds of the sale are used to enhance the value of other assets, concessionary relief is available in ESC D22 which treats the expenditure as expenditure incurred on acquiring new assets, if:

(i) the other assets are used only for the purposes of the trade;
(ii) on completion of the work on which the expenditure was incurred, the assets are immediately taken into use and used only for the purposes of the trade.

Furthermore, where the trader uses the proceeds from the disposal of the old asset to acquire a further interest in another asset which is already in use for the purposes of the trade, ESC D25 applies to treat that further interest as a "new asset" which is taken into use for the purposes of the trade.

A final concession with respect to this provision is in ESC D16 which provides that, where a person sells a business or a business asset, and, for purely commercial reasons subsequently repurchases the same asset, that asset will be regarded as a new asset.

---

[1] Sir John Vinelott at p32.
[2] At p33.
[3] *Ibid.*
[4] *Ibid.*

S152(1) stipulates that, in order for this relief to be available, the new asset must be taken into use for the purposes of the taxpayer's business at the time when it is acquired. This requirement has been applied strictly by the courts. So for example, Knox J held in *Campbell Connelly and Co Ltd v Barnett (HMIT)*[1] that, when a new asset is acquired in January, but is only taken into use for the taxpayer's business in September, the provision is not satisfied. Even if the taxpayer was anxious to take the asset into use immediately on its acquisition, if the taxpayer was in fact unable to do, then his intention is irrelevant. What matters is what actually happened.

The principle that an asset must be taken into use at the time when it is acquired makes the timing of an acquisition very important, especially in respect of disposals under a contract. S28 provides that where an asset is disposed of and acquired under a contract, the time of the disposal and acquisition is the time when the contract was made, and not, if different, the time when the asset is conveyed or transferred. This would have meant that, in cases where assets were disposed of under contract but the time of delivery was much later than the date of the contract, claims for relief under s152 would have failed automatically. However Knox J accepted in *Campbell Connelly and Co Ltd v Barnett* that the timing provision in s28 was not intended to apply here. According to him, there seems to be "enough internal evidence in s152 to lead to the conclusion that the acquisitions being aimed at are complete acquisitions, not ones which still lie in contract".[2]

In order to temper the rigours of the requirement that the new asset be taken into use immediately, ESC D24 gives a measure of relief in certain cases in which the new asset is not taken into use immediately, by treating the new asset as having nevertheless qualified for the relief given by s152. There are a number of conditions before this concession will be available:

(i)    the owner proposes to incur capital expenditure for the purposes of enhancing the value of the new asset, and

(ii)    any work arising from such capital expenditure begins as soon as possible after acquisition, and is completed within a reasonable time, and

(iii)    on completion of the work the asset is taken into use for the purpose of the trade and for no other purpose, and

(iv)    the asset is not let or used for any non-trading purpose in the period

[1] [1992] BTC 164; STC 316 (upheld by the Court of Appeal, [1994] BTC 12).
[2] [1992] BTC 164 at 172.

between acquisition and the time it is taken into use for the purposes of the trade.

The concession extends to cases where a person acquires land with a building on it, or with the intention to construct a building on it. In such cases the land will qualify for relief provided that:

(i) the building itself qualifies for relief;
(ii) the land is not let or used for any non-trading purpose in the period between its acquisition and the time that both it and the building are taken into use for the purposes of the trade.

The assets in respect of which a claim is made must be one of those specified in s155 which lists six Classes of asset. Class 1 is divided into two "Heads"—A and B. Head A covers (subject to restrictions in s156) any building or part of a building, any permanent or semi-permanent structure in the nature of a building occupied (as well as used) only for the purposes of a person's trade, and any land occupied (as well as used) only for the purposes of the trade. Head B covers fixed plant or machinery which does not form part of a building or of a permanent or semi-permanent structure in the nature of a building. Class 2 concerns ships, aircraft and hovercraft. Class 3 concerns satellites, space stations and spacecraft (including launch vehicles). Class 4 concerns goodwill. Class 5 concerns milk quotas and potato quotas, and Class 6 concerns ewe and suckler cow premium quotas.

Class 1 has attracted some attention in the cases. First, with respect to land, case law indicates that the requirement that the land be occupied and used for the purposes of the trade, is to be taken strictly. This approach is illustrated by *Temperly (HMIT) v Visibell Ltd.*[1] The taxpayer company purchased some land on which it intended to build a factory specially designed for its trade of the forming and printing of plastic guide-cards, and some offices. Planning permission was obtained for the construction, but during negotiations on the commencement of building works, and as a result of observations on visits to the site, it became apparent that the adverse conditions on the site would necessitate considerable expenditure before production could be commenced. A more suitable site was therefore acquired, and the old one was disposed of. The company claimed roll over relief. Relief was denied on the

[1] [1974] STC 64.

grounds that the old site had not been occupied as well as used for the company's trade. Mere visits to the site, coupled with an intention to build, and an application for planning permission, were not enough, and could not constitute use and occupation for the purposes of the company's trade.

When the land has actually been occupied as well as used for the purposes of the taxpayer's trade, it is essential that it was used *only* for those purposes. In *Anderton (HMIT) v Lamb* [1] Goulding J applied a strict interpretation of the phrase "land occupied (as well as used) only for the purposes of the trade" in Head A. He held that buildings occupied partly for use as homes could not qualify for relief because they were not occupied as well as used only for the purposes of the trade.

Secondly, with respect to plant, Nourse J held in *Williams v Evans (HMIT)* [2] that the phrase "fixed plant and machinery" under Head B meant "fixed plant" and "fixed machinery". So when the taxpayer sold earth-moving machines and used the proceeds to buy new earth-moving machines, this transaction was not eligible for roll over relief because the earth-moving machines were not fixed machinery but movable machinery. Thus the gain on the sale of the old machines was chargeable. According to Nourse J [3]:

> ... head B is referring to fixed plant which does not form part of a building etc and to machinery which does not form part of a building etc. On that footing I think it would be unnatural to read "fixed" as qualifying only plant and not machinery as well, because it would be rather strange, if not actually ridiculous, for the provision to contemplate that movable machinery might form part of a building. On the other hand it is perfectly natural for it to contemplate that fixed machinery might form part of a building.

There are a number of statutory restrictions with respect to this relief. By virtue of s152(5), the section will not apply unless the acquisition of the new asset was made for the purpose of its use in the trade, and not wholly or partly for the purpose of realising a gain from the disposal of the new asset or of an interest in it. Also, if the old assets were not used for the purposes of the trade throughout the period of ownership, s152(7) requires apportionment of the consideration in order to determine the

[1] [1981] STC 43.
[2] [1982] STC 498.
[3] At p503.

part which represents use for trade purposes. Only this part will qualify for relief. Finally, "period of ownership" in the section does not include any period before 31 March 1982.[1]

### Replacement of Compulsorily Acquired Land

S247 provides relief in cases of compulsory acquisition of land. The conditions for the relief are specified in s247(1):

(a) land is disposed of by a landowner to an authority exercising or having compulsory powers;
(b) the landowner did not take any steps, by advertising or otherwise, to dispose of the land or to make his willingness to dispose of it known to the authority or others; and
(c) the consideration for the disposal is applied by the landowner in acquiring other land.

If these conditions are satisfied and the landowner makes a claim, s247(2) provides, in cases where the whole of the consideration for the old land was applied in acquiring the new land, that he will be treated as having disposed the old land for a no gain/no loss consideration, and having acquired the new land for a consideration reduced by the held over gain. If only a part of the consideration was applied for the purpose of acquiring the new land, then if the part of the consideration which was not so applied is less than the amount of the gain, there will be an apportionment, if the landowner so claims (s247(3)).

These provisions do not affect the tax treatment of the authority which acquired the old land or the other party to the transaction involving the acquisition of the new land (s247(4)). There is a further restriction in s248 which provides that these provisions do not apply to private residences qualifying for the "main residence" relief.

### Gifts of Business Assets

s165(1) provides that if an individual makes a disposal, otherwise than by way of a bargain at arm's length, of certain qualifying assets, then on a claim by both the transferor and transferee, the chargeable gain on the disposal, and the acquisition cost of the transferee, will be reduced by the

---

[1] See s152(9); cf *Richart (HMIT) v Lyon* ([1989] STC 665), in which the Court of Appeal held that "period of ownership" in the predecessor of s152 included a period before 6 April 1965.

held over gain. The qualifying assets are described in s165(2). An asset qualifies if:

(a) it is an asset or an interest in an asset, used either for the purposes of a trade, profession or vocation, carried on by the transferor, or his personal company, or a member of a trading group of which the transferor's personal company is the holding company; or
(b) the asset consists of shares or securities of a trading company or of the holding company of a trading group, and the shares are unlisted, or the company is the transferor's personal company.

For definitions, s165(8) refers to definitions contained in Schedule 6, paragraph 1.

(a) *Personal company*, in relation to an individual, means a company in which the individual himself can exercise not less than five per cent of the voting rights (Schedule 6 (1)(2)).
(b) *Trading company* means any company whose business consists wholly or mainly of the carrying on of a trade or trades (Schedule 6(1)(2)).
(c) *Trading group* means a group of companies the business of whose members, taken together, consists wholly or mainly of the carrying on of a trade or trades (Schedule 6(1)(2)).

### Company Reorganisations

There are a number of provisions which govern the CGT consequences of company reorganisations. First, s127 provides that a reorganisation of a company's share capital shall not be treated as involving any disposal of the original shares or any part of it, or as involving any acquisition of the new holding. Rather, the original and new shares, each taken as a single asset, shall be treated as the same asset acquired as the original shares were acquired. Secondly, s135(1) extends this principle to situations where a company exchanges its shares or debentures for shares or debentures in another company. In such cases s135(3) provides that s127 shall apply (with any necessary adaptations) as if the two companies were the same company and the exchange were a reorganisation of its share capital. Thirdly, in cases involving disposals by one member of a group of companies to another member of the group, s171(1) provides that both members shall be treated, for the purposes of corporation tax on chargeable gains, as if the asset acquired by the disponee were acquired for a consideration of such amount as would secure that neither a gain nor a loss would accrue to the disponor. However, by s171(3), this provision does not apply to a transaction treated by sections 127 and 135 as not involving a disposal by the disponor company. This means that disposals between members of the same group take place at a "no gain/no loss" consideration except where the disposal involves an exchange of the shares of one company in the group for the shares of another company in the group.

The policies underlying these provisions have been explored in the cases. According to Hoffman J in *Westcott (HMIT) v Woolcombers Ltd*[1], the policy of (what is now) s171(1) is:

> ... to recognise that in the case of transactions between members of a group of companies, the legal theory that each company is a separate entity does not accord with economic reality. It gives effect to that policy by, broadly speaking, ignoring transactions within the group, computing the gain as the difference between the consideration given when an asset was acquired by the group and the consideration received when it left the group and charging the tax on upon whichever company made the outward disposal.[2]

In the light of s171(3), this policy seems to have now been abandoned in respect of inter-group share exchanges. While s171 is aimed at transactions within a group, s127 and s135 are directed at the position of a shareholder who is as likely to be a private individual as a company, and the underlying philosophy is to "secure that shareholders in companies which are involved in reorganisations of share capital or which are the subject of amalgamations or takeovers do not incur chargeable gains on disposals over which they have little or no control. Only when they later dispose of the new shares will a chargeable gain arise."[3]

The courts have had the opportunity to examine these provisions. Since s171(1) no longer applies to group reorganisations, we will examine the cases in the context of sections 127 and 135. In *Westcott (HMIT) v Woolcombers Ltd*[4] Fox LJ said[5] that the combined effect of these

---

[1] [1986] BTC 130 at 138 (approved by Lord Keith in *NAP Holdings UK Ltd v Whittles (HMIT)* [1994] BTC 450 at 456).
[2] Compare *NAP Holdings UK Ltd v Whittle (HMIT)* ([1994] BTC 450); Lord Keith of Kinkel at p458, and Lord Jauncey of Tullichettle at p459.
[3] Lord Jauncey of Tullichettle in *NAP Holdings UK Ltd. v Whittle (HMIT)* [1994] BTC at p459.
[4] [1987] STC 600; 60 TC 575.
[5] At p603.

provisions is to impose two fictions. The first is the "no disposal fiction". This is the consequence of the words ". . . shall not be treated as involving any disposal of the original shares or any acquisition of the new holding . . ." He said that those words seem to assume that a share reorganisation or reduction can give rise to a disposal, and the provision is artificially displacing that assumption. The second fiction is the "composite single asset fiction". This is the consequence of the words ". . . the original shares (taken as a single asset) and the new holdings (taken as a single asset) shall be treated as the same asset acquired as the original shares were acquired". These fictions are however only applicable to a case which is within s135 "with any necessary adaptations". Fox LJ said [1] that cases to which s127 apply can be described as the "one company situation". Here, the shareholder starts and finishes with shares in the same company. They may, wholly or in part, be shares of a different nature to those originally held, but he remains a shareholder in the same company. Cases to which s135 apply can be described as the "two companies situation". Here the shareholder starts with shares in one company and ends with shares in a different company.

According to Fox LJ [2] there is no difficulty in applying the two fictions to the "one company situation". The purpose of s127 is to exclude any claim for capital gains tax on the reorganisation or reduction of the company's share capital. This is achieved in effect by treating the new shareholding as if it were the original shareholding. However the matter is not so straightforward in the "two companies situation". Some adaptations of the provisions of s127, which were designed for the one company situation, will be required here. The "composite single asset fiction" cannot be applied fully, and s135 does not require that the exchange be disregarded. The requirement is that it be treated as a reorganisation. In this respect, Fox LJ noted that shares in the hands of one person cannot be treated as the same asset as other shares in the hands of another person. The position of the company which transfers the original shares is different. The original asset and the new asset cannot be treated as the same asset in the hands of such a transferor.

In order to determine the adaptations necessary for the two companies situation, Fox LJ went on to consider the purpose of s135. The section is concerned to ensure that where a shareholder in company A exchanges that shareholding for an issue of shares in company B, the shareholder is

---

[1] *Ibid.*
[2] At p604.

not taxed on that transaction. The shareholder in company A is treated as continuing to own the same asset, but company B cannot be treated as owning the shares which it has issued in consequence of the exchange. Furthermore, company B has become the owner of the shares in company A and so the composite single asset fiction cannot operate in relation to company B. If one of the fictions cannot be applied to company B, neither can the other. The position with the fictions is that they are both part of a single hypothesis and go together. The purpose of this hypothesis is to relieve the shareholder in a one company situation, and the transferor in a two companies situation from liability to tax. Thus the proper solution in the two companies situation is to limit the fictions to the tax consequences of the transaction to the owner of the original shares. [1] This decision was approved by the House of Lords in *NAP Holdings UK Ltd v Whittles (HMIT)*. [2] Lord Keith of Kinkel said [3]:

> It is plain that [s127] can apply only to the tax position of a shareholder who as a result of a company reorganisation disposes of his original holding in it and receives in exchange, a new holding in it. It cannot affect the company which is the subject of the reorganisation ... I am of the opinion that [s135] is likewise intended to affect only the tax position of the shareholder who disposes of his shares in one company in exchange for shares in another company, and not the tax position of that other company.

## Partnerships

### Introduction

S59(a) provides that, where two or more persons carry on a trade or business in partnership, they are to be charged and assessed on gains accruing on the disposal of partnership assets, separately. The principle extends to Scotland (*ibid*). By s59(b), partnership dealings are treated as made by the partners and not by the firm as such. The approach of the Revenue to CGT and partnerships is detailed in an important and lengthy statement of practice (D12, of 17 January 1975). Many of the principles discussed below are derived from this statement of practice.

---

[1] The effect of this decision has subsequently been reversed in part by s171(3).
[2] [1994] BTC 450 (Lord Lloyd of Berwick dissenting).
[3] At p458.

*Partnership Assets*

Each partner is regarded as owning a fractional share of each of the
partnership assets and it is this fractional share that the partner disposes of
when a partnership asset is sold. Thus when an asset is disposed of by the
partnership to an outsider, each of the partners will be treated as having
disposed of his fractional share of the asset. The same principle applies in
respect of part disposals of partnership assets. In these cases each partner
will be treated as having made a part disposal of his fractional share.

In computing the gains or losses on the disposal, the consideration
received for the disposal is allocated between the partners in the ratio of
their shares in asset surpluses at the time of the disposal. In the absence of
any surplus sharing provision, regard is had in the first instance to the
actual destination of the surplus as shown in the partnership accounts, or
to the ordinary profit sharing ratio. When a new partnership asset is
acquired, the expenditure on the acquisition is allocated between the
partners in similar fashion at the time of the acquisition.

*Dealings Between Partners*

It is important here to note that by s286(4) partners are connected with:

1. each other;
2. each other's spouses; and
3. each other's relatives.

The only exception to this is with respect to "acquisitions or disposals of
partnership assets pursuant to bona fide commercial arrangements".
Thus, in many instances dealing between partners will be subject to the
market value rule in s17.

*Changes in Profit-Sharing Ratios*

A change in the profit-sharing ratios, including one occurring when a
partner joins or leaves the firm is a disposal by some partners of a fraction
of their interests in partnership assets, and a corresponding acquisition by
other partners. More specifically, a partner who reduces or gives up his
share in asset surpluses will be treated as disposing of part or the whole of
his share in each of the partnership assets, and a partner who increases his
share will be treated as making a similar acquisition. Where no
adjustment is made through the partnership accounts, the disposal is

treated by the Revenue practice statement as being at a consideration equal to the disposing partner's CGT cost, and thus there will be neither a gain nor loss at that point. It results in a reduction of the base cost of the partner whose share is reduced, and an increase for one whose share is increased.

## General Notes on Consideration

### Deferred Payments

There is no discount for deferment of the consideration for the disposal of an asset. S48 provides that the disposal consideration shall be brought into account without any discount for the postponement of the right to receive any part of it, and without regard in the first instance to a risk of any part of the consideration being irrecoverable, or to the right to receive any part of the consideration being contingent. However, if any part of the consideration brought into account subsequently proves to be irrecoverable, any necessary adjustment will be made. These provisions have the potential to result in transactions being treated for CGT purposes in a way that departs from economic or commercial reality. [1] One problem is "acceleration" (that something which has not yet been paid is deemed to have been paid). In this respect, Lloyd J said in *Goodbrand (HMIT) v Loffland Bros North Sea Inc* [2]:

> [I]f a disposal is in whole or in part for deferred consideration, that element of business reality is ignored at the outset, and tax is payable on the false assumption that there is no postponement, and on the assumption (which may or may not turn out to be false) that the whole amount is in fact paid. If, however, some part is contingent, and the contingency is not satisfied, or if the debtor defaults on some part of the price, an adjustment is to be made to reflect the non-payment. No adjustment, however, is to be made to counteract the deemed acceleration of the deferred instalments which are in fact paid. This led Lord Wilberforce [in *Marren (HMIT) v Ingles*] to apply the epithet "draconian" to this provision.

Acceleration produces an "anomaly"—that the consideration deemed to

[1] See generally *Goodbrand (HMIT) v Loffland Bros North Sea Inc* [1997] BTC 100.
[2] [1997] BTC 100 at p105.

be paid is worth more than its real financial value because of there being no discount for postponement.[1] According to Lloyd J,[2] the phrase "subsequently shown to be irrecoverable . . ." covers both the risk of part of the consideration being irrecoverable on the default of the debtor and the possibility that the right to receive part of it may be contingent, and the contingency may not be satisfied. However, the section is only concerned with acceleration (for which there is no discount or adjustment) and, with presuming that all the consideration will be received (for which an adjustment can be allowed if it is not received).[3] Consideration may be shown to be irrecoverable for this purpose, only if, although due, it is not received (presumably because of the default of the debtor), or if the right to receive it is subject to a contingency which, in the event, is not satisfied.[4] Thus, Lloyd J rejected the taxpayer's argument that, where an asset is disposed of for a cash sum payable in foreign currency, and the sterling value of the proceeds when received is less than its value at the time of the disposal, the difference is "irrecoverable", and an adjustment falls to be made under this provision. According to him, the section was not directed at changes in exchange rates or other changes in valuation after the original valuation. The taxpayer had anticipated receiving and did receive the full amount of the original consideration, no part of which became or proved to be irrecoverable—and this was the case regardless of the fact that the depreciation of sterling during the payment period resulted in the amount received at the end being worth less than it was at the beginning.[5]

### Relief for Instalment Payments

S280 gives some relief where consideration is payable instalmentally for more than eighteen months from the disposal. At the option of the person making the disposal, the tax on a chargeable gain accruing on the disposal may be paid by such instalments as the Board may allow, over a period not exceeding eight years, and ending not later than the time when the last of the instalments of the disposal consideration is due.

---

[1] Lloyd J at 107.
[2] [1997] BTC 100 at 107.
[3] *Ibid.*
[4] At p108.
[5] See pp107–108.

*Self-Check Questions*

1. In what circumstances will the market value rule of s17 TCGA 1992 apply to a disposal?
2. What is meant by "roll over relief"?
3. Discuss the principles governing the availability of roll over relief on the replacement of business assets.
4. In what circumstances will roll over relief be available in respect of company reorganisations?
5. Discuss the CGT treatment of disposals by a partnership.

## Further Reading

Venables R, *Capital Gains Tax on Gifts—A Critique*, (1989) BTR 333–347.

# 12
# Allowable Expenditure

## Introduction

The factors discussed in the preceding chapter are taken into account in the determination of the amount of the consideration which a person who has disposed of an asset will be taken to have received in return for the asset. The amount so determined will invariably be gross in the hands of the disponor, and since the TCGA charges tax only on gains there will be a need to deduct expenses from the gross receipts. The types of expenditure which can be so deducted are specified in s38 and are the subject of this chapter.

## Acquisition Cost

Expenditure which is deductible as the acquisition cost of an asset is described in s38(1)(a) as the consideration given wholly and exclusively for the acquisition of the asset. This refers to the amount of the consideration if it is in money, or its value in money's worth, if it is not in money. [1] As far as possible, the matter should be determined according to normal business principles. [2] The acquisition cost will normally be the actual price paid for the asset. [3] Where non-monetary consideration is given, the value of the consideration will normally be the market value except if the transaction was by way of a bargain made at arm's length. In the latter type of case, the value of the non-monetary consideration will be that which was placed on it by the parties, which need not be the market value. This principle is established by *Stanton (HMIT) v Drayton Commercial Investment Ltd* [4] where assets were acquired at a consideration fixed at

---

[1] See Lord Fraser in *Stanton (HMIT) v Drayton Commercial Investment Ltd.*, [1982] STC 585 at 588.

[2] Lord Wilberforce in *Aberdeen Construction Group Ltd v IRC* ([1978] 1 All ER 962 at 966; 52 TC 281 at 296).

[3] See Carnwath J in *Garner (HMIT) v Pounds Shipowners & Shipbreakers Ltd* ([1997] BTC 223 at 230); ". . . in the case of an arm's length disposal for a monetary consideration such consideration is the starting point for the computation of the gain."

[4] [1982] STC 585.

nearly £4m, to be satisfied by a share issue (about 2.5m shares at £1.60 each). It was held that, since the transaction was a bona fide one made at arm's length, the acquisition cost was that fixed by the parties, and not the market value of the shares (£1.25 each on flotation, totalling £3,125,000). It has also been held in *E V Booth (Holdings) Ltd v Buckwell (HMIT)* [1] that where parties to a transaction had, as a result of negotiations between them, provided for a certain consideration for the disposal, they cannot subsequently seek to change it for tax purposes.

In those situations wherein a market value is specified by the Act (e.g. in cases where the transaction is not by way of a bargain at arm's length under s17(1)), the acquisition cost will be the market value. This will be the case even in the case of an acquisition which is not matched by a corresponding disposal. In *Harrison (HMIT) v Naim Williamson Ltd* [2] the Court of Appeal held that, in computing the acquisition cost of the taxpayer, the market value rule (in respect of transactions not by way of a bargain at arm's length) applies not only to transactions where there was an acquisition and a disposal (i.e. where the acquisition is the consequence of a disposal), but extends to cases where there was an acquisition by the taxpayer, without a corresponding disposal by the person from whom the asset was acquired (as in for example, an original subscription for stocks or shares in a company). According to Buckley LJ, [3] where there are both an acquisition and a disposal, the subsection will apply to both the acquirer and the disposer; where there is only an acquisition it will apply only to the acquirer, there being no disposal to be affected.

By virtue of s38(1)(a) where an asset was not acquired (e.g. goodwill and paintings) the allowable expenditure will be "any expenditure wholly or exclusively incurred ... in providing the asset". Thus in the case of paintings created by the disponor for example, the costs of the canvas, the brush, the oil paint, etc. used for the painting, will be deductible as part of the acquisition costs.

### Incidental Costs of Acquisition

In many cases, the purchase price of an asset will not be the only costs that will have been incurred in acquiring the asset. There are sometimes fees and commissions to be paid, and there may well be sundry petty expenses. The CGT regime recognises the existence of these expenses and attempts to relieve them. In this respect s38(1)(a) provides for the deductibility of

[1] [1980] STC 578.
[2] [1978] STC 67.
[3] At p71.

the incidental costs of acquiring an asset. This are defined in s38(2) as expenditure wholly and exclusively incurred for the purposes of the acquisition, being fees, money paid to a surveyor or valuer, auctioneer or accountant, agent or legal adviser, and costs of transfer or conveyance including stamp duties, together with the advertising costs to find a seller. Apart from the items specifically enumerated in the subsection, the provisions should be wide enough to include items such as fees paid to the lands registry.

## Enhancement Expenditure

Most people who have held an asset for more than a brief period would as a matter of course have spent money on maintenance, repair, improvements and other similar matters, either for the purpose of maintaining or increasing the value of the asset, or for the purpose of keeping it from being run down. If such expenditure serves to increase the value of the asset beyond what it would have been without the expenditure, this will inevitably lead to a higher profit figure and enure to the benefit of the Revenue. If while so benefiting the Revenue the taxpayer is unable to claim the expenditure as a deduction, the result will be a grossly unfair tax situation. The tax legislation therefore tries to provide relief for people who have incurred expenditure in this way. The relief so provided is not an open invitation to taxpayers to spend money freely on their assets. While all the types of expenditure just mentioned may well be legitimate items of expenditure in the views of asset owners, the CGT legislation is selective about the ones that will be relieved.

The relieving provision is found in s38(1)(b) which provides for the deductibility of the expenditure wholly and exclusively incurred in enhancing the value of the asset, which is reflected in the state or nature of the asset at the time of the disposal. With regard to disposals under a contract, even though s28(1) provides that the "time of disposal" is the time when the contract was entered into, for the purposes of s38(1)(b) (particularly with regard to the question whether the expenditure is reflected in the state of the asset at the time of disposal) the timing may be more flexible. Nicholls J said in *Chaney v Watkis (HMIT)* [1] that the context in which the phrase "at the time of the disposal" is found in s38(1)(b) compels the conclusion that that phrase does not exclude expenditure which is first reflected in the state or nature of the property after the date of the contract, but before completion.

[1] [1986] STC 89 at 94.

There are a number of restrictions on the deductibility of an item of expenditure under the heading of enhancement expenditure. First, the expense concerned must not be one which is an ordinary incident of the taxpayer's ownership or usage of the asset. Thus it was held by the Court of Appeal in *Emmerson (HMIT) v Computer Time International Ltd*[1] that a tenant who incurred expenditure in discharging his obligations under a lease, which obligations were an incident of his title, could not claim the expenditure as enhancement expenditure, or as expenditure for establishing, preserving or defending his title to the lease. Explaining the position, Orr LJ said[2]:

> ... in my judgment the phrase "expenditure wholly and exclusively incurred ... in establishing, preserving or defending his title to, or to a right over, the asset" applies to such matters as evicting a squatter or registering a charge over property, but has no application to the performance of a tenant's obligations under a lease.

Furthermore, the expenditure sought to be deducted must actually have been incurred: it must reduce taxpayer's estate in some quantitative way. Thus for example, it does not include the estimated cost of the taxpayer's own labour. The principle in point here was examined in *Oram v Johnson*.[3] The taxpayer had bought some property which he improved and enlarged by himself. He decided to deduct as enhancement expenditure the cost of his own labour and skill in improving the property, which he estimated at £1,700 on the basis of 1,700 hours work at £1 per hour. It was held that this sum was not deductible. Walton J explained[4]:

> It seems to me that, although one does in general terms talk about expenditure of time and expenditure of effort, ...where the expenditure is to be a "deduction", the primary matter which is thought of by the legislature in [s38(1)(b)] is something which is passing out from the person who is making the expenditure. That will most normally and naturally be money, accordingly presenting no problems in calculation; but that will not necessarily be the case. I instance the case (it may be fanciful, but I think it is a possible one and tests the principle) of [the taxpayer employing] a bricklayer to do some casual bricklaying about

---

[1] [1977] STC 170.
[2] At p175.
[3] [1980]2 All ER 1.
[4] At pp5–6.

the premises, the remuneration for the bricklayer being three bottles of whisky at the end of the week. It seems to me that that would be expenditure by the taxpayer, because out of his stock he would have to give something away to the person who was laying the bricks, and I do not think that that would present any real problems of valuation or other difficulty.

But when one comes to his own labour, it does not seem to me that that is really capable of being quantified in this sort of way. It is not something which diminishes his stock of anything by any precisely ascertainable amount ... I think that the whole group of words, "expenditure", "expended", "expenses", and so on and so forth, in a revenue context, mean primarily money expenditure, and, secondly, expenditure in money's worth, something which diminishes the total assets of the person making the expenditure ..."

Contrast this case with *Chaney v Watkis (HMIT)* [1]. The taxpayer owned a house which his mother-in-law occupied as a protected tenant. He wished to dispose of this property and agreed to pay her a sum (which under the agreed formula amounted to £9,400) in return for her vacating the property. This agreement would have the effect of increasing the value of the property because of vacant possession. Between the time of the agreement and the actual completion of the sale of the property, the taxpayer agreed to provide his mother-in-law with rent-free accommodation for life, in return for her releasing him from the obligation to pay the £9,400. He claimed this sum as an allowable deduction in respect of the sale of the property. The commissioners held that the sum was not allowable because it had not been paid by the taxpayer. Reversing the commissioners, Nicholls J said [2]:

> ... what one finds in this case is that the debt of £9,400 was never paid. Instead, the taxpayer agreed with Mrs Williams that in lieu of paying that sum he would provide her for life with rent-free accommodation ... I can see no reason in principle why the obligation thus undertaken by the taxpayer is not capable of being valued in money terms. It is not suggested that because of the domestic nature of the arrangement there was not a genuine, legally binding contract for the provision of the rent-free accommodation. That being so, I would have thought that, equally as if this accommodation arrangement had

[1] [1986] STC 89.
[2] At p94.

been made at arm's length with a stranger, a figure, albeit of a very approximate nature, could be placed on this agreement as the measure in lump sum terms of the cost of such an agreement . . . The obligation to pay £9,400 was the price of obtaining vacant possession of the property. If payment in cash of that sum for that purpose by the taxpayer would have been expenditure wholly and exclusively incurred on the asset by the taxpayer for the purpose of enhancing its value, so must have been payment by the taxpayer for the like purpose made not in cash but by providing money's worth at his expense, regardless of the precise nature of the benefit provided in lieu of money.

There had however been no evidence before the commissioners quantifying the amount of the expenditure represented by the financial detriment suffered by the taxpayer in undertaking the obligation to provide rent-free accommodation. In this respect Nicholls J said [1] that if the parties had been at arm's length he might have been attracted to the view that, unless evidence to the contrary were forthcoming, it could and should be assumed that the cost of providing the alternative benefit was of the order of £9,400. But given the relationship between the parties, considerations other than merely financial ones may have influenced the substitution of one arrangement for the other. Nicholls J therefore remitted the case to the commissioners to determine the value of the obligation.

The questions (a) what can be regarded as "expenditure" for these purposes, and (b) what is meant by "reflected in the state or nature" of the asset, were faced by the Court of Session in *Aberdeen Construction Group Ltd v IRC.* [2] The taxpayer company made loans totalling £500,000 to one of its subsidiaries, Rock Fall, the share capital of which it had acquired at a total cost of £114,024. When the subsidiary's business ran into difficulties, the taxpayer company agreed to sell it for £250,000 on the condition (demanded by the purchaser) that the loan of £500,000 was waived. The taxpayer company thus wrote off the loan in its books. One of the questions that arose was whether the making of the loan, or the waiver of the loan, was expenditure incurred on the assets (i.e., the shares) for the purpose of enhancing the value of the assets. The Court of Session answered the question in the negative. [3]

Lord President Emslie [4] outlined the company's contention in this

[1] At pp94–95.

[2] [1977] STC 302.

[3] The taxpayer's appeal against the judgment of the Court of Session was allowed on other grounds ([1978] 1 All ER 962; 52 TC 281; [1980] STC 127).

[4] At p310.

respect. The taxpayer company took the view that the money laid out by way of the loans was "expenditure" wholly and exclusively incurred "on" the share capital for the purpose of enhancing its value. It argued that the words "state or nature" must be applicable to incorporeal property and are wide enough to include every circumstance which can affect the value of such property. It follows that, on the extinction of the loans, the "expenditure" was reflected "in the state or nature" of the shares sold, for they were then shares in a debt-free company and, having been worthless, they had acquired the value for which they were eventually sold. Lord President Emslie was unable to accept these arguments. He said[1] that, although it was permissible to suppose that the extinction of the debt owed by Rock Fall enhanced the value of its shares, to describe the making of the loans, or their waiver, as expenditure within the meaning of the section, was quite unacceptable. The making of the loan created rights and obligations, and the waiver constituted an abandonment of the rights; but in neither case was there any kind of expenditure with which the section is concerned. In any event, by no reasonable stretch of the imagination was it possible to classify the making of the loans or their waiver, as expenditure wholly and exclusively incurred "on" the shares, and it was impossible to say that either was reflected in the state or nature of the shares which were sold. The waiver of the loans may well have enhanced their value but what the section is looking for is, as the result of relevant expenditure, an identifiable change for the better in the state or nature of the asset, and this must be a change distinct from the enhancement of value.

## Preservation of Title

It is not uncommon for a person's title to an asset to be contested, sometimes leading to litigation, or for a person to have to take some other type of action to protect his or her investment in the asset. With respect to the expenses that would necessarily be incurred in such event, s38(1)(b) further provides for the deductibility of expenses wholly and exclusively incurred in establishing, preserving or defending title to the asset or to a right over it. This will for example cover situations where a person has had to defend his or her claim to an asset against a person who has challenged the title. It should also cover cases where a property owner has to take action against squatters. Other possible situations can be seen in the case law. In *IRC v Richards' Executors*[2] for example, costs incurred by

---

[1] At pp310–311.
[2] [1971] 1 All ER 785; 46 TC 626.

personal representatives in valuing shares and securities for estate duty were held to be deductible because the main purpose was to obtain probate of the will, which established their title to the assets.

On the other hand, where a residuary legatee under a will paid some money to the executor upon which the executor agreed to transfer property to the legatee, the payment could not be classified as expenditure incurred in establishing, preserving or defending the legatee's title to the property. Rather, it was expenditure incurred in acquiring the title. This is because the residuary legatee did not acquire any legal or equitable interest in the estate on the testatrix's death. The time of the agreement to transfer the property was the time when the legatee acquired any title to the property. Thus the payment could not be deducted under s38(1)(b) (see *Passant v Jackson (HMIT)*).[1]

## Incidental Costs of Disposal

Just as a person who is about to buy an asset may have to incur some additional costs incidental to the cost of acquiring the asset, a person who is about to dispose of an asset is likely to incur some expenditure on the venture. More likely than not, there will be a need to advertise to find a buyer. There may also be a need to have valuation, and there may be commissions to be paid. S38(1)(c) provides for the deduction of the incidental costs incurred in the disposal of an asset. Such costs are defined in s38(2) as expenditure wholly and exclusively incurred for the purposes of the disposal, being fees, commission or remuneration paid for the professional services of any surveyor or valuer, auctioneer, accountant, agent or legal adviser, and the costs of transfer or conveyance, including stamp duty. S38(2)(b) adds to this list the costs of advertising to find a buyer and costs reasonably incurred in making any valuation or apportionment required for the purposes of the computation of the gain, including expenses reasonably incurred in ascertaining market values where required by the Act. The provisions should cover most of the genuine expenses that fall on a seller of property. However, the phrase "expenses reasonably incurred in ascertaining market value where required by this Act" in s38(2)(b) does not include the costs of appealing to a Special Commissioner against the Revenue's valuation of an asset. In *Couch (HMIT) v Caton's Administrators*[2], the taxpayers, administrators of the estate of a certain Mr Caton, were deemed to have acquired his holding

---

[1] [1986] STC 164. However the payment fell to be taken into account as part of the acquisition cost of the asset.

[2] [1996] BTC 114. Upheld by the Court of Appeal ([1997] BTC 360)

of 14.02 per cent of the issued share capital of an unquoted company on his death for a consideration equal to their then market value. About seven months after the death, all the issued shares in the company were sold and the taxpayers received £3,269,173 in respect of Mr Caton's shares. The taxpayers appealed to a Special Commissioner against the Revenue's decision on the market value of the shares on Mr Caton's death. The Commissioner having decided that the costs of that appeal were deductible as expenses reasonably incurred in ascertaining the market value of the shares, the Revenue appealed. Rimer J, allowing the Revenue's appeal, held that the costs referred to in the relevant part of [s38(2)(b)] include the costs of the initial valuation carried out by the taxpayer in order to determine the value of the relevant shares "so as to enable him to compute the chargeable gain and to comply with his statutory obligations to make the requisite return".[1] With respect to the taxpayers' argument that the relevant words extended beyond the costs of that initial valuation to the costs in cases involving a negotiated valuation with the Revenue, or, if there is none, to the costs of any appeal in so far as it is concerned with the issue of valuation, Rimer J said[2]:

> I do not, however, regard the costs which a taxpayer may subsequently incur in (a) negotiating (whether successfully or not) the question of value with the Revenue or (b) pursuing an appeal against an assessment, being an appeal which involves a question of the value of the shares, as being costs "incurred in making [a] valuation" of the shares or as being "expenses . . . incurred in ascertaining [their] market value". If the valuer retained to produce the initial valuation were to be asked what he was being paid by the taxpayer to do he could quite properly and naturally reply that he was making a valuation of the shares, or was ascertaining their value. If the solicitors, counsel and expert witnesses retained by the taxpayer for the purposes of an appeal against an assessment were to be asked what they were being paid to do it is in my view most unlikely that they would answer that they were making a valuation of the shares or ascertaining their value. They would not so answer because that is not what they were doing. It is more likely that they would answer that they were together playing their respective roles in presenting to the special commissioner the taxpayer's case on the question of value. They would so answer because that is what they were doing.

[1] At p141.
[2] *Ibid.*

According to Rimer J, this description of the functions of the lawyers and expert witnesses does not involve a mere playing with words. Rather, it reflects a material and relevant difference between their task and that which is performed by the valuer doing the initial valuation. Rimer J said that, at the appeal stage, the only person who could with any accuracy be described as making the relevant valuation, or as making a relevant ascertainment of the market value of the shares, is the special commissioner. Thus, the costs incurred by the taxpayers for the purposes of the appeal were nothing more than costs incurred for the purposes of conducting a tax controversy with the Revenue.[1]

A final point to note with respect to the incidental costs of disposal concerns some restrictions in s38, which in subsection (3) establishes a general rule (subject to exceptions in s40) that no payment of interest will be allowable, and in subsection (4) provides that where there is a deemed disposal and re-acquisition, this does not imply that any expenditure is incurred as incidental to the sale and re-acquisition.

## Expenditure Not Allowable

Expenditure which does not fall within the broad headings discussed above will not qualify for deduction. However, in cases where an item of expenditure *prima facie* falls within those categories, it may still be disallowed, or have its scope restricted by statute. There are several examples of such types of expenditure. The discussion that follows examines some of them in outline.

### Payments of Interest

S38(3) disallows the deduction of payments of interest, subject to the provisions of s40, which provides for the deduction of interest payments (charged to capital) by companies in certain circumstances. The conditions imposed by s40(1) are that the company should have paid the interest on a loan to finance expenditure on the construction of any building, structure or works, being expenditure allowable under s38 in computing the company's gains on the disposal of the building, structure or work or the disposal of any asset comprising such building, structure or work. If these conditions are satisfied, then the sums allowable under s38 will include the interest payment, if such payment is referable to a period or part of a period

[1] *Ibid.*

ending on or before the disposal. This relief is subject to s40(2) which provides that it shall not apply to interest which is a charge on income.

### Revenue Expenditure

We have seen in our discussions on income tax that expenditure of a capital nature is not deductible for income tax purposes. The corollary of this is that expenditure of an income or revenue nature will not be deductible for capital gains tax purposes. For this purpose s39(1) provides that there shall be excluded from the sums allowable under s38, any expenditure which is allowable for the purpose of computing the profits of a trade, profession or vocation, or any other income tax profits or gains, and expenditure which would have been so deductible but for an insufficiency of profits.

Extending this further, s39(2) disallows expenditure on an asset which, if the asset had been used as part of the fixed capital of a trade, would have been allowable for the purposes of computing the profits or losses of that trade.

### Capital Allowances: Restriction of Losses

The general rule is that expenditure is deductible even where capital allowances have been granted. S41(1) provides that the restrictions in s39 (above) shall not require the exclusion from the sums allowable as a deduction of any expenditure, simply because it is expenditure in respect of which a capital allowance or renewals allowance is made. This provision applies in cases of disposals which turn in a gain. However, where a loss accrues on a disposal, different considerations apply. This is because s41(1) also provides that the amount of any losses accruing on the disposal of an asset shall be restricted by reference to capital allowances and renewals allowances.

The main restriction is in s41(2) which provides that, in computing the amount of a loss accruing on a disposal, there is no allowable deduction in respect of any expenditure on which capital or renewal allowances have been given or may be given.

### Expenditure Reimbursed out of Public Money

S50 disallows the deduction of any expenditure which is to be met directly or indirectly by the Crown, or any government, public or local authority, in the United Kingdom or elsewhere.

*Premiums on Insurance Policy on an Asset*

S205 provides, without prejudice to s39, that there shall be excluded from the sums allowable as a deduction in the computation of the gain accruing on the disposal of an asset, any premiums or other payments made under a policy of insurance of the risk of any kind of damage or injury to, or loss or depreciation of, the asset.

## Wasting Assets

*General Principles*

The allowable expenditure on the disposal of wasting assets is subject to special rules which are examined in this section. For CGT purposes, a wasting asset is an asset with a predictable life not exceeding 50 years (s44(1)). Thus for example, a lease for a term of less than 50 years is a wasting asset. The following general rules apply with respect to wasting assets (see s 44(1)):

(a) freehold land is never a wasting asset;
(b) plant and machinery are always wasting assets;
(c) a life interest in settled property shall not be a wasting asset until the life tenant's predictable life expectation (ascertained from actuarial tables approved by the Revenue) is 50 years or less.

Since wasting assets will normally be depreciating assets, it is entirely possible, or even likely, that the sale of a wasting asset that is only a few years old will result in a loss or in a very small profit figure. For this and other reasons special rules apply to the computation of the gains/losses on the disposal of wasting assets. S46(1) provides that any residual or scrap value of the asset is to be deducted from the acquisition cost, and the resulting sum is written off at a uniform rate over the predictable life of the asset. Enhancement expenditure is similarly written off from the time it first becomes reflected in the state of the asset. This increases the amount of any chargeable gain on the disposal.

The formulae for determining the "wasted" expenditure (i.e. a fraction of what would have been the allowable expenditure, which will now be disallowed) are presented by s46(2).

With respect to the acquisition cost and the incidental costs of acquisition the formula is:

$$\frac{T\ (1)}{L} \times (\text{Expenditure} - \text{Scrap Value}$$

Where:

T (1) = the period from acquisition of the asset to its disposal
L      = the predictable life of the asset at the time of acquisition.

Which can be translated into:

$$\frac{\text{Period of ownership}}{\text{Predictable life}} \times (\text{Expenditure} - \text{Scrap Value})$$

Example:

Emily bought an asset for £350. It had a predictable life of 40 years. She kept it for 10 years, after which she sold it for £450. Its scrap value was £50.

1. On a normal calculation, the gain on this disposal would have been:
   £450 − £350 = £100
2. Applying the "wasting asset" rules:
   S46(2) calculation for the "wasted" expenditure—
   $$\frac{10}{40} \times (£350 - £50) = £75 \text{ ("wasted expenditure")}$$
   The gain on the disposal will be:

| | |
|---|---|
| Disposal consideration | £450 |
| *deduct* | |
| Allowable expenditure: | |
| Acquisition cost | £350 |
| *less* | |
| Wasted expenditure | £75 |
| Gain | £175 |

*Short Leases of Land*

A lease with an unexpired term of 50 years or less is, in general, a wasting asset (Schedule 8 paragraph 1(1)). This is so even if there exists the possibility of the lease being extended under statute, as is shown by *Lewis*

*(Executor of F H Lewis) v Walters (HMIT)* [1]. The taxpayer's lease had 16
years left to run, and when the leasehold interest was disposed of, the
Revenue assessed him to capital gains tax on the basis that the lease was a
wasting asset. The Leasehold Reform Act 1967 gave tenants the right to
extend their lease for a further term of 50 years by notice given to the
landlord. Furthermore Schedule 3 paragraph 8(5) of the CGTA 1979
(Schedule 8 paragraph 8(5) TCGA 1992) provided that, where the terms
of the lease include provision for the extension of the lease beyond a given
date by notice given by the tenant, the paragraph will apply as if the term
of the lease extended for as long as it could be extended by the tenant, but
subject to any right of the landlord to determine the lease by notice. The
taxpayer argued that, on the basis of these provisions, the overall result
was that the at the date of disposal the duration of the lease for capital
gains tax purposes was not 16 years but 66 years, i.e. the unexpired term
of 16 years plus the extension of 50 years under the Leasehold Reform
Act 1967. Thus the lease was not a wasting asset because it had a
predictable life exceeding 50 years. Rejecting the taxpayer's contentions,
Mummery J said [2] that the relevant provisions, read in their ordinary and
natural sense, require that the provision for the extension of the lease
should be included among the "terms of the lease". The provision for
extension relied on by the taxpayer was not in "the terms of the lease".
Rather, it was in the Leasehold Reform Act 1967. This term was not
implied into the lease by that statute. According to Mummery J, [3] even if
the statutory right were to be regarded as a "term of the lease" it would
not constitute a provision "for the extension of the lease beyond a given
date". Close examination of the Leasehold Reform Act reveals that what
is envisaged is a new tenancy for a term expiring 50 years after the term
date of the existing tenancy. Thus, the new tenancy would not be an
"extension of the lease" within the meaning of the provision.

With respect to new tenancies, an Extra-Statutory Concession has been
made by an Inland Revenue Press Release of 17 October 1991. This is to
the effect that the surrender of a lease before its expiry and the grant of a
new lease for a longer term will not be regarded as a disposal or a part
disposal of the old lease where all of the following conditions are met:

(i)     the transaction is between unconnected parties bargaining at arm's

---

[1] [1992] BTC 76.
[2] At p81.
[3] At p82.

   length;
(ii) the transaction is not part of or connected with a larger scheme or series of transactions;
(iii) a capital sum is not received by the lessee;
(iv) the extent of the property in which the lessee has an interest under the new lease does not differ in any way from that to which the old lease related;
(v) the terms of the new lease (other than its duration and the amount of rent payable) do not differ from those of the old lease.

As wasting assets, leases have a special regime. Allowable expenditure for CGT purposes is treated as wasting away over the length of the lease, in accordance with a table contained in Schedule 8 paragraph 1.

*Self-Check Questions*

1. What factors are taken into account in respect of the acquisition cost of an asset?
2. Discuss the principles governing the deductibility of enhancement expenditure.
3. What items of expenditure are specifically disallowed by the CGT legislation?
4. How is the allowable expenditure on the disposal of wasting assets determined?

## Further Reading

Stopforth D, *Events Affecting the Deduction of Trading Losses from Capital Gains,* (1992) BTR 384–394.
Burgess R, *The Capital Gains Tax Expenditure Rules,* (1978) BTR 291–308.

# 13
# Exemptions and Reliefs

## Introduction

In addition to the issues already discussed there are some further factors which have to be taken into consideration in the computation of the amount on which capital gains tax is charged. In some cases the disposal consideration and/or allowable expenditure fall be apportioned. In other cases there are further deductions which do not fall strictly within the description of allowable expenditure, and finally there are sundry exemptions and reliefs which may be available to the taxpayer. This chapter examines some of the available deductions, exemptions and reliefs.

## Losses

### Introduction

One of the most important reliefs relates to losses. S2(2) provides that capital gains tax shall be charged on the total amount of the chargeable gains accruing to a person in the year of assessment, after deducting:

(a) any allowable losses accruing to that person in that year of assessment, and
(b) unused allowable losses of the previous years.

Capital gains tax losses are generally computed in the same way as gains (s16(1)), and, except as otherwise expressly provided, all the provisions of the Act which distinguish between chargeable and non-chargeable gains shall also apply to distinguish losses which are allowable from those which are not (s16(2)). References to an allowable loss are to be so construed.

*Loss Relief: General*

The scope of allowable losses is restricted by s16. S16(3) provides that a loss which accrues to a person who is neither resident nor ordinarily resident in the United Kingdom shall not be an allowable loss unless the person would have been chargeable under s10 (gains made on the disposal of assets used for branch or agency within the United Kingdom) if there had been a gain instead of a loss on the relevant occasion. Furthermore s16(4) disallows losses incurred by persons who are not domiciled in the United Kingdom, on the disposal of foreign assets. Finally, in order to claim loss relief, the taxpayer must give notice to "an officer of the Board", quantifying the amount of the loss (s16(2A)).

As seen above, past losses which have not been relieved can be set against current gains (s2(2)). Current losses cannot be carried backward to set against gains of earlier years (s2(3)), except on death (s2(3) and s62(2)). If a loss occurs on a disposal to a connected person, s18(3) provides that it will only be deductible from chargeable gains accruing on a disposal to the same person, made at a time when they are connected persons. Exception is made for gifts made into settlements for education, cultural or recreational purposes, for the benefit of persons all, or most of whom are not connected persons.

*Loss Relief on Death*

By s62(2) allowable losses sustained by the deceased in the year of death will first be deducted from chargeable gains accruing in that year, and any excess can be carried back to set off against gains of the three years of assessment preceding the year of death, taking later years before earlier years.

## Annual Exemptions

As is the case with the Income Tax Acts, the TCGA allows some chargeable persons a certain amount of tax-free gains every year. This amount varies with the type of chargeable person.

*Individuals*

S3(1) provides that an individual shall not be chargeable to capital gains tax in the respect of so much of his taxable amount for any year of assessment as does not exceed the exempt amount for that year. S3(2) fixes the annual exempt amount, which varies from year to year (for example, for 1996–97, it was fixed at £6,300, and, for 1997–98, it was fixed at £6,500). By s3(3), this amount is index-linked. S3(5) provides that an individual's taxable amount is the amount on which he is assessed under s2(2), but where the chargeable gains less allowable losses accruing to an individual in a year are less than the exempt amount for that year, no deduction shall be made for that year in respect of losses carried forward from past years.

## Personal Representatives

Personal representatives have the same annual exemption as an individual in the tax year of the deceased's death and the next two tax years after death (s3(7)). Thereafter, they have no more annual exemptions.

## Trustees

Schedule 1 paragraph 2(1) and (2) provide that trustees are entitled to half the annual exemption of an individual. If the trust is for a mentally or physically disabled person, Schedule 1 paragraph 1 provides that the same annual exemption as that of an individual will be available. Where a settlor has created more than one settlement, the annual exemption is either 10 per cent of an individual's exempt amount, or 50 per cent of the individual's exempt amount, divided by the number of settlements, if this would yield a higher figure (Schedule 1 paragraph 2(4)).

## Indexation Allowance

### Introduction

The indexation allowance was introduced by the Finance Act of 1982 to give relief for the effects of the high rates of inflation witnessed in the late 1970s, thereby preventing the taxation of paper gains (i.e. "gains" which were only attributable to the effects of inflation, as opposed to "real" gains).

The relevant legislation is contained in ss53–56 and s109 TCGA 1992. The system works by linking items of relevant allowable expenditure to rises in the retail prices index (RPI). The allowance is deducted from the unindexed gain or loss (i.e. the gain/loss computed on normal principles).

For these purposes "relevant allowable expenditure" means the sums which are deductible by S38(1)(a) (see s53(2)). These are the acquisition costs (including incidental costs of acquisition), enhancement expenditure, and expenditure on preservation of title. The incidental costs of the disposal are not indexed.

With respect to assets owned by a person on 31 March 1982, the indexation allowance works by deeming that the asset was disposed of, and immediately reacquired, on that date, at its market value on that date (s55(1)). This means that, the base cost of an asset which was acquired before 31 March 1982 is, for the purposes of the indexation allowance, taken to be its market value on that date. Where, however, the indexation allowance would otherwise be higher (e.g. if there was a fall in the value of the asset between the date of its acquisition and 31 March 1982), then, unless the taxpayer has made an election under s35(5), the deemed disposal of s55(1) will not apply (see s55(2)). The purpose of this exception is to ensure that the taxpayer is not unduly prejudiced by the re-basing provisions of s55(1).

*Calculation*

In order to calculate the indexation allowance, the RPI for the month in which expenditure was incurred is compared with that of the month of disposal of the asset. The indexed rise for each item is ascertained separately, and then aggregated to get the total indexation allowance (S54). The formula to be applied for determining the indexed rise of each item (S54(1)) is:

$$\frac{RD - RI}{RI} \times \text{allowable expenditure}$$

where:

RD = RPI for the month of disposal
RI = RPI for month of incurring the expenditure or the RPI for March 1982, whichever is the later.

Where the RPI of the month of expenditure exceeds, or is equal to, the RPI for the month of disposal, the indexed rise is nil (S54(2)(b)). This is because this situation will only occur in cases of zero inflation, or where prices are falling. The indexed rise has to be expressed as a decimal figure, and is rounded to the nearest three decimal places (S54 (3)).

*Application*

The indexation allowance is applied by setting it against the unindexed gain. This is the gain calculated on normal CGT principles prior to deduction of the indexation allowance. The provisions for indexation do not apply to a disposal on which a loss accrues (s 53(2A)), thus the indexation allowance cannot be used to increase the amount of a loss. By virtue of s 53(1) the indexation allowance can be used to reduce the amount of a gain which accrues on a disposal, and, if the indexation allowance exceeds or equals the unindexed gain, then the gain is extinguished, and the disposal is taken to be one which, after taking account of the indexation allowance, neither a gain nor a loss accrues.

Example:

Melina bought some property in January 1988 for £100,000. She sold it in January 1997 for £250,000. The RPI for January 1988 was 300 and the RPI for January 1997 was 360. She has already used up her annual exemption.

(a) The unindexed gain on this transaction will be:

£250,000—£100,000 = £150,000

(b) The indexation fraction will be:

$$\frac{RD\ (360) - RI\ (300)}{RI\ (300)} = 0.2$$

(c) The indexation allowance will be:

0.2 × £150,000 = £30,000

(d) The indexed gain will be:

£150,000 − £30,000 = £120,000

## Apportionments

*Introduction*

In some situations the TCGA grants exemptions and reliefs in the form of an apportionment of the gains made on the disposal of an asset. We will examine two main reliefs given in this way. The first is in respect of assets held on 6 April 1965 (which relief is now largely obsolescent) and the second is in respect of assets held on 31 March 1982.

### Assets Held on 6 April 1965

CGT is charged only on gains accruing after the 6 April 1965 (Schedule 2 Paragraph 16(2)). Thus where an asset was acquired before that date, the gross gain on the disposal would fall to be apportioned, and only that part which is referable to the period after 6 April 1965 will be liable to tax. In such cases, Schedule 2 paragraph 16(3) indicates that the gain will be presumed to have grown at a uniform rate, from nothing at the date of acquisition, to its full amount at the date of disposal.[1] The chargeable gain is then calculated by applying the following fraction to the gross gain:

$$\frac{T}{P + T}$$

where:

T = period between 6th April 1965 and the date of disposal
P = period from acquisition to 6 April 1965.

This translates to the following formula:

$$\text{Gross Gain} \times \frac{\text{Period of ownership since 6 April 1965}}{\text{Total period of ownership}}$$

The figure that is arrived at is the chargeable gain.
Example:

Sean bought some property in 1960 at a cost of £20,000. He sold this property in 1975 for £60,000. The gross gain on this disposal (assuming all other allowances had been used up) would have been be £40,000. The taxable fraction would, applying the rule under discussion, be:

$$£40,000 \times \frac{10}{15} = £26,666$$

[1] By Sch. 2 para 16(6) the gain is deemed to grow from a period not earlier than 6 April 1945.

The indexation allowance in these cases is to be deducted from the gross gains accruing throughout the whole period of ownership, and not just from the gains accruing since 6 April 1965. Thus, the time-apportionment formula is to be applied to the gain after the indexation allowance is used, making the allowance less valuable—i.e. the indexed gain is the gain that has to be apportioned.[1]

### Election for 6 April 1965 Value

Schedule 2 paragraph 17(1), permits the taxpayer to make an election for the value of the asset on 6 April 1965 to be used, instead of the time apportionment formula. If the election is made it applies for all purposes both in relation to the taxpayer and other persons. It is irrevocable (Schedule 2 paragraph 17(4)) and it is given effect by treating the taxpayer as having disposed of and immediately reacquired the asset at its market value on 6 April 1965. This means that the base cost of the asset is now its market value on 6 April 1965, extinguishing all accrued gains on that date. There are restrictions in this respect. The election may not be used to increase a loss, or to convert a gain into a loss. In such circumstances a no gain/no loss figure is used (Schedule 2 paragraph 17(2)). However, this no gain/no loss rule will not apply *unless* the election for the 6 April 1965 value has been made in the first instance. If no such election has been made, the time apportionment rule will still apply, even if the conditions of paragraph 17(2) are satisfied.[2] Note that the election may be used to reduce or increase a gain and to reduce a loss.

The 6 April 1965 value also becomes the base value of the asset in another case, this time, automatically. Schedule 2 paragraph 9 (1) and (2) provide for a deemed disposal and re-acquisition at the market value on 6 April 1965 if the consideration for the disposal of an interest in land situated in the United Kingdom, and held on 6 April 1965, exceeds the current value of the asset at the time of disposal (i.e. if the disposal consideration reflected development value). The market value of the land at the date of disposal will fall to be assessed partly on the footing that no material development (defined as "the making of any change in the state, nature, or use of the land"[3]) is permissible or will ever be permissible.[4] In this case, development value includes "hope value", i.e. an increase in

[1] See *Smith v Schofield*[1993] BTC 147 (House of Lords, reversing the Court of Appeal).
[2] See *Whitaker v Cameron (HMIT)* [1982] STC 665.
[3] Sch. 2 para 13(1).
[4] See Scott J in *Morgan (HMIT) v Gibson* [1989] BTC 272 at 279; STC 568.

the disposal consideration, based on the hope that development permission would be forthcoming. [1]

*Assets Held on 31 March 1982 (including assets held on 6 April 1965)*

### The General Rule

The Finance Act 1988 introduced new rules applying to disposals which take place on or after 6 April 1988. Relief is given for pre-1982 inflation by re-basing assets held on 31 March 1982 to their market value on that date. S35 treats the owner as having disposed of the asset, and as having immediately re-acquired it at its market value on 31 March 1982 (see s35(2)). The effect of this is to extinguish any pre-March 1982 gain. Thus where the asset was acquired before 1965 and was disposed of after 6 April 1988, the 1965 rules (discussed above) will generally be redundant.

### Exceptions to the General Rule

Although the deemed disposal and reacquisition at 31 March 1982 values will normally be automatic, there are statutory exceptions which may prevent such a deemed disposal in specific cases. By virtue of s35(3) the re-basing will not apply where:

(a)  it would increase the amount of a gain or convert a loss into a gain (i.e. the taxpayer should not be unduly prejudiced by re-basing);
(b)  it would increase the amount of a loss or convert a gain into a loss (i.e. the taxpayer cannot unjustly benefit from re-basing);
(c)  a no gain/no loss situation would apply on the facts, under the 1965 rules, or under some other specified statutory provisions.

Where the effect of the re-basing would be to substitute a loss for a gain or a gain for a loss, and the re-basing provisions are excluded by s 35(3), then the disposal will be taken to have been made for such consideration as will secure that neither a gain nor a accrues (s35(4)). Thus the 1988 rules will normally be used only for the purposes of reducing the amount of a loss or reducing the amount of a gain.

Example:

Ewing bought a house in 1977 for £100,000. The house is not his

---

[1]  See *Morgan (HMIT) v Gibson, supra.*

main residence. On 31 March 1982 the house was worth £180,000. He sold the house in 1997 for £165,000.

Applying normal principles (assuming that the indexation factor is nil, because of deflationary trends), the sale in 1997 would have resulted in a gain of £65,000.

If house were re-based to the value on 31 March 1982, £180,000 would become the base cost, and there would be a loss of £15,000. This would then be a case in which the re-basing would have the effect of converting a gain of £65,000 into a loss of £15,000. It would fall within the exceptions mentioned in above, and thus the re-basing to the 31 March 1982 value will not apply here.

Instead, s35(4) will apply to deem the house to have been sold for a no gain/no loss consideration.

*Election for 31 March 1982 Value*

The exceptions to the re-basing rules listed above show the need for taxpayers to keep pre-1982 records. They also show the complexity of tax calculations which would have to be made on alternative bases in order to determine whether the exceptions apply. However, s35(5) enables a person to make an election for the operation of the exceptions in s35(3) to be displaced. This means that the relevant asset will just simply be re-based to 31 March 1982 values without any consideration of the likely capital gains tax consequences. By s35(6) the election must be made before 6 April 1990, or within certain specified periods from the "first relevant disposal" (i.e. a disposal to which s35 applies). Once made the election is irrevocable.

## Other Exemptions and Reliefs

In addition to the reliefs already discussed, there are a number of other sundry exemptions and reliefs in the CGT legislation, in respect of gains which would otherwise have been fully chargeable. Some of the reliefs operate to remove the tax burden completely, while some others are, in effect, partial reliefs. Some of the so-called exemptions are in fact nothing more than measures to ensure that loss relief will not be available in respect of certain transactions which are almost always likely to result in a loss. The discussion that follows examines some of these exemptions and reliefs. Most of them will be discussed in outline only, but a number of them are, because of their relative importance, discussed in greater depth.

*Debts*

The general rule in S251(2) is that the satisfaction of a debt is a disposal of the debt at the time when the debt is satisfied. However, S251(1) provides that no chargeable gain shall accrue on a disposal of a debt, except in the case of a debt on a security. The policy underlying s251(1) was explained by Templeman LJ in *WT Ramsay Ltd v IRC*[1]:

> An original creditor who lends money repayable by the debtor at any time or on demand by the creditor can never make a capital gain because in the hands of the original creditor the debt can never be worth more than the sum advanced. Such a creditor can, however, make a loss, particularly if the debtor becomes insolvent. The creditor may never recover the whole of the debt or may be forced to sell or may choose to sell the debt for less than the sum advanced. Since capital gains tax is calculated on the amount by which annual chargeable gains exceed chargeable losses it would be illogical to include, in the ambit of tax, assets the disposition of which can result only in a loss and never in a gain. A loan to a corporation may also take the form of a debt in respect of which the original creditor can sustain a loss but cannot earn a capital gain. One example is a bank overdraft repayable on demand. On the other hand there are certain types of loan to a corporation, whether protected by a charge on property or not, which constitute forms of investment and which are capable of being realised by the original creditor at any time either at a profit or at a loss depending on the circumstances at the time of disposal ... In order to constitute a coherent system of capital gains taxation it was therefore necessary to exclude the effect of dispositions of debts by owners where the dispositions cannot give rise to a gain but to include dispositions of debts in the form of investments which may result in gains or losses in the same way as dispositions of other investments.

The provision that no chargeable gain accrues on the disposal of a debt relates to the original creditor. It does not affect the original creditor's assignee for value, and an assigned debt is an ordinary asset which is therefore chargeable. According to Templeman LJ in *WT Ramsay Ltd v IRC*[2], even though, for example, the original creditor cannot make a gain on a simple debt, if he assigns the debt for an amount which is lower than

[1] [1979] 54 TC 101 at 131.
[2] 54 TC at 132.

the amount of the debt, the assignee will make a gain if he recovers more than the amount for which the debt was assigned to him, or if he assigns the debt for more than that amount. He would however make a loss if he recovers less than that amount. In the case of an assigned debt, there is no allowable loss if the assignee is connected to the original creditor (S 251(4)).

The term "debt on a security" is pertinent, but it is not defined in the Act. There is a statutory definition of "security" but no definition of "debt". It has been held, however, that a mere contingent liability which may never ripen into a present debt, is not a "debt".[1] The term "security" is defined in s132(3)(b) by way of inclusion—it includes any loan stock or similar security of the United Kingdom or foreign government, or of any public or local authority in the United Kingdom or elsewhere, or of any company, and whether secured or unsecured. The context of this definition is the conversion of securities held, in the typical case, as an investment, although this context may not by itself be a reliable guide.[2] The term "security" is itself imprecise and takes its colour from its setting (in this case, investments). The word should not be approached with any preconceptions as to its primary meaning.[3]

In the absence of a statutory definition of "debt on a security", the courts have endeavoured to provide answers to the determination of the distinction between an ordinary debt, and a debt on a security—a question which, according to Lord Wilberforce in *WT Ramsay v IRC*[4], "many learned judges" have found "baffling". Lord Wilberforce said in *WT Ramsay v IRC* that the legislature seemed to be endeavouring to distinguish between mere debts, which normally (although there are exceptions) do not increase but may decrease in value, on the one hand, and debts with added characteristics which may enable them to be realised or dealt with at a profit, on the other hand.

In *IRC v Cleveley's Investment Trust Co*[5] Lord Cameron said that "debt on a security" is not a synonym for a secured debt. Lord Migdale provided a more detailed explanation[6]:

The word "security" has two meanings. It may refer to some property deposited or made over or some obligation entered into by or on behalf

---

[1] *Marson (HMIT) v Marriage* [1980]STC 177 (House of Lords).
[2] Robert Walker J in *Taylor Clark International Ltd v Lewis* (HMIT) [1997] BTC 200 at 209.
[3] *Ibid.*
[4] 54 TC 101 at 189.
[5] [1971] 47 TC 300.
[6] At p315.

of a person in order to secure his fulfilment of an obligation he has undertaken. Or it may refer to a document held by a creditor as evidence or a guarantee of his right to repayment . . . I think that the words "the debt on a security" refer to an obligation to pay or repay embodied in a share or stock certificate issued by a government, local authority or company, which is evidence of the ownership of the share or stock and so of the right to receive payment. This reading of this section enables me to give some effect to the words "and whether secured or unsecured". If I take the words "security" and "secured" as meaning the same thing, these last words "and whether secured or unsecured" have no meaning at all. "The debt on a security" means debt evidenced in a document as a security.

What this means is that unsecured debts may be included within the term "debt on a security". This view is reinforced by *Aberdeen Construction Group Ltd v IRC*[1] which involved unsecured loans from the taxpayer company to a subsidiary, which loans were not acknowledged in any document or certificate. Lord Wilberforce said[2] that the use of the words "whether secured or unsecured" in the definition of "security" means that "debt on a security" must include some unsecured debts (repeating Lord Cameron's words that the phrase is not a synonym for a secured debt). But which types of unsecured debt will be included? According to Lord Wilberforce, the only basis on which a distinction can be drawn is between a pure unsecured debt as between the original borrower and lender on the one hand, and a debt (which may be unsecured) which has, if not a marketable character, at least such characteristics as enable it to be dealt in[3], and if necessary, converted into shares or other securities. When this case was in the Court of Session, the Lord President (Lord Emslie) had said[4] that, in order to have a debt on a security, one must have "a security" on which there is a debt. Referring to the statutory definition of security, he had concluded that, on a proper construction of the subsection, what is in contemplation is the issue of a document or certificate by the debtor institution, which would represent a marketable security as that expression is commonly understood, the nature and character of which would remain constant in all transmissions. However,

---

[1] [1980] STC 127.

[2] At p133.

[3] In *Taylor Clark International Ltd v Lewis (HMIT)* ([1997] BTC at 219) Robert Walker J said that this distinction could not have been intended as a statement of two categories which between them comprehensively covers the whole ground.

[4] [1977] STC 302 at 309.

in *WT Ramsay v IRC*[1] Lord Wilberforce said that documentary evidence is not a necessary condition, saying:

> I am not convinced that a debt, to qualify as a debt on a security, must necessarily be constituted or evidenced by a document. The existence of a document may be an indicative factor, but absence of one is not fatal.

He also doubted[2], on reflection, the usefulness of a test (propounded by him in *Aberdeen Construction Group Ltd v IRC*) enabling the debt to be converted into shares or other securities.

From these *dicta*, this much is clear. A "debt on a security" is not necessarily the same thing as a secured debt, and may include unsecured debts. That the debt is evidenced in a document is "indicative" of it being a debt on a security—however, the absence of a document is not fatal. Thus, it seems that the phrase "debt on a security" refers either to debts which are evidenced in a document which constitutes a marketable security, or which are marketable in character, or which possess characteristics that enable them to be dealt in.

### Sterling

S21(1)(b) provides that sterling is not an asset for CGT purposes. This means that no chargeable gain accrues on the disposal of sterling.

### Foreign Currency for Personal Expenditure

A gain accruing on the disposal (e.g. by reconversion into sterling) by an individual of foreign currency acquired for personal expenditure abroad for himself or family, is not chargeable (s269).

### Wasting Chattels

S45(1) provides that no chargeable gain shall accrue on the disposal of an asset which is tangible movable property and which is a wasting asset. Because of restrictions in s45(2)(a), this exemption will not apply to cases in which the asset has been used throughout the period of ownership solely for the purposes of the trade, profession or vocation of the person

[1] 54 TC at p190.
[2] *Ibid.*

disposing of it, and that person has claimed or could have claimed any capital allowance in respect of the costs of acquiring or enhancing the value of the asset.

S45(2)(b) contains a further restriction, in cases where the person making the disposal has incurred any expenditure on the asset which has qualified in full for any capital allowance. This restriction was considered in *Burman (HMIT) v Westminster Press Ltd.*[1] The taxpayer company purchased a printing press and obtained capital allowances in respect of the instalments of the purchase price which it had paid. Five years after its acquisition, the press was sold, never having been brought into use in the company's trade. Because of this, the capital allowances previously obtained were withdrawn retrospectively. A gain was realised on the sale of the press and the Revenue sought to tax it. The Revenue rejected the company's claim that the gain was exempt under s45(1) on the basis that the exemption was negatived by s45(2)(b), because the asset had qualified in full for capital allowances. The company contended that all the conditions leading to the making of a capital allowance had to be continued to be satisfied at the time of the disposal in question, while the Revenue claimed that they only had to be satisfied at some point in time. Knox J upheld the company's argument. According to Knox J, not only the asset, but also the expenditure on it has to qualify for capital allowances, and the conditions must continue to be fulfilled at the time of the disposal. Since the capital allowances given had already been withdrawn retrospectively, they were to be treated as never having been made, and so the exemption applied.

### Chattel Exemption

S262(1) provides that a gain accruing on the disposal of an asset which is tangible movable property will not be chargeable if the amount or value of the consideration for the disposal does not exceed £6,000. Where a chattel is disposed of for more than £6,000, the gain is computed in the normal way, but there is some relief in s262(2) limiting the gain to five-thirds of the difference between the consideration and £6,000.

Example:

Ming bought an ancient Abyssinian hunting knife for £3,000. She later sold it for £8,000, realising a gain of £5,000. Applying the provisions of s262(2), the chargeable gain will be limited to:

[1] [1987] STC 669.

$$\frac{5}{3} \times £8,000 - £6,000 \,(£2,000) = £3,333.33$$

S262(3) restricts loss relief where a chattel is disposed of for less than £6,000 by deeming it to have been disposed of for £6,000.
  Example:

Anastasia bought what she thought was a Mayan golden pipe for £14,000. It turned out to be a forgery, and she was only able to sell it for £2,000, incurring an actual loss of £12,000.
  By s262(3), the disposal consideration is deemed to be £6,000, so the loss is limited to:
  £14,000—£6,000 = £8,000

The proper approach to the predecessor to this provision (s128(3) CGTA 1979, which set the limit at that time at £2,000) was examined in *Neeley v Ward.*[1] The taxpayer claimed loss relief in respect of some antiques and other chattels which had been stolen from his home, and in respect of which the insurance payments were insufficient to replace the items. There was no evidence that any of the stolen items cost more than £2,000. It was held that the taxpayer was not entitled to loss relief in respect of those items. Nicholls V-C held that the effect of s20(1)(a) of the CGTA 1979 (now s22(1) of the TCGA 1992) is that a capital sum received by way of compensation for any loss of assets falls to be regarded as an occasion of the disposal of that property, but relief for any loss incurred on such deemed disposal was restricted by s128(3) in cases where the consideration for the disposal was less than £2,000. According to Nicholls V-C[2] the effect of this provision is that there can be no question of an allowable loss [or chargeable gain] in respect of tangible movable property unless the acquisition cost exceeds £2,000 (now £6,000). Although this observation will not always be true, this is a helpful way of looking at the question. This restriction applies only to reduce the amount of the allowable loss claimable if the asset is disposed of for less than the specified sum. If the asset was acquired for less than the specified sum (presently £6,000) a loss will be normally incurred only if it is disposed of for less than the acquisition cost (except perhaps in cases where unusually

[1] [1991] BTC 408; STC 656; affirmed by the Court of Appeal ([1993] BTC 110).
[2] [1991] BTC 408 at 412.

high enhancement expenditure was incurred). Since the acquisition cost was itself less than the limit, it follows that the provision will always apply in such cases, if the asset is disposed of for less than its acquisition cost.

Where, as in this case, more than one asset is involved, each item falls to be considered separately for the purposes of the restriction.[1]

## Motor Cars

By virtue of s263, a motor car (described in the section as a "mechanically propelled road vehicle constructed or adapted for the carriage of passengers, except for a vehicle of a type not commonly used as a private vehicle and unsuitable to be so used") is not a chargeable asset. Thus, no chargeable gain or allowable loss will accrue on its disposal. This may appear at face value to be a generous exemption but since most motor cars are depreciating assets, it is more of a denial of relief in respect of the inevitable losses that will be incurred on the sale of the cars.

## Gambling Winnings

S51(1) provides that winnings from betting, including pool betting, lotteries, etc., are not chargeable gains.

## Personal Injury Compensation

Sums obtained by way of compensation or damages for any wrong or injury suffered by an individual in his person or in his profession or vocation are not chargeable gains (s51(2)).

## Decorations for Valour or Gallantry

S268 provides that a gain accruing on the disposal by any person of a decoration awarded for valour or gallant conduct shall not be chargeable unless the decoration was purchased (for example, by a collector).

## Gilt-Edged Securities

S115(1) exempts gains on disposal of gilt-edged securities or qualifying corporate bonds or on disposal of an option or contract to acquire or dispose of any of these.

---

[1] Nicholls V-C at p412.

## Works of Art

S258 exempts gains accruing on a gift of works of art to an organisation falling within s26(2) of IHTA 1984, if the Treasury gives a direction in relation to the asset under s26(1) of IHTA. The Treasury may in this sort of case require an undertaking to be given with respect to the proper maintenance and preservation of the asset, and reasonable public access thereto.

## Disposals by Charities

A gain is not a chargeable gain if it accrues to a charity and is applicable and applied only for charitable purposes (s256(1)). For this purpose, a charity which gives money to another charity is applying the funds for charitable purposes and is therefore entitled to the exemption. The principle, according to Slade J in *IRC v Helen Slater Charitable Trust Ltd*[1] is that:

> Any charitable corporation which, acting *intra vires*, makes an outright transfer of money applicable for charitable purposes, in such manner as to pass to the transferee full title to the money, must be taken, by the transfer itself, to have "applied" such money for "charitable purposes", within the meaning of [s256(1)], unless the transferor knows or ought to know that the money will be misapplied by the transferee.

This was upheld by the Court of Appeal.[2]

## Superannuation Funds, Annuities and Annual Payments

S237 exempts gains accruing on the disposal of a right to, or to any part of:

(a) any allowance, annuity or capital sum payable out of any superannuation fund or scheme established solely or mainly for persons employed in a profession, trade, undertaking or employment, and their dependants;

(b) an annuity, granted otherwise than under a contract for a deferred

---

[1] [1980] 1 All ER 785 at 795–796.
[2] [1981] STC 471.

annuity, by a company, as part of its business of granting annuities on human life; and

(c) annual payments, which are due under a covenant made by any person, and which are not secured on any property.

In *Rank Xerox Ltd v Lane (HMIT)*[1] the House of Lords held that the word "covenant" (in paragraph (c) above) could not be construed in isolation. What fell to be construed was the whole phrase "annual payments which are due under a covenant made by any person".[2] According to Lord Wilberforce,[3] as a matter purely of grammar, the words "due under" and "made by any person" suggest a unilateral promise which is enforceable in spite of the absence of consideration. They are not apt to refer to bilateral agreements in which the annual payments are consideration for some obligation undertaken by the payee. The term should be understood as referring only to unilateral promises of a voluntary character. Lord Russell said with respect to the same issue:[4]

In my opinion "due under a covenant" is fairly to be construed as something narrower in scope than "due under an agreement" would have been. I construe the phrase as meaning due by reason of the fact that the promise is under seal, because of the existence of the seal. If the presence of the seal adds nothing to the obligation to make the annual payments, [e.g. if it is already enforceable because of consideration] I do not consider that the payments were "due under a covenant made by a person". This construction is in my view legitimate as avoiding the wholly capricious outcome of exclusion or non-exclusion from chargeable gains depending on the chance of an unnecessary seal.

The House of Lords also decided in the case that, in Scotland, the phrase should be understood as referring to enforceable gratuitous promises,[5] or to situations "where the gratuitous nature of the undertaking to pay requires it to be evidenced by the writ of the undertaker".[6]

---

[1] [1979] 3 All ER 657.
[2] Lord Wilberforce at p660.
[3] *Ibid.*
[4] At p664.
[5] Lord Wilberforce at p661.
[6] See Lord Russell at p665; Lord Keith at p666.

## Private Residencies

*Introduction*

Private residence relief is one of the major reliefs available under the CGT legislation. Home ownership has always been seen as something desirable and worthy of encouragement, and the reason is clear. Every one in every society needs a home. And this means that after the daily bread, homes constitute the next major concern of mankind. A society of home-owners is a society that does not rely on the state for its housing needs. This means that scarce resources which are thereby freed, can be diverted elsewhere. Also, property ownership has traditionally been regarded as one of the soundest forms of investment. Such sound investment ensures future stability and security. Furthermore, when a person sells his home, he frequently needs to acquire a new home elsewhere. [1] There are other rationales which were succinctly expressed by Brightman J in *Sansom v Peay* [2]:

> The evil of inflation was evident even in 1965. It must have occurred to the legislature that when a person sells his home to buy another one, he may well make a profit on the sale of one home and lose that profit, in effect, when he buys his new home at the new, inflated price. It would not therefore be surprising if Parliament formed the conclusion that, in such circumstances, it would be right to exempt the profit on the sale of the first home from the incidence of capital gains tax so that there was enough money to buy the new home.

For these and other reasons, relief is given in respect of capital gains made on the sale of a person's home. S222 describes the types of property which qualify for relief in this manner:

(i) a dwelling-house or part of a dwelling-house
(ii) which is or has at any time been an individual's *only or main residence*
(iii) together with and land enjoyed with the residence as its garden or grounds, up to the permitted area.

By virtue of s222(2), the permitted area, subject to subsections (3) and (4)

---

[1] Brightman J in *Sansom & Anor v Peay (HMIT)* (1976) 52 TC 1 at 6; [1976] 3 All ER 375 at 397.
[2] *Ibid.*

is, inclusive of the site of the dwelling-house, 0.5 of one hectare. Where the area required for the reasonable enjoyment of the dwelling-house as a residence is (having regard its size and character) is larger than 0.5 of one hectare, then that larger size shall be the permitted area (s 222(3)). The relief that is available here is found in s223(1), which provides that any gain on the disposal of a dwelling-house is exempt if it has been the only or main residence, either throughout the period of ownership or throughout the period of ownership except for the last 36 months of ownership.

### Dwelling-House

Whether a particular building constitutes a dwelling-house or not is a question of fact. There are a number of decided cases on this point and most of them turn on their own facts. One such example is *Makins v Elson (HMIT)* [1] where a caravan was held to be a dwelling-house. The taxpayer had purchased for £1,800 a building plot of three-quarters of an acre in respect of which planning permission for a dwelling-house had been granted. The taxpayer had then moved to the site in a mobile caravan. Subsequently essential services—water, electricity, and a telephone, were installed. Although the caravan had wheels, the wheels were actually not on the ground, because the caravan had been jacked up and rested on some sort of supports. The taxpayer then claimed relief in respect of a gain on the sale of the caravan. It was held by Foster J that the caravan was exempt as a dwelling-house. Factors which he considered important were the facts that services had been installed, and that the wheels were not on the ground.

Contrast however *Moore v Thompson (HMIT)* [2]. The taxpayers had bought an old detached farm house, which had not been inhabited for two years, and which did not have an electricity supply, for use as their family home. The husband later purchased a wheeled caravan which had a sink, table, some chairs, and a settee that could turn into a bed. This caravan was towed into the courtyard of the farm house. It was not connected to any services. The taxpayers stayed in this caravan for various periods, the husband sometimes staying for several weeks, while renovating the farm house. They claimed private residence relief in respect of the caravan. The commissioners decided that, on the facts,

[1] [1977] STC 46; 1 All ER 572.
[2] [1986] STC 170.

neither the farm house nor the caravan in its courtyard was ever a "dwelling-house" capable of being regarded as the taxpayers' main residence. They were upheld by Millet J.

Whether ancillary buildings fall to be included as part of the dwelling-house or not is also a question of fact. In *Batey (HMIT) v Wakefield*[1] for example, it was held that a separate bungalow, which was adjacent to the tax payer's house and within the grounds, and which was occupied by a caretaker was exempt as part of the dwelling-house. This decisions can be contrasted with *Green v IRC*[2] where the taxpayer's mansion consisted of a central block, and two wings, each of which contained a self-contained flat with its own entrance, but was linked to the central block by connecting passages. One of the wings was occupied by a gardener and his family. The General Commissioners decided that the two wings were not part of the taxpayer's residence, and the Court of Session felt unable to reverse them.[3]

It should be noted that, for the purposes of the main/private residence relief, a dwelling-house could comprise more than one building, and that these separate buildings need not be physically connected. This principle is well established but the problem is how it is to be applied. The courts have, in a long line of cases, grappled with this problem. In *Markey (HMIT) v Sanders*[4], the taxpayer had a small country estate consisting of a main house with three bedrooms, and a bungalow, which also had three bedrooms. The bungalow was sited about 130 metres from the main house and was separated from it by a large paddock. The bungalow had been thus sited for privacy, that is deliberately sited in order to take it away from the main house. It had its own garden and was protected by a belt of trees deliberately screening it from the main house. The commissioners held that it constituted part of the taxpayer's dwelling-house, but they were reversed by Walton J.

According to Walton J[5] two conditions were laid down by the Court of Appeal in *Batey (HMIT) v Wakefield* (above) in order for a separate building to qualify as part of the main residence. First, the occupation of the building in question must increase the taxpayer's enjoyment of the main house. This is a necessary but not a sufficient condition. Secondly, the other building must be "very closely adjacent" to the main building. This

---

[1] [1981] STC 521.

[2] [1982] STC 458 (Court of Session).

[3] In *Honour (HMIT) v Norris* [1992] BTC 153 at 160, Vinelott J said that *Green v IRC* was a case that "turned on very special facts".

[4] [1987] STC 256.

[5] At p263.

again is a necessary but not sufficient condition. Walton J himself would prefer to ask the question "looking at the group of buildings in question as a whole, is it fairly possible to regard them as a single dwelling-house used as the taxpayer's main residence?". He felt that this was a preferable approach, because the concept of "very closely adjacent" does not of itself indicate that the scale of the building must be taken into consideration, which would appear to be fairly obvious. The expression "very closely adjacent" was, according to him, too imprecise. [1]

In this case the first test was very clearly satisfied but the second was not. According to Walton J [2] although it is true that the test of "very closely adjacent" is an elastic one which is for the commissioners to decide, merely because it is an elastic test does not mean that the commissioners are entitled to apply it absolutely, regardless of the facts. "It is no use the commissioners describing in great detail what is clearly recognisable as an elephant and then concluding that it is a giraffe". [3] Walton J's conclusion was that either the commissioners had applied no test at all beyond the first condition, or they had applied the wrong test.

In *Williams (HMIT) v Merrylees* [4], Vinelott J, referring to *Markey v Sanders* said that he found it difficult to spell out of the *Batey* decision two distinct conditions, each of which must be satisfied, before a separate building can be considered part of a single dwelling-house. He felt that both Browne-Wilkinson J at first instance, and the Court of Appeal intended to lay down only one test – "the entity which in fact constitutes the residence of the taxpayer". According to Vinelott J [5] what one is looking for is an entity which can be sensibly described as being a dwelling-house though split up into different buildings performing different functions. In deciding whether this test is satisfied on the facts of a particular case, the commissioners must look at all the circumstances and, of course, the propinquity or otherwise of the buildings, having regard to their scale, is a very important factor to be weighed. It however does not seem right to isolate a single factor as one which must be present if the commissioners are to be entitled to conclude that a building physically separate from the taxpayer's main dwelling-house, but occupied in such a way that it may be said to increase his enjoyment of the main dwelling-house, is part of his residence. The question is one of degree. [6] In this case, a gardener's/

---

[1] *Ibid.*
[2] At p264.
[3] *Ibid.*
[4] [1987] STC 445 at 453.
[5] At p454.
[6] *Ibid.*

caretaker's lodge, situated some 200 metres from the main house was held by the commissioners to constitute a single dwelling-house with the main house. Vinelott J did not feel able to reverse them even though he doubted whether he would himself have arrived at the same conclusion.

More recently, in *Lewis (HMIT) v Lady Rook*[1] the Court of Appeal in deciding that a cottage, situated some 175 metres from the main house and occupied by the tax payer's gardener, did not constitute one residence with the main house, emphasised the question of the proximity of the cottage to the main house. After reviewing the case law, Balcombe LJ confessed that he found the current state of the authorities unsatisfactory, and that it was hardly surprising that different sets of commissioners have reached conclusions which are not always easy to understand.[2] In these circumstances it was necessary to go back to the words of the statute. Balcombe LJ said that what first had to be decided was what in the particular case constituted the "dwelling-house", an ordinary English word defined in the shorter *Oxford English Dictionary* as a "house occupied as a place of residence". Following the decision in *Batey v Wakefield*, a dwelling-house could consist of more than one building even if the other building itself constituted a separate dwelling-house. Nevertheless, he would agree with Vinelott J in *Williams v Merrylees* that what to look for was an entity which could be sensibly described as a dwelling-house, though split up into different buildings performing different functions.

How, then, can this entity be identified in any given case? Balcombe LJ said that attention must first be focused on the dwelling-house which is said to constitute the entity. According to him, to seek to identify the taxpayer's residence may lead to confusion, because where, as in the present case, the dwelling-house forms part of a small estate, it is very easy to consider the estate as his residence and from that to conclude that all the buildings on the estate are part of his residence. Balcombe LJ said that in so far as some of the statements made in *Batey v Wakefield* suggest that one must first identify the residence, they must be considered to have been made *per incuriam*.

According to Balcombe LJ, the proposition that no building can form part of a dwelling-house which includes a main house unless that building is appurtenant to, and within the curtilage of, the main house, was a helpful approach.[3] It involves application of well-recognised legal concepts, and may avoid somewhat surprising findings of fact which were reached in *Markey v Sanders, William v Merrylees*, and the present case. This

---

[1] [1992] BTC 102.
[2] At p108.
[3] At p108.

approach coincides with the close proximity test to which the other cases refer: "very closely adjacent"—per Browne-Wilkinson J in *Batey v Wakefield*, and also avoids the difficulty that a separate lodge or cottage which by any reasonable measurement must be outside the one acre "permitted area" of garden or grounds, can nevertheless be part of the entity of the dwelling-house. [1] Thus the correct test in this case was "was the cottage within the curtilage of, and appurtenant to, [the main house], so as to be a part of the entity which, together with [the main house], constituted the dwelling-house occupied by the taxpayer as her residence"? [2] In this case it was impossible to answer the question in the affirmative.

The principles stated by Balcombe LJ in *Lewis v Lady Rook* were applied by Vinelott J in *Honour (HMIT) v Norris* [3] where the question was whether four separate flats, situated in different buildings, in Ovington Square, Kensington, and occupied by the taxpayer and his family, could be regarded as part of a single dwelling-house. The particular flat which was the subject of the dispute was called "Flat 10" and it was situated some 60 to 95 yards by road from the others, but within the same Ovington Square. Answering the question in the negative, Vinelott J said [4] that the proposition that Flat 10, together with the others formed part of a single entity which could sensibly be described as a dwelling-house split into different buildings and performing different but related functions, was an affront to common sense. According to him [5] Flat 10 was acquired because it was a separate dwelling-house conveniently close to the taxpayer's main dwelling-house and with a view to it being used to provide occasional bedroom accommodation for the taxpayer and his wife. It was no more part of a dwelling-house than for example a guest house bought in a neighbouring village by the owner of a country house who found that his house was not always adequate to accommodate his children and guests.

### Land Used with the House

The exemption in respect of land used as garden or grounds applies where it is used in connection with the dwelling-house. Where the dwelling-house is sold *first* and then the garden/grounds is/are sold

---

[1] At 109.
[2] *Ibid.*
[3] [1992] BTC 153.
[4] At p162.
[5] *Ibid.*

afterward, it will not qualify for exemption. In *Varty v Lynes*[1] Brightman J held that, in order to be exempt, the garden must be occupied at the time of the disposal. In *Varty* the taxpayer first sold the house and a part of the garden, and then sold the rest of the garden 11 months later, with the benefit of planning permission. It was held that the latter disposal was not exempt.

### "Home"

In order to qualify for main residence relief, a building which is acknowledged to be a dwelling-house also has to constitute the taxpayer's home. In *Owen v Elliot (HMIT)*[2] Fox LJ said that the section is concerned with dwelling-houses that can reasonable be called "homes". Leggatt LJ said that the concept of occupation as a home is derived not from the use of the term "residence" by itself, but from its use in the phrase "his only or main residence".[3] In *Sansom v Peay (HMIT)*[4] Brightman J said that the scheme of the provision is to exempt from liability to capital gains tax "the proceeds of sale of a person's home". This apparent gloss on the statutory words received close attention in *Goodwin v Curtis (HMIT)*.[5] This case involved the acquisition and sale of three properties by the taxpayer within a nine-month period in 1985. The property which is relevant to this discussion ("the Farmhouse") had its purchase completed on 1 April 1985, but the taxpayer had instructed estate agents to sell it in March 1985 (i.e. before his purchase of the property was completed). At about the time of completion, the taxpayer separated from his wife and took up temporary residence in the Farmhouse. On 11 April 1985 the Farmhouse was advertised for sale in *Country Life*. In the same month, it was advertised for sale in a number of other publications. A buyer was found almost immediately, and the sale was completed on 3 May 1985. The commissioners decided that, in order to qualify for relief, the taxpayer must provided evidence that his residence at a property showed some degree of permanence, some degree of continuity or some expectation of continuity. Accordingly, since the taxpayer had not intended to occupy the Farmhouse as his permanent residence when he moved into it, the Farmhouse had not been occupied as his home, and did not qualify for relief as his main residence.

[1] [1976] 3 All ER 447.
[2] [1990] BTC 323 at 326; Ch 786; 3 WLR 133; STC 469.
[3] [1990] BTC at p327; compare Fox LJ at p326.
[4] *Supra.*
[5] [1996] BTC 501.

Vinelott J, upholding the commissioners, referred to the Court of Appeal's decision in *Fox v Stirk*[1], in which it was held that students at the Universities of Bristol and Cambridge were "resident" at their halls of residence for the purposes of entry into the electoral register. In that case, Lord Denning MR referred to three principles[2]:

> The first principle is that a man can have two residences. He can have a flat in London and a house in the country. He is resident in both. The second principle is that temporary presence at an address does not make a man resident there. A guest who comes for the weekend is not resident. A shortstay visitor is not resident. The third principle is that temporary absence does not deprive a person of his residence ... I think that a person may properly be said to the "resident" in a place when his stay there has a considerable degree of permanence.

Vinelott J also referred to Widgery LJ in *Fox v Stirk*. Before the passage referred to by Vinelott J, Widgery LJ had said that a man cannot be said to reside in a particular place unless in the ordinary sense of the word one can say that for the time being he is making his home in that place[3]. Vinelott J then referred to Widgery LJ's statement that this conception of residence is of "the place where a man is based or *where he continues to live, the place where he sleeps and shelters and has his home*",[4] and that it is imperative to remember in this context that "residence" implies a degree of permanence:

> In the words of the Oxford English Dictionary, it is concerned with something which will go on for a considerable time ... Some assumption of permanence, some degree of continuity, some expectation of continuity, is a vital factor which turns simple occupation into residence.[5]

In the present case, Vinelott J said[6] that the commissioners were distinguishing permanent residence from mere temporary accommodation and amongst the factors to be weighed by the commissioners are the

---

[1] [1970] 2 QB 463; 3 All ER 7. Applied in *Hipperson v Electoral Registration Officer for the District of Newbury* [1985] 2 All ER 456 (see Sir John Donaldson MR at page 461).

[2] [1970] 2 QB at 475; 3 All ER at 11–12.

[3] [1970] 3 All ER at 13.

[4] *Ibid*. Emphasis added.

[5] [1970] 2 QB at 477; 3 All ER at 13.

[6] [1996] BTC at 518.

degree of permanence, continuity, and the expectation of continuity. The facts found by the commissioners were that the taxpayer had decided to sell the Farmhouse and had advertised it widely before completion of the sale to himself, that it was a nine-bedroomed house wholly unsuitable as the residence of a single man who was separated from his wife and in financial difficulties. In the light of these facts, Vinelott J held that the commissioners were entitled to take the view that the Farmhouse was used not as a residence but as merely temporary accommodation for a period that the taxpayer hoped would be brief and which in fact was very brief.

One result of this type of reasoning may be that occupation of a dwelling-house for a brief period would be regarded as not satisfying the "home" principle. While, in most cases of brief occupations of dwelling-houses, the houses concerned would not have been occupied as the individual's "home", problems may arise in cases where people have to sell their home shortly after buying it, either as a result of an emergency, or as a result of a realisation that the property in somehow not adequate. The same problems might arise in cases where a house is purchased as a temporary measure while the search for the "dream home" continues. In this type of case, if the "dream home" is subsequently found quickly, the taxpayer may be faced with the assertion that the temporary residence was not occupied as a home. In these types of case, there might well be no permanence, continuity, or expectation of continuity. Would it then be right to deny main residence relief? If this were the result achieved by decisions such as *Fox* and *Goodwin*, then the gloss introduced by these cases on the statutory provisions would be unsupportable. However, it may be that escape might be found in the principle that the decision of the matter is a question of fact and degree, and that it would be open to the commissioners to find evidence that a dwelling was occupied as a home even in the absence of permanence, continuity or expectation thereof.

### Multiple Residences

Where an individual has more than one residence, he may determine which is to be treated as his main residence for any period, by notice to the inspector within two years from the beginning of that period, subject to a right to vary that notice by a further notice to the inspector in respect of any period not earlier than two years before the time when the further notice is given (s222(5)(a).

This provision appears straightforward enough, but the case of *Griffin*

*(HMIT)* v *Craig-Harvey*[1] shows that that appearance may be deceptive. The taxpayer in the case acquired a farmhouse on 12 August 1985. On 9 July 1986 he completed the sale of another house, and, on the same day completed the purchase of yet another one ("7 Sibella Road"). On 21 January 1988 he gave written notice to the inspector of taxes pursuant to s101(5) CGTA 1979 (now s222(5) TCGA 1992) that the farmhouse should be treated as his main residence for capital gains tax purposes. On 26 January 1989 he sold the farmhouse. Since the notice was given more than two years after the acquisition of the farmhouse, the question arose as to when the notice could take effect. The taxpayer contended that the notice was effective for a period of up to two years before it was given. The gist of his argument was that the words "from the beginning of that period" in [s222(5)(a)] relate back to the words "for any period" in the opening part of [s222(5)], that there is no restriction on the date chosen as the beginning of that period, and that a taxpayer may therefore give notice at any time that a residence is to be treated as his main residence for the period beginning two years before the giving of the notice. Thus, the taxpayer's election would take effect from 21 January 1986 (two years before the notice was given). The Revenue, on the other hand, argued in effect that, a taxpayer who fails to make an election within two years of acquisition of a residence cannot thereafter make any election in respect thereof unless and until he acquires a new residence or makes a change in residence. This meant that the taxpayer's notice could not take effect to make the farmhouse his main residence before the date when he acquired 7 Sibella Road (9 July 1986). It followed that, from 12 August 1985 when the taxpayer acquired the farmhouse, until 9 July 1986 when he acquired 7 Sibella Road, the farmhouse was not his main residence, and that period of ownership did not qualify for relief.

Vinelott J upheld the Revenue's argument. Counsel for the taxpayer put forward a number of examples which illustrated the arbitrary and irrational consequences of the Revenue's argument. The first example was that of a taxpayer who owns two houses, each of which he occupies as a residence. After more than two years, he begins to use a third house as a residence. A new two-year period begins to run at that time so that he can make an election between all three residences during that two-year period. The second example was, if given the same facts as before, the taxpayer ceased, after acquiring a third residence, to use one of them as a residence, a new period will begin at the time of cesser so that, again, he

[1] [1994] BTC 3.

will have a period of two years during which he can elect between the remaining residences. Vinelott J's answer to these illustrations was that they did no more than illustrate the inevitable consequences of [s222(5)], namely, that it becomes necessary to determine which of two or more residences is an individual's main residence whenever there is a change in the number of properties which he occupies as a residence. [1]

The decision that the two-year period begins to run from the acquisition of the property to which the notice relates seems to be right. It does not seem that Parliament would give taxpayers a *carte blanche* in respect of the time during which they may give notice of their election. Vinelott J said [2] that the reference to "any period" in the opening part of [s222(5)] and to "that period" in paragraph (a) are most naturally read as referring to "the whole or any part of the period of ownership in question". This is obviously correct. If a taxpayer owned two residences in the period between 1 January 1990 and 1 January 1998, any reference to "the period" in s222(5) would obviously relate to that eight-year period. A notice of election given after 1 January 1992 would be out of time. It cannot possibly be right that the taxpayer may give a notice in respect of this period on 1 January 1997, and then have that notice take effect from 1 January 1995 (the effect of the taxpayer's argument in this case). This decision illustrates the need for prompt action by people who acquire other residences. It may be thought imprudent to commit oneself in this way at the early stages of ownership of new properties—especially when it may not be clear which of them would yield a higher profit figure when they are eventually disposed of, and which should therefore be chosen for main residence relief. However, s222(5)(a) does provide some amount of relief for those who make their election promptly, by allowing them to vary the earlier notice, by a further notice, with retrospective effect, at any time. This variation notice is also subject to a two-year time limit—but the limit this time attaches to the time when the further notice is given, to make it effective for the preceding two-year period.

While the decision that a fresh two-year period begins each time a change in residence (or acquisition of a new residence) occurs may seem astounding, it could be of benefit to a well advised taxpayer with sufficient means in that it provides a possible escape route for those who had earlier been tardy. Presumably, all that they would need to do in order to obtain a fresh start would be to acquire another residence.

[1] [1994] BTC at p10.
[2] At p9.

## Married Couples

A husband and wife can only have one residence or main residence if living together (s222(6)). Concessionary relief is available in cases wherein the parties are separated or divorced. ESC D6 applies where a married couple are separated or divorced, and one partner ceases to occupy the matrimonial home, and, subsequently as part of a financial settlement, disposes of the home or an interest in it to the other partner. In these cases, the home may be regarded for the purposes of the main residence relief as continuing to be a residence of the transferring partner from the date his or her occupation ceases, until the day of the transfer (subject to the condition that the home was the other partner's only or main residence throughout this period). According to the text of the concession this means that where a husband leaves the matrimonial home while still owning it, the usual CGT exemption or relief for a taxpayer's only or main residence would be given on the subsequent transfer to the wife, provided that she has continued to live in the house and the husband has not elected that some other house should be treated for capital gains tax purposes as his main residence for this period.

## Residence Used for Trade Purposes

S224(1) provides that, where part of the dwelling-house in respect of which relief is being claimed is used exclusively for the purposes of a trade or business, or of a profession or vocation carried on by the taxpayer, the gain on the house will be apportioned, and the exemption will be applied to the part which is not so used.

## Letting

Where the property or part of it has been let to tenants, this in effect means that the exemption is lost because the property is not the taxpayer's own residence. There is however a measure of relief. S223(4) provides that, with respect to houses qualifying for the main residence relief, if the house is or has been either partly or wholly let by the owner as *residential accommodation*, the gain which would otherwise have been chargeable because of the letting would only be chargeable to the extent that it exceeds the lesser of (a) the part of the gain attributable to the owner-occupation, and (b) £40,000.

What does "residential accommodation" mean in this respect? Some answers were forthcoming from the Court of Appeal in *Owen v Elliot*

*(HMIT).* [1] The taxpayer in this case and his wife purchased the Gleneagles Hotel in 1976, and carried on a business of a private hotel and boarding house on the premises. The hotel consisted of two parts, first, a main building, which consisted of ten bedrooms, a kitchen and a lounge, and secondly, an annexe, which consisted of two bedrooms, a lounge, a kitchen and some ancillary facilities. During the period from Easter to September, the hotel received guests who stayed for short terms—usually less than two weeks. During these periods, the taxpayer and his family occupied the annexe. During the period from October to Easter, guests stayed for longer periods, typically three to four months and the taxpayer and his family occupied the whole building together with their guests. The taxpayer sold the whole property on March 24 1982. The inspector agreed that one-third of the gain on the sale of the hotel should be treated as exempt from capital gains tax under [s222 and s223 TCGA 1992]. The taxpayer then claimed further relief in respect of dwelling-houses let as residential accommodation under [s223(4) CGA 1992].

The Crown accepted that as a matter of the ordinary use of the English language "residential accommodation" includes such lettings as were made by the taxpayer, but argued that the provision must be read in its context. It was designed to extend the relief in ss222 and 223. The concept of a home is central to s222 and is carried into s223(4). It is therefore consistent with the relief to extend it to taxpayers who have some surplus accommodation in their homes and which they are proposing to let to a person as his home. Millet J at first instance accepted the Crown's argument but the Court of Appeal disagreed. Fox LJ [2] said that the concept of a home is not conveyed by the use of the word "residence" alone. A person may well have a residence or several residences which are not his home. The language of [s222] plainly indicates a home, but that of [s223(4)] is completely different. Fox LJ could see no reason why it should be assumed that because the main residence relief is granted in respect of the home of the taxpayer, the additional relief should only attach to a letting to third parties as their homes. There is no necessary connection between the two. According to him, the provision was designed to encourage householders who had surplus accommodation in their dwelling-houses, to make it or some of it available to other persons. The language of the provision is such that the lettings made by the taxpayers in their hotel were within the words "residential accommodation".

[1] [1990] BTC 323; Ch. 786; 3 WLR 133.
[2] At p326.

Leggatt LJ concurring[1] said that "residential accommodation" does not directly or by association mean premises likely to be occupied as a home. He said that it means living accommodation, by contrast, for example, with office accommodation. According to him:

> No relevant distinction can be drawn between a letting to an undergraduate or nurse or lodger, such as the judge thought would be entitled to relief, and a letting to anyone else. All are lettings of residential accommodation indistinguishable from that which is provided by boarding or guest houses or indeed by hotels, and all are conducted on what the judge called a "commercial basis". They differ from each other, if at all, only in the average length of letting, but it is accepted on behalf of the Crown that the length of the letting is not determinative. This conclusion will not result in relief being extended to a taxpayer the whole or part of whose dwelling-house is exclusively used as an hotel or boarding house. It will apply only where a dwelling-house has at any time been used wholly or partly for that or a like purpose by a person whose only or main residence it is ... [T]here is no limitation imposed by the statute on the scope of residential accommodation entitled to relief ...

### Periods of Absence

Normally, if an individual is absent from the dwelling-house, it will not satisfy the residence requirement. However, some periods during which the taxpayer may not have occupied the dwelling-house may still qualify as periods of occupation.

### The Last 36 Months of Ownership

S223(1) provides that a gain accruing on the disposal of a dwelling-house will not be chargeable if it has been the individual's only or main residence throughout the period of ownership, or throughout such period except for the last 36 months. This particular provision covers both periods of absence, and periods during which the house was used for any other purpose, for example letting.

---

[1] At p327.

*Qualifying Periods of Absence*

In addition to the last 36 months of ownership the following periods of absence are treated by s223(3) as periods of owner-occupation if, both before and after such periods, there was a time when the dwelling-house was actually the individual's only or main residence:

(a) a period, or periods of absence not exceeding three years;
(b) any period of absence throughout which the individual worked in an overseas employment in which all the duties were performed abroad;
(c) any period or periods of absence, not exceeding four years, throughout which the individual was prevented from living in the house because of the situation of his place of work, or because of a reasonable condition imposed by his employer, requiring him to reside elsewhere, being a condition reasonably imposed to secure effective performance of his job.

Concessionary relief is available in ESC D4, to the effect that the requirement of occupation after the period of absence is satisfied where, on a person's return, he is not able to take up residence in his previous home because the terms of his employment require him to work elsewhere.

"Period of absence" is defined in s223(7) as a period during which the house was not the individual's only or main residence, and throughout which he had no residence eligible for relief under (this) section. This does not include any period before 31 March 1982.

*Job-Related Accommodation*

S222(8) provides that, if at any time during an individual's period of ownership of a dwelling-house, he resides in a job-related accommodation (within s356 ICTA 1988—i.e. those within the exception to income tax charge on living accommodation) and he intends in due course to occupy the dwelling-house as his only or main residence, ss222–226 shall apply as if the dwelling-house were occupied by him as a residence.

*Trustees*

By s225, the relief applies also to a gain accruing to trustees on a disposal of settled property which is an asset within s222(1), where during the trustee's period of ownership, the house has been the only or main residence of a person entitled to occupy it under the terms of the settlement. In *Sansom v Peay*[1] it was held that, when beneficiaries under a discretionary trust occupied a house as their main residence in pursuance of an exercise by the trustees of powers to permit those beneficiaries to go into and remain in occupation, the trustees were entitled to main residence relief in respect of accrued gains when they disposed of the dwelling-house, under what is now s225.

## Dependent Relatives

S226(1) extends the relief to a gain accruing to an individual on a disposal of a house which, on 5 April 1988, or at any earlier time in his period of ownership, had been the sole residence of a dependent relative, provided rent-free and without any other consideration. The relief is limited to one dependent relative. The requirement that the provision of the accommodation be rent-free is satisfied where the dependent relative pays all or part of the occupier's rates and the cost of repairs attributable to normal wear and tear (ESC D20). Additionally, the benefit of the relief will not be lost where the dependent relative makes other payments in respect of the property, either to the taxpayer or to a third party, provided that no net income is receivable by the taxpayer, taking one year with another.[2]

"Dependent relative" is defined in s226(6) and (7) as:

(a) a relative of the individual, or of his/her spouse, who is incapacitated by old age or infirmity from maintaining himself; and
(b) the widowed, divorced or separated mother of the individual, or of his/her spouse, or a single woman in consequence of dissolution or annulment of marriage.

## Other Use of the Dwelling-House: Apportionment

Where the dwelling-house has not been the taxpayer's only or main residence throughout his period of ownership (excluding the last 36 months which will invariably attract exemption), only a fraction of the

---

[1] [1976] STC 494.

[2] *Ibid.* Because of the time limit of the dependent relative relief, this concession is now obsolescent in the sense that the number of persons who can claim it cannot now increase, and will diminish over time.

gain is exempt. The fraction is determined according to a formula in (s223(2)), which can be thus expressed:

$$\frac{A}{B} \times C$$

where:

A = period of owner-occupation (including last 36 months)
B = total period of ownership
C = gross gain

## Motive

S224(3) provides that the relief will not apply to a gain if the acquisition of the house was made wholly or partly for the purpose of realising a gain from the disposal of it.

## Roll Over Relief on Transfer of Business to Company

S162 provides for roll over relief where an unincorporated business is transferred to a company as a going concern, together with all the assets of the business (other than cash), in consideration wholly or partly of shares in the company. ESC D32 extends the relief to cases where liabilities are taken over by the company on the transfer. In cases qualifying for relief, the gain accruing on the disposal to the company is "rolled over" (deferred) into the shares, resulting in a postponement of CGT until when the shares are eventually disposed of. It works by deducting the gain on the disposal from the cost or value of the shares, thus reducing their base cost. Where the consideration is partly shares, and partly cash, the gain is apportioned, and the part attributable to the cash payment is chargeable immediately.

The formula for determining the part which qualifies for relief is found in s162(4):

$$\frac{A}{B} \times \text{gain on old assets (the business)}$$

where:

A = the cost of the new assets (the shares)
B = total consideration for the transfer

The purpose of this provision was explained by Lord President Hope in *Gordon v IRC*[1]:

> It is clear that the section is intended to enable persons who are carrying on a business as individuals or as a partnership to transfer the business to a company without having to pay capital gains tax immediately on the disposal which must then inevitably occur. That company may be one which is controlled by others, or it may be one which the persons have incorporated themselves for the particular purpose of accepting the transfer of the business. It does not seem to me to matter for present purposes which of these alternatives applies . . .

Two other points emerge from the judgment of Lord President Hope. First, when determining whether or not a business was transferred to a person as a "going concern" the question is whether the transferee's activities could be carried on without interruption, at the date of the transfer.[2] Encompassed within that principle is the second point—timing. According to Lord President Hope[3] the roll over relief does not depend on the date at which the disposal was made, which for example will, in cases of disposals under contract, be the date when the contract was made (s28(1)). Neither does the relief depend on the state of the business at the date fixed by the contract for the transfer, if the transfer did not in fact take place on that date. What is important is whether the business was a going concern at the date when it was actually handed over from one party to the other.

This leads to another principle. The only thing that must be considered is the state of the business at the date of actual transfer. According to Lord President Hope, there is no requirement that the business shall answer the description of being a going concern at any future date, or that it shall continue to be a going concern for any period after the date of the transfer, nor is the relief said to be affected by what the transferee company may do with the business once it has been received by it. It was Lord President Hope's view that the words "going concern" do not in

---

[1] [1991] BTC 130; [1991] STC 174.
[2] [1991] BTC at p143.
[3] At p142.

themselves carry any implication about what may happen in the future or about the length of time which the business must remain in that condition once it has been taken over by the transferee.

## Retirement Relief

### Introduction

When an individual who has built up a business throughout his or her life wishes to retire from the business, the options available with respect to the business are either to pass the business on (to a member of the family or other beneficiary), or to sell it. If the business had enjoyed anything vaguely resembling financial success, either of these options will normally attract a charge to CGT. Depending on how one looks at it (the political or economic viewpoint) such tax consequences on the results of a lifetime of toil may either be a desirable thing (redistribution of wealth) or, alternatively, a chilling prospect which will discourage investment, stifle enterprise, encourage planning, and which must therefore be avoided or minimised. The latter is the current philosophy of the CGT legislation which therefore provides what is known as retirement relief. S163(1) provides that relief shall be granted to an individual who makes a material disposal of business assets and who either:

(a) has attained the age of 50, or
(b) retired on grounds of ill health below the age of 50.

Two important concepts are encompassed within this prescription—a disposal of business assets, which is also a material disposal. We shall examine these concepts in turn.

### Disposal of Business Assets

A disposal of business assets is defined by s163(2) as:

(a) a disposal of the whole or part of a business;
(b) on cessation of a business, a disposal of assets used for the purposes of that business;
(c) a disposal of shares or securities in a company.

*Material Disposals*

What constitutes a material disposal depends much on the type of asset, and the proportion of the asset that is being disposed of.

*The Whole or Part of a Business—s163(3)*

A disposal of the whole or part of a business is a material disposal if throughout the period of at least one year ending with the date of the disposal, [1]

(a) the business is owned by the disponor, or
(b) if the business is owned by a company, the company is a trading company, which is either the disponor's personal company (or a subsidiary thereof), and he is a full-time working officer or employee thereof. [2]

It should be noted that the provisions of s163(3) relate to a disposal of the whole business or a part of it. [3] They do not relate to a mere disposal of business assets (except on cessation). So for example it is not enough for the taxpayer to establish that he had disposed of an asset, or even an important asset used in his business [4]. Thus Peter Gibson J said in *Atkinson (HMIT) v Dancer* [5]:

> [T]he fact that a farmer sells some land alone which has has been using for a farming business prima facie will not amount to a sale of his farming business or any part thereof because it is only the sale of a chargeable business asset and not in itself the sale of the business or any part of it notwithstanding that it will be virtually inevitable that the sale of land on which the business has been conducted will reduce the activity of the farmer and probably his profits.

Although when a business is disposed of there is almost inevitably a

---

[1] There is no relief where the conditions are satisfied for only part of the specified period—see *Davenport (HMIT) v Hasslacher* [1977] STC 254.

[2] For definitions see *Sch. 6 para 1(2)* which defines a "personal company", in relation to an individual, as a company in which not less than 5% of voting rights are exercisable by that individual. A "full time working officer or employee" is an officer or employee who is required to devote substantially the whole of his time to the service of the company in a managerial or technical capacity.

[3] Note that this does not mean that the business must of necessity be sold as a going concern (see Jonathan Parker J in *Pepper (HMIT) v Daffurn* [1993] BTC 277 at 283).

[4] Knox J in *Jarmin (HMIT) v Rawlings* [1995] BTC 3 at 9.

[5] [1988]STC 758 at 764.

disposal of one or more individual assets which are used in it or which form part of it, there is an essential difference in that a business is an entity distinct from the sum of its parts [1]. Whether a particular disposal amounts to a disposal of the whole or part of a business, or whether it is merely a disposal of business assets is a question of fact. [2] The distinction between the two was discussed in *McGregor (HMIT) v Adcock* [3]. A farmer sold some five acres out of a farm of 35 acres with the benefit of planning permission. There was nothing to suggest that the scale of his farming business had been significantly altered by the sale. It was held that he was not entitled to retirement relief because he had only sold a business asset, and not a part of the business. Fox J said [4] that the provision requires the taxpayer who is seeking relief to establish that he has disposed of "the whole or part" of his business and that in the ordinary use of language, land is not the same thing as a business. According to him, a business connotes an activity, but land is merely an asset of a business. Fox J said that, although in order to bring the section into operation the taxpayer must dispose of the whole or part of a business, for the purposes of computation, the gains are calculated by reference to the "chargeable business assets" (i.e. assets used for the purposes of a trade, profession, etc) comprised in the disposal. According to Fox J, the provision is therefore merely recognising a distinction which in fact exists:

> In my view there is thus a clear distinction between the business and the individual assets used in the business. Prima facie, therefore, it seems to me wrong to assert that the mere sale of farmland is a disposal of part of the farm business. The true position, I think, is that the sale is merely a factor which the court has to consider in deciding whether there has been such a disposal.

In his view, the test was "whether there has been such an interference with the whole complex of activities and assets as can be said to amount to a disposal of the business or part of the business". [5]

Concerning this test, Peter Gibson J in *Atkinson (HMIT) v Dancer* [6]

---

[1] Knox J in *Jarmin (HMIT) v Rawlings* [1995] BTC 3 at 9. A business connotes an activity (*ibid*, at p14).

[2] See Fox J in *McGregor (HMIT) v Adcock* [1977] STC 206 at 209; Peter Gibson J in *Atkinson (HMIT) v Dancer* [1988] STC 758 at 765.

[3] [1977] STC 206.

[4] At p209.

[5] [1977] STC at 209.

[6] [1988] STC at 765.

doubted whether it was particularly helpful or illuminating to rephrase the simple and clear test posed by the wording of the section by a test in terms of interference with the whole complex of activities and assets. [1] However, since both counsel in the case were agreed that this was the appropriate test, he would, in spite of his reservations, follow the test, leaving it to a higher court, if it thinks fit, to lay down some other test. As far as applying the test was concerned Peter Gibson J accepted that the only relevant matters to be considered in relation to the interference are those that are caused by the sale. According to him Fox J was clearly contrasting the position immediately before the sale and the position immediately after the sale. When posing the test of an interference with the whole complex of activities and assets, Fox J was plainly looking to the sale constituting that interference. It was thus implicit in Fox J's remarks that changes in activities and assets caused by something other than the sale are irrelevant. [2] Elaborating on this point Peter Gibson J said [3]:

> But unless the change in [the taxpayer's] activities is attributable to the disposal by way of sale it is simply not material that prior to the sale there had been a connection between the activity that has ceased or been reduced and that which is sold. What the commissioners must do if applying Fox J's test is to look at the position before the sale and the position after the sale and ask the question whether the sale caused any changes in the activities and assets. If the changes caused by the sale lead to the conclusion that the position is wholly different from the position before the sale, then in Fox J's words "it may well be" . . . that an inference will be drawn of the sale of a business or part of a business.

Problems arise where the taxpayer disposes of assets in a number of transactions, and then claims that these transactions constitute a disposal of part of his business. The question in this case is whether the transactions ought to be taken as one single transaction involving a disposal of the business or part of it (therefore qualifying for relief), or as single and independent transactions which are just mere disposals of business assets (therefore not qualifying for relief). The issue arose in *Mannion (HMIT) v Johnston.* [4] In this case the taxpayer, after some

---

[1] Compare Jonathan Parker J in *Pepper (HMIT) v Daffurn* [1993] BTC 277 at 282.
[2] *Ibid.*
[3] At p766.
[4] [1988] BTC 364.

deterioration in his health, decided to retire partially. He farmed 78 acres of land and in April 1984 he sold some 17 acres of his farm to a neighbouring farmer. In December 1984, he sold a further 18 acres of the farm to the same purchaser. These transactions were undertaken by the taxpayer in order to sell part of his farm. Counsel for the taxpayer argued that, where there were a number of disposals, these could and should be taken together in deciding whether there had been a sale of a business or part of a business. Counsel argued that this was so even if there was no contractual connection between the disposals, or any other link which made the disposals part of the same transaction—otherwise, a taxpayer who chooses to dispose of his business by a number of disposals to obtain a better price would be treated less favourably than a taxpayer who disposes of his business by a single sale. The commissioners accepted the arguments and held that the disposal of 45 per cent of the taxpayer's farm acreage was a disposal of part of the business and thus he was entitled to retirement relief. The Revenue's appeal against this decision was upheld. Peter Gibson J said [1]:

> Where there are two separate disposals not part of the same transaction, I cannot see anything in [s 163] or in the capital gains tax legislation in general which allows or requires such disposals to be treated as one. They are two separate disposals occurring, it may be, in different fiscal years and having separate fiscal consequences accordingly. Unless there be some evidence to enable the two disposals to be treated as one, such as evidence that they were part of the same transaction, they must be treated separately.

Peter Gibson J said [2] that the commissioners appeared to have treated the two disposals as a single substantial disposal, having referred to the sale (in the singular) of the land and to the disposal of a substantial proportion (also in the singular) of the farmland. He said that this was not correct, and that, each disposal, being a separate transaction, must be treated separately.

This decision is not authority for the proposition that multiple disposals must always be treated separately. The question depends on the facts of each case, and it is quite possible for a number of separate disposals to be taken together as a sale of part of a business. This happened in *Jarmin*

[1] At p373.
[2] At p375.

*(HMIT) v Rawlings.* [1] The taxpayer, who was then 61 years old, was a dairy farmer who owned some 64 acres, with a milking parlour and yard, a hay barn, implements shed, cattle sheds and a herd of 34 cattle. He also had the benefit of a milk quota. In October 1988 he sold the milking parlour, yard and storage barn at an auction. Completion took place in January 1989. None of the cattle was sold at the auction (which was solely concerned with the land and buildings) but between the auction and completion 14 cows were sold. At completion, the rest of the cattle were transferred to the taxpayer's wife's farm. He retained ownership thereof, but he did not have any financial benefit from their milk. They were eventually sold after a period of time. After completion, the taxpayer ceased dairy farming, but he continued farming on the farm by rearing and finishing store cattle. The commissioners held that the dairy business was a separate and distinguishable part of the taxpayer's business and that, in selling the means of dairy production and the dairy herd, he was disposing of the dairying part of his business. They also found that the sale of the milking parlour and the buildings made it impossible for the taxpayer to continue his business after the sale, and that there was sufficient interference to satisfy the "interference test". Thus the taxpayer was entitled to retirement relief.

Knox J upheld the commissioners. One issue that arose in this case concerned timing. S 28(1) TCGA 1992 provides generally that, where an asset is disposed of and acquired under a contract, the time of the disposal and acquisition is the time when the contract is made and not, if different, the time at which the asset is conveyed or transferred. In this respect the Revenue argued that it was only permissible to have regard to what happened at the time of the relevant disposition, which, under s 27 CGTA 1979 (now s 28 TCGA 1992) was the date of the auction in October 1988. According to this argument, all that was disposed of at the auction was milking parlour and yard, most of the other disposals having taken place after the auction but before completion. Thus, it was not possible to find that part of a business, as opposed to an asset of a business, was disposed of. The taxpayer on the other hand argued that the proper subject of inquiry was what was disposed of when the transaction in question took effect and that this could only realistically be assessed by comparing the position immediately before the auction with the position at and immediately after completion. This was all part of the disposal which had to be looked at realistically and included all that happened

[1] [1995] BTC 3.

between contract and completion. He argued that s 27 CGTA 1979 (s 28 TCGA 1992) was only a timing provision which enabled a date to be fixed for capital gains tax purposes of a disposal. Knox J preferred the taxpayer's argument, saying [1]:

> It would . . . be highly artificial to look only at the date of a contract in order to assess whether there was or was not a sale of part of a business, more especially if the proper subject of enquiry is whether the disposal effected by a contract followed by completion amounted to a disposal of part of a business. To ignore events after the making of the contract would be to ignore the performance of the disposal itself and that in my view cannot be right.

Therefore the sales of cattle between contract and completion could properly be taken into account by the commissioners. However, in respect of the sales subsequent to completion, he felt that the conclusion that there was a disposal of part of a business could not be supported unless there was some connection established at the date of completion, which enabled a subsequent sale of cattle to be treated as part of the same transaction. For these purposes, the fact that the cattle were no longer being used by the taxpayer for his daily farming business would not be a sufficient connection.

On the question of whether the disposals constituted the disposal of a business or part of a business, Knox J said that the right question was whether the sales of cattle were part of the same transaction as the disposal of the farmyard and the milking shed. [2] He said that it was not an easy question [3], and that it could be tested by postulating simultaneous sales by the owner of a business to a wide variety of purchasers not connected between each other, of the totality of the assets of a business:

> An obvious example would be a sale by auction of all the assets used in a business. As regards any individual business asset it would only be possible to say that the disposal was a sale of part of a business if all the other sales of other business assets were taken into consideration. The auction could be regarded as a single transaction at least from the vendor's point of view and it is to be remembered that it is a disposal

[1] At p13.
[2] At p13.
[3] At p14.

that is the subject matter of inquiry and not the consequential acquisition by another party.[100]

Knox J said that it is legitimate to have regard to simultaneous disposals entered into of other assets used in the business in assessing whether or not a particular disposal can be categorised as a sale of part of a business. In this case, it was not material that the taxpayer still retained some assets after the disposal because it was not necessary that, for a business or part of a business to be disposed of, all the assets used in the business must be sold. Knox J thus concluded that, on the facts as found by the commissioners, it was open to them to find that the dairy farming was a separate business from the rearing and finishing of store cattle and that the dairy farming business was disposed of by the sale of land at auction coupled with the cessation of milking for profit at completion of that sale.[1] According to him, the critical factor is that a business connotes an activity. The activity in this case was the production and sale of milk, which ceased at completion as far as the taxpayer was concerned. The fact that cows which still belonged to him continued to be milked for other persons' profit, and that he still owned the milk quota (although he did not use it for his own milk production) did not detract from the conclusion that, on completion, the taxpayer's dairying business ceased. Concluding the matter, Knox J said[2]:

> The sale of the milking parlour was a vital ingredient in that cessation so far as to make it indeed possible to say that that sale caused such an interference with the whole complex of activities and assets as to amount to a disposal of part of a business, if that is the correct test. For my part I would prefer to look at it somewhat more broadly and say that the sale by auction and completion of that sale of the milking parlour and yard coupled with the cessation at completion of all milking operations for Mr Rawlings' benefit amounted to a disposal by him of his dairy farming business.

On the facts of this case, this was obviously the correct decision. However, the point still needs to be emphasised that everything depends on the facts of each case, and that no general rule can be made, as the recent decision of *Wase (HMIT) v Bourke*[3] shows. Here, the taxpayer, having decided to

[1] *Ibid.*
[2] At pp14–15.
[3] [1996] BTC 3.

give up farming, sold his entire dairy herd in March 1988 at which time he was aged 59 years and four months. At that time the qualifying age for retirement relief was 60 years. After the herd had been sold, the young cattle that remained were fattened up and sold. He leased his milk quota to a third party and then sold it in February 1989, at which time he was 60 years old. The delay in selling the milk quota was due to financial reasons. While the quota remained unsold the taxpayer could have resumed his dairy farming, but did not do so. The only question that arose in this case was whether the disposal of the milk quota was a disposal of the whole or part of a business. It was common ground that the dairy business ceased to be carried on when the taxpayer sold his herd in March 1988. The commissioners found that the taxpayer's decision to give up dairy farming was primarily motivated by the fact that he had developed arthritis in his shoulder, and that each of the transactions were steps taken in implementation or further implementation of that decision. They thus held that the sales were all part of one transaction—the disposal of the taxpayer's dairy farming business. In reaching this conclusion they had asked themselves what it was that amounted to a "major interference with the whole complex of activities carried on by the taxpayer". They decided that this was the disposal of the farming business, of which the sale of the milk quota was an integral part. The judge (Anthony Grabiner QC sitting as a deputy judge of the High Court) held that the commissioners had erred by failing to ask themselves the correct question—which was, whether the disposal by the taxpayer of his milk quota amounted to the whole or part of his business.[1] If they had asked themselves the correct question, they would have concluded that the disposal of the milk quota was simply the disposal of an asset which had formerly been used in or which was part of the dairy farming business, and that it was not by itself the disposal of the whole or part of the business. According to Anthony Grabiner QC, the relevant business activity consisted of the production and sale of milk, and that activity ceased upon the disposal of the dairy herd. The subsequent disposal of another asset does not, in the circumstances of this case, amount to a disposal of part of the business. Anthony Grabiner QC said that this case fell on the *Atkinson v Dancer* and *Mannion v Johnston* side of the line, and that the sale of the milk quota does not satisfy the "simultaneous disposals" test identified by Knox J in *Jarmin v Rawlings*. The taxpayer in this case had specific financial reasons for delaying the sale of the milk quota for almost

[1] At p12.

a year after he had sold his herd and given up dairy farming, and these two matters could not be properly described as amounting to a single transaction.

## Cessation: Disposal of Assets Used for Business

As seen above, s163(2)(b) includes in the definition of "disposal of business assets" a disposal of assets which, at the time when a business ceased to be carried on, were in use for the purposes of that business. S163(4) provides that a disposal of business assets on cessation is a material disposal if:

(a) throughout a period of at least one year ending with the cessation, the business was owned by the disponor or his personal company (as in s163(3) above) and
(b) on or before the cessation he had either attained the ago of 50 or retired before attaining that age on grounds of ill health, and
(c) the date of cessation falls within the permitted period before the date of the disposal.

"Permitted period" is defined by Schedule 6 paragraph 1(2) as a period of one year, or such longer period as the Board may allow by notice in writing.

By virtue of the decision in *Plumbly v Spencer (HMIT)* [1], it is necessary for the purposes of s163(2)(b) that the business in which the asset was being used belonged to the individual seeking the relief. In *Plumbly v Spencer* itself, H granted a lease of land to a company which was a trading company and his family company, and of which he was a full time working director. The letting was for the use of the company's trade, and the company paid rent to H. Within one year of the company ceasing to carry on its trade, H disposed of the land. The question was whether, upon the true construction of (what is now) s163(2)(b), use of the land for the purposes of the business carried on by the company was sufficient, or whether it was necessary that the land was used for the purposes of the business carried on by H himself. Lightman J held that, while the subsection on its face required only a disposal of an asset for the purposes of "a business", and not "a business of the individual making the disposal", due regard must be had to the context of the provision and its place in the scheme of the relevant legislation as a whole. Thus, the starting and (in this case)

---

[1] [1997] BTC 147.

finishing point is reading the section in its context and in its place in such scheme.[1] According to Lightman J it is clear that the words in [s163(2)(a)] "a disposal of the whole or part of a business" mean, and can only mean "a disposal of the whole or part of a business of the individual claiming relief".[2] He said that s163(2)(a) is concerned with the situation where the individual on attaining the specified age disposes of the whole or part of his business as a going concern. However, s163(2)(b) is concerned with the situation where the individual on attaining the specified age, instead of disposing of the business as a going concern, ceases to carry on the business and sells one or more assets previously used in the business.[3] In short, s163 in the two subsections is concerned with:

> two different scenarios, either of which may occur when the businessman decides to retire from his business: he may dispose of his business as a going concern or he may merely dispose of the assets used in such business. The tax relief is rendered available in both cases. In both cases the expression "a business" is used to denote any business of the individual making the disposal.[4]

## Shares or Securities in a Company

S163(5) provides that a disposal of shares or securities in a company is a material disposal if throughout a period of at least one year ending with the operative date:

(a) the disponor owns the business, which at the date of the disposal is owned by the company or, if the company is the holding company of a trading group, by any member of the group; or

(b) the company is the disponor's personal company, (or a subsidiary) and the disponor is a full time working officer or employee of the company.

Except in situations where either s 163(6) or s 163(7) applies, the operative date is the date of the disposal.[5] S163(6) provides that, where cessation (of trading) occurs during the permitted period, and on or before cessation

---

[1] At p154.
[2] *Ibid.*
[3] At 154–155.
[4] At p155.
[5] s163(5).

the disponor was 50 or retired on ill health grounds before that age, the operative date is the date of such cessation. This date is also deemed to be the date of disposal for the purposes of s163(5)(a). Where the disponor has ceased to be a full-time working officer or employee of the company, the date when the disponor ceased to be a full-time working officer or employee is the operative date (S163(7)).

## Other Disposals

S164(1) extends retirement relief to assets held for the purpose of an office or employment (other than director of a personal company) and s164(3) extends it to disposals by trustees of settled property, being disposals of shares or securities in a company or of business assets where the conditions attached under subsections (4) and (5) of the section apply to a beneficiary having an interest in possession.

## Associated Disposals

Where relief falls to be given under s163 in respect of a material disposal of business assets which is either a disposal by an individual of his interest in partnership assets, or a qualifying (under s163(5)) disposal of shares or securities of a company, relief is also given in respect of associated disposals made by that individual (s164(6)). S164(7) provides, for these purposes, that a disposal is associated with a material disposal if it takes place as part of a withdrawal of the individual concerned from participation in the business (carried on by the partnership, or the company, as the case may be). Further conditions are that, immediately before the material disposal (or, if earlier, the cessation of the relevant business), the asset was in use for the purposes of that business, and during any part of the individual's ownership of the asset being disposed of, the asset had been used for the purposes of the business or some other qualifying businesses. Although s164(7)(b) refers to the asset being in use for the business immediately before the material disposal or cessation, there is some amount of flexibility in the timing. In *Clarke (HMIT) v Mayo* [1] the Revenue argued that the use of the word "immediately" required that the property must have been in use at the instant immediately before the cessation, such that, when the disposal of property took place four weeks before the cessation of the business, the condition in

_____
[1] [1994] BTC 225.

respect of immediacy was not satisfied. Evans-Lombe J rejected the argument in the following terms [1]:

> The words "immediately before ... the cessation of the business" should not be construed in isolation but in the context of the provisions of [s163 and 164] as a whole. From those sections it is in my judgment plain that the legislature intended that relief from capital gains tax should be available for associated disposals of assets where those disposals were part of a withdrawal by a taxpayer from participation in a relevant business where he has attained the [prescribed age] or retired earlier on grounds of ill health. The requirement that the asset being disposed of must have been in use in the relevant business immediately before the interest in the business itself was disposed of or that business ceased seems to me to have been provided for so as to ensure that the associated disposal was genuinely part of the withdrawal. It seems to me that where the commissioners are satisfied that such is the case they are justified in so construing the relevant words of subs. (7)(b) so as not to require precisely that at the instant before the material disposal or cessation the asset was in use in the business. The words "immediately before" may be construed as meaning "sufficiently proximate in time to the material disposal or cessation so as to justify the conclusion that the transaction in question formed part of it".

In respect of the principle of "withdrawal from participation", the withdrawal itself must constitute the relevant material disposal of business assets, [2] and "participation" in this context means holding an interest in the business concerned. [3] Whether the required association exists or not is a question of fact for the commissioners. [4]

## Amount of Relief

The amounts on which retirement relief is granted change from time to time. However, the general scheme is to provide relief in relation to a lower monetary limit and an upper monetary limit (e.g. for 1996/97 and

---

[1] At p234.
[2] At p233.
[3] At p234.
[4] *Ibid.*

1997/98 the upper limit was £1,000,000). Relief is available on gains of up to that upper limit (Schedule 6(13)(1)).

According to Schedule 6 paragraph 13(1), the available relief is the aggregate of:

(a) so much of the qualifying gains as do not exceed the appropriate percentage of £250,000 (the lower monetary limit), and
(b) half of so much of the gains as exceed the appropriate percentage of the lower monetary limit, but do not exceed that percentage of £1,000,000.

i.e. the appropriate percentage of the first £250,000 is exempt and half of the appropriate percentage of the next £750,000 is exempt. Any excess over £1,000,000 is chargeable.

The "appropriate percentage" is one which is determined according to the length of the qualifying period rising arithmetically from 10% for one year to 100% for ten years, i.e. relief is available in respect of:

(a) £25,000 for each full year, for the first £250,000 and
(b) half of £75,500 for each full year, for the remaining £750,000.

*Self-Check Questions*

1. What is meant by "indexation allowance", and how is it applied?
2. What reliefs are available in respect of the disposal of chattels?
3. In what circumstances will separate buildings constitute one single dwelling-house?
4. What periods of absence will be considered as periods of owner-occupation for the purposes of the main residence relief?
5. In what circumstances will retirement relief be available?
6. What is the difference between the disposal of part of a business and, a mere disposal of a business asset?

**Further Reading**

Pearce-Crump D, *Paddocks Lodge Revisited (or Private Residence Relief Again)*, (1993) BTR 12–23.
Norris W, *Capital Gains Tax: More About Residences*, (1993) BTR 24–41.
Nobes CW, *Capital Gains Tax and Inflation*, (1977) BTR 154–163.

# Part Four — Companies and Corporation Tax

# 14

# Companies and Corporation Tax

## Introduction

Companies resident in the United Kingdom are liable to pay corporation tax on all "profits" wherever arising.[1] "Profits" are defined to include both income and chargeable gains. It is convenient that income and chargeable gains are computed in accordance with income tax principles and capital gains tax principles—thus much of the work has been completed in previous chapters. In this chapter we are going to focus on the problems peculiar to companies. In particular we will consider the issues raised by "groups" of companies; "close" companies; and the problems created by the relationship between the company and its shareholders and any returns (dividends) that shareholders might receive. Before we consider these issues and problems we must first consider why we tax companies.

## Why Do We Tax Companies?

This question was considered by the Royal Commission in its Final Report on the Taxation of Profits and Income in 1955.[2] In its own discussion of and reply to that question the Royal Commission appeared to place emphasis on the fact that a company enjoys a personality of its own: it is a legal person distinct and separate from the members, the shareholders, who make up the company.[3] As a legal person perhaps a company like other legal persons should be subject to taxation. However, this reasoning does not explain why a company should be subject to a different regime of taxation nor does it explain why there was a time "lag" between the recognition of the separate legal personality of a company

---

[1] TA 1988, s6.

[2] Cmn 9474, para. 45.

[3] For a discussion of the separate legal personality of a company see *Salomon v A Salomon & Co Ltd* [1897] AC 22.

and the introduction of a tax on company profits and gains. The "time lag" is always difficult to explain and account for. The separate legal personality of a company had been recognised for a long period before revenue law caught up with the concept and introduced a separate taxation of companies.[1] In the UK special taxes were introduced and imposed on companies from 1915–1924 and from 1937 onwards. Once again, the initiative for the introduction of these special taxes was the need to finance warfare. In 1965 those special taxes were replaced by a system of corporation tax—it is not applicable to unincorporated associations (partnerships, sole traders) and it recognises the legal status of the company and its separation from the individuals who make up the company. It also provides greater flexibility in allowing the government to operate its fiscal policy knowing that corporation taxes are separate from income taxes. Their independence can be used to promote and encourage investment.

Some believe that the separate taxation of companies is a fair charge for the benefits and privileges that a corporate status confers. One presumes that those benefits or privileges includes the ability to access wider sources of finance, and the privilege of the protection of limited liability. The measure and extent of such privileges is difficult to assess. In many ways those privileges are under threat or, at least, enjoyed at a cost. For example, the registration procedure and the annual disclosure requirements impose a cost or charge on the benefit of incorporation. Similarly, increasing statutory regimes impose liability on individuals instead of or in addition to the company[2]: it is not always possible to "hide" behind the company's existence.

If one still accepts that "incorporation" is a privilege, then a charge for that privilege in terms of a licence and licence fee rather than the inclusion of an uncertain and unquantifiable privilege element in a system of corporation tax is the preferred method of charge. Another major problem of taxing on the basis of benefit or privilege is the difficulty of ascertaining who really pays for that privilege. The incidence of corporation tax or of a benefit charge might fall on the company employees, company owners or the consumers and customers. These might not constitute the intended target.

---

[1] It is believed that in Europe, the practice of recognising a separation of the business and its owners was present in the thirteenth century.

[2] See section 213, 214, Insolvency Act 1986.

## Systems of Corporation Tax

There are three recognised systems of corporation tax: (1) classical, (2) imputation, and (3) integrated. Under the classical system double taxation of the same income often occurs. The company profits are subject to corporation tax and if the company pays dividends out of those taxed profits those dividends are taxed once more in the hands of the recipient shareholder. Thus we find that the same income is taxed twice. First in the hands of the company as corporation tax and then in the hands of the shareholder as income from his investment (the "dividend on his shareholding). The UK operated a classical system of taxation in 1965–73. The main objection against such a system is the inequitable double-taxation of income. It raises a disadvantage of incorporation if one considers the tax treatment of unincorporated businesses, and it might discriminate against entrepreneurial risk-taking. It also creates a bias against the distribution of dividends: the larger the distribution, the larger is the total tax borne by a company and its shareholders.

The imputation system of taxation mitigates the double-taxation problems of the classical system by imputing to the shareholders some or all of the tax paid by companies. An imputation system was introduced in the UK in 1973 and is present in most EC countries. Imputation systems operate because the income that has been subject to corporation tax and is then distributed as dividends to shareholders will be distributed with a tax credit attached to it. For example, if £1.00 profit had been subject to a corporation tax rate of 35 per cent and then 30 pence dividend had been declared out of the net profit, the money representing the dividend would not be subject to further tax charges in the hands of the shareholder. Instead, the shareholder would receive the dividend (at a grossed-up amount) together with a tax credit to offset against any personal tax liability attending to that income receipt.

The problem that the UK faces is that we enjoy a partial rather than a full imputation system. Under a full imputation system the shareholder would receive a tax credit that equated with both the company's corporation tax liability and the shareholder's individual tax liability. Some countries, such as Germany, do operate full imputation tax systems. Under a partial imputation tax system (UK, France) the taxpayer receives a tax credit equivalent to basic rate liability. For example, if we assumed a basic rate of 25 per cent and a higher rate of 40 per cent a shareholder would receive a dividend plus 25 per cent tax credit. If the shareholder is a basic rate tax payer no tax liability would ensue, whereas if the shareholder is a higher rate taxpayer, tax liability of 15 per cent (40 per cent rate minus the tax credit) would remain. Thus double taxation at the marginal rate would result. [1]

Finally, before we leave the imputation system of corporation tax we must consider the peculiarities of advance corporation tax (ACT). In essence ACT was introduced to maintain the government's cash flow under the imputation system of corporation tax. Generally when a distribution is announced a company must pay ACT equivalent to the tax credit granted to the shareholder on that distribution. This ensures that the shareholder's tax credits have always been paid for. The ACT is then set-off against the company's corporation tax liability. Two problems have occurred with ACT. First, the recipient shareholder may actually be another company. Those companies cannot benefit from the tax credits in the same way as the "non-corporate" shareholder. In this situation the dividends received by the "corporate" shareholder is classed as Franked Investment Income (FII). This FII can be used by the recipient company to reduce any ACT due on its own distribution of dividends—thus reducing the amount of tax that it needs to pay in advance.

The second problems caused by the ACT system relates to "surplus ACT". Surplus ACT is, in essence, ACT which a company is unable to set-off against its corporation tax liability—it is sometimes regarded as a dividend tax, Surplus ACT normally occurs in one of two ways. First because a company pays dividends out of reserves, common in a recession, pays ACT on those dividend payments but finds that the ACT payments exceed the company's mainstream corporation tax liability; or, second, in those companies that earn most of their profit overseas, UK tax liability is usually reduced by the amount of foreign taxes that they pay. Consequently, such companies also find that the amount of mainstream corporation tax liability that remains, if any, is insufficient to offset any ACT paid. Thus it appears that foreign profits are taxed twice, abroad and at home. In recognition of this problem the Chancellor has recently announced the issuing of a consultative document based on a proposal that dividends paid out of overseas profits should be separately classified as "foreign income dividends"; companies would be entitled to a refund if the dividend payment gives rise to surplus ACT. [2] Significantly, it is proposed that no tax credit would be available to shareholders who enjoy

---

[1] In the UK the current tax credit of 25 per cent is to be reduced to 20 per cent in 1993–94. This will increase the liability of higher rate taxpayers (40 per cent) by 8.5 per cent. Thus increasing the double-taxation element and, according to Mr Lamont, the Exchequer's revenue by some £200m a year.

[2] Announced by the Chancellor in his Budget Speech, 16 March 1993.

such dividends. The absence of a tax credit might influence investment decisions.

Finally, the integrated system of company taxation involves an integration of the company's tax liability with the personal income tax liability of the shareholders. Shareholders would pay personal income tax on their share of corporate income or profits irrespective of whether that income is distributed or undistributed. Such a system removes any discrimination between distributed and undistributed income or profit, and it assists in removing any tax deferral control and opportunities of corporations.

An integrated system is similar in operation to the manner in which we deal with the "profits" of a partnership and has recently reared its head in the manner in which we tax European Economic Interest Groupings (EEIGs).[1] In situations where the taxpayer has little (real) control over the declared distributions of a company, an integration system could result in a tax liability in excess of receipts.

## The Tax Base, Assessment and Rates

Before we discuss European influences on the development and reform of corporation tax, it is important to appreciate the tax base of corporation tax. The tax base and its importance is often overlooked, and was overlooked at European level, when considering the reform of corporation tax. The tax base represents the definition of taxable income. In some countries, particularly France and Germany, the tax base (taxable income) is linked to accounting profit and thus varies with the particular country's rules on the calculation of accounting profit. In the UK, the tax base is not so interrelated with accounting income and profit. The tax base and taxable income is calculated in accordance with statutory requirements and currently consists of a requirement that corporation tax falls on the "income and chargeable gains of a company".[2] Thus the administration of corporation tax is closely linked with that of income tax and capital gains tax.

The tax period for corporation tax is levied by reference to "financial years", not "years of assessment". Financial years begin on 1 April and end on 31 March. They are known by a calendar year of reference being the year of the commencement of the financial year, i.e. 1 April of that year (calendar year 1997 for a year running 1 April 1997 to 31 March

[1] TA 1988, S510A.
[2] TA 1988, s6(4).

1998). Apportionment of profits will take place where the company's accounting year does not correspond to the "financial year". Generally, assessment is based on a current year basis, and a system of "Pay and File" operates whereby a company "files" a return with the Revenue within twelve months following the end of its accounting period and a final assessment is made, albeit that a company initially must comply with a requirement to pay corporation tax within nine months following the end of its accounting period based upon its own assessment: clearly some adjustments may be necessary to accommodate differences in the the initial self-assessment and the subsequent "file".

When considering the rate of corporation tax, it is important to consider both mainstream rate, the "small companies rate" and the rate of ACT (advance corporation tax). The rate of mainstream corporation tax has seen a steady decline from 52 per cent in 1982 to the current rate of 33 per cent, introduced in 1991. Similarly, ACT has been reduced but not as dramatically. ACT used to be linked to the basic rate of income tax for the relevant year, but in 1993 the detail was changed permitting ACT to be related to the lower rate of income tax thereby improving the cash flow of many companies. Finally, a "small companies rate" exists. The measure is based on the size of the company profits in the relevant year, not asset value. The rate applies to companies with profits not exceeding £300,000 and the rate currently stands at 24 per cent, a reduction from 38 per cent in 1982.

In computing a company's profits, the income and capital gains principles discussed elsewhere in this book generally apply (sections 8 and 9 of the Taxes Act confirm this). For example, a company's income will be allotted to the various Schedules and Cases with the relevant rules for determining assessment and expenses being applied just as they would be for determining the position of an individual. It is then the several classes of income of a company together with the total of its chargeable gains that constitutes the total profits of the company.

One broad exception to the application of income tax and capital gains principles to the assessment of corporate profits relates to "loan relationships". Changes were introduced through Chapter II of Part IV of the Finance Act 1996 to loan relationships involving companies as either the borrower or lender. The changes treat all such profits and losses for companies as income, not capital gains nor losses as might previously have been the case. An obvious example of the changes can be illustrated in relation to interest paid on loan capital, debentures. Previously interest paid by a company on its debentures would be treated as a charge on income and thus deductible from profits: the position has now changed. Sections 82 and 83 of the Finance Act 1996 provides that where companies enter into loan relationships (widely defined in section 81) for the purposes of a trade, the profits, losses and expenses relating to those relationships will be treated as receipts of the expenses of that trade and thus be part of the Schedule D Case I computation. In the case of profits and losses arising from other (non-trading) loan relationships, any net profit will be taxable under the rules of Case III of Schedule D: Schedule C and Schedule D Case IV are no-longer applicable. Any net loss from a non-trading loan relationship can be used in one of four ways: (i) it can be set against profits for corporation tax of the year in which the loss occurred; (ii) it can be used by way of "group relief", (iii) it can be carried back against similar non-trading profits of the preceding three years; (iv) it can be carried forward against non-trading profits of the company for succeeding accounting periods.

Finally, a special note on "distributions". Some payments made by a company are termed as distributions, for example dividends paid to its shareholders. To the individual taxpayer the receipt of such income is chargeable to income tax under Schedule F.

The meaning of a distribution can be found in sections 212 and 218 of the Taxes Act. Broadly it includes dividends and other distributions made in respect of shares, the distributions being made out of the assets of the company and involve a cost falling on the company. It does not cover the situation of the repayment and reduction of capital, nor the situation where the company issues bonus shares, because no cost falls on the company, except where that bonus issue is followed by a repayment of share capital: the latter repayment will then be treated as a distribution up to the extent of the value of the bonus issue. Similarly a rights issue is not included because it is not made out of the assets of a company but involves the company receiving fresh consideration for the issue.

A distinction has been drawn between distributions which are qualifying and distributions which are non-qualifying. Section 14(2) of the Taxes Act declares that a "qualifying distribution" means any distribution other than (a) bonus redeemable shares and bonus securities; and (b) any share capital or security which the company making the distribution has directly or indirectly received from another company in the form of bonus redeemable shares or securities. Thus these non-qualifying distributions confer no immediate benefit to the shareholder although, of course, the benefit can eventually confer a cash benefit, for example through the sale of the bonus shares.

Why make a distinction? The importance lies in the fact that if the distribution is a qualifying distribution, advance corporation tax becomes due from the company and the recipient gets a tax credit. A non-qualifying distribution does not attract advance corporation tax and no tax credit is given.

## European Harmonisation

It has been suggested that the importance of bringing VAT rates into line is insignificant in comparison to harmonising corporation tax.

> ... The only effect of differences in VAT rates is the encouragement of some cross-border shopping. Differences in corporation taxes affect the location of business and the flow of capital. [1]

Empirical studies and evidence from the Confederation of British Industry appear to support the perceived tax influences on location decisions and actions. Early recognition of the influences of corporation tax and the possible distorting effects were present at European level. Corporation tax systems, tax bases and tax rates differ between EU member countries. Some countries follow the classical system, some the imputation system and some adopt a mixture of the two. Tax bases vary because different countries have different rules determining taxable profits; and differences exist in corporation tax rates of the different member states. [2] At various times the European Commission has published reports and proposals on the reform of corporation tax. [3] These proposals have essentially concentrated on tax systems rather than tax bases (although the 1980s did witness consideration of the harmonisation of tax bases), and the earlier proposals did favour the classical system but have been replaced with proposals and a draft Directive focusing on Union-wide adoption of an imputation system of corporation tax. [4] The draft Directive proposed that an imputation system should operate with a single tax rate between 45 and 55 per cent. Imputation credits would be available and compensatory tax like ACT or a pre-compte should be introduced. This draft Directive

---

[1] M Wilson, *Taxation*, at p130.

[2] For example, in 1990 corporation tax rates stretched from 35 per cent in the UK, Spain and Portugal, to 50 per cent in Germany and Denmark.

[3] Early reports include the Report of the Neumark Committee in 1963 (The EEC Reports on Tax Harmonisation) and the van den Tempel Report in 1974.

[4] Official Journal of the European Communities 5/11/1975 No C253/2.

has received criticism on a variety of grounds. [1] Concerns have been expressed at the failure to consider the treatment of capital gains. This might encourage the wasteful manoeuvring of capital gains in order to gain favourable tax treatment in some member states. Similarly, it is suggested that corporation tax must include "turnover and local taxes" if it is to minimise differences in total tax burdens. It has been suggested that total harmonisation is inappropriate. Corporation tax and its influences on location decisions ought to permit regional differences (and favourable treatment) to encourage investment in the "needier" areas and regions of the Union.

Despite this draft Directive and the early recognition of the need to harmonise corporation tax, progress to date has been slow. In fact, some member countries have regarded the Directive as having little influence or contraint on their activities and corporation tax developments [2]— although the situation might be changing. [3]

Two major constraints on the harmonisation of corporation tax are apparent. First, the issue of harmonising tax rates as opposed to tax systems. The determination of corporation tax rates provides an important fiscal tool and opportunity for the governments of each member state. Any request for them to surrender (if they have not already done so) that fiscal and political tool is likely to continue to meet strong opposition—although it has been suggested that a two-stage approach to the harmonisation of "rates" would be appropriate. [4] Second, the need to consider the harmonisation of tax bases has often been repeated. Commenting on the draft Directive, Nobes concluded that:

> Perhaps the most important criticism is that there are some major differences in the calculation of taxable income which it is not proposed to harmonise. [5]

At long last, the Commission has begun to accept concerns in this area

---

[1] See A Easson, "Tax Harmonisation in the EEC: the Commission's Programme", [1981] BTR 329; C W Nobes, "EEC Imputation Systems of Corporation Tax and the Proposal for a Directive on Harmonisation" [1979] JBL 306.

[2] For example, the Irish Commission on Direct Taxation reported that they did not consider the EC draft Directive to be a significant constraint on their recommendations. First Report of the Commission on Taxation, 1982. Similarly, the UK Green Paper on Corporation Tax (1982, Cmnd 8456) made little reference to EC constraints or recommendations.

[3] The European Commission have reported and recommended the need to revise and continue the harmonisation programme. (Guidelines on Company Taxation—SEC (90) 601).

[4] Easson, supra n15, at p338–339.

[5] Nobes, supra n15, at p309.

and the harmonisation of tax bases—as well as rates and tax systems—is now firmly on the agenda.

Finally, one should not assume that the harmonisation programme has not resulted in tangible changes Products of harmonisation and change exist; for example, the EC Directives on cross-border mergers and parent/subsidiary companies are beginning to influence practice. [1] What we have yet to experience is the expected, and needed, harmonisation of tax systems and tax bases (and perhaps even tax rates). [2]

## Groups and Consortia

It is common for companies to operate their business activities through a group of companies. Groups often involve complex organisational and control structures, especially in the United Kingdom. A group basically involves one company (or individual) acquiring control of another company. The controlling company is known as the holding or parent company and the controlled company is known as a subsidiary company. "Control" is normally achieved through the purchase of shares or through the acquisition of management appointments and rights. Groups of companies exist for a variety of reasons—often very sensible economic decisions in that they might facilitate economies of scale; they might present a steady flow of supplies or of outlets; they might facilitate the "risk-taking" often associated with new ventures or diversification. Groups of companies might also provide a convenient structure for unwanted business practices and unwarranted financial protection of investors, directors and company officers. It has been the task of many areas of English law to try to recognise the reality of groups and to recognise and control potential abuse. Unlike some of our European neighbours we do not enjoy a "Law of Groups". [3] We rely on aspects of competition law, company law and revenue law to provide ad hoc recognition and control of groups. In this section we shall attempt to provide an insight into aspects of revenue law that try to provide some recognition of the group structure and form of business organisation. However, before we begin we must issue a word of warning: "Groups" and "control" do not enjoy the

---

[1] See Saunders, *Solicitors Journal*, 1992 at 318.

[2] One interesting suggestion is that if the aim of the harmonisation programme is to prevent "distorted" location decisions, then the solution is not to consider corporation tax rates but to instigate and achieve a change from profits-source to residence-based taxation (See Wilson, *supra*).

[3] Germany, in particular, enjoys a Law of Groups. This has influenced EC debate and proposals in this area.

same meaning in all aspects of revenue law and statutory provision. For example, you will find that we will refer to "51 per cent groups", "75 per cent groups" and to "100 per cent consortia". All should become clear!

## Loss Relief (ss402, 403 TA 1988)

The provisions for loss relief are perhaps the most economically significant group relief provisions. These allow one member (the surrenderer) of a group or consortium to set its losses against the profits of another member (the claimer) of the same group or consortium.

For the purposes of "loss relief", a group consists of a United Kingdom resident parent company plus United Kingdom resident subsidiaries in which the parent company enjoys a 75 per cent interest (essentially "ordinary share capital"). A "consortia" consists of a 75 per cent interest held by member who each own at least five per cent in the consortium company.

Restrictions on loss relief demand that the relief must be claimed, with the agreement of all the companies involved, within two years of the end of the surrendering company's relevant accounting period [1]: the claimant company must use the relief in the year of surrender. In the case of a consortia, the claimant is only entitled to that part of the trading loss which is proportionate to the claimant's share in the consortium.

Anti-avoidance controls exist, through sections 409 and 410, to control a temporary group membership or temporary group formation. If a company enjoys temporary membership of a group, loss relief will be time apportioned or adjusted to reflect a just and reasonable allocation of the loss relief. Similarly, if a company is to cease to be a member of a group and "arrangements" are in place to effect this change, that "member" is not entitled to participate in the loss relief provisions. The latter control combats temporary and convenient group formations.

## Surrender of ACT (s240, TA 1988)

A parent company may surrender any ACT paid in the current year to a subsidiary in which it owns more than 50 per cent. The surrender can constitute all or part of any surplus ACT and, where there are a number of subsidiaries, it can be surrendered in such proportions as is desired. The recipient subsidiary can use this surrendered ACT to reduce its own mainstream corporation tax liability. This ability enables the parent

---

[1] See *Gallic Leasing Ltd v Coburn*, [1991] STC 151.

company to find relief for surplus ACT and it assists the transfer of funds within a group situation.

These provsions also apply to a consortium consisting of a 75 per cent holding in another company by the consortium in which each member has a minimum interest and holding of at least five per cent.

### Transfers of Assets (s171, TCGA 1992)

Relief for capital gains tax purposes is available on the transfer of assets between members of the group: the transfer is deemed to result in neither a gain nor a loss. An "exit" disposal will trigger a charge. This occurs when the asset is disposed of outside the group or the company owning the asset leaves the group—provided, in the latter case, that a six year period from the aquisition date has not elapsed. When calculating the gain or an exit disposal, the purchase price must reflect the price paid by the original owner within the group.

For the purposes of the "transfer of assets" provisions, a "group" consists of a 75 per cent group as per the "loss relief" provisions.

## Close Companies

Perhaps in an attempt to prevent the abuse of the corporate form and in an attempt to encourage neutrality of tax in the choice of business organisation and form, provisions have been in existence since 1922 to control close companies.

Close companies are in essence small family companies or similar where the control and the activities of the company are in the hands of a few individuals. The complex statutory definition of close companies essentially provides that a close company is

> one controlled by five or fewer participators, or by participators who are directors. [1]

"Control" is widely defined to include control over the company's affairs (for example, through voting rights) or control through the right or acquisition of the right to receive share capital which confers an entitlement to a majority of the distributable income of the company, or confers the right to the majority of its assets upon winding-up. [2] Rights

---

[1]  s414, TA 1988.
[2]  s416, TA 1988.

invested in associates or nominees are deemed to belong to the participator.

"Participator" is defined to include a shareholder and a loan creditor excluding bank's lending in the ordinary course of their business. [1]

"Director" [2] includes a person occupying that post; a shadow director; and a manager who, together with his associates, controls 20 per cent of the company's ordinary share capital.

Certain companies are declared as not being close companies. These include non-resident companies, and companies controlled by the Crown.

Controls on close companies inlcude the following.

### Loans to Participators and their Associates (s419, TA 1988)

When a close company advances a loan to a participator (or their associates) the company is obliged to pay to the Revenue a sum that corresponds to the rate of advance corporation tax (ACT). It is important to appreciate that this sum is not ACT, it is merely paid at the corresponding rate of ACT. If the participator repays the sum lent, the Revenue will repay the sum that is received. If, however, the loan is released or written-off, the sum paid to the Revenue is forfeited and the borrower is deemed to have received income equal to the grossed-up equivalent of the amount released or written-off. This might result in higher rate tax liability for the borrower.

The purpose of these controls is to prvent a close company being used to confer loans to participators on advantageous terms. [3] Of course "genuine transactions" are not prohibited. These include loans made by a close company in the ordinary course of its business which includes the lending of money; and loans to directors or employees of amounts not exceeding £15,000, provided the borrower works full-time for the close company (or its associate) and does not enjoy a material interest in the company. A material interest is five per cent of the ordinary share capital.

### Expenditure on Facilities for Participators and their Associates (s418, TA 1988)

Whenever a close company incurs expenses in providing living accommodation or other benefits or facilities, for a participator or his associates, that expense is treated as a distribution and must be taxed as such (i.e. the

---

[1] s417, TA 1988.
[2] *Ibid.*
[3] Complimentary controls can be found in the Companies Act 1985, s330.

expense it not tax deductible to the company, ACT must be paid; the value of the benefit plus the tax credit is taxable income of the participator).

This provision will not apply if the benefit provided is subject to taxation under other provisions—normally as benefits in kind to directors or higher-paid employees. [1]

Treating the conferment of benefits as a distribution removes the possibility of providing tax advantageous or tax free benefits to participators or their associates.

### Statutory Apportionment of Income

One of the perceived opportunities of close companies was the ability to hoard profits in response to high tax rates. Rather than receiving a distribution, and thus taxable income, a participator might be influenced to declare little or no distribution and retain that profit in the company until income tax rates or personal circumstances favoured dividends or distributions. For example, in 1976/77 a declared distribution might have attracted the top marginal rate of income tax on unearned income of 98 per cent whereas retention of the same profit in the company might attract the main rate of corporation tax of 52 per cent.

In order to influence proper decision-making, the position was that if a close company did not distribute a required proportion of its profits to its shareholders, the Revenue were entitled to apportion the undistributed profits among shareholders and tax them as if the company had distributed a dividend of that amount. This statutory deemed apportionment ought to have influenced proper retention and investment decision-making, although one suspects that it may have tipped the balance in favour of distributable profits.

As income tax rates, capital gains tax rates, and corporation tax rates began to reach almost the same level, it became apparent that the "old" advantages of retention had been reduced or removed and that the regime of statutory apportionment was no longer required. In his 1989 Budget Speech, the Chancellor of the Exchequer confirmed this view and announced the abolition of the statutory apportionment regime. However, the Chancellor did announce the need to introduce controls on a smaller number of close companies known as Close Investment Holding Companies. Close Investment Holding Companies are not trading

[1] TA 1988, ss153–168.

companies nor are they members of a trading group: they are normally viewed as passive investment companies and as such they are denied access to the small companies' rate of corporation tax.[1] It is hoped that this control will remove the use of small companies for non-trading, passive investment purposes.

## Taxation and the Choice of Business Medium

A number of factors influence the choice of business medium. These include issues of retention of control; costs of complying with any statutory requirements, particularly annual returns and publicity; statutory restrictions on the number of members; the desirability of limited liability; and financial requirements and access to funds. Tax influences on the choice of business medium might also be apparent. These often involve a comparison of the tax treatment of companies and partnerships. In making such a comparison it is likely that the following will be considered:

1. *Tax Rates*

   If the business is carried on as a partnership, the profits are treated as distributed for income tax purposes. Therefore the partners (and proprietors) will pay up to 40 per cent income tax (at current rates) on marginal trade income and on capital gains.

   If the business is carried on as a company, all profit (including capital gains) will be taxed at the appropriate corporation tax rate (currently 25–35 per cent).

2. *Remuneration and Distributions*

   The remuneration that a company pays its employees or the salaries and fees that it pays to its directors are deductible business expenses. It is thus possible to reduce the corporation tax bill, and applicable rate, by the payments to its directors.

   In a partnership, increased fees and payments to the partners would simply be reflected in their marginal rate of tax. The deemed distribution of profits would also be reflected in their marginal rates of tax.

3. *The Treatment of Share Capital*

   If the proprietors of a company take their return and profits in the form of shares and dividends then they ought to consider two matters. First, although dividends are treated as though basic rate tax has been

[1] See FA 1989, s105.

paid (grossed-up), tax liability still remains for those subject to higher rate tax liability. This represents "double-taxation" of the company's (and the proprietor's) profits. Second, an eventual sale of the share capital might result in capital gains tax liability.

Careful use of the capital gains tax exemptions must be considered. The double-taxation of capital gains is a real danger.

### 4. *Pension Arrangements*

Pension scheme arrangements have traditionally been more generous to company employees as opposed to the self-employed. Payments by a company to an employee pension scheme are generally tax deductible to the company, and non-taxable benefits to the employee.

### 5. *National Insurance Rules*

If the proprietor of a business in the form of a company takes out a salary as an employee, Class I National Insurance Contributions are payable (by both the employer and the employee/director).

A self-employed person pays National Insurance Contributions in Class 4. The rules allow up to half of the Class 4 contribution to be deductible for tax purposes. The different rates coupled with the rules on deductibility normally favour the self-employed person.

*Self-Check Questions*

1. Why should we tax the profits of a company?
2. Distinguish between (a) classical; (b) imputation; and (c) integration systems of corporation tax.
3. To what extent does corporation tax recognise the fiscal reality of groups and consortia of companies?

## Further Reading

Watters RM, *To Incorporate or Not to Incorporate—That is the Question*, (1977) BTR 34–47.

Chown J, *The Harmonisation of Corporation Tax in the EEC*, (1976) BTR 39–48.

*The Reform of Corporation Tax: Some International Factors*, (1971) BTR 215–29.

Knatz T, *Corporation Tax Systems*, (1972) BTR 32–50.

Nobes CW, *EEC Imputation Systems of Corporation Tax and the Proposal for a Directive on Harmonisation*, (1979) JBL 306.

Oliver JDB, *Company Residence – Four Cases*, (1996) BTR 505.

Williams DV, *The Corporation Tax Acts: Time to Realise a Myth*, (1997) BTR 268.

# Part Five — Inheritance Tax

# 15

# Chargeable Persons and Activities

## The Background

The tax which is now known as inheritance tax began its life in 1894 as estate duty, which was a tax on a deceased's property, whether passing under a will, or on intestacy. The Labour Government in 1974 announced its intention to abolish estate duty and to replace it with a tax which would operate in relation not only to transfers on death, but also life-time gifts. This was capital transfer tax (CTT), introduced in 1975, and which lasted until 1986. The genealogy of the tax up to the introduction of capital transfer tax was thus traced by Fox LJ in *Inglewood v IRC*[1]:

> From 1894 to 1975 the main instrument of capital taxation was estate duty. It has been described as a voluntary tax. That goes too far but certainly it contained loopholes which enabled its impact to be much reduced. First, it was a tax on death only and while gifts of property or dispositions of life interests were, in effect, taxable on death though made inter vivos, that, in general, only applied to gifts or dispositions made during the statutory period (which was latterly seven years before death).
>
> Second, discretionary trusts were an effective means of avoiding estate duty. There was normally no charge on the death of one of the discretionary objects leaving more than one other such object surviving him (since no property interest passed or determined by reason of such death); this was so though the deceased had been receiving part or even the whole of the income during his lifetime. The position was altered to some extent by the Finance Act 1969 which imposed a charge for duty on the death of a discretionary object which was geared to the proportion of income which had actually been paid out to him during the statutory period.

---

[1] [1983] STC 133 at 135.

The Finance Act 1975 revolutionised the position. It abolished estate duty and created CTT, which was a tax not merely in relation to death but also to other dispositions of capital. Thus a voluntary disposition of property inter vivos to an individual will attract CTT.

Capital transfer tax was replaced with inheritance tax, with respect to transfers on or after 18 March 1986. Inheritance tax is similar to capital transfer tax and estate duty in varying ways, but it is also unlike them in some other ways. Like estate duty, it charges transfers on death, but unlike estate duty, it also imposes an immediate charge on some *inter vivos* transfers. Like capital transfer tax, it imposes a charge on life-time transfers, but unlike capital transfer tax, most life transfers are not immediately chargeable. In effect, inheritance tax is a tax on transfers which occur on death and in the seven-year period immediately preceding death. The Capital Transfer Tax Act 1984, rechristened Inheritance Tax Act 1984 (by s100 FA 1986) is the basic law. Unless otherwise stated all references to statutory provisions are references to provisions contained in the Inheritance Tax Act 1984 (IHTA).

## The Charge to Inheritance Tax

*Introduction*

The charge to inheritance tax is contained in s1 of the IHTA 1984, which provides that inheritance tax is to be charged on the value transferred by a chargeable transfer. From this statement two clear ideas emerge. First, that there must be a chargeable transfer, and, secondly, that what is to be taxed is the value thereby transferred. What then is a chargeable transfer? S2(1) defines a chargeable transfer as any transfer of value which is made by an individual, and which is not an exempt transfer. The second element of this definition of chargeable transfer indicates that inheritance tax is primarily a tax which is imposed on individuals. However there are special provisions in respect of transfers by trustees and close companies, which we shall examine later. The first and third elements of the definition are of more immediate importance. There must be a transfer of value, which is not an exempt transfer. It is clear that these terms relate to specific concepts in the inheritance tax regime and, thus, we need to examine them more closely.

*Transfer of Value*

The term "transfer of value" is defined in s3(1) as a *disposition* made by a person, as a result of which the value of his estate immediately after the disposition is less than it would be but for the disposition. The amount by which the estate is so reduced is the value which is transferred by the disposition. What then is a disposition for these purposes? The term "disposition" is not defined in the Act, but taken in its ordinary sense, it appears to be wide enough to cover any transaction by which a person disposes of an interest in an asset. In addition to the ordinary meaning there is an extended definition in s3(3) which provides that, where a person's omission to exercise a right leads to a decrease in the value of his estate, and an increase in the value of the estate of another person (for example, a failure to sue on a debt until the limitation period has elapsed), the person whose estate is so reduced will be treated as having made a disposition, unless it is shown that the omission was not deliberate. This disposition will be deemed to have taken place at the time, or the latest time when he could have exercised the right the exercise of which was omitted. This is the only occasion when the estate of someone other than the transferor is relevant for inheritance tax purposes, i.e. by the transferor's omission to exercise a right, the other person's estate was increased. But even so, the value transferred is not the amount by which the other person's estate was increased, but rather, the amount by which the transferor's estate was diminished.

As is evident from the above discussions, the reduction or diminution in the value of the transferor's estate is central to the theme of inheritance tax (see e.g. s3(1)). This would mean for example that the sale of an asset at full market price, while being a disposition, will not be a transfer of value since, because of the full price paid, there is no reduction in the transferor's estate. In other words, inheritance tax is basically a tax on gifts, particularly those made within seven years of death. A reduction in a person's estate can occur however, without any element of gift, for example a commercial arrangement which is a bad bargain, or the purchase of an immediately depreciating asset such as a new car [1]—these would *prima facie* be transfers of value and chargeable to inheritance tax. Such situations would however be covered by one of the instances of statutory non-transfers of value. S10(1) provides that a disposition is not a transfer of value if it was not intended to confer *any* gratuitous benefit on *any* person, *and* either (a) was made in a transaction at arm's length between unconnected persons, or (b) it was such as might be expected to

---

[1] See Lord Jauncey in *Macpherson v IRC* [1988] 2 All ER 753 at 757.

be made in a transaction at arm's length between unconnected persons (emphasis added).

The term "connected persons" for these purposes has the same meaning as under s286 of the TCGA 1992. S286(2) of the TCGA 1992 provides that individuals are connected with their own spouses, their own relatives and their spouses, and with their spouses' relatives and their spouses. The term "relative" is defined by s286(8) of the TCGA as meaning a person's brother, sister, ancestor, or lineal descendant, but s270 of the IHTA 1984 also includes the words "uncle, aunt, nephew and niece". [1]

An example of a situation to which s10(1) of the IHTA 1984 would apply is a sale at an undervalue because of an emergency. There was however another poignant example in *IRC v Spencer-Nairn* [2], a case which also tries to explain the purpose and effect of the provision. The taxpayer had sold a farm for £101,305 after he had received advice from his accountant to the effect that he as landlord was obliged to incur expenditure of about £80,000 on replacing farm buildings. Unknown to both the taxpayer and the accountant, at the time of sale, the purchaser had been "connected" with the taxpayer for the purposes of capital gains tax and inheritance tax, which meant that for capital gains tax purposes he fell to be treated as having disposed of the farm at market value. For the purposes of valuation for capital gains tax purposes, the case was referred to the Land Tribunal. The Tribunal took the view that the taxpayer had not been obliged to replace the farm buildings and valued the farm at £199,000. The Revenue claimed that the sale of the farm was a transfer of value to the extent that the Land Tribunal's valuation exceeded the sale price. The taxpayer on the other hand claimed that since he had no intention to confer a gratuitous benefit by the sale, and since the sale transaction was one which might be expected to be made in a transaction at arm's length between unconnected persons, the sale was not a transfer of value.

The special commissioner upheld the taxpayer's argument, holding that the advice that the taxpayer was obliged to replace the farm buildings was reasonable given the unclear state of the law at the time, and that it was unlikely that anyone would have been interested in the farm in a run-down condition. The commissioner was upheld by the Court of Session.

---

[1] With respect to the meaning of "connected persons" in the context of trustees, partnerships and companies, see s286(3), (4) and (5) of the TCGA 1992, respectively.

[2] [1991] BTC 8003; STC 60.

According to Lord President Hope [1] it is clear that transactions which are gratuitous or which were for less than the open market value of the property may nevertheless be taken out of charge if they satisfy the tests laid down by the s10(1). The fact that the transaction was for less than the open market value cannot be conclusive of the issue, otherwise the subsection would be deprived of its content. The gratuitous element in the transaction becomes no more than a factor, which must be weighed in the balance with all the other facts and circumstances to see whether the onus which is on the taxpayer has been discharged. Lord President Hope accepted that the question of open market value is crucial to the question whether there has been a diminution in value of the transferor's estate [2]. But the purpose of the subsection is to enable the transferor, if he can, to escape from a rigid application of the open market test, in cases in which there was no intention to confer a gratuitous benefit on anyone, and the other conditions are satisfied. This is necessary if the inevitable bad bargains which occur from time to time are not to be subjected to the tax, and if the great mass of transactions which take place at arm's length between persons not connected with each other are to be exempted from scrutiny. In this case, it was important that the taxpayer and his adviser were both unaware that they were dealing with a connected person, that the accountant's advice was sound, and that the actions of the taxpayer were reasonable in all the circumstances.

Another example of a statutory non-transfer of value is s11, which relates to dispositions for the maintenance of family. S11(1) provides that a disposition is not a transfer of value if it is made by one party to a marriage in favour of the other party or in favour of a child of either party, and is (a) for the maintenance of the other party, or (b) for the maintenance, education training of the child, while he is under 18 or, if above that age, while he is undergoing full-time education or training. S11(2) similarly excludes a payment for the education, maintenance or training of a child who is not in the care of a parent, who is under the age of 18, or who is receiving full-time education or training if over that age, and who has, for substantial periods, been in the care of the person making the disposition. Furthermore s11(3) covers dispositions for the reasonable care and maintenance of a dependent relative.

For the purposes of s11, a "child" includes a step-child and an adopted

[1] [1991] BTC at p8012.
[2] At p8014.

child, and "parent" shall be construed accordingly.[1] "Dependent relative" means, in relation to any person, any relative of his, or of his spouse, who is incapacitated by old age or infirmity from maintaining himself, or the widowed, divorced or separated mother of the person or of his spouse.[2]

Sections 12–17 contain examples of other sorts of dispositions which are not transfers of value.

## Exempt Transfers

As seen earlier in this chapter, a chargeable transfer is a transfer of value, made by an individual, which is not an exempt transfer. Implicit in this statement is the proposition that some transfers of value are exempt—and there are numerous examples, for example s18, which relates to transfers between spouses, and s23, which relates to gifts to charities. These exemptions are explored more fully in our discussions on exemptions and reliefs.

## Potentially Exempt Transfers (PETs)

Apart from exempt transfers, there are some transfers which are only chargeable if they occur within seven years of death, i.e. they are not immediately chargeable. These are referred to as potentially exempt transfers, even though the term "potentially chargeable transfers" may be more appropriate. Most life-time gifts by individuals, and certain favoured trusts, fall within this category of transfer (see s3A). If the transferor dies within seven years of the transfer, the transfer will be said to have "proved chargeable", and tax will be levied at death rates. References to "chargeable transfer" do not include PETs.

## The Value Transferred

S3(1) provides that the value transferred by a disposition is the amount by which the transferor's estate is less than it would be but for the disposition. For these purposes, "estate" is defined by s5(1) as the aggregate of all the property to which a person is beneficially entitled. The consequences of

[1] S11(6).
[2] *Ibid.*

the provision that the value transferred is the amount by which the transferor's estate is reduced by the transfer are:

(a) The relevant estate is that of the transferor and not that of the transferee. Thus, the value transferred by the transferor is not necessarily the same as the value received by the transferee.

Example:

> Elena has a set of three pearls, worth £5,000 each, but £30,000 as a set. She gives one to Yannish. Yannish receives a pearl worth £5,000 but Elena has now two pearls, which, because the set is no longer complete, are worth not £25,000, but £10,000. Thus Elena's estate has been diminished by £20,000, and that is the value transferred.

(b) Any consideration received for the transfer will be taken into account in determining how much decrease there has been in the value of the estate.

## Grossing Up

In calculating the value of a transferor's estate immediately after a transfer, any liability of his to inheritance tax (but not any other tax) on the transfer falls to be included (s5(4)). This means that the transferor's estate diminishes in value by the value of the transferred property *plus* the inheritance tax due on the transfer, i.e. the value of the property itself is net of inheritance tax (unless the tax is to be borne by the transferee, in which case it is gross) and must be grossed up to determine the total fall in the transferor's estate.

The formula for grossing up the net transfer is:

$$\frac{100}{100 - R} \times \text{Value of the gift}$$

where:

R = the rate of tax at which the transferor will be chargeable on the gift.

Example:

Mokhtair makes a gift of £15,000 after he had already made gifts taking him above the nil rate of tax. He is to pay the tax on the gift.

Grossed up at "life" rates, the total amount transferred by him will be:

$$\frac{100}{100 - 20} \times £15,000 = £18,750$$

This is the figure that inheritance tax is charged on.

## Valuation

### Market Value

As a general rule, the value of any property is the price which it might reasonably be expected to fetch on a sale in the open market (s160). This "market price" will not be reduced on the ground that the whole property is to be placed on the market at one and the same time (even though such reduction would normally occur if an actual sale were to take place in an open market in the real world). A number of principles can be gleaned from the cases. According to Peter Gibson LJ in *Walton v IRC*[1], the valuation required is on the basis of a hypothetical sale in the open market. The hypothesis must be applied to the property as it actually existed and not to some other property, even if in real life a vendor would have been likely to make some changes or improvements before putting it on the market.[2] The concept of the open market automatically implies a willing seller and a willing buyer, each of whom is a hypothetical abstraction. However, the willing buyer reflects reality in that he embodies whatever was actually the demand for the property at the relevant time.[3] Whilst both the seller and the buyer are assumed to be willing, neither is to the taken to be over-eager. Rather, each will have prepared himself for the sale, the seller by bringing the sale to the attention of all likely purchasers, and honestly giving as much information

---

[1] [1996] BTC 8015 at 8020.

[2] Hoffman LJ in *IRC v Gray* [1994] BTC 8034 at 8036. To this extent only, the express terms of the statute may introduce an element of artificiality into the hypothesis (*ibid*).

[3] Peter Gibson LJ in *Walton v IRC* [1996] BTC 8015 at 8020.

to them as he is entitled to give; and the buyer by informing himself as much as he can properly do. [1]

According to Peter Gibson LJ the statute does assume a sale, and this assumption has a number of implications. First, however improbable it is that there would ever be a sale of the property in the real world, for example, because of restrictions attached to the property, the sale must be treated as capable of being completed, the purchaser then holding the property subject to the same restrictions. [2] This is because the property must be assumed to have been capable of sale in the open market, even if in fact it was inherently unassignable or held subject to restrictions on sale. [3] In this respect, the question is what a purchaser in the open market would have paid to enjoy whatever rights attached to the property at the relevant date. [4] Secondly, the vendor, if he is offered the best price reasonably obtainable in the market, cannot be assumed to say that he will not sell because the price is too low as inadequately reflecting some feature of the property—nor can the buyer be assumed to say that he will not buy because the price is too high. [5] One does not have to ask whether the hypothetical parties would have been pleased or disappointed with the result, for example, by reference to what the property might have been worth at a different time or in different circumstances, because such considerations are irrelevant. [6] Because the market is the open market, the whole world is to be assumed to be free to bid—however, the valuer will inquire into what sort of person will be in the market for the property in question and what price the possible purchaser would be likely to pay. [7] According to Peter Gibson LJ in *Walton v IRC*, the statute requires one to assume a sale, but it should be assumed to take place in the real world. [8] This is more or less the same thing as the statement of Hoffman LJ in *IRC v Gray* [9] that, although the sale is hypothetical, there is nothing hypothetical about the open market in which it is supposed to have taken place. The "practical" nature of this exercise, according to Hoffman LJ, will usually mean that, although in principle no one is excluded from

---

[1] *Ibid.*

[2] *Ibid.*

[3] Hoffman LJ in *IRC v Gray* [1994] BTC 8034 at 8036.

[4] *Ibid.*

[5] Peter Gibson LJ in *Walton v IRC* [1996] BTC at 8020.

[6] Hoffman LJ in *IRC v Gray*, at p8037.

[7] Peter Gibson LJ in *Walton v IRC* [1996] BTC at 8020.

[8] [1996] BTC at 8021.

[9] [1994] BTC 8034 at 8037.

consideration, most of the world will usually play no part in the calculation. [1] Thus:

> The inquiry will often focus upon what a relatively small number of people would be likely to have paid. It may arrive at a figure within a range of prices which the evidence shows that various people would have been likely to pay, reflecting, for example, the fact that one person had a particular reason for paying a higher price than others, but taking into account, if appropriate, the possibility that through accident or whim he might not actually have bought. The valuation is this a retrospective exercise in probabilities, wholly derived from the real world but rarely committed to the proposition that a sale to a particular purchaser would definitely have happened. [2]

### Related Property

S161 provides a special regime for "related property", in order to counter the avoidance opportunities presented by asset-splitting. This special regime relates to situations where assets are worth more as a set than they are worth as separate items (e.g. shares, interests in land, etc). The avoidance in these situations could be achieved by splitting the sets between two or more tax payers, in a situation wherein transfers between them would be exempt, e.g. between spouses. The related property rules apply to frustrate such schemes.

In this respect, s161(1) provides that, where the value of an asset would be less than its value when aggregated with any related property, the value of the asset will be the appropriate portion of the value of that aggregate. For the purposes of this rule, property is "related" to the property comprised in a person's estate if it is comprised in the estate of the person's spouse, or if it was, within the preceding five years, the property of a charity, or property held on charitable trusts, etc (see s161(2)). Example:

> Jake has a five-piece vintage train set, worth £100,000 as a set, but only £5,000 per piece. Jake gives one piece of the set to his wife

---

[1] [1994] BTC at 8037.
[2] *Ibid.*

Winifred. Winifred receives an asset worth £5,000. Jake's estate falls in value by £80,000, because he has lost the set and now only has four pieces, worth £5,000 each; but this transfer is exempt as an inter-spousal transfer. Winifred later gives the asset to their son Wilf. Wilf receives an asset worth £5,000, and Winifred's estate is reduced by £5,000. However, on the related property rules, the asset is valued as one-fifth of a £100,000 five-piece set (£20,000), and that is what Winifred's estate is reduced by.

## Close Companies

As we have seen earlier, s2(1) provides that a chargeable transfer is a transfer of value made by an individual. This means that transfers by companies are not chargeable, opening up planning opportunities, whereby a company could for example make transfers to donees specified by an individual. There are special provisions in the Inheritance Tax Act to combat the use of close companies in this way. Generally, s94(2) provides that, where a close company makes a transfer of value, the value so transferred shall be apportioned to each participator according to his rights and interests in the company immediately before the transfer. Any amount which happens to be apportioned to a close company in this manner shall be further apportioned among its participators, and so on. The participators are treated as having made net transfers of value, so that the values apportioned to the participators must be grossed up at their respective inheritance tax rates (s94(1)). For these purposes a participator's estate shall be treated as not including any rights or interests in the company.

Note that for these purposes a bona fide commercial transaction by a close company will not fall to be treated as a transfer of value (see s10(1)). By s3A(6) the definition of PET does not extend to deemed transfers of value such as this, and thus the values apportioned to each participator will be chargeable transfers.

"Close company" has the same meaning as it has for corporation tax purposes (s102(1)). It is defined by s414(1) of the ICTA 1988 as a company which is under the control of five or fewer participators, or of participators who are directors. For inheritance tax purposes, it also includes non-resident companies (s102(1) IHTA 1984).

"Participator" also has the same meaning as it has for corporation tax purposes, except that, here, it does not include a loan creditor (s102(1)). It is defined s417(1) of the ICTA 1988 as any person having a share or interest in the capital or income of the company.

## Calculation of Inheritance Tax

*Rates of Tax*

There are basically three relevant rates, found in Schedule 1 and s7 of the Act. The first rate is a nil (or 0 per cent) rate, which applies to chargeable transfers of value not exceeding a specified threshold. This threshold generally increases from year to year. Thus, for the 1996/97 year of assessment, it was £200,000, and for the 1997/98 year of assessment, it was £215,000. Taking account of the variations in the nil rate threshold from year to year, the tax rates are:

(a) for chargeable transfers of value up to the threshold, tax is charged at a nil rate;
(b) for any excess over the threshold, tax is charged at 40 per cent.
(c) "life" rates of 20 per cent, i.e. half of the normal rates—this is provided for in s7(2) which provides that tax is charged on a chargeable transfer made during the life of the transferor at half of the normal rates.

Where death occurs between three and seven years of the transfer, there is relief in form of a tapering reduction in the tax rate. This relief is given under s7(4):

1. Where the transfer was made between three and four years of death, there is relief of 20 per cent of the normal rates. This means that tax is charged at 80 per cent of the death rates (80 per cent of 40 per cent) instead of the full death rate of 40 per cent.
2. Where the transfer was made between four and five years of death, there is relief of 40 per cent.
3. Where the transfer was made between five and six years of death, there is relief of 60 per cent.
4. Where the transfer was made between six and seven years of death, there is relief of 80 per cent.

Where death occurs less than three years from the date of the gift, tax is levied at the full 40 per cent rate.

*Cumulation*

Inheritance tax involves a principle of the cumulation of all the chargeable transfers made by an individual. S7(1) requires the tax chargeable on a transfer by an individual to take account of the chargeable transfers already made by him. This principle of cumulation applies to all chargeable transfers made in the seven-year period ending with the relevant one. Transfers made more than seven years previously fall out of the cumulation. The latest transfer is treated as the top slice of the cumulative total and taxed as such.

Example:

On 1 January 1988, Seamus made a transfer of £400,000 (the transferee to pay the tax). If this was his first transfer of value, he would have a cumulative total of £400,000. On 1 January 1992, he made another transfer, this time of £100,000. He would then have a cumulative total of £500,000. On 1 January 1997 he made a further transfer of £50,000. The cumulative total at this time would be £150,000. The 1988 gift, having been made more than seven years previously, has fallen out of cumulation.

PETs are not cumulated in this way during the life of the transferor.

## Liability for Inheritance Tax

*Introduction*

One curious feature of inheritance tax is that more than one person may be liable for the tax chargeable on any particular transfer of value. In this respect, s205 stipulates that, except as otherwise provided, where two or more persons are liable for the same tax, each of them shall be liable for the whole of it. This seemingly draconian provision is tempered by limits imposed on the quantum of the liabilities that fall on the various persons who may be subject to tax. The issue of liability to tax depends partly on when the transfer of value took place, (i.e. *inter vivos* or on death) and partly on the nature of the transferred property, (i.e. was it settled property or not). The applicable rules are contained in ss199–204 and the discussion that follows addresses first the question of liability to tax on life-time transfers, followed by liability on death.

*Liability on Life-time Transfers*

Generally speaking, liability to tax on life-time transfers depends upon whether the transfer was made by an individual, by trustees or by close companies.

*Individuals*

In the case of chargeable life-time transfers by an individual, s199(1) provides for the liability of:

(a) the transferor;
(b) the transferee;
(c) any one in whom the transfer vests the property or who has an interest in possession therein;
(d) where the property becomes settled property, the beneficiary.

With respect to potentially exempt transfers which later become chargeable, and chargeable transfers made within seven years of the transferor's death which then become subject to a supplementary charge on the death, s199(2) replaces the reference to the transferor in (a) above with a reference to his personal representative.

   The liabilities so indicated, of persons who are not the transferor or the transferor's personal representative, are supplemental in the sense only that the persons lower down the list are only liable to the extent that the tax has not been paid by the transferor at the time when it ought to have been paid. Thus for example, the transferor is primarily liable and the transferee only becomes liable if the full tax has not been recovered from the transferor, and so on (see s204(6)).

*Trustees*

When chargeable transfers are made by trustees, s201(1) provides for the liability of:

(a) the trustees of the settlement;
(b) any person entitled to an interest in possession in the settled property;
(c) any person for whose benefit any of the settled property or the income thereof is applied at or after the transfer;
(d) in cases of transfers made during the life of the settlor and in which the trustees are not resident in the United Kingdom, the settlor.

For the purposes of these provisions the trustees of a settlement shall be regarded as not being resident in the United Kingdom unless the general administration of the settlement is carried on in the United Kingdom, and the trustees or a majority of them are resident in the United Kingdom (s201(5)).

As with the case of transfers by individuals (above) the liability of persons who are not trustees attach only to the extent that the tax remains unpaid by the trustees after it ought to have been paid (s 204(6)).

## Close Companies

When a close company makes a chargeable transfer of value the persons liable are, primarily, the company making the relevant transfer, and, so far as the tax remains unpaid after it ought to have been paid, the persons to whom any amounts have been apportioned under s94, and any individual the value of whose estate is increased by the transfer.

## Liability on Death Transfers

S200(1) provides for liability to tax in cases in which a chargeable transfer is made on death. Generally, the persons who may be liable to inheritance tax on death are personal representatives, trustees, and beneficiaries/legatees.

## Personal Representatives

By virtue of s200(1)(a), so far as the tax is attributable to the value of property which either was not comprised in a settlement immediately before the death, or consists of settled land situated in the United Kingdom which devolves upon or vests in the deceased's personal representatives, the persons liable to tax are the deceased's personal representatives. This provision relates to the tax due on the estate itself. In relation to the extra tax payable on transfers made within seven years of the transferor's death, the transferee alone is liable to pay the extra tax. [1] There are further limits on the liability of the personal representatives under s200(1)(a). In cases where the tax is attributable to settled land in the United Kingdom, s204(1)(b) provides that a personal representative's liability is limited to so much of the property as is at any time available in

---

[1] s199(2), s204(6) & (7).

his hands for the payment of the tax, or might have been so available but for his own neglect or default. In cases where the tax is attributable to the value of any other property, s204(1)(a) limits the liability of a personal representative to the assets (other than settled land in the United Kingdom) which he has received as personal representative or which he might have so received but for his own neglect or default.

For these purposes the liability of a personal representative is a personal liability. It was thus explained by Scott J in *IRC v Stannard*[1]:

> ... the liability in respect of capital transfer tax for which a personal representative becomes liable is not and could never have been a liability of the deceased. It is necessarily an original liability which is in terms imposed on the personal representative. There is nothing in the statutory scheme which in express terms limits the liability of the personal representative to assets of the estate except in so far as such limitation is found in [s.204] of the Act which I have just read. There is, in my judgment, nothing in [s.200(1)] which justifies limiting the liability of a personal representative to liability in a representative capacity only.

### Trustees

With respect to settled property in which the deceased had an interest in possession (other than settled land in the United Kingdom) s200(1)(b) provides for the liability of the trustees of the settlement. The liability of a trustee of any property is limited by s204(2) to:

(a) so much of the property as he has actually received, disposed of, or is liable to account for to the persons beneficially entitled thereto, and
(b) so much of any other property as is for the time being available in his hands as trustee for the payment of the tax, or which might have been so available but for his own neglect or default.

### Beneficiaries / Legatees

The above provisions specify those who are liable to tax in the first instance. There are others who may be liable to tax on death. S200(1)(c) provides that, so far as tax chargeable on death is attributable to the value of any property, any person in whom the property is vested or who is

[1] [1984] STC 245 at 249–250.

beneficially entitled to an interest in possession in the property at any time after the death is liable for the tax. S200(1)(d) further provides that, so far as the tax is attributable to the value of any property which was comprised in a settlement immediately before the death, any person for whose benefit the any of the property or the income thereof is applied after the death is liable for the tax. The quantum of the liability is limited by s204(5) to the amount of the property or income so applied for his benefit.

### General Limitations of Liability

S204(6) imposes limitations (some of which have been mentioned above) on the liabilities of persons who are liable otherwise than as transferor, personal representative, or trustee of a settlement. Such persons are only liable if the tax remains unpaid after it ought to have been paid. However, by s204(7) this limitation does not apply where the tax is more than it would have been if the transferor had died more than seven years after the transfer, i.e. it does not apply in relation to potentially exempt transfers—here, the transferee is equally liable to the tax arising on death.

### Duty to Render Account

We have spoken at length about transfers of value and liability to tax thereon. One may begin to wonder how the Revenue will acquire information about the occurrence of a transfer so as to be able to levy tax. The answer is in s216 which provides that any person who is liable to inheritance tax on a chargeable transfer must render an account of the transfer to the Board. This must generally take place within 12 months of the transfer, and there are penalties, in s264, for late reporting of transfers, and, in s245, for failure to deliver an account.

## Death and Inheritance Tax

### Introduction

Inheritance tax is primarily a tax on the property of a person on his death. The reason for the charges on life-time transfers is to prevent taxpayers from enjoying the benefit of property until the moment before death, and then making death bed transfers free of inheritance tax. This is the reason for the incentives to make gifts as soon as possible (PETs), and for gifts dropping out of cumulation after seven years, if the transferor is still alive.

The charge on death arises by treating the death as a deemed transfer of value. S4(1) provides that, on the death of any person, tax shall be charged as if, immediately before his death, he had made a transfer of value equal to the value of his estate immediately before his death. For the purpose of s4, where it is uncertain which of two or more people died first, they shall be assumed to have died at the same instance (s4(2)).

### Gifts with Reservation

The rules relating to gifts with reservation are designed to combat the obvious planning device of making a life-time gift, and then "borrowing" the asset for the rest of one's life. If the original gift was made to an individual more than seven years before death, this would, without more, have been a successful PET. The rules here provide generally that property which is subject to a reservation is to be treated as continuing to form part of the transferor's estate at his death. The applicable law is in s102, FA 1986, which applies where an individual disposes of any property by way of gift, and either possession and enjoyment of the property is not *bona fide* assumed by the donee, at or before the beginning of the relevant period; or, at any time in the relevant period the property is not enjoyed to the entire exclusion or virtually to the entire exclusion of the donor, and of any benefit to him by contract or otherwise. [1]

"The relevant period", during which "significant" benefits to the donor are forbidden, is the period of seven years ending with the date of the donor's death (s102(1) FA 1986). By s102(3) any property which is subject to a reservation is treated as still continuing to be comprised in the donor's estate. This means that the so-called transfer has no effect whatsoever, and that the donor will, in effect, just be "borrowing" his own property. It will still be part of his estate for the purposes of valuation. If the property ceases to be subject to a reservation during the relevant period, that occasion is treated as a PET (s102(4) FA 1986).

It is important to note here that there are exceptions in S102(5) to this "gifts with reservation" rule. The exceptions apply mainly to exempt transfers, for example, transfers between spouses, transfers to qualifying political parties, charities, small gifts, and other sundry exempt transfers. Presumably, these exceptions exist because it would make no sense to tax gifts with reservation in situations where gifts made without reservation would be exempt.

[1] See s102(1).

It is clear from the definition in s 102(1) that substantial enjoyment by a donor of the donated property would fall to be considered as a "reservation". But does this indicate that *any* enjoyment of the property would be so treated? We note here the phrase "enjoyed to the entire exclusion or *virtually* to the entire exclusion of the donor" in the definition.[1] This seems to indicate that a question of degree arises. The principle of virtual exclusion implies the applicability of the *de minimis* rule. While a significant or substantial benefit would cause a gift to fail, the Inland Revenue's interpretation[2] indicates that a gift will not fail in situations where a benefit to the donor is "insignificant" in relation to the donated property. Obviously, the determination of whether a benefit enjoyed by the donor is "insignificant" or not would be a question of fact and degree. The intention however is clear—that donors are not prevented unreasonably from having limited access to property which they have given away. The Revenue statement itself gives examples, such as stays in the absence of the donee for not more than two weeks each year, and stays with the donee for less than one month each year.

## Other Consequences of Death

There is, in general, no grossing up on death. Chargeable transfers (already taxed at 20 per cent) made within seven years of death become liable to a supplementary charge at death rates (40 per cent), with credit for the tax already paid, and subject to tapering relief for transfers between three and seven years from death. Chargeable transfers made more than seven years from death escape the death supplementary charge. PETs made within seven years of death become chargeable at death rates (40 per cent) subject to tapering relief where available. The PETs are deemed to have been made at the time of the original disposals and fall into cumulation during that period. This will involve a recalculation of tax.

## Variations of Dispositions Made on Death

S142(1) provides that where, within the period of two years after a person's death any of the persons who would benefit under the dispositions made on the death make an instrument in writing varying the

---

[1] Emphasis added.
[2] RI 55, November 1993.

dispositions or disclaiming the benefit conferred by any of the dispositions, the Act shall apply as if the variation had been effected by the deceased, or (as the case may be) as if the disclaimed benefit had never been conferred. Subsection (2) of the section requires an election by written notice to the Revenue within six months of the date of the instrument, either by the persons making the variation, or, in cases where the variation results in additional tax being payable, by the personal representatives of the deceased.

The typical type of situation in which it may be helpful to make such a variation would be in a case where a person leaves property to another by will, in circumstances giving rise to no tax liability (e.g. husband and wife), and the legatee wishes to pass on the property, so that it will not fall to be aggregated with the rest of his own personal estate. [1] This may result in a lower inheritance tax burden. Note that for these purposes when a will has already been varied, a variation which merely varies that earlier variation is not within this section. [2]

*Self-Check Questions*

1. What is a transfer of value?
2. What is the effect of a disposition, by a person, of a set of antique china, the effect of which is to break up the set?
3. What is the principle of cumulation?
4. Who is liable for inheritance tax on life transfers?
5. What are the inheritance tax consequences of the death of a transferor within seven years of a transfer made by him?

**Further Reading**

Dobris J C, *Marshalling the Arguments in Favour of Abolishing the Capital Transfer Tax*, (1984) BTR 363–378.

McCutcheon B, *Partnerships and Capital Transfer Tax*, (1980) BTR 417–434.

Goodhart W, *Too Good to be True? A Proposal for the Reform of Taxes on Gifts and Inheritances*, (1980) BTR 473–481.

Wheatcroft G S A, *First Thoughts on the Capital Transfer Tax*, (1974) BTR 265–281.

---

[1] See e.g. *Lake v Lake* [1989] BTC 8046.
[2] *Russell v IRC* [1988] 1 WLR 834; BTC 8041 (Knox J); *Seymour v Seymour* [1989] BTC 8043 (Mervyn Davies J at 8045).

MacDonald G, *From Estate Duty to Inheritance Tax—Towards an Income Tax on Capital?* (1973) BTR 306–322.

# 16
# Exemptions and Reliefs

The inheritance tax legislation features a host of exemptions and reliefs from the full rigour of the tax. This chapter examines a selection of these exemptions and reliefs.

## Potentially Exempt Transfers (PETs)

The PET is a device to implement the principle that inheritance tax is largely a tax on death. It is designed to encourage the transmission of property as early as possible, by operating to relieve completely transfers made within a certain period from a person's death. S3A(1) provides that a PET is a transfer of value, made by an individual on or after 18 March 1986, which apart from the section would be chargeable, and which constitutes either a gift to another individual, or a gift into an accumulation and maintenance trust or a disabled trust. S3A(4) provides that a PET which is made seven years or more before the transferor's death is an exempt transfer, and that any other PET is a chargeable transfer. Thus, people of substantial means who have dependants/heirs will be able to avoid the charge to inheritance tax by giving away their property while still young.

It is normally presumed (until the contrary is shown) that a PET will prove to be an exempt transfer [1]. If a PET later proves chargeable, tax is payable as if the deceased had made a chargeable transfer at the time of the original disposition. Tax is then calculated by reference to the cumulative total of chargeable transfers made by the transferor in the seven years prior to the transfer.

## Conditionally Exempt Transfers

A conditionally exempt transfer generally involves a designation by the Treasury under s31 and is dependent upon a claim for designation being made by the taxpayer. For these purposes, s 30(1) of the IHTA 1984

[1] S3A(5).

exempts a transfer of value if the value transferred thereby is attributable to property which has been designated by the Treasury under s31, and in respect of which an "undertaking" has been given. Conditional exemption also includes transfers of value which are exempt under s76 FA 1976[1]. One restriction is that, subject to certain exceptions, the exemption applies only to the deemed transfers of value occurring on death, under s4 IHTA 1984[2]. The restriction is removed in certain cases, making the transfers of values in those cases conditionally exempt. First, the restriction does not apply in cases where the transferor and the transferor's spouse, have, jointly or severally, been beneficially entitled to the property throughout the period of six years immediately preceding the transfer[3]. Secondly, the restriction does not apply in cases in which the transferor acquired the property on the occasion of the death of another person, if the deemed transfer of value occurring on the death of that person was conditionally exempt.[4]

As earlier indicated, s31 requires designation by the Treasury, and undertakings by the taxpayer. Under s31, the Treasury may designate such articles as pictures, prints, books, manuscripts, works of art, scientific collections, or other non-income-yielding items which appear to the Treasury to be of national, scientific, historic or artistic interest; land, which in the opinion of the Treasury is of outstanding scenic, historic, or scientific interest; buildings which in the opinion of the Treasury require special steps to be taken in respect of their preservation, by reason of their historic or architectural interest, etc. In cases in which a claim for designation is made in respect of a potentially exempt transfer which has proved chargeable, the question whether a designation is appropriate falls to be determined by reference to circumstances existing after the death of the transferor[5]. With respect to undertakings by the taxpayer, the required undertakings vary according to the type of property concerned. With respect to items like books, pictures, and manuscripts, the required undertakings are, first, that until the death of the owner of the property, or until the disposal of the property, the property will be kept permanently in the UK (except temporarily, for a purpose and period approved by the Treasury); and, secondly, that the person giving the undertaking will take steps, agreed with the Treasury, to preserve the property and allow the

---

[1] S76 applies to other types of property which have been designated by the Treasury, which are also the subject of specific undertakings by the taxpayer.

[2] S30(3).

[3] S30 (3)(a).

[4] S30(3)(b).

[5] S31(1A).

public reasonable access thereto [1]. If the property concerned is land of historic or scenic or scientific interest, an undertaking is required, until the death of the owner, or until disposal thereof, to take steps, agreed with the Treasury, to maintain the land and preserve its character. Other properties require an undertaking in respect of the maintenance, repair and preservation thereof. [2]

Where the designation and undertakings have been made, a transfer of value in relation to the property concerned is an exempt transfer. [3] The transfer is exempt even if the property concerned is comprised in a discretionary trust [4] and, in such cases, the exemption extends to the "ten-year anniversary charge" which is levied on trusts in which there is no qualifying interest in possession. [5] The exemption is lost if certain events occur, triggering a tax charge. For example, s32(2) provides for a loss of exemption if the Treasury is satisfied that there has been a failure in a material respect to observe an undertaking given in respect of the property concerned, and s32A(3) provides for a loss of exemption if there is a failure to observe materially an undertaking for the maintenance, repair, preservation, access or keeping of the associated properties of certain buildings. With respect to other types of property, the death of the owner of the property and the disposal of the property are also "chargeable events", unless either the transfer of value thereby effected is also conditionally exempt, or any undertaking given in respect of the property is replaced by a corresponding undertaking by such persons as the Treasury considers to be appropriate in the circumstances. [6]

The relief given in respect of conditionally exempt transfers is disregarded in determining whether a transfer of value is a PET (s30(3A)), and a transfer which is a PET cannot be the subject of a claim for conditional exemption under s30(1) until the transferor has died (s30(3B)). Furthermore, a PET cannot be conditionally exempt if the property transferred has been disposed of by sale between the date of the transfer and the death of the transferor (s30 (3C)). Exemptions given to transfers between spouses under s18, and to transfers to charities under s23 (see below) have priority over conditional exemption (s30(4)), in the sense that conditional exemption would apply only where the transfer of value is not otherwise exempt under those provisions.

[1]  S31(2).
[2]  S31(4).
[3]  S30(1).
[4]  S78.
[5]  S79.
[6]  S32(3) & (5).

## Husband and Wife

S18(1) exempts transfers between spouses from inheritance tax, without limit, whether the transfer took place during the lifetime of the transferor, or on the transferor's death. However, by virtue of s18(2) if the transferor is domiciled in the United Kingdom but the spouse is not so domiciled, the relief is limited to £55,000.

## Annual Exemption

Like the income tax and capital gain tax legislations the Inheritance Tax Act allows transferors an annual tax-free amount. S19(1) provides that, transfers of value made by a transferor in any one year are exempt to the extent that the values transferred by them (calculated as values on which no tax is chargeable—i.e. as gross sums) do not exceed £3,000. If the value transferred in any year falls short of £3,000, the unutilised portion may be carried forward to the next tax year only (s19(2)).

Where a particular transfer is a PET, this will be ignored in the original allocation of the annual exemption since it is assumed that the PET will not require the exemption. Rather, the exemption will conferred on other transfers which are immediately chargeable (s19(3A)). If the PET later proves to be a chargeable transfer, it will be assumed that it was made later than any transfer in the same year which was immediately chargeable, so that it obtains relief only to the extent that the relief has not already been exhausted in that year.

## Small Gifts

Transfers of value made in any year by way of outright gifts to any one person are exempt if the values transferred do not exceed £250 (s20(1)). Thus it is possible to make gifts to the value of £250 to different people in the same year, and to have them each of them exempt. The gifts must not exceed £250 in value, and this sum cannot be severed from a larger sum. Thus if the value transferred by the gift is worth £251, no part of it is exempt. This is quite independent of the £3,000 annual exemption.

## Normal Expenditure out of Income

A transfer of value is exempt if it is made as part of the normal expenditure of the transferor, was made out of his income, and, after allowing for all transfers of value forming part of his normal expenditure, leaves the transferor with sufficient income to maintain his usual standard of living (s21(1)). This exemption was examined in *Bennett v IRC*[1]. The case involved two series of payments, each of which amounted to substantial sums, made to B's children (£9,300 to each child, and £60,000 to each child, in two consecutive years) under a "form of authority" to trustees, of income accruing to B from a trust, which was surplus to her financial requirements. B was 87 years old and in good health when the form of authority was made by her solicitor. She died suddenly and unexpectedly shortly after the second series of payments were made. The question was whether these payments were exempt as normal expenditure out of income. Lightman J held that they were so exempt. Lightman J[2] referred to the Oxford English Dictionary, which defined the word "normal" to mean "constituting, conforming to, not deviating from or differing from, the common type of standard; regular, usual". He then referred to the decision of the Court of Appeal of Northern Ireland in *A-G for Northern Ireland v Heron*[3] on the interpretation of s59(2) FA 1910 which exempted from estate duty *inter vivos* gifts made by the deceased which were both part of the normal expenditure of the deceased and were reasonable. In that case, Lowry J (at page 4) said that the adjective in the subsection is used in a qualitative and not a quantitative sense, and that it seemed to refer to type or kind, and not size. Lightman J said[4] that in the context of s21 of the IHTA 1984, the term "normal expenditure" connotes expenditure which at the time it took place accorded with the settled pattern of expenditure adopted by the transferor. According to him, the existence of the settled pattern may be established in two ways:

> First, an examination of the expenditure by the transferor over a period of time may throw into relief a pattern, e.g. a payment each year of ten percent of all income to charity or members of the individual's family or a payment of a fixed sum or a sum rising with inflation as a pension to a former employee. Second, the individual may be shown to have assumed a commitment, or adopted a firm resolution, regarding his future expenditure and thereafter complied with it. The commitment may be legal (e.g. a deed of covenant), religious (e.g. a vow to give all earnings beyond the sum needed for subsistence to those in need) or moral (e.g. to support aged parents or invalid relatives). The

---

[1] [1995] BTC 8003.
[2] At p8007.
[3] [1959] 63 TR 3.
[4] [1995] BTC at p8008.

commitment or resolution need have none of these characteristics, but none the less be likewise effective as establishing a pattern, e.g. to pay the annual premiums on a life assurance qualifying policy gifted to a third party or to give a pre-determined part of his income to his children. [1]

Lightman J said that there need be no fixed minimum period during which the expenditure should have been incurred in order for it to be "normal'. All that is necessary is that the totality of the evidence shows that the pattern of actual or intended regular payments has been established, and that the relevant expenditure conforms with that pattern. [2] He said that, if a prior commitment or resolution can be shown, then a single payment implementing it may be sufficient, but that, if no such commitment or resolution can be shown, then a series of payments may be required before the existence of the necessary pattern will emerge. According to Lightman J, although the pattern does not need to be immutable, it must be established that it was intended to remain in place for more than a nominal period. Barring unforseen circumstances, it must be shown that the pattern was intended to remain in force for a "sufficient period" in order for any payment to be fairly regarded as a regular feature of the transferor's normal expenditure. This means that a death bed resolution to make periodic payments "for life", and a payment made in accordance with such a determination, will not suffice. He also said that the amount of the expenditure need not be fixed. It is sufficient that a formula or standard has been adopted by application of which the payment (which may fluctuate in amount) can be quantified (e.g. ten percent of the earnings, whatever they may be, or the costs of a sick and elderly dependant's residence at a nursing home). Furthermore, the recipients need not be the same. It is sufficient that their general character, or the qualification for benefit, is established (e.g. members of the family, or needy friends). [3] Lightman J also said that there is no need for the expenditure to be reasonable or to be such that an ordinary person might have incurred in the circumstances (although the existence or non-existence of this characteristic may be relevant in deciding whether the evidence establishes the necessary pattern). Finally, he said that the fact that the objective behind the expenditure is tax planning (e.g. to prevent an accumulation of income in the hands of the transferor liable to inheritance tax on his death) is no impediment. Rather,

[1] *Ibid.*
[2] *Ibid.*
[3] *Ibid.*

[w]hat is necessary and sufficient is that the evidence should manifest the substantial conformity of each payment with an established pattern of expenditure by the individual concerned—a pattern established by proof of the existence of a prior commitment or resolution or by reference only to a sequence of payments.[1]

Lightman J referred in *Bennett v IRC* to premiums for life insurance policies. It is important to note that, by s21(2), a life insurance premium or a gift which is applied directly or indirectly to pay such premium will not be regarded as normal expenditure if an annuity has been purchased on the transferor's life at any time, unless it can be shown that the purchase of the insurance and annuity were not associated operations.

## Gifts in Consideration of Marriage

S22 exempts gifts made in consideration of marriage, up to certain limits, depending on the relationship between the transferor and the transferee. The limits are £5,000 in the case of gifts by a parent of either party to the marriage, £2,500 in the case of gifts by remote ancestors (e.g. grandparents) of either party to the marriage, £2,500 in the case of gifts by one party of the marriage to the other, and £1,000 in any other case. A disposition by way of outright gift will not be treated as a gift in consideration of marriage under this section unless it is a gift to a person who is a party to the marriage (s22(3)).

## Gifts to Charities

S23(1) provides an exemption for transfers of value to the extent that the values transferred by them are attributed to property which is given to charities. Property is "given to charities" for the purposes of this exemption either if it becomes the property of charities, or if it is held on trust for charitable purposes only (s23(6)). The latter requirement is taken strictly. According to Lord President Hope in *Guild v IRC*[2] it is not sufficient that one of the purposes of the relevant trust is seen to be charitable, since what the exemption requires is that the property be held in trust for charitable purposes only.[3] This makes it necessary to examine

---

[1] *Ibid.*
[2] [1991] BTC 8055; [1991] STC 281 (Court of Session sitting as the Court of Exchequer).
[3] [1991] BTC 8055 at 8060.

the relevant gift bearing in mind that what one is looking for is whether, viewing the matter in a reasonable sense, its *predominant or sole* purpose is charitable.[1] In *Guild*, the testator had left the residue of his estate to a local authority for use in connection with its sports centre or "for some other similar purpose in connection with sport". The first part of the bequest was held to be a charitable purpose. However, with respect to the second part, while the bequest may have been wide enough to enable the property to be applied in the provision of, or to assist in the provision of, facilities which are charitable, there were no words of restriction or limitation to prevent their being used in some way which falls outside the scope of what may be regarded as charitable purposes. Lord President Hope said that any non-charitable element which is merely incidental or ancillary to the bequest can be overlooked.[2] But here there was a provision of such width and generality that the possibility of some benefit which is non-charitable was both real and substantial. Thus, according to a majority of the Court of Session, the Revenue were right to refuse to grant the exemption. While this outcome was reversed on appeal to the House of Lords[3] the principles remain valid. The House of Lords differed from the Court of Session only on the point whether the words "for some other similar purpose . . ." in the bequest were so wide that they might include non-charitable purposes. On this point Lord Keith accepted the submission that the court should adopt the "benignant" approach which has regularly been favoured in the interpretation of trust deeds capable of being regarded as evincing a charitable intention.[4] Adopting this benignant construction of the bequest, he inferred that the testator's intention was that any other purpose to which the local authority might apply the bequest or any part of it, should also be charitable. This meant that the whole bequest was for charitable purposes only and qualified for exemption. Lord Keith also said that a Scottish court, when faced with the task of construing and applying the words "charity" and "charitable" in a United Kingdom tax statute, must do so in accordance with the technical meaning of those words in English Law.[5]

There are further restrictions in s23(2). The exemption in respect of gifts to charities will not apply in relation to any property if the testamentary or other disposition by which that property is given either:

[1] Emphasis added.
[2] At p8064.
[3] [1992] BTC 8046; [1992] 2 All ER 10.
[4] [1992] BTC 8046 at 8052.
[5] [1992] BTC at 8048.

(a) takes effect on the termination of any interest or period which is subsequent to the transfer itself, or

(b) depends on a condition which is not satisfied within the 12 month period subsequent to the transfer, or

(c) is defeasible.

For these purposes, any disposition which has not been defeated 12 months after the transfer, and which is not defeasible after that time, will be treated as not being defeasible.

## Gifts to Political Parties

Gifts made to a qualifying political party are exempt from inheritance tax (s24(1)). For this purpose, a "qualifying political party" is one which at the last general election preceding the transfer either had two members elected to the House of Commons or had one member elected to the House of Commons and not less than 150,000 votes were given to candidates of that party (s24(2)).

## Gifts for National Purposes

S25 exempts gifts made to certain bodies listed in Schedule 3 to the Act. Examples of bodies mentioned specifically include the British Museum, the National Museums, of Scotland and Wales, the Ulster Museum, local authorities and local authority museums and art galleries, universities and university libraries, museums and art galleries, and government departments. However, the Schedule also refers to "[a]ny other similar national institution which exists wholly or mainly for the purpose of preserving for the public benefit a collection of scientific, historic or artistic interest and which is approved for the purposes of this Schedule by the Treasury".

## Agricultural Property

*General*

Relief for agricultural property is contained within sections 115–124. "Agricultural property" is defined in s115(2) as meaning agricultural land or pasture, including woodland, and any building used in connection with the intensive rearing of livestock or fish, if that building is occupied with agricultural land or pasture, and that occupation is ancillary to that of the agricultural land or pasture. The term also includes such cottages, farm buildings and farmhouses, together with the land occupied with them, as are of a character appropriate to the property.

According to Blackburne J in *Starke (Executors of Brown deceased) v IRC*[1], the expression "agricultural land or pasture" is a composite one. Pasture is bare uncultivated land used for the grazing of animals, and "agricultural land" when used in association with pasture suggests land of a broadly similar nature (i.e. undeveloped land in the sense of land) without buildings or other structures, used for agricultural purposes such as the cultivation of crops. He therefore held that buildings on a piece of land used for agricultural purposes (a six-bedroomed farmhouse, outbuildings used for egg production, a Danish piggery and a covered yard with loft over for housing cattle) did not fall within the definition of agricultural property. The Court of Appeal affirmed the decision[2] although not necessarily agreeing with the narrowness of the approach. Morritt LJ said[3] that it is common in some parts of the country for pasture to include buildings for the storage of winter feed or to provide shelter for the animals using the pasture. Also, the Interpretation Act 1978 (which in s5 defines "land" to include a number of structures, unless the contrary intention appears) requires the word "land" to be read as including "buildings or other structures" unless the contrary intention appears. Thus, neither by itself nor in conjunction with the word "pasture" can the words "agricultural land" be read as bare land. Morritt LJ said that the intention that "buildings or other structures" should not be read into the word "land" must appear, if at all, from other parts of the definition or the Act. Morritt LJ could find no assistance in the part of the definition in s115(2) which defines incorporated woodland and any building used in connection with the intensive rearing of livestock or fish, saying that that was required so that woodland might be included, and to resolve doubts which might be entertained as to the status of buildings used for intensive farming whether of livestock or fish. However, the part which referred to "cottages, farm buildings and farmhouses . . ." was very important since it referred expressly to the buildings and structures which would most obviously be included in the words "agricultural land" if the Interpretation Act applied in full.[4] This seemed to him to be an indication contrary

[1] [1994] BTC 8029 at 8032.
[2] [1995] BTC 8028.
[3] At p8032.
[4] [1995] BTC at 8032.

to the inclusion of the relevant words said to be derived from the Interpretation Act. Another indication of a contrary intention could be found in s115(4), which referred to the breeding, rearing and grazing of horses, and buildings used in connection with those activities. Morritt LJ said that this indicated that Parliament thought it necessary to deal with the buildings used in connection with those activities, which treatment would not be necessary if the words "agricultural land" included "buildings and structures" and the breeding and rearing of horses was taken to be agriculture.[1] According to Morritt LJ it is necessary to consider the structure of the definition as a whole:

> With the exception of the inclusion of "woodland" all that follows the words "agricultural land or pasture" is concerned with the buildings of one sort or another which are to be included. In such a context it would be surprising to find that buildings were already included in the phrase "agricultural land or pasture". It is as though the draftsman had started with the land and then dealt with what should be treated as going with it.[2]

Morritt LJ concluded that the indications earlier referred to, and the general structure of the definition, together show a contrary intention sufficient to exclude the words "buildings or other structures" from the definition of the word "land" otherwise required by s5 of the Interpretation Act.[3]

Thus, while the term "agricultural land" is not necessarily limited to bare land, in the context of this relief, there is sufficient indication in the statute that it should be so limited (i.e. the term could include buildings or other structures, but in this instance it does not).

The relief in respect of agricultural property is given by reducing the value which is transferred by a transfer of value by various amounts, such that the tax chargeable will be reduced or eliminated. The available relief is specified in s116(1) which provides that, where any part of the value transferred by a transfer of value is attributable to the agricultural value of agricultural property, that value will be reduced by the appropriate percentage. "Agricultural value" is defined by s115(3) as the value of property, if it were subject to a perpetual covenant prohibiting its use

---

[1] At 8032–8033.
[2] At p8033.
[3] *Ibid.*

"otherwise than as agricultural property" (i.e. it has no development value whatsoever). The "appropriate percentage" is 100 per cent (i.e. there is a 100 per cent reduction in the value transferred) if certain conditions are fulfilled, and, generally, 50 per cent in any other case.[1] The conditions for 100 per cent relief are:

(a) immediately before the transfer, the transferor had the right to vacant possession, or the right to obtain it within the next 12 months, or
(b) the transferor had been beneficially entitled to his/her interest before 10 March 1981, and certain other conditions (specified in s 116(3)) are satisfied, or
(c) the transferor does not have the interest specified in paragraph (a) above only because the property is let on a tenancy beginning on or after 1 September 1995.

The Inheritance Tax Act specifies a minimum period of ownership or occupation before the agricultural property relief can apply. S117 denies relief in respect of any agricultural property unless:

(a) it was occupied by the transferor for the purposes of agriculture throughout the period of two years ending with the date of the transfer, or
(b) it was owned by the transferor throughout the period of seven years ending with that date and was throughout that period occupied (by him or another) for the purposes of agriculture (i.e. if the land is tenanted, then there is a seven-year ownership period required for the transferor).

### Agricultural Property Relief on Death

S124A provides extra conditions to be met where a PET of agricultural property proves chargeable, or where extra tax becomes due on a chargeable transfer on account of death within seven years of the transfer. S124A(3) provides in such cases that, first, the original property must have been owned by the transferee throughout the period between the transfer and the transferor's death (the relevant period) and must not have been subject to a binding contract for sale at the time of death. Secondly, the original property must still be agricultural property immediately before

[1] S116(2).

the transferor's death and occupied by the transferee or another for agricultural purposes, throughout the relevant period. And, thirdly, where the original property consists of shares in or securities of a company giving the transferor control of the company before the transfer, the value of which reflects the agricultural value of agricultural property owned by the company, that agricultural property must have, throughout the relevant period, been owned by the company and occupied (by the company or another) for the purposes of agriculture.

## Business Property

Sections 103–114 give relief for transfers of relevant business property. The types of property that constitute "relevant business property" are described in s105(1), subject to exceptions in s105(3), and the amount of the available relief (either 100 per cent or 50 per cent) differs in respect of each type.

### 100 Per Cent Relief

There are three main types of property which qualify for 100 per cent relief. The first type is property which consists of a business, or an interest in a business (s104(1)(a) and s105(1)(a)). For the purposes of this relief s110(a) and s110(b) provide that the value of a business or an interest in a business shall be taken to be its net value, and that the net value of a business is the value of all the assets used in the business (including goodwill), reduced by the aggregate amount of any liabilities incurred for the purposes of the business. The types of problem that may arise in connection with the assets that fall to be included in such a valuation are highlighted by *Finch v IRC*[1]. The deceased was a life tenant of settled land which he had used for the purposes of his farming and forestry business. It was common ground that the business constituted relevant business property for the purposes of relief, but the question was whether the value of the land used by the deceased for his farming and forestry business fell to be included in the value of the business. Vinelott J held that it did not. According to him[2]:

> . . . the phrase "assets used in the business" cannot be construed in isolation. It is part of a provision the stated purpose of which is to

[1] [1983] STC 157.
[2] At p160.

prescribe a rule for ascertaining the "net value of a business". That last phrase is one the meaning of which would be perfectly well understood if it stood alone. The net assets of a business are the balance of the assets after deducting the liabilities of the business. In striking a balance only those assets which can be said to be assets of the business would be brought in. [Section 110(b)] should not, I think, be read as giving the phrase "the net value of a business" an artificial meaning wholly divorced from its ordinary meaning . . . In my judgment, therefore, the words "assets used in the business" should be construed as meaning "assets of the business which are used in the business". So construed, [s110(b)] in effect excludes assets which in an exceptional case might be considered assets of a business and included in a balance sheet or statement of assets and liabilities but which at the relevant time were not used in the business; similarly [s110(b)] makes it clear that the liabilities to be deducted are only those "incurred for the purposes of the business". So construed, settled land occupied by a tenant for life and used by him in his farming business is not an asset of that business.

Other types of business property which qualify for 100 per cent relief are: securities of a company which are unquoted and which either by themselves or together with other such securities and any unquoted shares owned by the transferor give the transferor control of the company immediately before the transfer (s104(1)(a) and s105(1)(b)); and any unquoted shares in a company (s104(1)(a), s105(1)(bb)).

For these purposes, the word "quoted", in relation to shares or securities, means "listed on a recognised stock exchange", and "unquoted" means "not so listed" (s105(1ZA)). By s269(1), a person has "control" of a company at any time "if he then has the control powers of voting on all questions affecting the company as a whole which if exercised would yield a majority of the votes capable of being exercised on them". The word "them" in this definition refers to all questions affecting the company as a whole.[1] In *Walding v IRC*[2] the question was whether, in a case where W owns 45 per cent of the shares in a company, and her infant grandson owns 24 per cent of the shares, because of the infant's legal incapacity to exercise his voting rights, his shareholding is irrelevant to the question of control, and W has control of the company. It was argued for the taxpayer that the question is a subjective one, and that it requires the court to have regard to the personal capacity or incapacity of

[1] Knox J in *Walding v IRC* [1996] BTC 8003 at 8005.
[2] [1996] BTC 8003.

the registered proprietor, who is the person who has conferred on him the votes attached to the shares. The taxpayer contended that the words "capable of being exercised" in s269(1) must have been inserted for a reason, and that, that reason was to introduce the question of the capacity of the person who has the shares in question registered in his or her name. Knox J rejected this argument. He said [1] that the inclusion of the words "capable of being exercised" is attributable to the rest of the sentence (i.e. "on them"), and that the reason why the words are found in the section is by way of explanation of the category of votes that is being referred to. Knox J said that implicit in the subsection are two categories of votes that may exist—first, votes on questions that do not affect the company as a whole (e.g. a voting right attached to particular classes of shares); and, secondly, voting rights on all questions affecting the company (which are the rights that count for the purposes of s269). [2] Knox J pointed to serious practical objections to the taxpayer's contention. If one were to have regard to the personal capacity of the registered shareholders in order to determine whether the taxpayer has control under s269(1), this could lead to serious complications—people may suffer from incapacity on grounds of age, or mental incapacity:

> If it is right that one has to have regard to the personal capacity of the registered shareholder at the relevant time—the date of death—there must potentially be a substantial number of people who, at the date of death, are mentally incapable but who would not have a receiver appointed, notwithstanding the fact that they had substantial estates . . . There may be a mentally disabling disease that overtakes the deceased in question not very long before his or her death and there may not be time to get a receiver appointed. If the argument for the taxpayer is right, that would have the effect of disentitling the estate of that person to business property relief.
>
> From the point of view of considering what Parliament is likely to have intended, it also involves the very unfortunate investigation into the mental powers of the deceased at the date of his or her death. That would be both a difficult and, in many cases, invidious task which I suspect would not be welcomed either by the Revenue or taxpayer. [3]

While the taxpayer's argument in this case is understandable, Knox J is clearly right to reject it. The taxpayer's contention would have introduced

---

[1] At p8005.
[2] At 8005–8006.
[3] At 8006–8007.

a totally undesirable and unnecessary subjectivity to the test of control, and would only have served to complicate an otherwise straightforward provision.

## 50 Per Cent Relief

Quoted shares or securities which, either by themselves or together with other such shares or securities owned by the transferor, gave the transferor control of the company immediately before the transfer attract a 50 per cent reduction (s104(1)(b) and s105(1)(cc)). Land, building, machinery or plant which, immediately before the transfer, was used wholly or mainly for the purposes of a business carried on by a company controlled by the transferor, or by a partnership of which he was a partner, will also attract a 50 per cent reduction (s104(1)(b) and s105(1)(d)). So will any land, building, machinery or plant which, immediately before the transfer, was used wholly or mainly for the purposes of a business carried on by the transferor, and which constituted settled property in which the transferor had an interest in possession (s104(1)(b) and s105(1)(e)). There is a restriction in respect of the types of land, building, machinery and plant described above, to the effect that they will not constitute relevant business property in relation to a transfer of value unless the business or the transferor's interest therein, or the shares/ securities of the company carrying on the business, as the case may be, are relevant business property in relation to the transfer (s105(6)).

## Minimum Period of Ownership

S106 provides that property will not be regarded as relevant business property unless it was owned by the transferor throughout the two years immediately preceding the transfer. S107 applies to extend the relief to property which is acquired to replace other property which was owned for two of the five years immediately preceding the transfer. S113A provides extra conditions for transfers within seven years of the transferor's death. In this respect, the combined effect of s113A(1), s113A(3), and s113A(3A) is that, in cases where any part of the value transferred by a PET would otherwise be reduced by the business property reliefs, such reduction would be subject to the conditions that:

(a) the original property was owned by the transferee throughout the period between the transfer and the death of the transferor, and

(b) the original property would (apart from the period of ownership required by s106) be relevant business property, except to the extent that the original property consists of shares or securities, which were either quoted at the time of the transfer, or which were unquoted throughout the period between the transfer and the death of the transferee.

## Reliefs Available only on Death

There are a number of reliefs in the inheritance tax legislation which are available only on the death of the transferor. The discussion that follows examines some of them in outline.

### *Woodlands*

As has been seen above, agricultural property relief may be available in respect of woodlands the occupation of which is ancillary to occupation of other land used for agricultural purposes. However, even if no such relief is available under ss115–124, there may be some relief under ss125–130, available only on death. S125(1) and (2) provide that where any part of a person's estate immediately before his death is attributable to the value of land in the United Kingdom on which trees or underwood are growing but which is not agricultural property, an election can be made to leave the value of the trees and underwood out of account in determining the value transferred on death. The relief is subject to a qualifying period of ownership of five years immediately before death, unless the deceased had received the woodlands as a gift (s125(1)(b)), and there may be a charge when the trees and underwood are eventually disposed of (see s126).

### *Death on Active Service*

S154 provides that no inheritance tax is payable under s4 in relation to the death of a person where the Defence Council or the Secretary of State certify that he died from a wound inflicted, accident occurring or disease contracted at a time when he was engaged on active service against an enemy, or on other service of a warlike nature, or which in the opinion of the Treasury involved the same risks as service of a warlike nature. This relief is dependent on the condition that the deceased was a member of any of the armed forces of the Crown or, not being a member of any of those forces, was subject to the law governing any of those forces by reason of association with or accompanying any body of these forces (s154(2)). The exemption extends to the death of such a person from a disease contracted at some previous time, if the death was due to, or was hastened by, the aggravation of the disease during the specified periods of service.

## Quick Succession Relief

S141 provides relief where the value of a person's estate has been increased by a chargeable transfer, and that person (the transferee) then dies, or makes a chargeable transfer of the same property, within five years of the original transfer of the property to him. The relief is given as a reduction of a percentage of the tax which is charged on so much of the value of the original transfer as is attributable to the increase in transferee's estate, by the second transfer. The appropriate percentages are specified by s141(3). If less than one year has elapsed between the date of the first and last transfer the reduction is 100 per cent. If the elapsed period is between one and two years, the reduction is 80 per cent; if between two and three years, the reduction is 60 per cent; if between three and four years the reduction is 40 per cent, and if the elapsed period exceeds four years, the reduction is 20 per cent.

## Self-Check Questions

1. In what circumstances will be transfer of value be exempt as a gift to charity?
2. What are the conditions necessary for agricultural property relief?
3. Discuss the principles governing business property relief.
4. Which reliefs are available only on death?

# 17
# Settled Property

## Introduction

The inheritance tax treatment of settled property depends on whether or not there exists someone with an interest in possession in that property. Generally, settlements in which no one has an interest in possession are not favoured by the inheritance tax regime, with the exception of certain favoured trusts like accumulation and maintenance trusts. The tax that is chargeable upon the creation of a settlement is determined generally according to the ordinary rules relating to chargeable transfers of value. The subsequent tax treatment of the property comprised within the settlement may however differ significantly, according to the type of settlement. Most of the discussions that follow relate to the inheritance tax treatment of settled property, after the creation of the settlement.

## Settlement

The term "settlement" is defined in s43(2) as any disposition or dispositions of property whereby the property is for the time being:

(a) held in trust for persons in succession (e.g. to Clare for life and then to Emily)) or for any person subject to a contingency (e.g. to Clare when she attains 30); or
(b) held by trustees on trust to accumulate the whole or part of any income of the property or with power to make payments out of that income at the discretion of the trustees or some other person, with or without power to accumulate surplus income (e.g. discretionary trusts and accumulation trusts); or
(c) charged or burdened (otherwise than for full consideration in money or money's worth) with the payment of any annuity or other periodical payment payable for a life or any other limited or terminable period.

S43(3) further provides that a lease for life or lives granted otherwise than for full consideration shall be treated as a settlement (e.g. A grants B a lease of a house for B's life at a nominal rent).

Where there is more than one settlement, in circumstances in which the settlements may be seen as a "composite settlement", they may be regarded as associated operations within the meaning of s268(1) and they may therefore be taken as effecting a single disposition for the purposes of the Act[1]. In this respect s268(1) defines "associated operations" as:

(a) any two or more operations of any kind, being operations which affect the same property, or one of which affects some property and the other or others of which affect property which represents, whether directly or indirectly that property or income arising therefrom; or
(b) any two operations of which one is effected with reference to the other, or with a view to enabling the other to be effected or facilitating its being effected, and any further operation having a like relation to any of these.

Generally, where a transfer of value is made by associated operations carried out at different times, it shall be treated as having been made at the time of the last of those operations (s268(2)).

## Settlor

"Settlor" is defined in s44(1) to include any person by whom the settlement was made directly or indirectly and, in particular, it includes any person who has provided funds directly or indirectly for the purposes of or in connection with the settlement, or who has made with any other person a reciprocal arrangement for that other person to make the settlement. Where there is more than one settlor in relation to a settlement and the circumstances so require, the settled property shall be treated as comprised in separate settlements (s44(2)).

## Trustee

The term "trustee" should normally be taken according to its ordinary meaning in trust law. However there is an extended definition in s45, which provides that "trustee", in relation to a settlement for which there would be no trustee apart from this section, means any person in whom the settled property or its management is for the time being vested.

[1] See Chadwick J in *Hatton v IRC* [1992] BTC 8024 at 8043–8045; [1992] STC 140.

## Types of Settlement

There are three main types of settlement for inheritance tax purposes. First, there are those settlements in which a person has an interest in possession, e.g. where an annuity is payable to a person for life. Secondly, there are settlements in which there is no subsisting interest in possession, e.g. discretionary trusts. Thirdly, there are some settlements in which there is no subsisting interest in possession, but which are nevertheless treated more favourably than other "no-interest-in-possession settlements", e.g. disabled trusts and accumulation and maintenance trusts. The inheritance tax treatment of each of these types of settlement is quite different, and a change from one type of settlement to another will normally involve an "exit charge".

## Interest in Possession

The term "interest in possession" has featured prominently in the discussion on the different types of settlement above. The fact that settlements are classified and taxed by reference to the presence of an interest in possession indicates that the question whether or not a person has an interest in possession in settled property is of the utmost importance. However, the term "interest in possession" is not defined in the Act and an examination of the case law is therefore necessary. The leading case on this point is the decision of the House of Lords in *Pearson v IRC*[1] in which it was held that an interest in possession exists when a person who has an interest in settled property has an immediate entitlement to any income produced by that property as the income arises. In this case three beneficiaries were entitled to all the income arising under a settlement, subject to a power in the trustees to accumulate income. It was held that the overriding power in the trustees to accumulate the income was fatal to the existence of an interest in possession. There had to be a present right to present enjoyment of the income. Viscount Dilhorne said[2] that one should first seek to determine the ordinary and natural meaning of the words "interest in possession" and then consider whether there is anything in the context in which they are used to lead to the conclusion that the proper interpretation thereof involves a departure from the ordinary and natural meaning. He referred to Preston's Treatise on Estates which states that an estate in possession is one which gives "a present right of present enjoyment". This was

[1] [1980] STC 318.
[2] At p323.

contrasted with an estate in remainder which, it was said, gave "a right of future enjoyment". Viscount Dilhorne then referred to Fearne's "Contingent Remainders" where it was said that an estate is vested when there is an immediate fixed right of present or future enjoyment; that an estate is vested in possession when there exists a right of present enjoyment; that an estate is vested in interest when there is a present fixed right of future enjoyment; and that an estate is contingent when a right of enjoyment is to accrue on an event which is dubious and uncertain. In the light of these statements, it appeared that the words "an interest in possession" would ordinarily mean the possession of a right to the present enjoyment of something. This, was the meaning that it had to bear in the present case.

Lord Keith said[1] that the provisions appeared to contemplate that the entitlement to income which is spoken of is an entitlement which, for the time being at least, is absolute. If that is true of the part, it must also be true of an interest which extends to the whole of the property. In the present case, the beneficiaries certainly did not have an absolute right to any income of the property as it accrued. At that moment, their interest was qualified by the existence of the trustees' power of accumulation, to the effect that they had no immediate right to anything, but only a right of later payment of such income as the trustees, either by deliberate decision or by inaction for more than a reasonable time, did not cause to be subjected to accumulation. In his opinion, a right of that nature is not a present right of present enjoyment.

The gist of this decision is that an overriding power to accumulate (e.g. to Ben absolutely subject to the trustees power to accumulate income during the next 21 years) deprives a beneficiary of an interest in possession because he would only be entitled to the net income of the trust fund if the trustees decide not to accumulate. It cannot be said of any trust income, as soon as it arose, that it belongs to the beneficiary, since this would be the case only if the trustees decide not to accumulate. On the other hand, an appointment to Ben for life, and then to Emily, subject to a power in the trustees to revoke Ben's interest, would give Ben an interest in position because, although the trustees could revoke the right and thus deprive him of future income, they cannot deprive him of income which has already arisen, even if it had not yet been paid to him. This is the distinction drawn by Viscount Dilhorne[2] between the exercise of a power which prevents a present right of present enjoyment arising, and the exercise of a power to terminate a present right to present enjoyment.

[1] At p334.
[2] At p325.

The distinction here has sometimes been likened to a tap—if all that pours out goes to Ben, then he has an interest in possession even if there is a person who can deprive him of future income by turning off the tap. If on the other hand, someone can divert part of what is flowing out of the tap to Emily or some other person, then no interest in possession exists.

The question of interest in possession arose again in a different context in *Moore and Osborne v IRC*[1]. A settlor made a settlement directing the trustees to hold the income of the trust funds during the life of the settlor upon protective trusts and, in their discretion, to pay or apply the same to or for the benefit of the settlor, and any wife whom he may marry, and the child or children or issue of the settlor. The powers were to be exercised by the trustees only with the consent of the settlor during his life time. The settlor died without having married or having had any children. The question was whether he had an interest in possession in the settled property on his death. Peter Gibson J held that he did not. According to him[2], in the light of the decision of the House of Lords in *Pearson v IRC*, the expression "interest in possession" connotes a present right of present enjoyment, or "an immediate entitlement, which for the time being is absolute, to income as it accrues." In this case the settlor was, from the date of the settlement until his death the sole beneficiary in existence under the discretionary trust, but until his death there was always the possibility that the class of beneficiaries might increase were he to marry. According to Peter Gibson J[3]:

When income is received by the trustees of a discretionary trust of income, the sole object of a class which is not yet closed cannot in my judgment claim an immediate entitlement to that income. It is always possible that before a reasonable time for the distribution of that income has elapsed another object will come into existence or be ascertained and have a claim to be considered as a potential recipient of the benefit of that income. So long as that possibility exists, the sole object's entitlement is subject to the possibility that the income will be properly diverted by the trustees to the future object once he comes into existence or is ascertained. Indeed in strictness the entitlement of the sole object is only an entitlement that the trustees should consider whether to pay income to him. In respect of income already received it may be possible to say that such an entitlement has arisen, but for

[1] [1984] STC 237.
[2] At p241.
[3] At p243.

present purposes I must consider the position before the death of the settlor not in relation to income previously received by the trustees but in relation to the settlor's rights to income then or thereafter accruing. Such income as it accrued was subject to the possibility that it could properly be withheld by the trustees from the settlor and diverted to a future beneficiary, unlikely though the possibility of such beneficiary coming into existence or being ascertained undoubtedly was in the present case. On that footing the settlor did not immediately before his death have an interest in possession.

## Administrative and Dispositive Powers

The question whether a person has an interest in possession depends on the existence of a power in someone else to deprive him of trust income which has already arisen, and not on the exercise of that power. Furthermore, entitlement to trust income refers to the net income of the trust, not all (i.e. gross) income. [1] The concept of net income is designed to allow for the administrative expenses of the trust. Thus, a distinction is drawn between "administrative powers", that is the power of trustees to have recourse to income for purposes of administering the trust, (e.g. expenses incurred in the management of the trust), and "dispositive powers" (i.e. powers to dispose of the net income). A life tenant for example has an interest in possession, but his interest only extends to the net income of the property, that is to say, after deduction from the gross income of expenses, etc., properly incurred in the management of the trust by the trustees in the exercise of their powers. In *Pearson v IRC*, Lord Keith [2] summed up the matter thus:

> I consider that a distinction is properly to be drawn between powers directed to the preservation of the trust estate for the benefit of life tenant and remainderman alike, and discretionary powers the exercise of which is intended to have an effect on the actual benefits which the beneficiaries as such became entitled, by virtue of their several interests, to receive. It is not at all appropriate, in my view, to equate a power to execute repairs with a power to distribute income at discretion among a class of beneficiaries, from the point of view of a person who is entitled to receive any income not dealt with under the power. And the considerations applicable in the case of a discretionary power to

[1] See e.g. Viscount Dilhorne in *Pearson v IRC* [1980] STC at 323.
[2] At pp333–334.

distribute income apply equally to a discretionary power of accumulation, the exercise of which in effect rolls up income for the benefit of a class of beneficiaries or objects contingently entitled.

A problem arises in this respect where there is a power to have recourse to income for the payment of what will normally be a capital expense. In *Miller v IRC*[1] a trust deed provided for payment, to the beneficiary, of the free income of the trust property, during her life. The trustees had the power, before determining the free income of the trust for any year, to appropriate revenue to meet depreciation of the capital value of any of the assets, and for any other purpose thought advisable or necessary. When the beneficiary died the Revenue assessed tax on the basis that she was, on her death, entitled to an interest in possession in the whole of the funds held by the trustees. The trustees contended that their powers of appropriating revenue deprived the beneficiary of an interest in possession. The question therefore was whether the said powers were dispositive so as to be fatal to the existence of an interest in possession, or merely administrative, so that they would not deprive the beneficiary of an interest in possession. The Court of Session held that the powers were administrative and that the beneficiary had an interest in possession.

Lord Kincraig,[2] referring to *Pearson v IRC*, said that Lord Keith in that case considered that the feature of a dispositive power is that it is a power which, if exercised, has the effect of diverting the income so that it accrues for the benefit of others. The feature of an administrative power, on the other hand, is that it is a power the exercise of which is intended to preserve the estate for the benefit of both the income beneficiary and his successors. Administrative powers are those relating to prudent management in the discharge of the trustees' duty to maintain the trust estate. According to Lord Kincraig[3] the question whether powers contained in a trust deed were dispositive or administrative depends upon a construction of the declarations relating to those powers in the context of the trust deed as a whole. He concluded that, in this instance, the powers of the trustees were administrative powers, being intended to preserve the capital value of the trust estate by meeting the sum required to maintain those values.[4] He said that "appropriation" in this context means the setting aside for a particular purpose, and the use of the word "meet" limits the appropriation to what is necessary for keeping the value of the estate up to that

[1] [1987] STC 108.
[2] At p111.
[3] *Ibid.*
[4] At p112.

which it had when the trust fund vested in the trustees. It is not a power to set aside the income for any other purpose as, for example, to preserve it for the benefit of future beneficiaries, even though they might benefit incidentally from the exercise of the power. According to Lord Kincraig "[a] power to meet depreciation is not one to increase the capital value of the estate by diverting the income to those in right to the capital". [1]

## Settlements with an Interest in Possession

*Introduction*

S49(1) provides that a person who is beneficially entitled to an interest in possession in settled property shall be treated as being beneficially entitled to the property in which the interest subsists. Where the beneficiary is only entitled to part of the income of the settled property, s50(1) stipulates that he is to be treated as being entitled only to a proportionate part of the settled property. The effect of s49(1) and s50(1) is that a beneficiary who has an interest in possession in settled property is treated as owning the capital of the fund, or the settled property itself. Accordingly, the value of the beneficiary's estate will be increased by the full value of the settled property (or the appropriate proportion thereof).

With respect to close companies, s101(1) provides that, where a close company is entitled to an interest in possession in settled property, the persons who are participators in relation to the company shall be treated as being the persons entitled to that interest, according to their rights and interests in the company. This will mean for instance that, where the close company is not resident in the United Kingdom but the participator is so resident, exemptions based on the non-resident status of the transferee will be lost. [2]

An *inter vivos* creation of a settlement in which an individual has an interest in position is a PET since the settled property which he is thereby treated as owning will be property which increases the value of (and which is comprised in) his estate (s3A(2)). This would presumably apply also to those cases in which s101(1) treats participators in close companies as being entitled to an interest in possession.

Creation of a settlement with an interest in position on death will attract the usual charges that are raised on death.

---

[1] *Ibid.*

[2] See for example *IRC v Brandenburg* [1982] STC 555.

*The Charges to Tax*

## Death

On the death of any person, tax is charged as if, immediately before his death, he had made a transfer of value equal to the value of his estate immediately before death (s4(1)). Since the settled property in which a person has an interest in possession is treated as belonging to that person, the value of such property will form part of his estate on death for valuation and tax purposes.

## Exit Charge

S51(1) provides that where a person who is beneficially entitled to an interest in position in settled property disposes of it, the disposal is not treated as a transfer of value, but shall be treated as the coming to an end of his interest and tax shall be charged under s52. The charge under s52(1) is to the effect that where, during the life of the beneficiary, his interest comes to an end, tax is charged as if he had made a transfer of value equal to the value of the property in which his interest subsisted. S52(2) provides that any consideration received in respect of the termination of such interest will be deducted from the value transferred. Such a transfer would be a PET (see s3A(6)) if the property becomes part of the estate of another individual.

The charge also applies in cases wherein s101(1) attributes interests in possession held by a close company to the participators therein. This point is illustrated by *Powell-Cotton v IRC.*[1] The taxpayer had a life interest in some settled property. He sold his life interest to a close company in return for shares in the company. He later transferred some of these shares by way of gift to named individuals as the trustees of a registered charity. It was not disputed that at all material times the company had been a close company which was entitled to an interest in possession in the parts of the taxpayer's former life interest that it still had. It was also accepted that, immediately before the transfer, the taxpayer fell to be treated as if he had been entitled to a part of that interest in possession, and that the effect of the transfer was that the part of the interest to which he was to be treated as being entitled, had become smaller. The question that arose was whether in these circumstances the taxpayer must be deemed to have disposed of part of his interest under s51(1) (and was

[1] [1992] BTC 8086; [1992] STC 625.

consequently liable to tax under s52). Answering the question in the affirmative Vinelott J said [1] that the overriding purpose of s101(1) was to ensure that the participators in a close company which is entitled to an interest in possession are to be treated for all the purposes of inheritance tax as if they were entitled to interests in possession according to their rights and interests in the company. The legislative intention must have been to give rise to a charge whenever there is a change in the proportion of the settled property in which any participator is deemed to be entitled to an interest in possession—whether the change arises on death or on termination of the interest, or on a disposition or deemed disposition *inter vivos* and, in the latter case, whether as a result of a disposal by the company, or of a change in the participators or in the rights and interests of the participators *inter se*. According to Vinelott J this result could be arrived at by the ordinary process of construction and does not require recourse to "intendment or equity" or any presumption to tax in order to meet the obvious anomaly that would result if a taxpayer could avoid inheritance tax on a disposal of an interest in possession in settled property by first transferring it to a close company in which he owned all the shares, and then transferring the shares to the intended beneficiary. [2]

*Exceptions to the Charges*

*Excluded Property*

S53(1) provides that tax shall not be chargeable under s52 if the settled property is excluded property. "Excluded property" is defined in s48. S48(1) provides that a reversionary interest is excluded property unless (a) it has at any time been acquired for money or money's worth, or (b) the settlor or the settlor's spouse is or has been beneficially entitled thereto, or (c) it is interest expectant on termination of a lease treated as a settlement by s43(3). Where the settled property is situated outside the United Kingdom s48(3) provides that such property is excluded property unless the settlor was domiciled in the UK at the time of making the settlement (i.e. if the settlor was non-domiciled at the creation of the settlement, foreign settled property is excluded property).

---

[1] [1992] BTC 8086 at 8091–8092.

[2] The transfer did not fall within the exemption for gifts to charities in this case because of a restriction in s56(3) which denies exemption in cases where the property transferred is an interest in possession in settled property and the settlement does not come to an end in relation to that settled property on the making of the transfer.

*Beneficiary Acquiring Another Interest*

S53(2) provides another exception to the charge under s52 in cases in which the person whose interest in settled property comes to an end becomes on the same occasion entitled to that settled property or to another interest in possession in it.

*Reverter to Settlor*

Tax is not chargeable under s52 if an interest in possession in settled property ends during the settlor's life and on that occasion the property in which the interest subsisted reverts to the settlor (s53(3)).

*Reverter to Settlor's Spouse*

There is no charge under s52 if on the occasion on which the interest comes to an end the settlor's spouse (who is domiciled in the United Kingdom) becomes beneficially entitled to the settled property (s53(4)). This exception also extends to the settlor's widow or widower, who is domiciled in the United Kingdom, and who becomes beneficially entitled to the settled property not later than two years from the death of the settlor.

*Exemption from the Charge on Death*

S54(1) and s54(2) provide that if, on the death of the beneficiary during the settlor's life, the settled property reverts to the settlor, or to the settlor's spouse, or widow(er) (if domiciled in the United Kingdom), the value of the settled property shall be left out of account in determining the value of the deceased's estate immediately before his death.

## Settlements without an Interest in Possession

*Introduction*

The inheritance tax legislation looks upon settlements in which there is no interest in possession with particular disfavour and subjects them to a number of charges. The typical example of such a settlement is the discretionary trust—a type of trust which, because of its potential as a planning tool, has always been unpopular with the Revenue. Property comprised in these types of settlement will be "relevant property" for the purposes of the inheritance tax charges. S58(1) defines relevant property as settled property in which no qualifying interest in possession subsists. Certain items are excluded from this definition, for example accumulation and maintenance trusts, disabled trusts, and excluded property. The term "qualifying interest in possession" is defined by s59(1) as an interest to which an individual is beneficially entitled. Although the term is defined in the context of an interest owned by an individual, in certain cases a company can have a qualifying interest in possession. S59(2) indicates that, in order for a company to have an interest in possession, the business of the company must consist wholly or mainly of acquiring interests in settled property, and the company must have acquired the interest for full consideration in money or money's worth from an individual beneficially entitled to it.

## The Charges to Tax

### Creation of the Settlement

The creation of a settlement in which there is no qualifying interest in possession will be a chargeable transfer, since such a settlement does not fall within those types of transfer of value which are PETs.

### The Ten-Year Anniversary Charge

This ten-year anniversary charge is perhaps the most troublesome of all the consequences of creating a settlement without a qualifying interest in possession. The term "ten-year anniversary" in relation to a settlement means (subject to some exceptions) the tenth anniversary of the date on which the settlement commenced, and subsequent anniversaries at ten-year intervals (s61(1)). S64 provides that, where immediately before a ten-year anniversary, all or part of the property comprised in the settlement is relevant property, tax shall be charged on the value of that relevant property. The ten-year anniversary involves a notional transfer by a person who has the cumulative transfers of the settlor. This notional transfer is defined by s66(4) as the aggregate of:

(a) the value of the relevant property comprised within the settlement;
(b) the value immediately after coming into the settlement of non-relevant

property which has since not become relevant property while remaining in the settlement;

(c) value of property comprised in a related settlement immediately after being so comprised. [1]

This is a transfer of value made by a notional person having the cumulative transfers of (a) the chargeable transfers made by the settlor in the seven years before creating the settlement, and (b) any amounts charged under s65 (the exit charge).

The tax is charged at 30 per cent of the "effective rate" at which tax will be charged on that notional transfer (s66(1)). This effective rate is found by expressing the tax chargeable as a percentage of the amount on which it is charged.

Example:

> Justin sets up a discretionary trust in which there is relevant property to the value of £200,000. This transfer takes his cumulative total of chargeable transfers to £50,000 above the nil rate threshold. If the first £150,000 were taxed at the nil rate, and the last £50,000 at 20%, this would result in a tax liability of £10,000.
>
> The effective rate would in this case be:

$$\frac{10,000}{200,000} = 0.05 \text{ (or 5\%)}$$

> The ten-year anniversary charge will be levied at 30% of this effective rate (i.e. 30% of 5%, which equals 1.5%)

The highest rate at which the ten-year charge can presently be levied is 6 per cent because the highest rate for life-time transfers is 20 per cent (30% of 20% = 6%).

Where the whole or part of the property was not relevant property throughout the period of ten years ending immediately before a ten-year anniversary, or was not comprised in the settlement throughout that period, the rate at which tax is charged on that part will be reduced by

---

[1] For these purposes two settlements are related only if they are made by the same settlor and commenced on the same day (s62(1)). Two settlements are not related if all the property comprised in one or both of them was, immediately after commencement, held for charitable purposes only, without limit of time (s62(2)).

one-fortieth for each of the successive quarters in that period which expired before the property became or last became relevant property comprised in the settlement (s66(2)).

## The Exit Charge

S65 imposes a charge to tax on the occurrence of certain events in the midst of a ten-year period. S65(1) provides that tax shall be charged where the property comprised in the settlement, or any part thereof, ceases to be relevant property, whether because it ceases to be comprised in the settlement or otherwise (e.g. where an interest in position is acquired). A charge is also imposed under the subsection in cases in which the trustees make a disposition as a result of which the value of the relevant property comprised in the settlement is diminished. By s65(2) the tax is charged on the amount by which the value of the relevant property is diminished as a result of the event or, where the tax is payable out of relevant property in the settlement, on the grossed up sum. The tax is charged at differing rates, depending on whether the occasion is prior to the first ten-year anniversary (s68) or between ten-year anniversaries (s69).

There are a number of exceptions to this exit charge. First, there will be no charge where the triggering event occurs in the first quarter of a ten-year period (s65(4)). Even though this provision could lead to some undesirable results, it is applied strictly.[1] Secondly, the charge will not apply in respect of a payment of costs or expenses fairly attributable to relevant property, in respect of a payment which is (or will be) the income of any person for income tax purposes, or in respect of a liability to make such a payment (s65(5)). Thirdly, there will be no charge in cases in which s10 would apply if the trustees were an individual—i.e. if they can show that they did not intend to confer a gratuitous benefit on anyone (e.g. a bad bargain by trustees).

## Accumulation and Maintenance Trusts

### Introduction

As has been stated earlier in this chapter there are some types of settlement in which there is no qualifying interest in possession but which are nevertheless not treated as harshly as, for example, a discretionary

[1] See *Frankland v IRC* [1996] BTC 8034 (Rattee J).

trust. Examples are disabled trusts and accumulation and maintenance trusts. The discussion that follows examines the inheritance tax treatment of accumulation and maintenance trusts only.

S71(1) specifies the conditions that have to be satisfied before a settlement can qualify as an accumulation and maintenance trust. First, no interest in possession subsists in the settlement, and the income from it is to be accumulated so far as it is not applied for the maintenance, education or benefit of a beneficiary (s71(1)(b)). Secondly, one or more persons (i.e. the beneficiaries) will, on or before attaining a specified age, not exceeding 25, become beneficially entitled to the settled property or an interest in possession in it (s71(1)(a)). [1] Thirdly, either not more than 25 years have elapsed since the commencement of the settlement, or all present or past beneficiaries are (or were) grandchildren of a common grandparent, or children, or widow(er)s of such grandchildren beneficiaries who died before they would have become entitled to an interest in position.

As seen above, s71(1)(a) speaks about persons being entitled to an interest in possession at a "specified age" not exceeding 25. In most cases the age will be that imposed by s31 of the Trustee Act 1925—18 years. Thus that condition will be satisfied where s31 of the Trustee Act applies. The second condition (in s71(1)(b)—that the income is to be accumulated to the extent that it is not applied for the maintenance, education or benefit of a beneficiary) will also be satisfied where s31 of the Trustee Act applies. Indeed, s71 is really directed towards relieving cases where infant beneficiaries would have had an interest in position in settled property but for the interposition of s31 of the Trustee Act. S31 of the Trustee Act 1925 provides that, where an infant has an interest which is not reversionary, the trustees shall (even if the infant would otherwise have a vested interest) accumulate the income during the infancy of the beneficiary in so far as they do not use it for his maintenance, education or benefit. On reaching the age of 18, the beneficiary obtains an interest in position (a vested right).

Example:

Emily sets up a trust which provides that income from certain property

---

[1] Concessionary relief is available in ESC F8, to the effect that this particular requirement is regarded as being satisfied even if no age is specified in the trust instrument, provided that it is clear that a beneficiary will in fact become entitled to the settled property, or to an interest in possession in it, by the age of 25.

should be held on trust for such of Maria's children as attain the age of 30.

1. Maria's children are aged 10, 12, and 15.

   This is a case in which s31 Trustee Act 1925 will apply, because the beneficiaries are minors. The age of 30 which is specified in the trust instrument will be overridden, and the children will be entitled to an interest in possession when they attain 18 (under s31 Trustee Act 1925). Thus the provisions of s71(1)(a) IHTA 1984 are satisfied.

2. Maria's children are aged 20, 22, and 24.

   S31 Trustee Act 1925 will not apply because the children are all over the age of 18. Since the age specified in the trust instrument is above 25, the provisions of s71(1)(a) IHTA 1984 are not satisfied.

Apart from the effect of s31 of the Trustee Act 1925 discussed above, the requirement that the beneficiary "will" become entitled to the property or an interest is possession in it is taken strictly. This strict approach was evident in *Inglewood v IRC*[1], in which property was held on trust for such of the settlor's children then living, or born during the life of the settlement, as should attain the age of 21. The trustees also had powers of maintenance and accumulation, and powers to revoke (and reappoint in their discretion) any of the trustees appointed. The question was whether in these circumstances one or more persons will, on or before attaining a specified age not exceeding 25, become entitled to, or to an interest in possession in the settled property. The Revenue argued that, having regard to the power of revocation, it could not be postulated of any beneficiary that he or she "will" become entitled to an interest in possession in the settled fund on or before an age not exceeding 25. The trustees on the other hand claimed that the word "will" must be construed to mean "will if no event happens to disentitle him or her." The Revenue's argument was upheld. Fox LJ said[2] that the word "will" in [s71(1)(a)] does import a degree of certainty which is not satisfied if the trust can be revoked and the fund reappointed to some other person at an age exceeding 25. A trust for A if he attains 25 is within the provision. So also is a trust for A if he attains 25 and with a power of advancement. According to Fox LJ[3], if property is given to A for life but subject to a power of revocation, A is entitled to the income from the inception of the

---

[1] [1983] STC 133.
[2] At p139.
[3] At p141.

trust until it is revoked. That is an interest in possession. What the court is concerned with here is however something quite different. It is whether it can be said that somebody "will" become entitled to an interest if it is capable of revocation. With respect to this question, Fox LJ concluded [1]:

> [s71(1)(a)] leaves on us the strong prima facie impression that its provisions are not satisfied by a trust subject to a power of revocation and reapppointment under which the beneficiary's interest can be destroyed and reappointed to another person at the absolute discretion of the trustees. The word "will" involves a degree of certainty which is inconsistent with such a power.

He suggested however [2] that a power which is limited to permitting appointments to persons on attaining an age not exceeding 25 would be within the provision.

## The Tax Treatment of Accumulation and Maintenance Trusts

### Creation of the Settlement

s3A(1)(c) provides that a gift into an accumulation and maintenance trust (and a disabled trust) is a PET if made on or after 18 March 1986. Thus, there will be no charge on the creation of such a settlement, or on occasions in which further gifts are made into it. Furthermore, s58(1)(b) provides that property comprised in such a settlement is not "relevant property" for the purposes of the ten-year anniversary charge which is imposed on settlements in which there is no qualifying interest in possession. This means that accumulation and maintenance trusts will not be subject to the ten-year anniversary charges.

### Exit Charge

As said earlier in this chapter, a change from one type of settlement to another will trigger an exit charge. With respect to accumulation and maintenance trusts s71(3) imposes a charge in situations in which the settled property ceases to be held on accumulation and maintenance trusts

---

[1] *Ibid.*
[2] At p140.

as defined, and in situations in which the property does not cease to be held on such trusts, but the trustees make a disposition diminishing the value of the settled property. There are exceptions to the charge, in cases in which a beneficiary becomes entitled to settled property or an interest in position in it on or before the specified age (e.g. where the trustees make an advancement of capital to or for the benefit of an infant beneficiary or when a beneficiary obtains an interest in possession, for example on attaining 18 under s31 of the Trustee Act) and there will be no charge on the death of a beneficiary before attaining the specified age (s71(4)).

*Self-Check Questions*

1. What is an interest in possession?
2. What are the differences between administrative and dispositive powers, and what is the significance of these differences?
3. Discuss the inheritance tax treatment of settlements with an interest in possession.
4. What is an accumulation and maintenance trust, and how are such trusts treated by the inheritance tax legislation?
5. In what circumstances will a ten-year anniversary charge will levied in respect of settled property?

## Further Reading

Jopling J, *Interests in Possession*, (1982) BTR 105–113.
Goodhart W, *Capital Transfer Tax on Discretionary Trusts—A New Approach*, (1980) BTR 393–397.

# Part Six — Tax Planning and Tax Avoidance

# 18

# Tax Planning and Tax Avoidance

Tax planning normally involves an arrangement of the taxpayer's affairs in order to recognise fiscal opportunities and effectiveness presented by a mass of complex revenue law principles and their application. At times of high rates of tax, a tax avoidance and planning industry has thrived through its ability to present to the taxpayer (for an appropriate fee) "off the peg" tax planning schemes.[1] The success of these schemes lay in the recognition in *IRC v Duke of Westminster* that,

> [e]very man is entitled if he can to order his affairs so as that the tax attaching under the appropriate Acts is less than it would otherwise be[2]

and in the need to distinguish tax avoidance from tax evasion.[3]

The distinction between tax avoidance and tax evasion was considered by the Royal Commission on the Taxation of Profits and Income in 1955. In its Final Report, the Commission stated that tax evasion

> ...denotes all those activities which are responsible for a person not paying the tax that the existing law charges upon his income. Ex hypothesi, he is in the wrong, though his wrongdoing may range from the making of a deliberately fraudulent return to a mere failure to make his return or to pay his tax at the proper time....[4]

Tax evasion, therefore, is an illegal act and does not fall into the permitted "ordering of affairs" referred to by Lord Tomlin.

Tax avoidance is generally permitted. Tax avoidance consists of

---

[1] See *IRC v Plummer* [1979] STC 793; and *Vestey v IRC* [1980] STC 10 for an insight into the success of these schemes.

[2] [1936] AC 1 at 19 (per Lord Tomlin).

[3] There is growing recognition of a concept of "tax mitigation". This is an imported concept which we shall discuss later.

[4] Cmd 9474, para. 1016.

... some act by which a person so arranges his affairs that he is liable to pay less tax than he would have paid but for the arrangement. Thus the situation which he brings about is one in which he is legally in the right ... [1]

Tax avoidance is often equated with tax planning, because of its permitted nature and tax beneficial effects.

More recently, tax avoidance has started to evoke some concern and stirred the emotions of the general taxpayer. At one end of the spectrum tax avoidance appears to be widely and socially acceptable: at the opposite end of the spectrum some elements of tax avoidance stir emotions of inequity and unacceptability—at that end of the spectrum tax planning and avoidance schemes often represent artificial "loss" or "gain". They often lack genuine business and commercial intent other than the intent to avoid a tax burden and payment. It is that type of "unacceptable" avoidance that has been the focus of judicial debate and consideration in recent years. At times the judicial attempts to grapple with the situation have resulted in some apparent confusion over the concepts of "evasion" and "avoidance". [2]

Before we examine the judicial approaches to avoidance and evasion, there are a number of matters that we should note. First, accurate information about the level and practice of evasion and avoidance is difficult to obtain. The Inland Revenue have indicated that it is "not implausible" that incomes not declared for tax purposes could amount to 7.5 per cent of gross domestic product. Academic researchers have confirmed that tax evasion might be high and that professionals are keen to advise on tax avoidance schemes—albeit that there was some resistance to the consideration of complex artificial tax avoidance schemes. [3]

Second, just as accurate information on the extent of avoidance and evasion is difficult to obtain, so is accurate information on the causes of evasion and avoidance. High tax rates, imprecise and incomprehensive legislation, weak investigatory and legal penalties might all contribute to the encouragement of tax avoidance and evasion. Social attitudes are also

---

[1] *Ibid.*

[2] Most strikingly this was apparent in *Furniss v Dawson* [1984] AC 474, when Lord Scarman appeared to refer to unacceptable "tax avoidance" schemes as "tax evasion" (at 513). This drew a comment from Lord Goff that "... unacceptable tax avoidance schemes which Lord Scarman described as 'tax evasion'—a label which is perhaps better kept for those transactions which are traditionally so described ...".

[3] See Spicer 1975 BTR; Sandford, "Hidden Costs of Taxation", Institute for Fiscal Studies (1973).

important. In some countries tax evasion is perceived as a national sport or even a moral duty. In the United Kingdom the social penalties of evasion are probably high (as they also appear to be in relation to complex artificial tax avoidance schemes)—although we can all sympathise with the unintended evasion of the example of an elderly neighbour making and selling her home-made jam to a few close friends without any appreciation of the tax liability that should have attached to her "profits".

Third, one might question why we should be concerned over the practice of tax evasion and avoidance. The answer extends beyond the social unacceptability and inequity of evasion and avoidance. Included in the answer must be a consideration of the economic costs of the activity. These costs include the resource costs of the time and effort devoted to the development of evasion and avoidance schemes; the "loss" to any wealth redistribution and planning schemes; and the costs of policing and responding to evasion and avoidance developments. These costs provide sufficient reason to pursue and regulate evasion and artificial avoidance schemes and their creators.

## The Judicial Approach

We begin our journey through the changing and developing judicial approaches by examining what is often regarded as the "traditional approach"—an "approach" put forward by the House of Lords in *IRC v Duke of Westminster*.[1] The "traditional" or "*Westminster*" approach demands that the authorities impose a tax on the individual in accordance with the legal effect (or "form") of his arrangements. This approach demands recognition of the legal and tax result of the taxpayer's arrangements.[2] These arrangements and their legal effects are not to be undone or ignored—except in very rare circumstances, and certainly not for the sole purpose of imposing a greater tax burden on the taxpayer.

The facts of *IRC v Duke of Westminster* involved the Duke entering into a covenant to pay his gardener a yearly sum by weekly payments (£1.90 per week), for a period of seven years or during their joint lives. The covenant was expressed to be without prejudice to the gardener's normal weekly wage (£3.00), although there was an understanding that the gardener would only take the balance of £1.10 per week as his wage. The purpose

---

[1] [1936] 19 TC 490.

[2] See Lord Atkin, *ibid*, "... it has to be recognised that the subject, whether poor and humble or wealthy and noble, has the legal right so to dispose of his capital and income as to attract upon himself the lease amount of tax. The only function of a Court of Law is to determine the legal result of his dispositions so far as they affect tax...".

of the scheme was to enable the Duke to deduct the covenanted sum in order to avoid or reduce his liability for surtax. The Revenue claimed that the covenanted sum represented the gardener's wages and could not therefore be deducted for surtax purposes. The House of Lords disagreed with the Revenue's claim and held that the covenanted sums were annual payments under Schedule D Case III and thus were deductible for surtax purposes. Lord Tomlin emphasised the taxpayer's freedom to enjoy the benefits of the tax consequences of his affairs. The courts must recognise and tax the legal status and effects of the taxpayer's arrangements

> ... however unappreciative the Commissioners of Inland Revenue or his fellow taxpayers may be of his ingenuity, he cannot be compelled to pay an increased tax.

Thus the *Westminster* doctrine or approach invites the taxpayer to arrange his affairs so as to enjoy maximum tax benefits and invites the courts to recognise the status of those arrangements and apply any tax benefits or tax rules accordingly. Some writers have suggested that this is a recognition of form over substance. Although this might be a convenient way of explaining the *Westminster* case, it is not entirely accurate. The courts have always been willing to look beyond the presented "form" to ascertain the true status of the taxpayer's arrangements. This is formally apparent when the courts declare the form or label a "sham". Less formally it is apparent when the courts find that the substance dictates the form. In the determinant of legal status and in the attaching of the appropriate tax consequence the process demands recognition of both substance and form. For example, in the *Duke of Westminster* case Lord Tomlin cited the words of Warrington LJ in In *re Hinckes, Dashwood v Hinckes*[1] that in order to recognise substance one must recognise legal effects and form. Upon that basis the form put forward (the "covenant") was in substance correct.

> ... the substance is that which results from the legal rights and obligations of the parties ascertained upon ordinary legal principles, and ... the conclusion must be that each annuitant is entitled to an annuity which as between himself and the payer is liable to deduction of income tax by the payer and which the payer is entitled to treat as a deduction from his total income for surtax purposes. ...[2]

[1] [1921] 1 Ch 475 at 489.
[2] Supra.

The "sham" exception referred to above appears to enjoy a limited scope and limited application. The exception has become too technical in its requirements. In essence it demands evidence of an intention to conceal or deceive. If such an intention is present, the courts are able to ignore the label or appearance presented and disregard the "sham" transactions. [1]

It soon became apparent that a strict application of what might be regarded as the *Westminster* doctrine might not be appropriate in the circumstances of "off the peg", artificial tax. The purchasers of these "off the peg" schemes (or even tailor-made schemes) would seek to enjoy the tax consequences of each transaction examined in isolation from the whole. They would insist, relying on the *Duke of Westminster* case, that the courts should recognise the status and effects of each isolated transaction, and that such recognition should result in the application of appropriate, and often isolated, tax principles and concessions. This was an attempt to project the *Westminster* principle into an area of (perhaps) unacceptable and artificial tax avoidance schemes. It was an invitation to ignore the fiscal reality of the overall effects of the scheme: merely an invitation to recognise the legal status of each isolated transaction and step in the scheme. It soon became apparent that the courts would need to react to the artificiality of this situation and that they must react in a manner which would not undermine the taxpayer's freedom to organise his affairs to enjoy maximum tax benefits—a freedom strongly supported by Lord Tomlin in *IRC v Duke of Westminster*. It was clear that aspects of the *Westminster* principle must remain on the books, albeit with elements of restriction and qualification. [2]

*Ramsay v IRC* [3] is considered to be the starting point for the development of a "new approach" to tax avoidance schemes, although evidence of a change in judicial attitudes and approach can be found in the earlier case of *Floor v Davis* [4]. This case involved the disposal of shares from X to Y. In order to avoid capital gains tax, X set up a subsidiary

---

[1] See *Snook v London and West Riding Investments Ltd* [1967] 2 QB 786. See also, Lord Goff in *Ensign Tankers (Leasing) Ltd v Stokes* [1992] STC 226 where he declared that a scheme before him, despite its artificiality, was not a "sham", ". . . in the narrow sense in which that word has been used in this context . . ." (at 245).

[2] See Lord Diplock in *IRC v Burmah Oil Co Ltd* [1982] STC 30—where he emphasised the different types of schemes (and their artificiality) that face the courts today.

See also Lord Wilberforce in *Ramsay v IRC* [1981] STC 174, where he explained that ". . . While the techniques of tax avoidance progress are technically improved, the courts are not obliged to stand still".

[3] *Ibid.*

[4] [1978] STC 436.

company, and transferred shares to that company in consideration of the issue of shares. The subsidiary would then transfer those shares to Y. Subsequently, the subsidiary was dissolved and all its assets transferred to X. Thus, X had, indirectly, achieved the disposal of shares to Y through this subsidiary. On the issue of whether the "disposal" ought to be treated as one from X to Y, thus removing the capital gains tax advantages, or simply whether each step should be examined in isolation from the whole, the court erred on the side of the latter. The decision was perceived as being in keeping and consistent with the decision in *IRC v Duke of Westminster*. The dissenting speech of Eveleigh LJ provided an insight into changing attitudes. Eveleigh LJ suggested[1] that the courts were not required to consider each step in isolation. That the real issue was whether in reality they were faced with a disposal of shares from X to Y. If so, they should treat it as a transfer from X to Y and not a transfer by the subsidiary to Y—at least for tax purposes.

This suggestion was later confirmed as principle, albeit uncertain principle, in *Ramsay v IRC*.[2] *Ramsay v IRC* involved a complex series of transactions designed to create an "allowable loss" for capital gains tax purposes. The true position of things was that, at the end of the series of operations, the taxpayer's financial position was in reality just the same as at the beginning. Although the scheme produced a "loss", the taxpayer had not suffered any real or actual loss.

The House of Lords decided that such artificial schemes should be looked at as a whole for the purpose of determining their tax consequences. The courts should not look to each isolated transaction but to the fiscal reality of the series of related transactions, comparing the taxpayer's position at the beginning and at the end of the scheme. Lord Wilberforce remarked that:

> ... It is the task of the court to ascertain the legal nature of any transaction to which it is sought to attach a tax, or a tax consequence, and if that emerges from a series, or combination of transactions, intended to operate as such, it is that series or combination which may be regarded. ... To force the courts to adopt, in relation to closely integrated situations, step by step, dissecting approach which the parties themselves may have negated, would be a denial rather than an affirmation of the true judicial process. In each case the facts must be established, and a legal analysis made ...[3]

---

[1] *Ibid.*

[2] *Supra.*

[3] *Supra* at 180.

This "new approach" was followed in *IRC v Burmah Oil Co Ltd*[1]. This case also involved a complex scheme of transactions designed to create an "allowable loss" for capital gains tax purposes. In response, the House of Lords emphasised that the *Ramsay* case represented a new approach to artificial tax avoidance schemes. The new approach demands that the court

> . . . take the analysis far enough to determine where the profit, gain or loss is really to be found . . .[2]

Applying that analysis, the court was able to conclude that no "real loss" had been suffered by the taxpayer in this particular case.

It is interesting to note that Lord Diplock, in *Burmah Oil*, was careful to stress the differences between the tax avoidance scheme found as acceptable in *IRC v Duke of Westminster*, and the tax avoidance schemes declared unacceptable in *Ramsay* and in *Burmah Oil*. The former consisted of simple arrangements between two consenting (real) persons, whereas the later involved

> inter-connected transaction between artificial persons (limited companies) without minds of their own but directed by a single master-mind.

One appeared to be an acceptable arrangement of one's affairs whereas the other appeared to be an unacceptable artificial tax avoidance scheme.

The real problem is that of trying to ascertain when and in what circumstances the courts would adopt this "new approach". *Furniss v Dawson*[3] provided some insight into judicial thinking in this area. The facts involved a scheme to defer liability to capital gains tax. The taxpayers wanted to sell some shares to X Ltd. An outright sale would give rise to immediate tax liability under capital gains tax rules. The tax deferred scheme involved the taxpayers transferring shares (through a share exchange) to a newly incorporated company, Greenjacket Investments Ltd. Greenjacket Investments Ltd then sold its acquisition of the taxpayer's shares to X Ltd. The eventual sale price equated with the originally planned sale price of £152,000. The Revenue claimed that the reality of the scheme was a chargeable disposal from the taxpayer to X

---

[1] [1982] STC 30.
[2] *Ibid.*
[3] [1984] STC 153.

Ltd for £152,000. Applying the "new approach" the House of Lords agreed with the Revenue's assessment. The taxable disposal was a disposal of the taxpayer's shares to X Ltd. This invited immediate capital gains tax implications. Two distinct approaches were apparent in the court's analysis of the "new approach". The first approach is to be found in the speech of Lord Brightman, although Lord Brightman was careful to stress that he was adopting and following a formulation proposed by Lord Diplock in the earlier case of *IRC v Burmah Oil Ltd.* For the "new approach" to apply, Lord Brightman stressed that:

> First, there must be a pre-ordained series of transactions; or, if one likes, one single composite transaction . . . Secondly, there must be steps inserted which have no commercial (business) purpose apart from the avoidance of liability to tax . . . If those two ingredients exist, the inserted steps are to be disregarded for fiscal purposes. The court must then look at the end result. Precisely how the end result will be taxed will depend on the terms of the taxing statute sought to be applied . . . [1]

The second approach is to be found in the speech of Lord Bridge. Lord Bridge took strength from the United States Federal Courts experiences in suggesting that in areas of composite transactions it was perfectly legitimate for the court to draw a distinction between the substance and the form of the composite arrangement

> without in any way suggesting that any of the single transactions which make up the whole are other than genuine.

Following *Furniss v Dawson*, there was some concern over the way in which the "new approach" would develop. Would it confine its area of application to the rather mechanistic and legalistic requirements of Lord Brightman and Lord Diplock; or would it follow the US approach of enjoying a wide, but rather uncertain, application of searching for the substance and fiscal reality of the composite arrangement? The latter would provide wider scope for judicial discretion but suffered from uncertainty and imprecision of application. The US experience has been described as analogous to the search for the Holy Grail.

---

[1] *Ibid.* It is interesting to note that although many regard this formulation of the *Ramsay* principle as restrictive, Lord Brightman was intending, at one level, to present a wider meaning of the principle. For example, he was concerned to avoid the High Court and the Court of Appeal's confinement of the *Ramsay* principle to self-cancelling transactions.

In *Furniss v Dawson,* Lord Diplock resisted any attempt to provide an

. . . exposition of all the criteria by which . . . form and substance are to be distinguished.

It is possible that should that criteria be propounded the substance over form approach would face the danger of becoming as mechanistic and restrictive as the Lord Brightman approach!

The status of the "new approach" and the debate in *Furniss v Dawson,* was considered by the House of Lords in three co-joined appeals—*Craven v White; IRC v Bowater Property Developments Ltd; Baylis v Gregory.* [1]

Both *Craven v White* and *Baylis v Gregory* involved *Furniss v Dawson* type of share transfer schemes. In *Baylis v Gregory* it was originally intended that a sale to X would take place by the taxpayer transferring shares to an Isle of Man company and the Isle of Man company would then transfer those shares to X (as per *Furniss v Dawson*). However, following the transfer of the shares by the taxpayer to the Isle of Man company, X withdrew from the scheme. Eventually (some twenty months later) another buyer (Z) was found, and the sale to Z took place. The House of Lords unanimously held that the "new approach" did not apply: the sale was not one by the taxpayer to Z, but rather one by the Isle of Man company to Z.

In *Craven v White,* the taxpayers were considering either (1) a merger with X or (ii) a sale of its shares to Z. To start the ball rolling, the taxpayer transferred (a share exchange as per *Furniss v Dawson*) its share to an Isle of Man company.

Once again, the House of Lords held (Lords Templeman and Goff dissenting) that the "new approach" did not apply: the sale was by the Isle of Man company to Z, not one by the taxpayer to Z.

In *IRC v Bowater Property Developments Ltd,* a scheme was devised to provide the maximum tax benefits in a sale of land. *Bowater Property Developments Ltd* divided land into five parts and transferred each part to a separate company within its group. Each company then sold their part of the land to Z Ltd. The tax benefits of this arrangement enabled the five companies to enjoy individual statutory allowances under the development land tax regime. If Bowater had directly sold the land to Z Ltd, Bowater only would have enjoyed statutory allowances. The House of Lords unanimously held that the "new approach" did not apply, and that the transfers of land were transfer by the five individual companies; not a transfer from Bowater to Z Ltd.

[1] [1988] STC 476.

The importance of these three cases is reflected in how they interpreted *Furniss v Dawson* and applied the "new approach". It soon became clear that the court was willing to accept the rather mechanistic, Brightman and Diplock approach. For example, Lord Oliver carefully emphasised that *Furniss v Dawson* simply brought forth principles of statutory construction: it was not authority for any wider proposition such as

> . . . a general proposition that any transaction which is effected for the purpose of avoiding tax on a contemplated subsequent transaction and is therefore "planned" is, for that reason, necessarily to be treated as one with that subsequent transaction and as having no independent effect even where that is realistically and logically impossible. [1]

The mechanistic, or "new approach", of *Furniss v Dawson* was reformulated by the House of Lords to require the following:

1. that there exists a series of transactions which was, at the time when the intermediate transaction was entered into, pre-ordained in order to produce a given result; and
2. that that transaction had no other purpose than tax mitigation; and
3. that there was at that time no practical likelihood that the pre-planned events would not take place in the order obtained, so that the intermediate transaction was not even contemplated practically as having an independent life; and
4. that the pre-ordained events did in fact take place. [2]

If the above requirements are satisfied, Lord Oliver suggested that the court could then examine the true fiscal consequences of the scheme by comparing the taxpayer's financial status at the beginning and at the end of the scheme. It is only when such a comparison is made that the reality, or perhaps the "substance", of the scheme is realised and appreciated. This examination and recognition of the "substance" does not equate with the "substance" approach advocated by Lord Bridge in *Furniss v Dawson*. According to Lord Bridge's approach, the substance or fiscal reality will be assessed and determined because of the tax avoidance motive and actions of the taxpayer. According to the House of Lords in *Craven v White* (and associated appeals) the fiscal reality (or substance) will be assessed only if the pre-requisites identified above are satisfactorily established—

[1] *Ibid.*
[2] *Ibid* (per Lord Oliver).

there is no general right, or even qualified right, to search and tax the substance (especially on the grounds of the existence of a tax avoidance motive).

Elements of uncertainty and concern still remain. First, there is a need to understand the meaning and requirements of "pre-ordained". If events are pre-ordained, must the final outcome be guaranteed and indisputable?

The House of Lords approached this matter by examining whether at the time when the first step was entered into the taxpayer was able to secure the completion of the remaining steps of the scheme. The Lords concluded that an ability to absolutely secure the final stages was not necessary, but the occupation of a position that rendered the final steps and completion of the scheme "practically certain" or a "reasonable and practical likelihood" would suffice. Thus, for example, in *Craven v White*, the final step was not practically certain or likely because the taxpayer, at the time of the first step, genuinely believed that a sale to Z would not take place. The taxpayer believed that a merger with X was the more probable outcome. Similarly, in *Baylis v Gregory*, the breakdown of negotiations and the subsequent sale to a different purchaser some 22 months later indicated the absence of "certainty". In *IRC v Bowater Property Developments Ltd*, no "certainty" or pre-ordained nature was present. At the time of entering into the fragmentation of the land, the ultimate purchaser was not party to the fragmentation arrangements.

We have seen that in *Craven v White* (and associated appeals) different description of "likelihood" and "probability" were used. The absence of any unanimity of description is reflected in the dissenting speech of Lord Templeman in *Craven v White*:

> Two transactions can form part of a scheme even though it is wholly uncertain when the first transaction is carried out whether the taxpayer who is responsible for the scheme will succeed in procuring the second transaction to be carried out at all ...

and further that,

> ... if the ... undefined and indefinable expressions "practically certain", "practical likelihood", and "practical contemplation" possess any meanings, those expressions and those meanings are not to be derived from Furniss ...

On that basis, Lord Templeman was able to conclude that the intentions in *Craven v White* were eventually fulfilled as part of the planned arrangements. The case was indistinguishable from *Furniss v Dawson* and therefore, the scheme should fail in its tax avoidance intentions. Lord Templeman was concerned that the House's treatment of *Furniss v Dawson* was a narrowing of the principles and initiatives of that case. [1]

Second, we need to ascertain the meaning of "commercial" purpose. You will recall, that Lord Oliver stressed the artificial nature of the scheme by insisting that it must contain steps that were inserted for "no commercial purpose" (other than the avoidance of tax). Not only must we know and understand what constitutes a "commercial purpose" but we must also understand whether any commercial purpose, however slight, will be sufficient to defeat an application of the "new approach". [2]

Third, does the new approach apply to all taxes? We have some confirmation of this matter. [3]

Fourth, what remains of Lord Bridge's "substance" over "form" approach? Although in *Craven v White* (and associated appeals) Lord Brightman's mechanistic "pre-ordained" approach was preferred, the "door" for the development of Lord Bridge's approach was arguably left open. Lord Templeman in particular noted that

> Parliament cannot have intended that an individual taxpayer should be able to elect to carry out a taxable transaction without paying the tax which Parliament has imposed proportionately on all taxpayers. The court is entitled and bound to construe the taxing statute and to apply the taxing statute in relation to the scheme as a whole. [4]

This approach of looking to the reality of Parliament's intentions and to

---

[1] We shall see later, that it is probable that Lord Templeman has not given-up the initiative (*Ensign Tankers (Leasing) Ltd v Stokes. Ibid*).

[2] In *Ensign Tankers (Leasing) Ltd v Stokes* [1989] STC 770, the Commissioners had concluded that "the creation of two limited partnerships served no commercial or business purpose. Each was brought into existence as part of a tax deferral scheme."

Millet J declared this aspect of the Commissioner's findings as "untenable". "It was commercially essential for there to be some structure to regulate the relationship of the parties, . . . . The chosen structure was that of a limited partnership, which not only served a commercial purpose but became the taxable entity."

In the Court of Appeal, Sir Nicolas Browne-Wilkinson VC suggested that it would be wrong to decide the commercial purpose entirely from an objective view of the transaction in question. He suggested that "motive" was relevant in determining commercial purpose: to be a trading transaction the transaction must demonstrate the characteristics of trade and demonstrate, subjectively, a commercial purpose. [1991] STC 136.

[3] See *Gisborne v Burton* [1988] 3 All ER 760. *Countess Fitzwilliam v IRC* [1992] STC 185.

[4] *Supra*.

the reality (or substance) of the taxpayers' arrangements found some support in the later case of *Ensign Tankers (Leasing) Ltd v Stokes*[1]. This might also support a reconciliation with the *Duke of Westminster* case in that the *Westminster* principle often involved an assessment of the reality of the situation and the reality of the form of transaction—the reality of the form would often invite the court to disregard any labels given by the parties to the transactions or documents.

It is clear that in the future these uncertainties need to be resolved. One would like to believe that the courts will not get "bogged-down" in the mechanistic approach advocated by the "pre-ordained series of transactions" approach to statutory construction. One would suggest that Lord Templeman was correct in *Craven v White* (and associated appeals) when he appears to suggest that the issue is one of equity among taxpayers.[2] An issue later taken up in the "too much, too little" analysis in *Ensign Tankers*.[3] It is essentially the unacceptable (and perhaps inequitable) nature of these artificial tax avoidance schemes that has induced a reaction. One would hope that the logical and consistent, at least with the *Westminster* principle, response is to tax the reality of the situation irrespective of the presence or absence of "commercial purpose" or "pre-ordained" arrangements—although such factors might assist (but ought not to be definitive) the courts in determining the fiscal reality of the taxpayer's affairs.

---

[1] *Supra* n25 at 233–240. *Ensign Tankers* involved the creation of a partnership through which the producers of the film "Escape to Victory" were seeking to claim a first year capital allowance of $14,000,000 without, according to Lord Templeman, incurring the expenditure of $14,000,000. This was part of an arrangement whereby those who had contributed only 25% of the cost of the production of the film were hoping to enjoy the generous capital allowance scheme in this country to offset the total costs of production. In the words of the court, the scheme involved the "execution of a raid on the Treasury using the technicalities of revenue law and company law".

Relying on the *Duke of Westminster* case, the taxpayers sought to escape the true effect of the scheme by submitting that the court was not entitled to ignore or contradict the form of the various transactions that made up the scheme. Lord Templeman's response to this was that the court was entitled to look to the reality of the situation and impose tax accordingly:

> In the Duke of Westminster case the fiscal consequences claimed by the Duke corresponded to the legal consequences of the transaction ... In the present case the fiscal consequences claimed by the taxpayer company do not correspond to the legal consequences of the scheme documents read and construed as a whole.

Interestingly, Lord Templeman based his examination and application of the fiscal reality (or substance?) of the scheme as "consistent with the approach of the courts in recent cases, such as *Ramsay* and *Burmah*".

[2] See footnote (29) and the emphasis on proportionately on all taxpayers.

[3] *Supra.*

Two recent decisions of the House of Lords indicate the degree of uncertainty and confusion that remains. In *Fitzwilliam v IRC*[1] a narrow approach was taken to the *Ramsay* principle, whereas in *IRC v McGuickan*[2] a broad approach was taken. *Fitzwilliam* provides an example of a narrowing of the *Ramsay* principle through the adoption of narrow interpretations of the concepts of "pre-ordained" and "business purpose". The decision in *McGuickan* represents a fightback by the Lords, with Lord Steyn in particular adopting a more purposive approach to tax avoidance and statutory interpretation, and concluding with the warning that:

> Given the reasoning underlying the new approach it is wrong to regard the decisions of the House of Lords since the *Ramsay* case as necessarily marking the limit of the law on tax avoidance schemes.[3]

The story continues!

## Anti-Avoidance Legislation

Tax avoidance has also concerned the legislature. Although we do not have any general anti-avoidance provision[4], the legislature has at times begun to recognise potential planning and avoidance "loopholes" in statutory provisions and has sought to take anti-avoidance measures in relation to those, actual or potential, loopholes.[5] These anti-avoidance measures are limited in their application and they are broadly of two types. The first type apply irrespective of the intentions or motives of the

---

[1] [1994] STC at 153

[2] [1997] 1 WLR 991

[3] *Supra* 2 at 1000

[4] The practicalities and legitimacy of introducing a general anti-avoidance provision have been questioned (See Masters C, [1994] BTR 647).

[5] A recent example of this process can be found in the March Budget, 1993, when the Chancellor announced that he intended to "... close a number of loopholes which have been exploited to avoid tax."

Those "loopholes" related to the Business Expansion Scheme and to corporation tax matters. More recently the new Labour Government has intimated at the possibility of introducing new general anti-tax-avoidance provisions, although the practicalities of doing so have been questioned (see "Tax ploy warning", *Accountancy Age* (1997), 4 July p5).

taxpayer. The second type only apply when it is shown that there exists a tax avoidance purpose or motive behind the transaction.

Included in the first type of provision are these contained in the Taxes Act 1988, Part XV (ss660–694). These apply to settlements. For example, section 660 declares that dispositions for a short period (less than six years) are deemed to be made in favour of the disposer. Similarly, section 663 declares that income paid to or for the benefit of a child (who is unmarried and below the age of eighteen) is deemed to be income of the settlor.

Examples of the second type of provision can be found in Part XVII of the Taxes Act 1988. These include the provisions in ss703 to 709 which are designed to counteract tax avoidance schemes in relation to the distributable assets of a company. Sections 703 to 709 recognise the tax benefits and potential in relation to activities relating to the distributable assets of a company, but declare that those benefits cannot be enjoyed unless

> the person concerned can show that the transaction was carried out for either bona fide commercial reasons or in the ordinary course of making or managing investments and that the tax advantage was not his main objective.

## Tax Mitigation

In some jurisdictions the concept of "tax mitigation" has been developed and applied. The development in those jurisdictions is often explicit, entitling the taxpayer to the tax benefits of his actions only if his actions and transactions are genuine: he is entitled to the tax benefits of his actions because he has suffered the intended consequences. In the circumstances he deserves, or he will have earned, the tax benefits!

Increasingly, the term "tax mitigation" has crept into the English courts. In *Ensign Tankers*, Lord Templeman provided a useful definition by stating that tax mitigation occurs where a taxpayer "suffers a loss or incurs expenditure in fact as well as in appearance".[1] In the same case a distinction was drawn between tax mitigation and unacceptable tax avoidance:

> In the former the taxpayer takes advantage of the law to plan his affairs

---

[1] *Supra* at 240. For an earlier discussion, see Lord Templeman in *IRC v Challenge Corporation Ltd* [1987] 1 AC 155.

so as to minimise the incidence of tax. Unacceptable tax avoidance typically involves the creation of complex artificial structures by which the taxpayer conjures a loss, gain or expenditure, designed to achieve an advantageous benefit for the taxpayer. They are no more than raids on the public funds at the expense of the general body of taxpayers, and as such are unacceptable.[1]

It is interesting that no distinction was made (if one exists) between acceptable tax avoidance and tax mitigation. The key to tax mitigation appears to be its genuine, non-artificial nature. The above quote appears to equate tax mitigation with a permitted planning or ordering of one's affairs. This "ordering of one's affairs" appears to be similar to Lord Tomlin's dictum in the *Duke of Westminster* case[2]—although the "ordering of affairs" that Lord Tomlin was referring to was a description of acceptable tax avoidance. Logically this invites a conclusion that acceptable tax avoidance and tax mitigation are the same concept and must, therefore, be distinguished from tax evasion and unacceptable, (artificial) tax avoidance. This "logic" might, for the moment, be disturbed by suggesting that "acceptable" tax avoidance and tax mitigation are distinct and separate concepts because of the latter's insistence that the taxpayer "suffers" in fact as well as in appearance. However, if one points to the decision at the very heart of acceptable tax planning and avoidance, *IRC v Duke of Westminster*, one can see that the taxpayer did "suffer" in fact and in appearance. The covenant was for seven years, irrespective of the length of employment of the gardener. Thus, the gardener was entitled to receive the covenanted sum (per week) for seven years, even if his employment had terminated within that seven year period. The Duke of Westminster had, in fact, "suffered" this obligation to pay the covenanted amount. He might be regarded, therefore, as having earned his tax benefit.

### Self-Check Questions

1. Distinguish tax avoidance from tax evasion.
2. What is tax mitigation?
3. Explain the *Westminster* principle?
4. What is the "new approach" to tax avoidance? What uncertainties remain?

---

[1] *Supra*, at 227.
[2] *Supra*.

## Further Reading

Popkin WD, *Judicial Anti-Avoidance Doctrine in England: A United States Perspective*, (1991) BTR 283–310.

Mansfield G, *The "New Approach" to Tax Avoidance. First Circular, Then Linear, Now Narrower*, (1989) BTR 5–19.

Tiley J, *Judicial Anti-Avoidance Doctrines*, (1987) BTR; and (1988) BTR 63, (1988) BTR 108.

Kay JA, *The Economics of Tax Avoidance*, (1979) BTR 354–65.

Arnold BJ, *The General Anti-Avoidance Rule*, [1995] BTR 541.

Masters C, "Is there a need for General Anti-Avoidance Legislation in the United Kingdom?" [1994] BTR 647.

# Part Seven — Examination Technique and Preparation

# 19

# Examination Technique and Preparation

Having enjoyed the experience of discovering and discussing revenue law, most students will face the dreaded task of converting their knowledge and learning into suitable responses in the examination room. The purpose of this chapter is to provide some guidance on the type and nature of questions that one might face in a revenue law examination, and to provide some thoughts on how to prepare for and approach those questions. It is a frequent source of frustration to the examiner and lecturer that a student who has a good grasp of the subject fails to demonstrate that ability through poor examination technique and preparation.

## Review

One of the first tasks must be the need to review the syllabus (not the formal one but the one that you receive!) Review the focus of tutorial debate and discussion; review the types of questions on tutorial and past examination papers. At the very least this review will provide a sense of the relative importance and focus of topics covered during the course. It might also assist in the relatively dangerous sport of "question-spotting"— although an over-indulgence in that sport is not recommended!

## Practice

Preparation demands that you practice and develop your examination technique. Practice should also enable you to identify gaps in your knowledge and understanding well in advance of the formal examination. Included in this chapter are some typical examination questions. These could be used for practice purposes. The self-check questions at the end of each chapter should be used to review your reading and understanding and should identify your knowledge and understanding gaps—if any!

## Time management

Another frequent frustration for the examiner is the script of a "good" student which demonstrates poor time allocation. The statement "ran out of time" does little to assist the examination candidate and serves to confirm the suspicions of the examiner. One of the advantages of the review process is that it will enable you to be familiar with the requirements of the examination: is it four questions out of eight, or must I answer five questions out of nine?

The practice process will then be informed of the examination requirements and should be used to refine and develop your time management. You are strongly advised to avoid the situation where the formal examination is your first attempt at time management!

## Examination Rubric and Instructions

Become familiar with the rubric of your examiners. If you are asked to advise X, advise X and not Y and Z. If you are asked to discuss and advise on capital gains tax implications, do not write all you know about inheritance tax or other tax implications. Respond to the examiner's requests. An inevitable skill that the examiner will be testing is your ability to select and apply relevant principles only. A failure to consider and respond to the specific requests of the examiners will contribute to the danger that you include irrelevant discussion and debate, and fail to demonstrate one of the skills expected. It will also contribute to poor time management.

## Planning

Whatever the type of question, it is important that you practice and develop planning. The use of a plan should assist in the production of a well-structured answer. Such an answer would leave a good impression; it provides a basis to check that you have covered all points; it assists in time management; and it helps to avoid repetition.

## Types of Questions

Revenue law examinations traditionally contain two types of question: discussion type and problem type.

## Discussion Questions

Increasingly discussion questions involve a quote from an academic journal, a law reform committee, a member of the judiciary, or the examiner and request that you discuss the extract or opinion. For example, a question might read:

> Recent decisions on tax avoidance schemes indicate that the courts have lost the initiative and the willingness to control the effects of such schemes.
>
> Discuss.

Whatever the quote or extract, it is *not* an invitation for you to write all you know about the subject area (too easy and a waste of time and effort!). This type of question demands that you demonstrate your understanding and your ability to analyse the subject area and evaluate opinion in that subject area. The key to answering such questions is to begin by asking yourself:

- Have I explained the quote/opinion?
- Have I assessed the opinion? Do I agree or disagree with the opinion? How have I supported my assessment of the opinion? What are other commentators' views? How useful are those views?

Through your explanation and assessment of the opinion you will have demonstrated your understanding of the subject area.

The latter stage of analysis and evaluation is vital, but is often omitted by candidates. It provides a valuable opportunity to demonstrate your reading in the area; to illustrate your understanding of developments and criticisms in the subject area; and to offer opinions that you have developed and reviewed in your tutorial discussions and learning.

For example, in relation to the question asked above, you might consider the following self-check questions:

- Have I explained what constitutes tax avoidance and why aspects of it might cause concern?
- Have I explained the difficulties that the judiciary faced (*Westminster* doctrine) and how they started to overcome those difficulties?
- Did the judiciary really take the initiative? Has it been lost? (A need to assess the *Brightman v Bridge* approach and their respective requirements and receptions. The situation in *Craven v White* (and others) and

Templeman's views—re-appeared in *Ensign Tankers*).
- Have I reviewed commentator's opinions?
- Have I reviewed the scope for future development (the uncertainties of scope) and the role of the legislature (ad hoc, anti-avoidance provisions)?

## Problem Questions

Most students will be familiar with problem type questions (examples are provided below). They often demand that you demonstrate the following skills:

### (i) Identification

The ability to identify the relevant areas of law and relevant facts.

### (ii) Understanding

The ability to show understanding of the relevant principles and distinctions.

### (iii) Application

The ability to select and apply relevant principles in giving appropriate advice. This will assist in demonstrating your understanding and your ability to evaluate and select between conflicting principles.

### (iv) Conclusion

Your application should lead to the development of an appropriate and logical conclusion. An illogical or weak conclusion is evidence of weak application and/or understanding.

At the simplest level the above skills could provide a structure for your response. For example, if you are asked to advise X you might include the following stages in your answer:

### (i) Identification

"In order to advise X we need to consider the principles in Schedule D for the deduction of expenses".

This simple statement provides an introduction that demonstrates you have identified that the question concerns a Schedule D taxpayer and, more specifically, it involves the need to consider deductible expenses.

### (ii) Understanding

"The principles that govern the deductibility of expenses involve the need to consider that the expenses were 'wholly and exclusively' incurred for business purposes".

This stage would provide the opportunity to explain and illustrate the relevant principles. Quite often this involves the need to discuss case law and distinctions (and opinions on those distinctions). The danger in citing case law is in the need to be selective in the use of facts. Your discussion should not represent copious facts of cases strung together by meaningless introductory sentences or paragraphs. It is a matter of individual choice (hence the need for practice) to elect to discuss facts of analogous cases, but often an understanding of the case is implicit in its selective and relevant use. For example, one might refer to *Shilton v Wilmshurst* by citing the relevant facts and explaining the decision (if the problem question warrants such a detailed analogy to be made); or one could state, "... payments made by third parties might also be emoluments (*Shilton v Wilmshurst*) ..." A third approach would be to provide the briefest of details, "... in *Shilton v Wilmshurst* where a sum was paid to the taxpayer by his employer (to induce him to sign) and a further sum by an ex-employer (to induce him to leave) the court held both sums to represent emoluments ..."

The appropriate use of case law is another area where practice is important and should reap benefits.

### (iii) Application and (iv) Conclusion

"Applying the above principles, we can advise X that his expenses are deductible because ... Thus, we can conclude ..."

It is a useful test to ask yourself whether you have commenced a section of your answer that refers specifically to the application of the principles that you have discussed. The application should be specific to the facts and to the parties in the question. A specific approach confirms that you are answering the question and providing the advice to the parties.

You might now wish to test and develop your skill of answering problem questions by attempting the question below. You might find it convenient to divide your answer into (i) advice to Tom; and (ii) advice to Mary. You will often find that you are requested to advise more than one person and it is often convenient to divide your answer accordingly. When answering each part be careful to ensure that you follow the stages identified above and demonstrate the expected skills of identification, understanding, application and conclusion.

## Question

Tom and his wife, Mary, are employed by Woodlands (Private) School. Tom is the Headteacher and he receives an annual salary of £30,000. Mary is an administrative officer and she receives an annual salary of £6,500. They both live in rent-free accommodation consisting of a cottage in the School grounds. The School purchased and renovated the cottage in 1980 at a cost of £200,000. Tom is expected to entertain clients and guests in the cottage and he has devoted the whole of the ground floor of the cottage for the exclusive use of guests and clients of the School.

Tom and Mary have no children of their own, but they have arranged for their two nephews to attend the School at a reduced fee of 50 per cent. Tom receives a clothing allowance of £5,000 to enable him to purchase and wear the expected "academic" dress on official occasions. Tom also receives a travel allowance of £7,500 for conference attendance.

Tom and Mary have access to the School mini-bus and the School's holiday home in Cornwall. Tom and Mary occasionally use the mini-bus to take pupils on educational visits. They also use the mini-bus to enjoy a private holiday each summer in the School's holiday home in Cornwall.

Tom is entitled and expected to retire in December 1992. In recognition of the School's severe financial difficulties he has agreed to waive his entitlement to his full pension and to accept a 20 per cent reduction. In return the School has agreed to pay Tom a sum of £2,000 for his agreeing to act as a consultant until 1996.

Advise Tom and Mary on the tax consequences of the benefits and payments identified above.

## Your Answer

The substantive areas of law that you ought to have discussed include (i) fringe benefits, distinguishing between the common-law and statutory regime including specific discussion of accommodation, expense accounts and allowances, provision of motor vehicles, conferring benefits on relatives, and apportionment, and (ii) emoluments distinguished from compensation payments (*Hunter v Dewhurst*, etc). Other (peripheral) areas include the unit of assessment, and the nature of deductible expenses.

## Test Paper

You might find the following questions useful in practising and developing your examination skills.

*Question*

When commenting on the distinction between income and capital Greene MR suggested that:

> ... in many cases it is almost true to say that the spin of a coin would decide the matter almost as satisfactorily as an attempt to find reason. (*IRC v British Salmon Aero Engines* [1938] 2 KB 282)

Discuss the extent to which this is true and the extent to which the distinction between capital and income is still important.

*Question*

"The UK system of personal taxation contains many anomalies and loopholes which reflect its unsatisfactory *ad hoc* nature".
Discuss.

*Question*

"A system of expenditure tax has many advantages and ought to be introduced into the UK immediately".
Discuss.

*Question*

"Despite the decision in *W T Ramsay Ltd v IRC*, a taxpayer is still entitled to arrange his affairs and be taxed according to their **form** rather than their **effect**."
Discuss.

*Question*

"All payments and rewards received from your present, future or past employer are necessarily emoluments and taxable under Schedule E." Discuss.

*Question*

Bert is a partner in a firm of solicitors, BT & Co. He is required by the firm to attend an International Law Conference in Japan. Bert pays the conference fee of £2,500 and a travel fee of £1,200. The conference fee is inclusive of seven days accommodation and meals. The conference consists of four days of seminars and three leisure days. Bert decides to use one of the leisure days to meet with one of the firm's Japanese clients to discuss the recovery of bad debts. As an act of politeness, Bert purchased a kimono to wear at the meeting and, subsequently, invited the client out to an expensive dinner. It is unlikely that Bert will wear the kimono for social use on his return to the United Kingdom.

Two months following the conference BT & Co agree that Bert is to co-ordinate its international business activities. An international office is opened in Stratford and Bert is required to move there at his own expense.

Following the move to Stratford, Bert has decided to break away from BT & Co and set up his own international law consultancy. The consultancy business is successful and attracts clients away from BT & Co's Stratford office. Bert has agreed to pay £250,000 to BT & Co to compensate for BT's loss of business.

Advise Bert on whether any of the above expenses are deductible in determining his tax liability.

*Question*

Each Christmas since 1984, Eric has given his friend Jacko a painting from Eric's collection of eight famous British watercolours. Individually the paintings are worth £20,000 but as a set their value is £300,000.

Since 1987, Eric has imposed restrictions on the gifts. He has insisted that he be allowed to retain use and possession of the paintings for eight months per year.

In 1989, Eric becomes very ill. He immediately transfers the remaining watercolours to Jacko as a gift and removes any restrictions relating to use and possession. In 1989 Eric dies.

Jacko is arranging for his son to receive these valuable paintings. He is also applying to the Treasury to have the paintings declared to be of artistic and historic interest.

Discuss the inheritance tax implications of the above events.

*Question*

Jane is sole proprietor of an exclusive dress shop in Chester. She makes up her 12-monthly accounts to 31 December each year. During her business year ending 31 December her accounts included the following items:

(i) The purchase of a complete new set of window fittings and display stands at a cost of £40,000.

(ii) Entertainment expenses totalling £25,000. These include a sum of £5,000, the cost of accommodating the buyers from a well-known Dublin department store, whilst attending Jane's annual fashion show.

(iii) The sale of two mink coats for £50 each, both of which had been bought for £1,000. The first was sold to Jane's sister Mary. The second was sold to Clare, the senior executive of a leading wholesale clothing firm; shortly afterwards Clare supplied Jane with a new line in evening wear at a discount of 60 per cent.

(iv) Purchase of various personal clothing items for Jane at a cost of £5,000. These were all of the severe classical style which Jane considers desirable for business purposes. She has no great personal liking for this style as she considers it unflattering; she invariably dresses quite differently for purely social occasions.

(v) £15,000, the cost of an annuity for Ellen, Jane's long-serving maid, who retired during the year.

(vi) £1,000 in fees paid to Stephen, Jane's psychoanalyst and "confidant". Jane regards her weekly meeting with Stephen as a very necessary relief from business pressures and feels that she would not be able to carry on otherwise.

Discuss the relevance of the above mentioned items to Jane's tax position for the year ending 5 April.

## Question

Pat, a bookseller, owns a large country house and estate. He employs a gardener, Peter, who is provided with rent-free accommodation consisting of a bungalow in the grounds of the country estate. The bungalow was previously occupied by Pat and his family for a period of two years during which the building work was completed on the country house. In 1993 Peter leaves Pat's employment and Pat immediately sells the bungalow at a substantial profit.

In the same year, Pat sells his bookshop in Greendale to Sarah, at a profit of £120,000. He receives a further £30,000 in return for him agreeing not to open any bookshops in Greendale for the next two years. Pat uses the £120,000 to buy a new bookshop in Pontypandy.

In 1993, Pat sells to his cousin, Charlie, for £4,000 a rare book by a local author called Tubbard. Earlier in 1992, Pat had sold another Tubbard book to Charlie for £2,000. These books are the only books ever written by Tubbard and the market value of both books as a set is £8,000.

Discuss the capital gains tax implications of the above events.

# Index